"We all know that in the transition to the 21st century there are many paradigm shifts. Jeff Gates's book helps to understand the new direction."

—Professor Klaus Schwab, Founder & President,
World Economic Forum/Davos

"In this provocative study, Jeff Gates addresses a rich array of problems of fundamental human significance, and suggests approaches to them that should stimulate serious thought, and committed action, on the part of people who view the present world, and the possibilities for a better future, from many different perspectives."

—Noam Chomsky, author; professor,
Massachusetts Institute of Technology

"At a time when the need is great, Jeff Gates offers us a populist vision for the twenty-first century."

—Lawrence Goodwyn, author,
Democratic Promise: The Populist Moment in America

"Jeff Gates is a new kind of populist. He makes some folks uncomfortable by wanting to correct a capitalism in which the wealth of the wealthiest 1% exceeds what 95% of Americans have to live on. But he also wants to make capitalism worth conserving—by making it more civilized and more democratic, by making owners of all those who contribute to its success. *Democracy at Risk* is a tough diagnosis, with a fresh and future-oriented prescription attached."

—Harlan Cleveland, President,
World Academy of Art and Science; former U.S. Ambassador to NATO;
author, *Birth of a New World, The Global Commons*

"Jeff Gates is an insider who knows how wealth and the investment system really works — and it fills him with rage. Beneath his righteous anger, there's a deep sadness for what has happened to our democracy and also the conviction that it doesn't have to be that way. This is populist thunder that enthralls and educates and also ought to mobilize us."

—William Greider, author,
One World, Ready or Not: The Manic Logic of Global Capitalism

"With passion and precision, Jeff Gates reminds us that capitalism does not have to be an exclusive system. We make the rules! Here, from the man who helped bring us employee stock ownership is compelling commonsense for how we can make capitalism work for all of us by "ownerizing" it. Mind expanding. Hope inducing. And we need both!"

—Frances Moore Lappe, author,
Diet for a Small Planet, Rediscovering America's Values,
coauthor, *The Quickening of America*

"Jeff Gates is a phenomenon. He is turning the economics searchlight on ownership and demanding to know why the morally unbearable maldistribution of wealth and income is taboo in classical and contemporary economics. Jeff has achieved this focus, in two books two years apart, to the profound benefit of economics and democracy. He comes straight from top-of-the-mark work on Capitol Hill for Russell Long and the Senate Finance Committee to the crisis for democracy in which we Americans are all now mired, whether we want to be or not. American democracy is in great danger, if it's not already over the cliff, and Jeff Gates is making his special heroic effort to help save it and free enterprise. Can it be done? I don't know."

—Ronnie Dugger, founder, Alliance for Democracy;
former editor, *The Texas Observer*, author, *The Politician :
The Life and Times of Lyndon Johnson; On Reagan: The Man and His Presidency*

"Gives us hope that capitalism and humanism are not necessarily mutually exclusive."

—Paul Krassner, editor, *The Realist*

"Meticulously documents the need for broadening capital ownership in the United States—not only for overall efficiency and social development—but to fully release the talents and motivations of all our citizens in growing a more prosperous, just and ecologically sustainable society."

—Hazel Henderson, author,
Beyond Globalization and *Building a Win-Win World*

"In the aftermath of the citizen uprising against the World Trade Organization in Seattle, the need to bring democracy to our economic systems is clearer than ever. Gates reminds us that without democracy in our financial world we can't really expect to have real democracy anywhere. *Democracy at Risk* puts forth series of bold and practical proposals to re-design democracy and capitalism to be things the earth and future generations can afford. After Seattle, I think the world is ready to listen."

—David Brower, Founder and Chairman, Earth Island Institute;
author, *Let the Mountains Talk, Let the Rivers Run*

"In *Democracy at Risk*, Jeff Gates has presented us with an urgent and passionate polemic in support of a renewed democracy based on broadly shared ownership and economic power. He calls for an immediate populist insurgency to bring about a democratic sharing of wealth and power, and a broadening of the criteria of success to include the host of environmental, educational, cultural, community, intergenerational and global concerns which have the potential to threaten, or to enhance, the future of our civilization and, indeed, of our planet."

—Lynn R. Williams, president,
United Steelworkers of America (retired)

DEMOCRACY AT RISK

ALSO BY JEFF GATES

The Ownership Solution: Toward a Shared Capitalism for the Twenty-First Century

DEMOCRACY AT RISK

Rescuing Main Street from Wall Street

A Populist Vision for the Twenty-First Century

JEFF GATES

PERSEUS PUBLISHING
Cambridge, Massachusetts

Many of the designations used by manufacturers and sellers to distinguish their products are claimed as trademarks. Where those designations appear in this book and Perseus Publishing was aware of a trademark claim, the designations have been printed in initial capital letters.

A CIP record for this book is available from the Library of Congress.
ISBN: 0-7382-0326-2

Perseus Publishing is a member of the Perseus Books Group

Text design by Cynthia Young
Set in 11-point Galliard by the Perseus Books Group

1 2 3 4 5 6 7 8 9 10—03 02 01 00
First printing, April 2000

Printed on recycled paper with soy-based ink.

Perseus Publishing books are available at special discounts for bulk purchases in the U.S. by corporations, institutions, and other organizations. For more information, please contact the Special Markets Department at HarperCollins Publishers, 10 East 53rd Street, New York, NY 10022, or call 1–212–207–7528.

Find us on the World Wide Web at http://www.perseuspublishing.com

For the children

He will turn the hearts of the fathers to their children.

—BOOK OF MALACHI

Contents

Acknowledgments

The first draft of this book originated with a pair of two-week stays at Mesa Refuge, a writer's retreat in Point Reyes, California. I am particularly grateful for their gracious hospitality and the encouragement to settle in there to write "on the edge." Though many contributed to shaping both my thinking and my analysis, a particular thanks goes to several especially helpful people, including Peter Barnes, Bob Buchele, Harlan Cleveland, Chuck Collins, David Ellerman, Larry Goodwyn, Russell Long, Chris Mackin, Loren Rodgers, John Simmons, and Ed Wolff.

My agent, Joe Spieler of the New York–based Spieler Agency, was once again helpful. Likewise my editor Nick Philipson at Perseus Books, along with the production assistance of Marco Pavia and extraordinary editorial input from Patty Boyd.

The standard disclaimer applies: Any mistakes or omissions are my own. I am responsible both for what is said and how it's said.

Introduction

> We can have a democratic society or we can have great concentrated wealth in the hands of a few. We cannot have both.
>
> —SUPREME COURT JUSTICE LOUIS BRANDEIS

We live in the best of times and we live in the worst of times. At an ever-accelerating pace, things are getting both better and better and worse and worse. Contradiction and paradox confront us at every turn. The end of the Cold War and worldwide conflict. Capitalism triumphant yet the environment in trouble. Global integration and ethnic division. Great wealth amid widespread human misery. Longer lives but less wellness. More information but less communication. Greater possessions but fewer values. Larger houses but more broken homes. A knowledge economy and failing public schools. A common deficiency unites them all. If properly remedied, that one element alone could trigger an extended period of widespread well-being. That missing ingredient is a genuinely vibrant democracy. Although many of our triumphs are traceable to its spread, our many travails suggest that our democracy is under siege.

If you could step twenty years into the future and look back, what would you want to see? There lies the genius of democracy: It empowers us to choose our own future. With predictable uniformity, people choose peace and prosperity—in the same way that refugees "vote with their feet" by fleeing to countries that are stable and free because there lies their best chance for happiness. As I will show, the limits to human prosperity are now our own. Those limits lie in the realm of political choice. That makes them eminently solvable. The only thing keeping us from a peaceful, post-scarcity world is a lack of political creativity. The barriers are no longer physical but organizational. Even environmental constraints are now solvable with intelligent technologies, ecological design, and alternative fuels.

This doesn't mean a top-down, government-mandated change in the way that business does business. Quite the contrary. With a genuinely robust democracy, we can create—in a bottom-up fashion—a commercial culture with designed-in principles of equity and sustainability. At present, fairness and the environment are treated as ingredients we blend in later, like trying to add sweetener to a cake after it's baked. Equity and ecological common sense aren't options or add-ons. If we lived in a functioning democracy, both would already be embedded as design principles around which decision making turns. That remains the only sensible way to evoke the future we want.

Why hasn't this already been done? Look in the mirror. There's the primary constraint looking back at you. We've allowed our democracy to atrophy. And then we've become cynical because we claim the system isn't working. As I will show, the key constraints we now face are design constraints and in a democracy, *we* are the designers. That's what makes *us* the reason it's at risk. Democracy is not dysfunctional, but our attitude about it certainly is. Democracy doesn't change in response to cynicism, disillusionment, and alienation—no matter how well justified. Democracy is a contact sport; it wasn't designed to respond to the ironic detachment of a James Bond movie. It responds to hands-on participation. And to passion. And to energized imagination. That's its nature. It's designed to change as we choose, though not too quickly. That means *you* need to get into action. And stay there. In short, the risk is there because you aren't. By *you*, I mean not only leaders in business and politics but anyone concerned with the future of democracy and the environment. Here you will find both a chronicle of the risks and a litany of practical ways to address them.

Let me confess a key assumption. I view free enterprise as the best system known for organizing an economy. There's magic in capitalism. And that magic must not be lost. After advising on economic reform in thirty countries, I'm certain that free enterprise has no peer. That's not the point. We can still call it free enterprise regardless of whether the rules result in a system that works well for many or only for a few. What lacks all credibility is when, as now, it works best for a few and when they insist that their success and, by implication, the failure of others is somehow hard-wired into capitalism, an economic equivalent to the fate of the ancients or "God Wills It." That darkly pessimistic assessment reflects a blend of self-serving nonsense and monstrous arrogance. God doesn't make the rules of free enterprise; we do. That's why it's called a free-enterprise *democracy*. The invisible hand of the marketplace is not some disembodied cosmic entity; it operates within rules set by the very visible hand of democracy. The challenge lies in how to write the rules so that the market works well for as many people as possible without impairing its capacity for creativity and prosperity and without damaging the natural world.

My thesis is bone simple. Today's rules have created a business environment in which more than $17 *trillion* now resides in the hands of U.S. money managers who respond solely to values denominated in financial terms. As I will show, today's "people-disconnected capitalism" is woefully insensitive to personal and community-based concerns that must be addressed if we are to have a genuinely robust democracy. I argue here that the rules be rewritten to create a more inclusive and people-responsive economy. My goal is to smarten up free enterprise by fostering ownership patterns that enhance capitalism's capacity to learn from those whose lives are touched by its operations.

We Get What We Choose

Symptoms of the dangers to democracy show up in three key ways: profound inequality, dramatic environmental risk, and political gridlock. For instance, no sensible democracy would opt for an economic system in which the financial wealth of the top 1 percent of households exceeds the combined wealth of the bottom 95 percent.[1] Or one in which the wealth of the nation's four hundred richest families grew by an average $940 million *each* from 1997 to 1999, whereas over a recent twelve-year period, the modest net worth of the bottom 40 percent of households plummeted 80 percent.[2] For the well-to-do, that's an average increase in wealth of $1,287,671 *per day*.[3] If that run-up in riches were wages earned over a traditional forty-hour week, that would be $225,962 an hour or 43,876 times the $5.15-per-hour minimum wage. Who voted for *that*? Why would a functioning democracy allow just four hundred of its citizens to accumulate wealth equivalent to one-eighth of the gross domestic product (GDP)? How many of our 76 million baby boomers would knowingly choose a system in which at least two-thirds of us are destined to lack sufficient assets to sustain ourselves in retirement? Yet as of

1997, New York University economist Edward N. Wolff found that the median household financial wealth (net worth less home equity) was $11,700, a figure $1,300 less than in 1989.[4]

How many wage earners in a true democracy would endorse a system in which 1998 wages are 7 percent lower than in 1973—when Richard Nixon was in the White House?[5] Or a system in which the work year expanded by 184 hours over the past decade? That's another 4 1/2 weeks on the job for the same or less pay.[6] Or where one in every four preschoolers lives in poverty?[7] Or an economy whose present poverty rate remains above that for any year in the 1970s? Or a system in which the top-earning 1 percent in 1998 had as much income as the 100 million Americans with the lowest earnings?[8] Who voted for a system in which that 1 percent pocketed, on average, an *annual tax cut* of $40,000 since 1977? Their tax cut exceeds the average *annual income* of the middle fifth of households.[9] If this were a genuine democracy, how many votes could a candidate muster for *that*? Or for a system in which the pay gap between top executives and production workers skyrocketed from 42:1 in 1980 to 419:1 in 1998, excluding their lush stock options.[10]

With democracy on the march worldwide, how many votes would you expect for a globalized economy in which the world's two hundred richest people more than doubled their net worth in the four years to 1999, to more than $1 trillion—an average $5 billion each?[11] Their combined wealth (the top seven are Americans) now equals the combined annual income of the world's poorest 2.5 billion people.[12] How much is $5 billion? If invested at 5.2 percent, that's a steady income of $5 million *per week*. Who would vote for a system in which just three Americans—Microsoft cofounders Bill Gates and Paul Allen plus Berkshire Hathaway's Warren Buffett—have a net worth larger than the combined GDP of the forty-one poorest nations and their 550 million people?[13] Who would vote for a system in which the World Bank reports that 3 billion people live on less than $2 per day (1.3 billion on less than $1 per day) while 2 billion suffer from anemia?[14] Or a system where experts report that the wealthy have stashed away a staggering $8 trillion in tax havens, leaving us to pick up the tab?[15]

So, Just Whose Democracy Is It?

Who dares argue that these results reflect a robust democracy? Yet we endorse those results by our inaction. Some commentators insist that everything is fine. Never been better. And, besides, anything amiss will right itself if only we give markets a bit more time. And interfere a bit less. They point to consumer confidence, declining crime rates, more leisure travel, a steady growth in entertainment, even a greater amount of charitable giving. Or they suggest that fast-widening disparities are deceptive because they fail to take into account what people can expect under social security. Or they trot out the Horatio Alger exception to prove the rule that entrepreneurs can still succeed. After all, they say, Amazon.com's Jeffrey Bezos is now worth $7.8 billion. Or they complain that the statistics are deceptive because of the influx of immigrants and the growth in smaller households (more single households and higher divorce rates).

These commentators are being disingenuous, even deceitful. Their objections only prove the adage that for every Ph.D., there is an equal and opposite Ph.D. whose primary output is doubt. The facts are beyond doubt. We've created a mean economy—a sumptuous heaven for some, an ungodly struggle for most, and a living hell for many. Consumer debt-loads are at an all-time high, with bankruptcies to match. The United States imprisons far more of its citizens than does any other democracy. Social security is hardly an asset; it's an income transfer funded with a job tax. And to suggest that everyone become an entrepreneur is like advising that everyone become a chess prodigy. For every cyber-millionaire, there are hundreds of cyber-peons. We've always had lots of immigrants, but never so much economic disparity. As a proportion of their income, our beleaguered middle class gives far more to charity than does our pampered rich. And to suggest that the institution of marriage is at risk only confirms the all-pervasive impact of today's economic stress.

Though we have the luxury of productive capacity far in excess of what we can sell, we cruise the world shopping for cheap labor to boost financial returns instead of paying our people enough to clear the shelves. And now we're exporting this suspect model as our remedy for a failed socialist model that once swept the globe because of just such anomalies. Only this time around, we can add to human degradation the spectacle of fast-spreading environmental degradation that endangers both current and future generations.

Happily, these trends are not our destiny; they flow quite naturally from the rules we've chosen. Because those rules are so politically entrenched, change may require a resurgence of grass-roots activism and civil disobedience last seen during the 1960s. However, the immediate challenge lies in overcoming today's resistance to *waking up,* so that together we can choose a different future. My hope is that this book will serve as a wake-up call.

Choosing Environmental Damage

No informed majority would approve an economic design whose operations have forced every living system into decline. And the rate of decline is accelerating. Here's the WorldWatch Institute's 1998 assessment: "Forests are shrinking, water tables are falling, soils are eroding, wetlands are disappearing, fisheries are collapsing, rangelands are deteriorating, rivers are running dry, temperatures are rising, coral reefs are dying and plant and animal species are disappearing."[16] More specifically, over the past five decades, we've lost a fourth of the world's topsoil and a third of our forest cover. We are now poised to lose 70 percent of the ocean's reefs, home to 25 percent of all marine life. Ocean currents are already altered. Plant and animal species are dying 10,000 times faster than natural extinction rates, quicker than at any time in the last 65 million years (fifty to one hundred species become extinct each day).[17] And that's before we begin to experience the impact of chain reactions: When one part of the web of life is endangered, others are affected. The extinction of key pollinators, for example, can affect a myriad of plant species as well as those animal species dependent on them. At the current pace, 50 percent of the earth's plant and animal species will vanish before my nine-year-old son turns sixty. For what purpose shall I tell him this was done? And how shall I teach him to love a democracy so dysfunctional that it chooses not to cease this insanity?

James Hillman, noted Jungian psychologist, argues that it's time we grow up: "We are in a delusional state when we believe we are separate from and superior to nature."[18] Our current foundational ideas put us at great risk of what the Greeks called "hubris"—the terrible pride that comes before a catastrophic fall. In the United States alone, one-third of all plant and animal species are in jeopardy, including 70 mammals, 98 amphibians, 113 birds, and 318 freshwater fishes. We're losing our topsoil seventeen times faster than new topsoil is being formed. A dump-truck-load of topsoil floats by New Orleans every second, along with enough nitrate runoff to create in the Gulf of Mexico a New Jersey–sized, 7,000-square-mile "dead zone"—a marine desert where nothing lives.[19] We consume resources far faster than nature can replenish them. Every year the United States burns as much fossil fuel as the earth produced in a million years. It's too late to get into action to *save* our environment. Whole chains of DNA are certain to disappear. Entire ecosystems will be lost forever along with thousands of plant and animal species. All that can be done now is to make the decline less crude.

What's missing is two things. First, as Edwin Land put it, we need "a sudden cessation of stupidity." Second, we need remedial action to recover from the excesses of the past century. We can do both, but only if we choose policies that nudge us in that direction. The speed with which we begin the change is the central issue of our age—at least as important as our defense against Hitler or the campaign for civil rights.[20]

When the lifestyle of one species jeopardizes the possibility of life for others, we raise profound moral, ethical, and theological dimensions that few policymakers are willing to confront. Yet confront them we must if we are to embrace the changes now required. Our democratic soul must grow large enough and mature enough that we weave our responsibility to future generations into the very fabric of our daily relations. This intergenerational perspective must come to inform all aspects of decision making in both the commercial and the political realms.

Opting for Gridlock

No functioning democracy would put up with a political system paralyzed by stale and predictable partisan debate on matters of little substance while leaving unattended profound social inequities and fast-accelerating environmental tragedies. Yet that's what we face—a situation in which our very future is at risk alongside a legislature that immerses itself in self-imposed gridlock. The trends are far too clear and the implications far too ominous for us to endure the petty and pious bickering that now engulfs Congress.

We desperately need to draw on humanity's deepest insights in order to modify human behavior so that our presence will be life-giving and restorative. Instead we see a steadily widening gap between a detached decision-making elite and a disillusioned populace who are slowly awakening to just how little they've benefited from this two-decades-long policy-driven plutocratic boom—and how much that boom has damaged the natural world. Yet despite widespread dissatisfaction, only 5 of 435 House seats were lost in the 1998 elections. That's testimony not only to the power of the incumbent but also to our disengagement, even our lack of concern.

Happily, each of these three symptoms—inequity, ecological devastation, and political gridlock—can be remedied with a strong dose of the same prescription: your informed participation. For democracy and nature to flourish worldwide, this must become the decade of equity and sustainability. The politics of equity are essential to ensure the growth we need to create worldwide prosperity. And that growth will be sustainable only if undertaken in an environmentally sound fashion. At present, we're hurtling headlong in the wrong direction. We started out with a four-billion-year inventory of natural capital, including such freebies as an embedded capacity to convert the carbon dioxide we breathe out into the oxygen we breathe in.[21] That's a terrific design precisely because it's so clearly sustainable. The best things in life aren't free; they're priceless. They can't be bought or sold, only damaged or destroyed. Yet our standard of living presently depends on converting nature's capital (trees, minerals, oil, etc.) into "stuff" for our consumption (paper, appliances, plastics) before sending it off to the landfill in a form that nature can no longer use. Terrific design on nature's part, lousy design on ours.

Both our economic and our environmental trends are horrifically out of tune with the notion of a democracy meant to endure throughout the ages. Yet by allowing such vast economic inequalities—both here and abroad—we make collective decision making more difficult, because those in vastly different economic circumstances are affected in quite different ways. Someone making $150,000 a year has a very different perspective than someone living on $15,000 a year (or $1.50 per day)—on issues such as immigration, trade, the environment, and the notion of a living wage. If that gap continues to widen—as I show it will, absent our input—politics will become even more fractious. We can design our way out of this, but we must act quickly, as events are now spiraling wildly out of control. String together enough undemocratic moments, and soon you're living in a society that's both undemocratic and unsustainable.

Part of the answer lies in changing the law. Lots of laws. I crafted federal legislation for seven years, working with Senator Russell Long of Louisiana (son of America's most famous populist, Huey "Share Our Wealth" Long). Early on I learned a useful lesson about advising someone whom journalists routinely described throughout the 1970s as the most powerful man in Congress. One of the first meetings I staffed concluded with a contingent describing some reasonable course they wished to pursue but could not, because it was against the law. Long's response still rings true. "Don't tell me what the law says you can't do," he said. "Tell me what's right. We can change the law." That can-do attitude is precisely what's now needed. The laws we have are not delivering the democracy we deserve. In fact, they've put it at risk. By not insisting on change, we've imperiled democracy. The environment too. We made those laws. We can change them.

Prosperity by Design

Democracy is best known by its attributes, much as a strongman is known by his feats of strength. Our democratic deeds presently fall well short of our economic capabilities. The same is true abroad. Democracy stands little chance of success worldwide unless wedded to practical measures for ensuring, if not the prosperity, at least the survival of those whose lives it promises to improve. The UN Development Program reported in 1999 that eighty countries had per-capita incomes lower than they were a decade ago.[22] Sixty countries have been growing steadily poorer since 1980.[23] Yet if we blow away the cobwebs covering the heart of democracy, we find an unexplored generosity, a fundamentally moral impulse that seeks a world free of those forces by which it is presently imperiled. It is those dimensions of democracy that I intend here to explore. Serendipitously, the fostering of prosperity for others is the best way to defend our well-being here at home while also creating customers for what we produce, as any free trader will attest. It seems that in matters of lasting importance, the wiring is such that genuine goodness is the price we must pay for our freedom. And for our own prosperity.

The limits of democratic design are those we choose. With a combination of social justice and sensible policies on population growth, the frontiers of human prosperity become largely a matter of our willingness to live within nature's constraints. By all accounts, the best population policy is economic growth that is equitably shared and environmentally aware. We've long known that ecological strains worsen poverty and that poverty exacerbates ecological problems. Economic disparities between nations also play a role, according to *GEO 2000*, a September 1999 report by the United Nations Environmental Program (UNEP): "The continued poverty of the majority of the planet's inhabitants and excessive consumption by the minority are the two major causes of environmental degradation." The report included the assessment of 850 specialists and thirty environmental institutes.

We know we can do better. The ecological footprint of Americans is thirteen times that of the typical Indian. Yet "green designs" can cut by at least 75 percent the use of energy in our buildings, while drip irrigation can reduce water usage by as much as 90 percent. Alternative energy sources—solar, wind, biomass—could displace much of our climate-crazing hydrocarbons. We need only choose it.

Chronicling a litany of "full-scale emergencies" (water shortages, land degradation, air pollution, global warming), the UNEP's chilling report concludes: "Our present course is unsustainable—postponing action is no longer an option." Several of the world's major rivers—the Nile, the Ganges, the Colorado—now run dry during portions of the year, drained by irrigation and urban sprawl. Worldwide population hit 3 billion in 1960 and 4 billion in 1974. Our 5 billionth person is only thirteen years old. Our 6 billionth was born in October 1999. Sustainable worldwide prosperity is no longer just possible; it's now become essential. But that in no way means it's inevitable. Free-enterprise democracies have long found themselves on the losing end of the battle with human greed and political chicanery. Plus, environmental sensitivity remains far from the commercial norm. Common sense also remains in demonstrably short supply. Certainly our current political leadership is unburdened by brilliance, as they set low standards and regularly fail to achieve them.

In all these areas, the solution is the same: more people-responsive, people-connected systems. Today's widespread disconnectedness is the primary reason that democracy is at such risk. Democracy offers us the right to shape our destiny. It doesn't ensure that we'll use the right. Or use it well. Yet in the grand sweep of human history, democratic choice remains a very new concept and one well worth working to revive. We have enormous cause for optimism. With democracy spreading worldwide, the setting has never been better for a worldwide revolution in democratically driven design.

Toward a Democracy That Transcends Politics

The ability to diagnose a condition does little to improve it. One key challenge in moving from diagnosis to prescription is to anticipate and redirect the emotions that typically accompany the "populist" appraisal just outlined. Although the conditions I describe may upset you, as well they should, to overreact would only make the cure more distant. My hope is that the passions aroused will be put to positive ends because the promise of significant worldwide reform is now palpable and real. We do at last have the combination of societal tools, institutional insight, and ecological know-how to make widely shared prosperity an achievable reality. Analysis is the easy part, as you'll see. It's the broad synthesis of remedies required—and the complex politics their adoption demands—that presents the greater challenge. Yet there too participation is the cure. That's why I propose here an extensive populist education campaign along with a nationwide training program to evoke a populist style of broad-based, community-attuned leadership. Those two ingredients—education and leadership—are essential to move this message into the mainstream and there to engage us in reclaiming our democracy. Citizen concern is the only tool that works for changing democracies in a peaceful way. For this reason, I propose here a broad array of action-based programs to convert today's cynics into engaged citizens and our alienated pessimists into political optimists.

My message is permeated with a sense of urgency and even an occasional note of desperation. As I will show, we live in very dangerous times, with destructive, even deadly forces poised to jeopardize our future if we don't move promptly to address them. Yet this message is also one of great expectation. If we can get the ingredients right— and a robust democracy is a system *designed* to get them right—we can set the stage for a worldwide trend of sustainable prosperity and enduring peace. If the populist agenda I propose becomes a rallying point for political participation, we can revive democracy while also addressing the underlying economic and environmental trends that now endanger both democracy and us. At heart this is a hopeful book. Though I see this as a race and a rescue, the changes required are well within our capacity.

Be forewarned, however, the superficiality of today's political debate leads me to stray on occasion from the advice of those who urged that I "make it kind." Sometimes, watered-down just won't do. I speak here uncomfortable truths. And in a way that mainstreamers will find politically incorrect, even uncomfortable. I do so because democracy is meant to assist us in addressing just the sort of troublesome issues we face. Our policymakers have grown perilously timid at a time when courage is called for. We're selecting as leaders not visionaries, trailblazers, mythmakers, and dream weavers, but bean counters, scribes, and their ever-present pollsters who would substitute a pseudo-democracy for the real democracy of vigorous debates. They assure us "follow-ship" in place of leadership, like the fellow who tried to drive his car by gazing in the rearview mirror. Mediocrity shrinks from large problems. Yet if political pygmies now rule the land, what does that say of us?

Democracy is intended to be a living laboratory, with incessant creativity and experimentation. It implies risk and occasional failure, the hobgoblin of today's play-it-safe politicos. Rosa Parks didn't consult a poll on that day thirty-five years ago when she sat down for freedom. Likewise for what I propose here. Anyone who needs a poll to address these perilous trends has missed the point. In the times in which we live—with the resources and knowledge at our command— widespread, worldwide, environmentally sound prosperity should be considered a human right. Anything less is akin to forcing some to the back of the bus. That's not only unfair and unworkable; it undermines the dignity and underestimates the humanity of everyone else on the bus. What I suggest here is a course that challenges democracy to realize its full potential. It is in *that* direction that our destiny as a nation will be found—but not as long as political timidity reigns and a cautious incrementalism stalks the land.

Much of what I propose transcends partisanship because it requires of us a very new way of thinking. We don't face a political problem so much as a design problem. But democracies require political confirmation of support for any proposed design solution. That's a brilliant arrangement because the influence of an actively engaged democracy is the world's most powerful human force, capable of mustering not only the technical capacities but also the personal commitment, the stick-to-itness, and the essential *spirit* found at the heart of any successful movement. My goal is to make our democracy a day-to-day reality for as many Americans as possible and to extend that experience around the globe. Not only is that feasible and practical, but it's something we *must* do if we are to be left at peace to pursue happiness within our own borders.

Smartening Up Democracy

We live in a curious age. Some call it the information age, others the knowledge age. The "new economy" is the latest buzzword. Judging from the results, it might more aptly be called the age of ignorance. Why? Because the onslaught of information has been accompanied by less clarity. Our enhanced ability to describe is coupled with less capacity to make sense of what we see. Or where we mean to go. Yet that same information, if converted to insight and action, could help us tap the enormous potential of our times. That's why education and leadership training are essential as we step back for a moment to re-calibrate our political compass so that we might better chart a course that is both inclusive and sustainable. We must design for ourselves a system that curbs excesses from within—by conscious design. We can't expect peaches and continue to plant peanuts.

As I will show, the public support is there to turn this nation in a direction more consistent with values that are just, green, and, for lack of a better term, *feminine*—by which I mean idealistic, caring, "spiritual," and attuned to the benefits that accompany high-quality relationships and a balanced personal life. Sociologist Paul Ray iden-tifies a vast undercurrent of Americans—at least 50 million strong (120 million including Europeans)—whose lives are already guided by those values. They're quite puzzled why so few office-seekers em-body those values. And why those values are not yet reflected in our rules so that practicing these values becomes habitual rather than oc-casional. Enormous potential political leverage is found among those whom Ray calls the Cultural Creatives and who constitute 55 percent of the nation's strong activists (17 percent of the population).[24] Of the Cultural Creatives, 60 percent are women.[25] Many come from a background in the "moral movements" that emerged since the 1960s—civil rights, peace, the environment, women's issues, jobs, and social justice. In short, they know how to turn up the heat and turn out the vote, ingredients woefully lacking in today's uninspired political environment with its bland issues and matching candidates.

Most Cultural Creatives share a curious trait: They think they're alone in their views. That's because they don't see their values re-flected either in mainstream media or in the proposals of those run-ning for public office. This "Integral Culture" comprises a group "bigger than any comparable group seen at the birth of any previ-ous social renaissance," Ray notes. Its size suggests astounding im-plications for democratic renewal. The political challenge lies in mo-bilizing this "isolated many" around themes that reflect their shared concerns.

Twenty-First-Century Populism

Meaningful political debate has stalled in this country. That first be-came apparent to me in 1980, when I moved to Washington to work with Russell Long. By my reckoning, today's confused fog of unpro-ductive political posturing dates from that era. My rhetorical benchmark was the media's careless use of the term "populist." Jimmy Carter, a Democrat from my home state of Georgia, was then described as a populist, apparently because he was a peanut farmer who made it to the White House. Yet the term was also used to describe his 1980 presidential opponent, Ronald Reagan, whose policies set the stage for a rich-get-richer trend that continues today.[26] If that wasn't confusing enough, Tory Prime Minister Margaret Thatcher was also hailed as a populist, as were Mikhail Gorbachev, Texas billionaire Ross Perot, and now professional wrestler cum governor of Minnesota, Jesse Ventura. My conclusion: "Populist" is a label that politicians crave but that commentators too easily confer. A uniquely twenty-first-century populism is, I suggest, just the political tonic that democracy now needs. I describe here what populism really means and why it's uniquely well suited to revive and safeguard democracy. I also show how the public support is there to convert America's *innate populism* into a stunningly popular political reality.

My background is in ownership design. That's how I came to work with Huey Long's son in crafting the federal legislation that encourages employee stock-ownership plans (ESOPs) now found in some 10,000 U.S. corporations. I share the Longs' preference for broad-based versus concentrated ownership, believing simply that capitalism works far better when populated by many rather than just a few capitalists.

Right now we have far too few capitalists, despite Wall Street ad campaigns meant to persuade you otherwise. Broad-based ownership also has the potential to serve multiple purposes. Not only can it advance social justice and make markets work more smoothly (and with far less government interference), it can also address environmental issues in a very new way. I think of broadly "peoplized" ownership patterns as a tool, a *metatool*, if you will, that could involve more people in making decisions that affect them. Experience suggests that such personalized capitalism enhances both motivation and mindfulness while better aligning self-interest with the common interest, improving our foresight. There are lots of ways to do it—going well beyond ESOPs—as I show in Chapter 1.

2008 Is Too Late

As early as summer 1999, the political dynamics of the 2000 U.S. presidential election were already beginning to jell. An extraordinary confluence of events will be required for these populist themes to find a champion in the 2000 election, even though not long ago presidential campaigns were launched on Labor Day, just two months before the November election. If the next administration serves two full terms and these matters are not addressed until 2008, it may be too late. As I will show, today's economic, social, and environmental trends are demonstrably unsustainable. A vigorous campaign organized around the themes I describe could replace widespread cynicism with optimism as people rally around the promise of an inclusive future that is uniquely populist both in its outlook and in its policies. At various times, these populist themes have attracted support (though precious little action) from presidential candidates spanning the political spectrum—from Ronald Reagan, George Bush, and Jack Kemp to Ted Kennedy, Jesse Jackson, and Bruce Babbit. No one has yet made them a central focus of a presidential campaign. Modern-day populism offers a uniquely appealing political alternative because it places full confidence in a wisdom found neither in the distance that typifies governmental direction nor in the abstraction found in today's financial returns-obsessed economic model. Populism puts its confidence in the local preferences of real people living in genuinely people-empowered communities. People empowerment is the component now most missing in today's Wall Street–driven democracy.

Optimal solutions emerge when those closest to the problem possess the wherewithal to address them. Savvy business managers embrace this as a self-evident truth. They put decision making as close as possible to emerging problems because delayed feedback is the most costly. The more localized the control, the more precise and measured the response. That's how organizations learn to learn, as up-close decision making generates not only answers but also insights. Anita Roddick, founder of The Body Shop, captures the populist, people-first spirit embodied in this perspective: "We were searching for employees but people showed up instead." A democratic revival awaits a brand of politics that puts its priority on people and place. This priority is what free-enterprise democracy long ago promised and has yet to deliver.

Monocultures versus Democultures

Throughout our history, populists have opposed those who granted too much deference to the forces of finance. I hail from that tradition, but with two key differences. First, I'm a genuine insider. As counsel to the U.S. Senate Committee on Finance (1980–1987), I labored long in the inner sanctum of our financial system. I've seen firsthand the forces at work when its rules are written. And rewritten. Second, although my analysis includes traditional economic and social perspectives, it draws principally from modern systems analysis, once known as cybernetics. The word stems from the Greek *kybernetes*, meaning "that which steers" or the "helmsman"—who continuously adjusts the tiller in response to feedback received. My "systems" approach keeps this book ideology-free while also purging it of partisan politics—with a few exceptions. My aim is to preserve democracy, which means ensuring that people have a choice. The goal is not just to protect a diversity of views but also to *reflect that diversity* in the results that emerge. That's how you know the democratic process is working. Nature operates on a similar principle. Monocultures fare poorly in nature. In the face of environmental change, biodiversity provides a stabilizing force that buffers ecosystems against catastrophe, ensuring that a habitat is not overwhelmed or that native species are not driven into extinction.[27]

The finance monoculture that accompanies today's capital market-dominant economic model is similar to what's unfolding in nature after we imported the Japanese kudzu vine to control soil erosion. A virulent bioinvader (like water hyacinths or the zebra mussels of the Great Lakes), kudzu has taken over millions of acres in the American South, overwhelming the native habitat as it smothers flowering plants and shrubs, driving them to extinction. The success of this vine shows the impact of bioinvasion in natural systems as the newcomer out-competes native species, alters the habitat, or both.

The impact on democracy of a dominant *economic* factor is similar. Legitimate nonfinancial viewpoints are drowned out when money-based values become too controlling as a source of feedback. Although the impact of an "eco-invader" on democratic systems may take decades, as did kudzu, the effect can be just as devastating, driving other values to extinction before we can evolve survival mechanisms. Today's monoculture economics, with its compulsive fixation on financial factors, not only is drowning out the diversity of views essential to a vibrant democracy, but is also endangering domains that have no voice, including the environment and the rightful claims of future generations. Most disturbing of all, however, is the implication that the locus of authority in a democracy must now be found externally—in abstract financial signals—rather than internally in the community-sensitive self-governance envisioned at the heart of democratic society.

Yet even this systems analysis misses the full flavor of democracy because it makes it sound somehow mechanistic. It's hardly that. The genius of democracy lies in what physicists call "field-based thinking"—the notion that there's a quality of energy, attention, and shared values and meaning that permeate any society, giving it direction and momentum and creating an effect. The qualities that define democracy—freedom, equality, dignity, solidarity, and so on—reside not in mechanistic building blocks but in the dynamism of relationships.

As in modern physics, our policy focus must shift away from the study of things to the study of connections—from matter to patterns of relationships. Physicist Fritjof Capra provides a useful analogy. Sugar, he notes, is made up of three molecules: oxygen, hydrogen, and carbon.[28] In no single atom can the quality of sweetness be found; it emerges in the relationships among the molecules.

We're drawn to democracy because it's the smartest system we know. It evokes the best in us. Yet its intelligence is like the human brain whose substance is "notoriously unreliable," as systems pioneer Stafford Beer points out: "Neurons are extinguished without warning, synapses change their thresholds capriciously, and a single shot of alcohol alters the whole cerebral ecology. And yet we humans continue to operate fairly smoothly throughout it all."[29]

As with the design features that make human intelligence robust, a well-functioning democracy needs to be designed with abundant redundancy. "Redundancy" is used not in the sense of replicating fallible components until some of them work but in the sense of generating overlapping relationships so that the system learns from a multifaceted whole.[30]

An intelligent democracy clearly requires the mechanical element of democracy (the vote). However, we also need to think of democracy as we do our own holistic intelligence. In the same way that our intelligence is more than the meeting of neural synapses, democracy is a unified system made up of diverse networks of relationships and communication that direct its course. As an informed and passionate populace, we must do more than just vote. The relationships and connections typical of civil society make up the brain that both comprises and informs democracy's body politic.

Choosing a Sustainable Future

Our history, our common sense, and modern systems analysis confirm that the challenges we face would be far better addressed with a system that draws on more broadly participatory economic relationships. That's the best way to "smarten up" ourselves. Thomas Jefferson was quite outspoken on this point, insisting that the only remedy for the defects of democracy is *more* democracy. More democracy requires more connectedness, more interdependence, and input from more diverse views. To achieve this, we must create new ways for the system to communicate with itself. It's not only about smartening up the system, though that's important, but it's also about making the system *reliably* intelligent—a key component in sustainability. "Without good connections and a system-wide shared sense of what matters," author Myron Kellner-Rogers argues, "I cannot be trusted to act in a way that serves the whole."[31] Astute business managers know that. Our politicos are still trying to figure it out.

As you can see, this generic "systems" approach to democracy could form a key plank in the platform any of our various political persuasions—Democrat, Republican, Reform, Green, Libertarian, or whatever. Democratically derived solutions to very similar problems may look very different in Berkeley, Boulder, and Boston than in Baltimore, Birmingham, and Beverly Hills. That doesn't make one locale or one solution better than another. The point of democracy is not to have everyone arrive at the same solution, though it's easy enough to identify those in Congress who think so. Each community has its own experience and expertise from which its solutions emerge. Democracy values diversity, not only because of its richness but because it's also the most robust system we know. Like nature, democracy abhors a monoculture. When properly designed, tomorrow's free-enterprise democracy will mimic the wisdom found in nature's design, which recognizes that nothing is ever fully independent but exists in ever-shifting patterns of relationships.

True democracies constantly adjust to a variety of elements. Their architecture is that of a very large tent, with room enough to accommodate the Black Panthers and the Ku Klux Klan, evangelicals and scientologists, Muslims and Mormons, the greedy and the kind, vegetarians and junk-food junkies. There's no such thing as an ideal democratic result. Democracy is about empowering people to choose their own result, respectful of the right of others to do likewise. Although to the casual outsider the United States may look like a walking multiple character disorder, it was the tyranny of *any* monoculture that this nation was founded to escape.

Democracy is not a destination; it's our manner of traveling. It's not so much something we *do* as the way we *are*. And the way we are *in relation to others*. Therein lies its sweetness.

It's not accidental that "We the People" was the phrase chosen to identify the architect of democracy's design. It doesn't read "We the Capital Markets" or "We the Government" or "We a Certain Sort of People." Democracy is at risk because we've granted undue dominance to one very narrow perspective—finance. The nation's founders would find this narrow focus very curious indeed, particularly for a nation that has spent much of the twentieth century opposing political systems founded on very narrow perspectives. Happily, this time we don't need to rearm; we just need to reconnect. The operative agent of this solution is easy to identify. If you want to know it, go look again in the mirror. The Hopi elders put it succinctly: "We are the ones we've been waiting for."

Some commentators will dismiss this analysis. The dominantly cynical mode of present-day journalism assures criticism, even ridicule. The usual rhetorical gambit is to call it unduly alarmist. Or gloomy. Or grandiose. Even, heaven forbid, overly earnest. Or my personal favorite: yet another self-absorbed screed for a "cosmic justice" that must yield to the sober judgment of plainer folk.[32]

As any student of systems will attest, the greatest benefit flows from taking the broadest possible view of the various connections in a system and only then considering how to craft a fully integrated design. That was the approach taken when this nation was conceived; the Framers elevated the debate until they had a framework sufficient both for comprehension and for action.

Although we're clearly in the midst of another Gilded Age, exemplified by rampant selfishness and a fascination for trivial things, my point is not to stress the obvious—that we lack purpose and that we are distracted from accomplishing great things, particularly when compared to earlier eras or when measured against the challenges we face. This is not a judgment call, but a call for common sense. I wish to show that we endanger both ourselves and democracy when we indulge in anything less than democracy's highest calling. This is not some romantic vision, but part of the built-in design of democracy. To perform well over the long haul, democracy requires that we operate with certain key values, particularly the values of social equity and intergenerational sustainability. Until those core values are firmly encoded in this nation's rules and reflected in its results, democracy will remain at risk.

PART ONE

Out-of-Control Capitalism

1
The Populist Moment

I believe there are more instances of the abridgement of the freedom of the people by gradual and silent encroachment of those in power than by violent and sudden usurpations.

—JAMES MADISON

While self-interest is certain to remain a driving force in the success of free enterprise, democracy has long been animated by a latent generosity that longs to be unlocked. Humankind is predisposed to generosity. For the bulk of human evolution, we relied on cooperation and sharing to survive as hunter-gatherers, for whom survival depends on key psychological qualities—openness, attunement, solidarity, mutuality, appreciation. People still want to give of themselves to one another—to family, to friends, to their community—and thereby to live on in others. If democracy is to live on in the lives of our descendants, we must ensure that free enterprise, democracy's commercial component, is guided by rules that put some limits on greed so that more of us can afford to give expression to that innate yearning for connectedness.

Yet so long as we give such free rein to the unbridled forces of finance, we will be besieged by avarice and by the peculiar dictates of financial values. Finance has no way to calibrate what our relations should be with our fellow citizens or with the environment. Or what sort of society we should leave for the next generation. In the financial domain, those matters are of no concern. The answer lies not just in corralling greed, though that's a good start. Nor does the solution lie solely in encouraging broad-based ownership, though that's essential. The remedy—necessarily wide-ranging—can only emerge from a long-overdue national dialogue about the democratic values we share and how they can be reflected *throughout* our policy environment. In this chapter I provide an overview of suggested remedies meant to catalyze that dialogue.

It's helpful if we first "unpack" the sentiment (versus the feedback mechanism) that animates democracy and reflect on how far we've strayed from the inspiration that informed this nation's founding. At its core, democracy has to do with dignity, confidence, and respect. Genuine populists are easy to spot. They speak to you as an equal and in a straightforward way. Though compassionate in their dealings with others, they recognize that people are doubly victimized in a system that grants them the degradation of pity without the dignity of helping them earn genuine respect.[1] Populists understand that if we put too much faith in compassion, we are stuck with a "Have Mercy" argument—have mercy on others and give them what they did not produce. Not only does that degrade people, it also undermines market mechanisms and leaves people no better off. Populism suggests instead that government's role is to boost the capacity of people to produce so they can be confidently self-sufficient.

In announcing his candidacy in June 1999, George W. ("Dubya") Bush hid behind a rhetorical hybrid he labeled "compassionate conservatism," recalling his father's equally vacuous phrase from a decade earlier extolling "a kinder, gentler nation." Pundits were quick to skewer the phrase, labeling it "Right Lite"—particularly after Dubya clarified his position: "It is conservative to cut taxes and compassionate to give people more money to spend."[2]

In announcing his candidacy two weeks later, Al Gore attacked Bush for suggesting that people be left to fend for "crumbs of compassion," hinting that Bush's elitist attitude, like that of his father's, is akin to noblesse oblige. Yet what did Gore's "progressive" platform offer? Education and training—key ingredients in what he called practical idealism. Pundits quickly lampooned his position as "Limp Left," particularly after it was revealed that he was taking $15,000-per-month "masculinity lessons" from author Naomi Wolf.

Conspicuous by its absence was any mention of ownership. Neither candidate brought it up. Like two bald men fighting over a comb, neither offered an economic program with *any* hope of escape from today's plutocracy-prone trends. Instead they served up four largely interchangeable words akin to political pablum. Like preschoolers who learned only one way to draw a house, both imply there's no better way to organize free enterprise. Or to reinvigorate democracy. Or to address environmental concerns. We face a critical juncture in our approach to social progress. Yet rather than vision, ideas, inspiration, and leadership, we're offered political posturing and flashy presentation. A very new world requires very new solutions. Today's disturbing trends suggest there's much in our policy mix that should be tossed out. Yet rather than hint at the need for reform, we're assured they only plan to tweak the current model. New ideas are received with the same enthusiasm that the Flat Earth Society would show for a satellite photo.

The Politics of Respect

Populist arguments for sharing our wealth are multifold, but they cluster around two key beliefs. The first is that current wealth holders came by their riches unfairly or were granted an unfair advantage. That's why I include an explanation of today's rich-get-richer closed system of finance along with an insider's assessment of the role played by wealth-concentrating supply-side economics. I also explain the impact of corporate welfare on wealth patterns and document multiple deficits that endanger us all.

Second is the belief that although compassion is not to be dismissed as a safety net, it should be viewed as a profoundly weak foundation for a nation based on the principles of political equality and human dignity. That's where populists part ways with Clinton-Gore progressives in identifying the building blocks for a democracy. Democracy is not about marginally improving the plight of those adversely affected by capitalism. That's the progressive approach. Populism proposes instead to *transform* capitalism by "peoplizing" it so that Americans gain a personal stake in a system from which they've routinely been excluded. Its goal is to reconfigure free enterprise so that it becomes connected to people and their communities in a direct and authentic fashion. At its core, populism is about evoking a commercial environment, including a global economy, that exists to serve people and their communities rather than the other way around. Populists know that if we did a better job of sharing our wealth, we could get by with a lot less of today's so-called compassion—most of which is taxpayer-funded.

Populism proposes to restore authenticity and dignity to a democracy now bordering on crisis—as evidenced by the strains on civil cohesion, the breakdown of community, a prevalent sense of isolation, a corrosive addiction to consumption and endless economic growth, and a remarkable deference granted those whose devotion to Adam Smith depends on not reading him. Populists remind us that free-enterprise democracy is not just about free markets, but also about how to live free and how to create more possibilities for personal autonomy. That hunger lies at the heart of all democratic aspirations.

Autonomy Within Community

Autonomy is the pathway to genuine democracy. Paradoxical though it may seem, autonomy requires community. As Carl Jung put it, to be genuinely "I" requires "We." You cannot become fully human in isolation. Adam Smith agreed, advising that it is sensible to talk about the well-being of the self only within society.[3] Healthy societies encourage close social ties and mutual interdependence. Only within such a nurturing framework do individuals feel sufficiently confident and secure that they become genuinely free.

We're just now realizing how badly we've depleted our inventory of social capital, that unseen web of human relationships in which our personal liberty, and hence democracy, is embedded. That intangible element establishes the reach of societal connectedness and the boundaries of human trust. The outer limits of democracy are set not by geography, nor even by national boundaries, but by the level of one's confidence in the presence of those shared values (just imagine flying to London versus, say, Teheran).

A broadly shared capitalism *itself* has value because it helps combat today's radical individualism and its strident emphasis on personal rights with little regard for social responsibilities. Or for the needs of democracy. As we're belatedly discovering, that's a stance destined to breed distrust, disharmony, and lawsuits (the United States is now home to 70 percent of the world's lawyers). Populism rejects both the seductive politics of pity and the blind deference granted finance. The confidence essential to free and equal citizenship is found neither in the status of needy recipient nor in becoming an unwitting pawn in global capital markets. Populism embraces instead the politics of self-reliance wed to interdependence, secure in the knowledge that humankind is meant to be free and to live a life of dignity, security, and leisure. From that condition, we can explore the generosity that resides in the human heart. Rather than continue today's retreat from the promised vistas of democratic potential, contemporary populism insists that we pledge ourselves anew to their attainment. And that we do so within the confines of ecological limits.

It's essential to this goal that we assume an activist role in world affairs by demonstrating how the rules of free enterprise can be rewritten so that fast-widening prosperity becomes the global norm. We must show how modern living standards can be achieved in an environmentally sound fashion. That presents a daunting challenge in a world where physical and intellectual resources are unevenly distributed and where development has long been linked to harm to the natural world. Let me suggest only this: absent such a stance, we will prove ourselves unworthy of the demands of this age. If, in this post–Cold War era, we fail to seize opportunities for change that were won at such a high price, our indictment by history is richly deserved.

On these crucial issues, the recent legislative and diplomatic record has been profoundly poor. If we are to lead the global quest for a higher order of economic well-being, we must address not only the inequities in the U.S. system but also the cauldron of human misery that afflicts fully two-thirds of humankind. The stakes are huge and the window of opportunity perilously small. The continued spread of free enterprise may itself now be endangered by our failure to make it sufficiently inclusive that it meets commonly accepted standards of civilized behavior.

Peoplizing Capitalism

At the outset, let me assure readers that there is yet time to design a *peaceful* path out of this predicament, provided we turn quickly to crafting a *practical* cure. Conventional remedies won't work. For instance, the idea of people accumulating significant capital through personal saving is a particularly vigorous exercise in futility. Not only is our national savings rate negative, it's poised to worsen as we open up to the wage-dampening impact of foreign labor. The encouragement of dramatically inclusive financing techniques could help. That was a key recommendation in my 1998 book, *The Ownership Solution*.[4] However, the remedy falls well short for a very simple reason: The proceeds from any sale are destined to make the already-rich even richer—both by purchasing assets from them and by borrowing funds from them for the privilege.

These unconventional times call for highly unconventional remedies. There's no single answer to this multifaceted challenge. No societal silver bullet will magically cure our many ills. We must pursue a broad range of remedies and pursue them quickly. Brief descriptions of the populist policies I propose include the following (explained in more detail in later chapters):

Full-ownership policy. Today's full-employment economic policy needs a counterpart ownership policy. We need both widespread employment of our labor resources and widespread ownership of our capital resources.

Ownership impact reporting. Every policy pronouncement should be accompanied by an ownership impact report. We have a right to know when those we elect pass laws that make the rich richer. An international effort should compile and maintain a detailed global ownership registry.

Fiscally foresighted investment practices. Today's $8 trillion-plus in retirement-plan assets must be invested in a way that fosters broad-based ownership. Pensioners need to retire into a fiscal environment characterized by widespread financial self-reliance. Anything less endangers their retirement benefits.

Private wealth from public assets. Government contracting should favor broadly owned companies. The same should hold true for government-granted licenses (broadcasting, etc.) or anywhere private access is granted to public assets, such as commercial access to minerals, timber, and oil on public lands.

New ownership possibilities. Ongoing commercial relationships (supplier, distributor, customer, contractor, bank depositor, service provider) should be the priority focus for an array of policies designed to broaden wealth while improving enterprise performance by "ownerizing" those relationships.

Customer-owned utilities. Investor-owned utilities should become partially owned by their customers, gradually transforming bill payments into customer-owned equity.

Corporate localization. Today's megamergers should be restructured to ensure broad-based ownership, particularly within those communities where corporate operations are located.

Ownership-pattern-attuned tax policy. Fiscal foresight requires a tax policy ensuring that more of the nation's income-producing capital finds its way into the accounts of those now under-capitalized.

Monetary policy. The Federal Reserve's indifference to fast-widening economic disparities is destined to undermine long-term price stability as more people become dependent on the government. Both monetary and fiscal policy must be made more sensitive to ownership patterns.

Antitrust policy. Ownership patterns should be considered a key factor in assessing both the structure and the conduct of monopolistic firms.

Populist foreign policy. U.S. foreign policy should set as its top priority the worldwide alleviation of poverty. Plutocratic ownership patterns, now the global norm, pose a clear danger to global stability, to the environment, and to the continued advance of democracy.

Foreign assistance. Foreign aid, including assistance provided by the World Bank and the International Monetary Fund (IMF), should adopt ownership-pattern-sensitive development techniques.

Capital commons user fee. Global capital markets are a commons. An international effort should impose a capital commons user fee, directing the proceeds to fund human needs in the developing world. International law should extract a "freeloader's levy" from those who've hidden $8 trillion in the world's tax havens.

Resource productivity policies. All public policies should be designed to multiply the productivity of natural resources.

New assets for new owners. Limits should be placed on hydrocarbon emissions, property rights created in emission permits, and those permits used to capitalize households nationwide, linking energy conservation to income generation.[5]

Socially responsible investing. As with the antiapartheid screening of investments a decade ago, the investor community should screen for equity and sustainability.

Prosperity corps. A prosperity corps should be established to train Americans for missions abroad that implement best-practice development programs.

Culture corps. Americans should be sent abroad to share our diverse cultures with others while showcasing the world's cultures here.

Just say no to values-free free trade. Free trade, yes, but no more values-free free trade. Democracies must oppose injustice and unsustainability, whether here or abroad.

The rewiring of free enterprise for inclusion requires an extraordinary degree of political consensus, more than we've seen except during wartime. Yet even the strategies I propose may be insufficient if we hope to rely on personal capital as the route to broad-based economic autonomy. Given the extraordinary concentrations of wealth that policymakers embraced over the past two decades, an element of wealth reallocation has become not only advisable but essential, a subject to which we turn in Section 4.

A Glimpse of the Future

Is change possible? Yes, absolutely. We need only choose a different set of rules. Once we realize that the rules can be changed, then whether we do so becomes a question of ethics. How we answer that question cuts to the core of what it means to be a responsible member of the human community. We don't yet have leaders either with the gumption to propose needed changes or the grit to see them through. As those leaders emerge—as I'm confident they soon will—we'll at long last have an opportunity to choose inclusion and sustainability over a system that's now brutishly exclusive and alarmingly unsustainable.

A few examples show how "up-close capitalism" would differ from today's remote and disconnected capitalism. Up-close capitalism is more participatory, more personal, and more equitable and shares both the risks and the rewards far more broadly.

- In 1994, 55,000 employees of United Airlines purchased 55 percent of their employer for $4.9 billion. Tired of seeing their livelihoods subject to the whims of Wall Street, they decided to work for themselves. Peace of mind, they found, lies in using financial markets rather than being abused by them. The typical employee now has $40,000 in United Airlines stock plus competitive union wages and a diversified pension.
- When the North American Free Trade Agreement (NAFTA) was announced, the Canadian province of Manitoba rightly reckoned that local savings would flee to the major money centers, stripping the province of the means to create or maintain employment. The provincial government responded with incentives that encouraged local savings to stick around. The Winnipeg-based Crocus Investment Fund now has more than US$100 million invested in local businesses.
- Independent truckers at the Port of Savannah, Georgia, fed up with being pitted against one another by steamship and trucking companies, are organizing to form their own company to haul freight from the bustling port. Urged on by the International Longshoremen's Association, the strategy could mark the beginning of a new approach to labor organizing in the South, where only 7 percent of employed adults are unionized, versus a nationwide rate twice that.
- In response to 1998 legislation mandating the privatization of Ontario's electric power industry, a group called the Democratic Capitalism Study Group proposes the use of a customer stock ownership plan (CSOP) to purchase Ontario Hydro. for Ontario's 11 million citizens, relying largely on the firm's future revenues to finance the purchase.
- Several Internet companies (OWNERShop.com, MyOwn-Empire.com, and others) are beginning to sell a broad range of products with a unique twist: Rather than a cents-off discount coupon or a product rebate, customers will receive equity.
- In 1991, Real Goods Trading Corporation, a mail-order catalog firm, targeted a direct public offering (DPO) to its repeat customers. A second offering was completed two years later. Both were oversubscribed. Stakeholder-owners purchase twice the dollar amount of products as nonowner customers.[6]
- The Super Bowl champion Green Bay Packers football team has been anchored in a small Wisconsin town for eight decades with an ownership design that links the team to its

natural owners: local residents and fans. Contrary to other pro football franchises, collected like so many expensive doodads by the well-to-do, the Packers' ownership resides in a not-for-profit corporation first established in 1919. Shares can be left to relatives but can only be sold to outsiders after first being offered to the team. No one can own more than two hundred shares. If the team were sold (NFL franchises routinely fetch upward of $250 million), the proceeds must be used to construct a war memorial at the local post of the American Legion.

- Visa International is now the world's largest financial company, processing over 7 billion credit card transactions each year linking 14 million merchants and 750 million customers and producing $1.25 trillion in annual transactions across borders and currencies. Rather than being owned by one or a few owners, its nonstock membership stakes are held by more than 22,000 member banks, with each "owning" as much of the market as it can develop.

Continued Inaction Is Unacceptable

We're currently plagued by a policymaker corps unwilling to acknowledge that we live in a time of pending crisis. The implications of continued inaction are staggering—fiscally, socially, culturally, politically, environmentally—as I will show. Other nations are in even worse straits. Most alarming, however, is that this crisis—a crisis of our own making—is largely ignored both here and abroad. At home, policymakers are enthralled by a steadily rising stock market. Yet no one has pondered what becomes of this financial exuberance as those who've plowed funds into the market find that there are too few people with too few funds available to buy them back out. Any attempt at a massive sell-off would resemble a high-stakes game of musical chairs with few places to sit. People seem to forget that you don't really harvest the value of a security until you sell it.

During the twelve years of the Reagan-Bush administration, we passively watched while wealth and income disparities veered toward the unconscionable throughout the 1980s. Then we looked on complacently as those disparities worsened throughout the Clinton-Gore years of the 1990s. Because the policies of both camps brought this situation about, neither will address it. In politics, success has many fathers, whereas failure remains always an orphan. Happily, positive change truly is a matter of choice. Here I propose a way forward that is both politically practical and financially feasible. My goal is to reframe the political debate so that we choose more wisely—and so that we truly *have* a choice. That alone would be a major breakthrough in today's politics with its Tweedledum and Tweedledee candidates.

Today's unconscionable economic disparities not only affect us, but also reflect us. That should spur us to ponder just what sort of democracy we mean to leave for our descendants. Yet often I'm assured that the forces allied against the changes I propose are too strong, their influence too deep, the opposing interests far too entrenched. To that I say only this: Truth itself has power. And if the power of truth cannot prevail, then our democracy is not just endangered, but badly damaged and perhaps even doomed. If we but trust our common sense, embrace our common values, and remain true to our shared convictions, we can reclaim our country and ensure that never again will it be taken hostage by those forces by which it is presently imperiled. Contemporary populism faces the same paradox that has long bedeviled reform in a democracy: Though reform must be anchored in broad-based support, the stimulus for that reform requires inspired and committed leadership.

What Sort of Leader Is Required to Move a Populist Agenda?

The type of leader that democracy now needs is unlike anything we've yet seen. A populist presidential candidate would stand in sharp contrast to anyone now on the national political scene. If the candidate hopes to be a candidate in the near future, he or she will almost certainly enter the fray from well outside the mainstream political establishment. Because of the tightly closed nature of the modern presidential election process (expensive, front-loaded, party-driven primaries, party-organized nominating conventions, etc.), the person's candidacy will need to be a media phenomenon. That suggests someone with such a combination of fresh ideas and personal appeal that the other candidates pale by comparison. Happily, that's not a tall order, given today's short list of dull and shopworn wannabes. And the electorate's frustration with a nomination process that serves only to prove which candidates have lots of money and a fat Rolodex.

Yet these requirements also suggest someone quite unconventional and, as yet, largely unknown. Nor can the person be easily intimidated—by the job, other candidates, the media, or the political estab-

lishment. Many of these people or groups will be miffed that someone outside the guild is crashing their party—particularly someone
with no obligation to support *their* agenda and no commitment to
staff up with *their* people. Neither Democrat nor Republican nor
Reform nor Green nor even Libertarian, he or she will have to recast
the political mold, emerging as a "possibilitarian."[7] A possibilitarian is
someone with enough verve and vision to cure the nothing-can-be-
done disease that keeps voter turnout at historic lows among those
who fare the worst in today's economy, particularly Gen-Xers (the 50
million people born between 1965 and 1978) turned off by the
sleazebag nature of today's money-responsive politics.

American voters expect a touch of gravitas in their presidents, a trait
of somber reflection that former Treasury Secretary Lloyd Bentsen
once joked is readily achieved with a touch of gray hair and a freshly
pressed suit. That's a must. It precludes a serious bid by feather-boa-
attired former professional wrestlers. Yet the voting public is clearly
ready for a political upstart and will readily embrace someone who
takes the office seriously while taking himself or herself lightly. A keen
sense of fun and self-deprecating humor would be a huge plus.
Certainly a modern populist candidate would need to be well versed in
both domestic and foreign policy in order to have something useful to
say on the global applicability of populist principles. The person would
also need to be skilled at explaining new ideas in terms of the old so as
not to frighten anyone with what amounts to a fundamental reordering of the economy. It also suggests someone at ease with people and
whose heartfelt concerns shine through in what's proposed.

Though presidential candidates have typically had some experience
in a senior government job (governor, member of Congress, cabinet
secretary), this could prove a disadvantage today because of the prevailing cynicism about politics and the corrupting influence of money
in politics. A bit above the fray but a canny participant in it would be
the hallmark of an effective candidate. To keep from being co-opted
either by unwieldy political commitments or by the fund-raising required for a conventional presidential bid, the person will need to be
sufficiently provocative on the issues, as well as interesting in his or
her own right, so that ongoing media coverage and genuine popularity replace paid-for advertising as the way to access the public.
Although this may sound unlikely, it is also just the sort of initiative,
boldness, and change-of-pace personality one would expect from anyone willing to take on the powers-that-be in order to press a genuinely populist agenda.

It's no longer crucial for a candidate to have an Ozzie-and-Harriet family life. Anyone who fits the description above is certain to have had a broad range of life experience. A more complicated family situation would make the candidate more real, particularly for Gen-Xers, many of whom were raised in homes with divorced parents, stepparents, half siblings, and such. The United States is ready for the personal fallibility that such contemporary complexity suggests. The phony postcard perfection of the First Family lost its allure long ago. A blended family may even be an asset. The person may well be unmarried. Or divorced and have children who live with him or her. The candidate may be in a long-term committed relationship. It's a new century, after all.

In dealing with Congress, the candidate's independence from either party will prove a political plus, provided he or she remembers to appeal directly to the people when their support is needed to dislodge legislation from a paralysis-prone House and Senate. Bringing to office a wide array of new ideas (as you'll see herein), he or she will be a prolific initiator of legislation. With the presidency won on the appeal of a populist platform, he or she would enter office with the most significant election mandate given a president since Franklin Delano Roosevelt's election in 1932. The body of legislation introduced in the president's First Hundred Days would be sufficient to consume at least one full Congress (two years) and possibly two. Because populism embraces core values common to both major parties, the president would be well positioned to broker compromises when those prove essential. At the same time, however, the credibility of the office, as well as the momentum required to enact the administration's comprehensive program, will depend on the president's willingness to ensure that the Washington–Wall Street consensus bends in his or her own direction. That will generate an unusual reservoir of political strength seldom seen in American politics.

Like any genuine populist, the president would be a plain talker who exudes a palpable kindness, civility, and tolerance. He or she is likely to joke around a lot. An edge of genteel coarseness should endear the core constituency while engendering trust in those long suspicious of the sanitized good manners of the usual White House inhabitant. A blend of economic and cultural populism will make an appealing candidate for minorities and high-school-educated whites. Motivated by a real concern for the next generation, the president's popularity will remain strong, particularly with Gen-Xers and the elderly. A commitment to the baby boomers, from which he or she will doubtless emerge, should keep the president in good electoral shape for two full terms while paving the way for a successor to pursue any still-pending portions of the agenda. As a populist, this leader would be a genuine citizen-politician, someone elected not because he or she seeks office but because holding office is essential to enact the changes proposed. Once that's accomplished, our man or woman would happily head back home.

2
Reform or Rebellion?

A non-violent revolution is not a program of seizure of power. It is a program of transformation of relationships, ending in a peaceful transfer of power.

—MAHATMA GANDHI

I propose here an idea that some will find outlandish, particularly (as I write this) in the midst of the longest sustained stock market boom in history. The notion is this: Our democracy requires a revolution. Dramatic and fast-widening economic disparities suggest it's time that we again listen to Gandhi and to his followers such as Dr. Martin Luther King, Jr., who argued that for civil rights to be effective, it must have a counterpart in the domain of economic rights. King was assassinated soon after he began to shift his attention from civil rights and racial segregation to economic injustice with a focus on the Poor People's Campaign. He understood that, absent economic justice, we will never achieve what he called our beloved community. Gandhi also understood; he saw revolution as a change in relationships and a shift in power back to the personal and to communities. Echoing Thomas Jefferson from a century and a half before, he reminds us why unresponsive governments are much improved by an occasional encounter with rebellion.

Dr. King's peaceful but persistent revolution worked wonders for democracy, freeing both blacks and whites from the bondage that undermines democracy when some are denied their civil rights. Today's wrenching inequality and frightening environmental trends suggest that it's time we again demand an end to injustice. Indeed, I argue that rebellion is the only rational course and that today any realist must be a revolutionary. I don't mean armed rebellion in the streets—though the Framers would warn us not to rule that out. I mean revolution in the sense that evolution in the natural sciences occurs in fits and starts, progressing with long stretches of stability punctuated by periods of abrupt, even eye-popping change. Dramatic and rapid reform of the rules is now the only sensible course if we are to rescue our democracy.

Peer through the blizzard of ticker tape celebrating a rising stock market, and you'll see that the crowds lining the street are remarkably thin. Look closer, and you'll find that the parade is largely a charade. The real party is going on upstairs in a series of small, private rooms. In 1982, inclusion on the Forbes 400 list of the richest Americans required personal wealth of $91 million. The list then included 13 billionaires. By 1999, $625 million was required for inclusion on a list that included 268 billionaires.[1] While the number of households expanded 3 percent from 1995 to 1998, the number of households worth $10 million or more grew 44.7 percent.[2] Eighty-six percent of stock market gains between 1989 and 1997 flowed to the top 10 percent of households, whereas 42 percent went to the most well-to-do 1 percent.[3] Moreover, from 1983 to 1998, only the top 20 percent saw any appreciable increase in their income, whereas the middle class, if they lost their jobs, had enough savings to maintain their standard of living for just 1.2 months (thirty-six days), down from 3.6 months in 1989.[4] In *Luxury Fever* (1999), economist Robert Frank reports that the top 1 percent captured 70 percent of all earnings growth since the mid-1970s.[5]

Some party. Some parade—viewed by most with their noses pressed against the window as they watch confetti showers of cash engulf the few.

Trickle-Up Economics

Not since 1929 have the disparities in U.S. wealth and income been so wide. You will be dismayed at what you read. Alarmed also—perhaps even outraged. I hope so. "Ye shall know the truth," Aldous Huxley warned, "and the truth will make you mad." Yet that anger, I suggest, is a mask for sadness. For me, the trends evoke anguish at the inhumane impact of human forces, largely financial forces, that we've unleashed in the world. If we are to have a democracy, we must have reform. Either that, or our democratic conscience *requires* of us rebellion. Consider these facts:

- The combined net worth of the Forbes 400 was $1 trillion in September 1999, an increase from $738 billion just twelve months earlier. That works out to an average one-year increase of $655 million *each* for those who were already the nation's richest ($12.6 million per week).[6]
- Less than one-fifth of that increase ($48.4 billion) would have been enough to bring every American up to the official poverty line while still leaving each of our four hundred most-favored citizens with an average one-year increase of $534 million ($10.2 million per week).
- *Business Week* reports that in 1998, the average large-company chief executive was paid $10.6 million, a 36 percent jump over 1997.[7] That omits stock options that executives haven't yet exercised. That's a huge omission. Compensation expert Graef Crystal identifies five CEOs who each saw their wallets widen by more than $232 million in 1998. That works out to $116,000 per hour.
- In New York, the highest-income 5 percent of families gained nearly $108,000 between the late 1970s and the late 1990s, while the lowest-income 20 percent of New Yorkers lost $2,900 per family.[8]

You will search in vain for some rationale for these results. There isn't one. In no way are these results plausibly related to economic or social contribution. In 1998, the chief executive at Chrysler was paid 27 times that of the CEO at Volvo, yet Chrysler's net income was only 2.5 times that of Volvo. Colgate-Palmolive's CEO was paid 22 times as much as Unilever's, even though Unilever's net income was 6.6 times as large. Executive pay rose an average 481 percent from 1990 to 1998, while corporate profits rose 108 percent.[9] That's seven times faster than wage growth on the factory floor. When Daimler acquired Chrysler in May 1998, the European company realized that Chrysler's number two executive made more in one year from salary, bonus, and stock options than the top ten Daimler executives combined.

In 1998, Jack Welch, CEO of General Electric (GE), pocketed $86.3 million, making him the nation's sixth-best-paid employee. If his pay package were represented by the Empire State Building, how tall would the buildings representing other GE employees be? Eight inches. Had the typical worker's pay risen in tandem with executive pay, the average production worker would now earn $110,000 a year and the minimum wage would be $22.08. Turn-of-the-century financier J. P. Morgan, no stranger to greed, insisted that no executive should make more than twenty times what an average employee makes. Peter Drucker argues that a difference of more than fifteen to twenty times poisons the workplace and undermines productivity. Nevertheless, in 1998, Disney CEO Michael Eisner received a pay package totaling $575.6 million, 25,070 times the average Disney worker's pay.[10] How tall would the buildings of Disney employees be? Just over an inch. Yet despite the astronomical salaries of these CEOs—suggesting astronomical skills—corporate spending on consultants has increased by a factor of forty-four just since 1980, to $89 billion. Of that money, 60 percent is spent in the United States, where at sizable companies, there's now one consultant for every two executives.[11]

Of this I'm certain: Any system that makes it easier for a Bill Gates to amass another $50 billion than it does for a single mother to get $500 ahead of her bills (while trying to raise the next potential Bill Gates) is buying a lot of hogwash about the value of the contribution made to this nation by the superrich. And about the workability of a democracy that celebrates appropriation of this nation's prosperity by so few. Yet I've heard critics claim that my even raising this sensitive issue is the first step toward the Gulag. Far better, I'm told, if we focus instead on so-called social issues.

There's certainly ample precedent. In the 1920s, the issue evaders of that era insisted that alcohol was more important. So we amended the Constitution to prohibit it. And then amended it to permit it. That diversion allowed the Gilded Age to proceed unchecked—until it crashed. Today's masters of distraction urge that we do the same thing. They would have us deal instead with the dangers posed by flag burning, apparently hoping we'll wrap ourselves around yet another nonsensical, time-consuming congressional debate. Instead of the Anti-Saloon League, we now have the right-to-life missionaries. Instead of vilifying the town drunk, we have Murphy Brown and the welfare queen. What about fast-widening economic disparities, environmental devastation, and the powerfully fragmenting forces of modern economic life? Too sensitive. Too difficult. Too complex. Just cut taxes instead. After all, that's the only issue that *really* counts.

Keep it simple. Don't worry, the market will sort it all out. Just give it more time and a little longer leash. Although I understand the allure of such simplistic, single-issue politics, we can no longer afford to coddle those policymakers who are unable or unwilling to confront today's complex problems.

The World Is Not Enough

What's the point of prosperity in a democracy? Is it a success no matter who reaps its benefits? Apparently so. If the value of the Microsoft stock owned by Bill Gates continues to grow at the same torrid pace as it has since Microsoft's 1986 initial public offering (58.2 percent a year), he will become a trillionaire ($1,000 billion) in March 2005, at the age of forty-nine, and his Microsoft holdings will be valued at $1 quadrillion (that's a million billion) in March 2020, when he turns sixty-four.[12]

Or is prosperity an opportunity for widespread economic advance and social accomplishment?[13] Apparently not. Today's rules are clear: Making the already-rich endlessly richer is now the best use to which our expanding prosperity can be put. That's what today's policymakers have concluded. How much is a million billion? The 1998 gross world product was just $39,000 billion (less than 4 percent of a million billion). In May 1997, the journal *Nature* concluded that the planet's ecosystems provide a range of environmental and resource services worth $33,000 billion each year.[14] If that amount were capitalized using the interest rate paid on U.S. treasuries, that puts the value of all creation at about $500,000 billion, one-half Bill Gates's projected net worth in 2020.

What does our expanding prosperity look like from the perspective of the nonrich?

- From 1983 to 1997, only the top 5 percent of U.S. households saw an increase in their net worth, whereas wealth declined for everyone else.[15]
- According to the U.S. Census Bureau, today's record-breaking inequality means that the top fifth of households now claim 49.2 percent of our national income, whereas the bottom fifth get by on just 3.6 percent.[16]
- In the same year (1998) when one American (Gates) achieved the dubious distinction of amassing more wealth than the combined net worth of the poorest 45 percent of American

households, a record 1.4 million Americans filed for bankruptcy.[17] That's seven thousand bankruptcies per hour, eight hours a day, five days a week.[18] The pace is poised to quicken as household debt (figured as a percentage of personal income) continues to rise from 58 percent in 1973 to an estimated 85 percent in 1998 (personal bankruptcies totaled 1.3 million in 1999).[19]

How does today's prosperity look from an environmental perspective? Meteorological announcements that "this is the hottest year in history" are now routine. Eight of the ten hottest years on record were recorded in the past ten years (the 1990s were the warmest decade in a century of record keeping). Spring now arrives a week earlier than in 1970. In 1999, for the first time in recorded history, Chicago had no snow in November.

Escalating losses from severe storms, droughts, and floods are sending shock waves through the insurance industry, including a 318-mile-an-hour Category 5 tornado that terrorized Oklahoma in April 1999 and a Category 4 hurricane ("Floyd") that threatened the eastern seaboard in September. During the first ten months of 1998, weather-related damage caused $90 billion in losses worldwide. That's more than the entire decade of the 1980s, when damage averaged $2 billion per year. In December 1999, Western Europe suffered the ravages of the worst windstorm in a century.

Biodiversity is declining dramatically, according to a 1999 report by the U.S. Geological Survey, the first-ever large-scale assessment of the nation's heritage of natural resources. The report cited as the primary causes urbanization, conversion of wetlands to agriculture, draining of wetlands for development, and the fragmentation of forests.[20] From 1992 to 1997, land was converted to development at the rate of 3 million acres per year (6 acres per minute), more than twice the rate from 1982 to 1992. In the Pacific Northwest, 83 percent of the region's old-growth Douglas fir is gone, along with 75 percent of coastal rain forests in Washington State and 85 percent of California's old-growth redwoods.

According to the UN Environmental Program, the world water cycle probably cannot cope with demands in the coming decades. The organization also asserts that land degradation has negated many advances made by increased agricultural productivity, that air pollution is at a crisis point in major cities, and that global warming is now inevitable.[21]

Preserving the Magic While
Spreading the Prosperity

The principles of free enterprise are sound: private property, innovation, rewards linked to risk taking. What must change is the ideology that would have us limit the reach of prosperity that free enterprise can achieve. The question is no longer whether capitalism will prevail. The relevant question is *what sort of capitalism* do we mean to have? We can continue to do nothing. There's ample precedent for that. Inactivity is a choice in favor of a capitalism that remains highly exclusive and indifferent to its social and environmental effects. Or we can embrace a more inclusive capitalism, both modern and responsible, in which factors in addition to finance influence economic decision making.

The rules governing capitalism can change. As counsel to the Senate Committee on Finance during much of the Reagan-Bush era, I saw firsthand how dramatically they can change. That, too, is part of the creativity available in a free-enterprise democracy—we can change the rules. The same laws we amended then to make the rich richer could have encouraged broad-based ownership and widespread prosperity. Instead we wrote the rules in a way that was guaranteed to make an exclusive system dramatically more so. To my knowledge, I am the first insider to document the policy decisions that fueled that deficit-laden, rich-get-richer era.[22] Although rewriting the rules to create an *inclusive* capitalism may temporarily pinch the wingtips of the nation's most well-to-do, that's a price that must be paid. The changes proposed here are essential to ensure an equitable and sustainable system in place of one that's presently neither.

Let me be candid about my intentions. This is a populist challenge to our perilously complacent leadership. This book is a call to action to move us toward a more authentic form of democracy. It's addressed to those who are fed up and to those ready to wake up. And to those who sense that the current rules are unfair, unworkable, and unsustainable. They're right on all three counts. It's also about how to aspire grandly, and how to convert your personal longing into a collective dignity joined to an achievable level of real prosperity. We need only write the rules with those goals in mind. Though you may be pessimistic about the prospects for such a future, particularly as you ponder today's horrific trends, it's essential that we move rapidly into a post-pessimist period because there's much yet to be done and little time to do it. The 2000 election is upon us. With a new president to be elected, control of the House and Senate hinging on a margin of six seats each, the make-up of the Supreme Court in the balance, redistricting for the 2000 census under way, and political fund-raising at an all-time high, the political stakes just don't get any higher.

Prosperity Hijacked and Leisure Denied

Real change requires a real populist presidential candidate with sufficient courage and candor—and enough love of democracy—to insist that we reverse the current trends. Frankly, that seems unlikely. The word *courage* is taken from the French *coeur,* for "heart." The future of democracy may well depend on whether this election season—or the next—evokes a candidate with sufficient heart to fight these divisive forces and restore to free enterprise some semblance of fairness and ecological common sense.

Yet there's also much more at stake. Writing six decades ago in his "Economic Possibilities for Our Grandchildren," British economist John Maynard Keynes foresaw that labor-saving advances, what he called technological unemployment, would outpace the rate at which we could find uses for human labor. His forecast has born fruit, as the world's two hundred largest corporations now account for 28 percent of global economic activity while employing less than one-quarter of 1 percent of the global workforce.

As a result of steady advances in human ingenuity and design, he predicted, "This means that the economic problem is not, if we look into the future, the permanent problem of the human race." Rather than today's ongoing struggle for survival and economic security, we should by now be focusing (in Keynes's words) on "how to live wisely, agreeably and well." Instead, we've become steadily less secure and frantically more overworked as we've allowed a few to monopolize the nation's leisure by monopolizing the prosperity that makes leisure affordable. Surely that must rank among the most inhumane of acts in a century that will long be remembered for its many episodes of extraordinary inhumanity. Although the current results confirm the profound lack of a functioning democracy, they should also give us hope because today's results reflect the policy environment—and that environment can be changed.

Richard Goodwin, former special counsel to President Kennedy, argues that Bill Clinton and Al Gore abandoned the Democratic Party to keep themselves in office and, thus, the American majority no longer has a party.[23] That charge may be a bit harsh given the political choices they faced in the wake of the 1994 election blowout and ascendancy of the Newt Gingrich brand of radical-right conservatism. Yet regardless of whether Goodwin's claim of a political sellout is fair (I agree with him), the votes are there to put a genuine populist in the White House, as I will show. But that requires the emergence of an uncommonly courageous, even audacious candidate willing to address the challenges we face. Absent that, I fear for our democracy because today's centrist candidates—of both major parties—are clueless when it comes to the central issue: how to lead us back from a fast-emerging plutocracy to a robust and ecologically attuned democracy. Should the 2000 election proceed without the presence of a viable populist alternative—as seems likely—we must face the prospect that our democracy has become truly dysfunctional. That's why I show here how we can—and must—begin the task of restoring democracy by taking free enterprise back from those who would reserve it for themselves. And from those holding elective office who support them in that design.

Bread-and-Circus Politics

To lay the foundation for what follows, I offer below another "data dump" to indicate just how far we've traveled down the wrong road. Notice how curiously absent these facts are in today's political debates.

- In 1997, 142,556 people reported an adjusted gross income of $1 million or more, according to the Internal Revenue Service (IRS). That's up from 86,998 people for 1995.[24]
- In 1999, the Congressional Budget Office (CBO) indicated that the top 1 percent of income earners had an average before-tax income of $786,000 and an average after-tax income of $516,000.[25]
- In 1998, 9,257 new and existing homes sold for $1 million or more. That's triple the number of million-dollar homes on the market in 1995. Annual mortgage interest payments on a newly purchased $1 million home total $79,247 (assuming 10 percent down and a thirty-year adjustable rate mortgage at 8 percent).[26] The home mortgage interest deduction for those in the top 39.6-percent tax bracket saves on that house $31,382 a year in taxes. When that saving is added to the $40,000 average annual tax cut allowed the top 1 percent

since 1977, a $1 million house is all but paid for, leaving only $7,865 per year in outlays or $655 per month—barely enough to rent a one-bedroom apartment here in Atlanta.

- For every age group under fifty-five, home ownership remains below where it was in the early 1980s.[27]
- The after-tax income flowing to the middle 60 percent of households in 1999 is the lowest recorded since 1977. Among the bottom fifth of households, average after-tax income fell 9 percent from 1977 to 1999.
- The percentage of black households with zero or negative net worth (31.3 percent) is double that of whites.[28] As of 1997, the modest net worth of white families was eight times that of African Americans and twelve times that of Hispanics. The 1997 median financial wealth of African Americans (net worth less home equity) is $200, whereas that of Hispanics is zero.[29]
- The poverty rate among blacks, 26.1 percent, is 2.5 times greater than the rate for whites. For Hispanics, the rate is 25.6 percent.
- During the first quarter of 1999, for the first time since the Depression, the national savings rate turned negative.[30]
- If the richest 1 percent of the population were receiving the same share of after-tax income in 1999 as it did in 1977, it would have received $271 billion *less* in income in 1999— $226,000 less per household.[31]
- Congressional tax cuts targeted at the well-to-do mean that between 1977 and 1999, the *after-tax* income of our richest 1 percent actually grew faster (115 percent) than their *before-tax* income (96 percent).[32]

With help from an oddball assemblage of politicians, pundits, and academics, we've been seduced to think that the era of class conflict is over. Think again. We can't move beyond class-based politics until we remedy the structures that cause it. It's inconceivable that those who crafted the Declaration of Independence would pledge "their lives, their fortunes and their sacred honor" to create a system conducive to such social division. They knew it's impossible for a democracy consisting of political equals to survive alongside an economic oligarchy. Their intention was to resist the "economic royalists," not to condone, coddle, encourage, and celebrate them. They knew better. They warned that democracies must be ever vigilant in their opposition to what Jefferson and James Madison called "monarchial tendencies." Those tendencies are alive—as shown in Washington's insistence that we focus on bread-and-circus social issues so that we'll think there's a substantive debate ongoing in Congress. Or that matters of real importance are at issue between the Republican Congress and Democrats in the White House. Or in the race for the White House. To debate while saying nothing of significance has become a modern political art form. Meanwhile, issues of real, intergenerational substance remain well outside the sphere of consideration. Writing in *The Hungry Spirit*, British business philosopher Charles Handy puts today's leadership challenge in perspective: "Cathedrals inspire. Those who first worked on them knew for certain that they would never see them finished. We may not need any more cathedrals but we do need cathedral thinkers, people who can think beyond their own lifetimes."[33]

But What About the Booming Economy?

Defenders of the laissez-faire faith assure us that times have never been better: record-low employment and record-low inflation, along with a record-high 43 percent participation in a record-high stock market. A current best-seller predicts a 36,000 Dow. Another predicts 40,000. Yet another, 41,000. Even 100,000.[34] And, to top it off, the United States is enjoying a budget surplus for the first time since Lyndon Johnson occupied the Oval Office. In U.S. politics, it's long been a truism that "prosperity swallows up all criticism." Yet what we have today is the *perception* of prosperity. It's a thin veneer of prosperity, an illusion for most. Any objective assessment confirms that it's mostly optics.

Although unemployment, at 4.5 percent in 1998, was at its lowest level in decades, wages barely budged for the decade. The U.S. Census Bureau reports that the pretax median income was just $1,001 higher in 1998 than in 1989. For the entire decade of the booming 1990s, that's an average annual raise, adjusted for inflation, of $111.22, or a meager 0.3 percent. Meanwhile, income inequality climbed dramatically throughout the 1980s and early 1990s, holding roughly constant since 1994, locking in economic disparity at a record-high level.[35] Yet even that overstates the rise in living standards, because working hours steadily expanded from 1989 to 1998. Working hours reached 3,149 in 1998, roughly 60 hours a week for the average family, according to an analysis of census data by the Economic Policy Institute. That moves us into first place in the number of hours worked, surpassing even the workaholic Japanese.[36] "Finally we have *stemmed the tide* of rising inequality," Bill Clinton crowed in 1999, shining the best possible political light on these disturbing trends.[37] Not reversed it, mind you. Nor addressed it.

Amid today's widespread financial insecurity, is it truly an astute monetary policy that keeps a lid on inflation? More likely it's the stark terror of those afraid to press for a raise for fear of losing out on a steadily shrinking pool of middle-class jobs even as the official unemployment numbers hovered around a record-low 4.3 percent for much of 1999. Downsizing and "right-sizing" continue to take their psychic toll, silencing many who might have complained about stagnant pay, longer work hours, and deteriorating working conditions. Further down the income ladder, we find those resigned to the realization that they're stuck; no matter where they turn, they're locked into a very narrow range of low-wage jobs, largely in the service and hospitality industries. How do those struggling to cope with this "boom" describe it? With brutal candor: "You can always get a job but you can't always make a living."

Poverty and Prosperity

Meanwhile we continue to pretend that poverty in the United States is like ice that melts in the sun of overall economic growth. Nothing could be further from the truth. Census data confirms that recent declines in the poverty rate are a result of its decrease in the South with no change to speak of elsewhere except in the West, where it's on the rise. The South has long been a magnet for companies interested in moving their operations to a region (predominantly nonunion) where a large percentage of the population earns the minimum wage and thus benefited from modest increases in the minimum wage in 1997 and 1998. A forty-hour week at the 1999–2000 minimum wage ($5.15 per hour) nets a pretax annual income of $10,300. That's $6,355 below the 1998 poverty line for a family of four. Had increases in the minimum wage merely kept pace with inflation since the 1960s, the minimum would now exceed the earnings of nearly 30 percent of U.S. workers.[38] Does that sound like a boom?

Yet even these figures fail to portray the true picture. The current poverty formula was created for Lyndon Johnson during his War on Poverty. Except for inflation adjustments, it remains unchanged since 1965. The formula is geared to what was then required to address severe deprivation by providing barely sufficient nutrition and then only if "the housewife is a careful shopper, a skillful cook and a good manager who will prepare all the family's meals at home."[39] Facing widespread concern that the standard is out of date, the Census Bureau proposed experimental measures in July 1999, raising the poverty threshold to $19,500 for a family of four, well below the $21,000 to $28,000 that most experts agree is required not only to survive but to preserve a reasonable amount of self-respect. This political hot potato is already an orphan, particularly now that the Washington consensus took credit for a 12.7 percent poverty rate in September 1999, the lowest level in a decade. Raising the threshold to $19,500 boosts the poverty rate to a more realistic 17 percent, confirming that 46 million Americans scrape by on an income that fails to meet even that minimal level.

Ignoring the Fiscally Obvious

As for today's alleged budget surpluses, for the first time ever, White House budget projections extend over an impossible-to-predict fifteen years, even though everyone in Washington knows that any forecast beyond two or three years is mischievous malarkey. Though such ephemeral projections are innately irresponsible, they gained for Bill Clinton and Al Gore the political cover needed to propose costly changes in Medicare while also appearing to close the deficit. And they allowed congressional Republicans to propose yet another round of tax cuts, this time a $792-billion rich-get-richer giveaway sent to the White House for a certain veto in September 1999.[40] That political charade—akin to Oriental shadow boxing—follows in the wake of these joined-at-the-hip parties embracing in 1997 a nonsensical Balanced Budget Act. The act promised that unspecified categories of federal spending would be slashed by what everyone knew was an impossible 20 percent. At legislated fib encouraged budget estimators to consider this nonsensical assurance in their assumptions.[41]

Rosy-scenario economic projections are something to which we became accustomed during David Stockman's stint as budget director under Reagan. Stockman all but conceded that his phony figures were a backdoor ruse to de-fund the public sector. He was confident that the Reagan-Bush tidal wave of red ink would crowd out federal spending that Republicans lacked the votes to kill in Congress (events proved him correct). At least his figures were subject to debate on a range of shifting assumptions about the real world of economic growth and other influences. But rosy *legislative* assumptions are simply deceitful attempts to play the system for political gain. They bring to mind comedian George Carlin's quip that *bipartisan* usually means that some larger-than-usual deception is being carried out.

What legislators and budget estimators ignore is easily the most fiscally ruinous fact of all: inadequate assets accumulated by 76 million baby boomers, voters all. If they outlive their nest eggs, which are modest and shrinking, the economy will face a momentous fiscal shock. The boomers' combination of retirement-age insecurity and demographic political clout could generate wrenching demands on the rest of the country, converting any hoped-for, hyped-up surplus into a real and debilitating deficit. Though in their youth the boomers advised, "Don't trust anyone over thirty," they may soon adopt a new motto: "Don't mess with anyone over forty." What's brewing is a boomer backlash that's poised to make mincemeat of today's naively flush fiscal projections.

Meanwhile, the politically nimble Clinton-Gore team proposed a lockbox approach to deficit reduction, insisting that any surplus be applied to "Save Social Security"—even though many experts agree that surpluses have no effect on Social Security's health and that, indeed, no surplus may exist beyond what social security brings in. Never mind. The proposal was deemed politically brilliant by Washington's pundit-elite because a Democratic president, displaying keen fiscal conservatism, again preempted Republican calls for a tax cut. Influenced by six years of coaching from Treasury Secretary Bob Rubin, the Wall Street bond trader, the Clinton-Gore administration became staunch fiscal conservatives, their political antennae tightly attuned to financial markets. The problem, of course, is that this stance also means we either punt on needed public investments or call for new taxes to pay for them—which is madness when our fiscal cup runneth over. That brilliance may have fitted us for an even tighter fiscal straitjacket than during the Reagan-Bush era (witness Al Gore's attack on Bill Bradley when he proposed health-care reform similar to what Clinton offered in his first term).

What about the so-called largest intergenerational transfer of wealth in history—more than $12 trillion—that will take place from now until around 2020, as the World War II generation dies off and leaves its assets to the boomers? Don't hold your breath. The benchmark study by economists Robert Avery and Michael Rendall found that one-third of that transfer will go to 1 percent of the boomers

($1.6 million each), whereas another third will go to the next 9 per-cent ($336,000 per person). The final slice will be divided by the re-maining 90 percent (an average $40,000 apiece).[42]

What about the oft-claimed trickle-down benefits of this booming economy? Between 1983 and 1997, "there has been almost no trickle-down of economic growth to the average family," says New York University professor Edward N. Wolff. "Almost all the growth in household income and wealth has accrued to the richest 20 per-cent. The finances of the average American family are more fragile in the late 1990s than in the early 1980s."[43] Nine years into the longest economic expansion in the nation's history, labor's share of the na-tional income remains 2–4 percent below the levels reached in the late 1960s and early 1970s.[44]

By the standards of any functioning democracy, these disturbing and fast-accelerating trends would be addressed as a national crisis de-serving even a special session of Congress devoted to crafting a cure. Not so. At least not by the standards of the two reigning U.S. politi-cal parties: the Demopubs and the Republicrats. Neither mentions it. Both are firmly in denial, eloquent in their silence as they concentrate on partisan positioning rather than corrective policy. Among today's policymakers, these matters are simply of no concern. Leadership-wise, mediocrity reigns supreme while uninhibited selfishness and wanton greed roam the land, disguised as personal freedom, even lib-eration, as today's cramped view of freedom pushed democratic re-sponsibility into the shadows.

A Global Tragedy Unfolding

Although the domestic trends are unsettling, it's equally troubling to realize the impact of our leadership on other countries. As the world's mentor free-enterprise economy and chief cheerleader for fair-play-via-laissez-faire, the United States should not be surprised that iden-tical trends are emerging worldwide, where, as here, practically no one dares mention it. Although certain developments are hopeful, others are horrendous.

Lest we become unduly disheartened, it's important to acknowl-edge that global capitalism has lifted living standards in many places—improving nutrition, broadening education, and lengthen-ing life spans. In the 1950s the average woman bore 6 children, whereas in the 1990s she bore only 2.9. In the rich countries, birth rates are already below the replacement rate. Child death rates have fallen by half since 1965; a child born today can expect to live a decade longer than a child born then. Fifty years ago, 28 percent of children in developing countries died before age five; that's been reduced to 10 percent. Adult literacy rates continue to rise, from 48 percent in 1970 to 70 percent in 1997. Plus, more than 70 percent of the world's people now live under fairly pluralistic democratic regimes.[45] Yet these positive trends mask an unevenness that confirms widespread deprivation and fast-widening inequality. If as a nation we fail to address these trends, we risk becoming a caricature, a seedy barker for all that occurs, whether benign or malign, in a free-enterprise circus in which democracy is often on display but seldom demonstrated. Consider the following signs of fast-widening worldwide economic inequality:

- The assets of the world's eighty-four richest individuals exceed the GDP of China, with its 1.3 billion people.[46]
- In Indonesia, 61.7 percent of the stock market's value is held by the nation's fifteen richest families. The comparable figure for the Philippines is 55.1 percent and for Thailand 53.3 percent.[47]
- In 1960, the income gap between the fifth of the world's people living in the richest countries and the fifth in the poorest was 30 to 1. By 1990, the gap had widened to 60 to 1. By 1998, it had grown to 74 to 1.[48]
- With global population expanding by 80 million each year, World Bank President Jim Wolfensohn cautions that unless we address this "challenge of inclusion," thirty years hence we will have 5 billion people living on less than $2 per day.
- The UN Development Program reports that 2 billion people suffer from anemia, including 55 million in industrial countries. Current trends in population growth and prosperity hoarding suggest that in three decades, we could inhabit a world where 3.7 billion people suffer from anemia.

These interrelated phenomena led UN development experts to conclude that the world is heading toward "grotesque inequalities" and to offer this sobering appraisal: "Development that perpetuates today's inequalities is neither sustainable *nor worth sustaining.*"[49] Though our laissez-faire-obsessed economists predicted that globalization would lead to economic convergence, the past decade witnessed a steady increase in the concentration of income, resources, and wealth as ever more people got stuck in living standards just one notch north of survive.

It's generally agreed that six core ingredients are essential as minimal conditions for the flowering of human potential: safe drinking water, adequate sanitation, sufficient nutrition, primary health care, basic education, and family planning services for all willing couples. Sadly, these six core ingredients are lacking in much of the world. For example, the UN has reported that 1.3 billion people lack access to clean water, and one in seven primary-school-age children is out of school.[50]

How much would it take to provide the six essential ingredients? The UN Development Program calculates the cost at about $35 billion each year for fifteen years. That's about what the United States spent in 1999 to maintain its nuclear readiness, a decade after the fall of the Berlin Wall. If the world community were to bear the cost, it would total one-seventh of 1 percent of global income.[51] By comparison, every jet fighter sold by a developed country to a developing country costs the schooling of 3 million children.[52] The cost of a submarine denies safe drinking water to 60 million people. Though the Cold War may appear to have ended, it is far from over in the Third World.

What if those individuals who most benefit from the global economy were to bear the cost of providing the six essentials to all the world's population? An annual 3.5 percent levy on the $1 trillion in assets owned by the world's two hundred richest people (whose 1999 average individual wealth was $5 billion) would raise the requisite $35 billion. The UN Development Program indicates that three-quarters of those suffering from *affluenza* live in the 29 OECD (Organization for Economic Cooperation and Development) countries; 60 reside in the United States.[53] Imagine if the international community identified the $8 trillion in outlaw wealth sloshing around the world's tax havens in an estimated 1.5 million offshore corporations (up from 200,000 just since the late 1980s). An annual "freeloader levy" of just 3.5 percent (less than the typical sales tax) would generate $280 billion. That's 165 times the annual budget for UN development programs. Or 93 times the UN's annual expenditure for peacekeeping operations, now raised pass-your-hat style. That's enough to build 140,000 schools at $2 million apiece. That's also the bulk of the $300 billion that environmental researchers at Cambridge and Sheffield Universities report would be required each year to "save the planet."[54]

Tomorrow's Mothers

Globalization will not be reversed, because it's driven by advances in information technology and telecommunications that simply will not be undone. Yet the way globalization is proceeding invites instability, even insurrection. The trends also suggest a lingering inhumanity at large in the human community—a miserable and miserly self-indulgence that cloaks itself in the morality of the marketplace. Today's geopolitical forces point to the continued spread of values that embrace the freedom of free enterprise. Yet those who most benefit from its spread are unwilling to embrace the morality of *enough*. The consequences of that self-absorption threaten to overwhelm the adaptive capacities of societies around the world while also laying waste to the natural world. These pages bear witness to the reservoir of human pain, personal indignity, and ecological tragedy that accompanies continued denial and inaction by our elected leaders both here and abroad. The warning bell has been sounded. "It is a stupid society," Massachusetts Institute of Technology (MIT) economist Lester Thurow cautions, "that runs an experiment to see where its breaking points are." Or, as the elders of the Seneca tribe cautioned, "Every fire is the same size when it starts."

As another indication of how critical it is that these trends be addressed, consider the devastating impact on women and children:

- Eighty percent of the world's people live in developing countries.
- Ninety-five percent of the next generation's children will be born to women there.
- Seventy percent of those women live on less than $1 per day.
- Ninety percent of those women work as housewives who labor on average thirty-five hours more per week than the typical paid workman. None of their work is reflected in the GDP.
- Women in developing countries produce 80 percent of the food and receive 10 percent of the agricultural assistance.
- Seventy percent are illiterate.
- For every year that women attend school beyond the fourth grade, the birth rate declines 20 percent.
- Less than 1 percent of the world's assets are held in the name of women.

Poverty is not an abstraction; it's largely women and children in both developing and developed countries. Anyone who's traveled abroad has seen the phenomenon—the men sitting around the souks and the cafes with their coffee, cigarettes, and idle chatter while women toil the fields, haul the water, and do uncompensated "women's work" that includes raising the children and caring for their husbands. One of the most difficult and intractable elements in addressing poverty lies in the troubling reality that we live in a world where history's male/dominator model is all-pervasive. It's killing us, literally.

This prevalent mind-set poses one of the key barriers to any hope of a humane and sustainable future, yet it's little recognized and seldom discussed, particularly in those cultures where its operations are most apparent and its effects most cruel. As Riane Eisler argues in *Tomorrow's Children*, until "caring work" is compensated—in the sense of giving monetary value (versus psychological value) to that most essential of elements in any economy—it's difficult to imagine how we will lift the yoke of poverty from the backs of women and children worldwide.[55] By compensation, I mean the sort of pay such that you can afford to eat with it or sleep under it. Until caring work is seen as having genuine value, this divisive, even barbaric domination will continue to work its devastation on the poorest of the poor.

This is not meant as a put-down of men. Males have been educated and acculturated to differentiate themselves from women in ways too absurd for words. Nor is this a "women's issue." The issue is how to design humane and sustainable societies that give priority to human welfare and the quality of life.

The Duties of Wisdom

Gandhi once cautioned that "inaction at a time of conflagration is inexcusable." The agenda proposed here suggests that immediate action is required to head off conflagration. We face a crisis, yet no one wants to acknowledge it, much less address it. That's unacceptable. Tolstoy put it well: "Indifference to evil is violence." Although those are strong words, I suggest as a matter of conscience that we can no longer endure either the policies or the policymakers who brought us to this sorry state of affairs. The results chronicled above speak volumes for the callous indifference with which today's leaders have performed their tasks. Yet the demands of democracy require that we move quickly to get beyond dismay, alarm, and outrage to effective action.

I suggest here how to build support for reforms through the roll-out of a nationwide education campaign. My initial goal, however, is to persuade you that we face a crisis whose full dimensions are not yet widely appreciated. You'll be astounded at the scope of what's at stake. I then invite your embrace of a formula for change that I propose for the First Hundred Days following the election of what I suggest *must* be a genuinely populist president. We cannot afford yet another administration that remains aloof from these troubling issues.

Any objective outsider (say, a man from Mars) would surely conclude that we're presented in 2000 with a curious political choice for an avowed democracy: two professional politicians who are sons of professional politicians—even a grandson of a politician in Dubya's case. If our visitor from afar were to study the dynamics of today's democracy, he would surely note that both candidates are cut from the same cloth. They even look as though they're auditioning to be each other's double—born and bred to run for public office purely for the sake of holding office without regard to whether that might make a difference in people's lives.

For a nation raised on the notion that anyone can aspire to be president, this matched pair of candidates must appear to our visitor peculiar indeed. Both are political heirs born to privilege, fortunately educated and exuding a sense of casual entitlement that makes their occasional rhetorical forays into populist terrain seem all the more bizarre, even otherworldly. Surely our extraterrestrial visitor would ask if both do not in fact embody just the sort of hand-me-down, antiegalitarian political legacy that most frightened the nation's founders—style without substance, experience without meaning, character but no core, keen observers with no discernible vision, a clear grasp of procedure but no clarity of purpose, ambition all out of proportion to their understanding, knowledge of the pieces but no appreciation for the patterns that count. In short, the visitor surely would want to know, are we being offered all flower but no fruit? Either would make an able caretaker president were this a time when the nation needs the illusion of leadership without progress. Though this is not such a time, a caretaker president may be what we choose again to endure.

3
Killer Capitalism

The tendency of contemporary liberal democracies to fall prey to excessive individualism is perhaps their greatest long-term vulnerability, and is particularly visible in the most individualist of all democracies, the United States.

—FRANCIS FUKUYAMA

To make progress in this populist arena requires structural change. That can make people nervous. Sometimes I feel like a heretic in a land of true believers and recent converts. We can now see the clear outlines of tomorrow's version of capitalism. There's much not to like, at least not if we aspire to live in a robust democracy populated by political equals. Yet fundamental change goes against the grain of today's market-myopic economic model (it's difficult to imagine Dr. King calling his Poor People's Campaign the New Markets Initiative, a Clinton-Gore phrase). That's due to the remarkable success of a remarkably well funded political movement—disguised as an education initiative known as Law and Economics. The movement quietly, methodically, and effectively implanted today's purist market model in the minds of students, political leaders, business executives, and the judiciary. Originating at the University of Chicago, the campaign remains largely invisible, though I will chronicle some of its many successes.[1] Several deep-pocket individuals and well-funded foundations (Bradley, Joyce, Olin, Smith Richardson) provided generous support, including the publication of hundreds of the movement's books and generous payments to journalists to attend their seminars.

I consider one of its early victories a 1976 Supreme Court case *(Buckley vs. Valeo)* forbidding any restriction on how much of their own money political candidates or their supporters can spend, concluding that *spending is itself a form of political speech* entitled to protection by the First Amendment to the Constitution. However, the court upheld federal limits on contributions that congressional candidates can accept from others, agreeing that limits are justified to safeguard the integrity of the election process.[2] As we'll see later, that decision ensured the plutocratization of U.S. politics as the well-heeled and the financially well connected were guaranteed an advantage, and as ownership of our once-democratic media outlets shifted into fewer and fewer hands.

In a land of political equals, Steve Forbes is more equal than most. In a world of the free press, media baron Rupert Murdoch is considerably more free than most. The partnering of money and democracy has long been an uneasy one. We continue to struggle with how to draw the line between the Constitution's *absolute* guarantee of free speech and the fairness implied by our commitment to political equality and open debate. Cynicism is assured when you see both political parties announce in the summer of 1999 their intention to raise over $200 million in soft money for the 2000 presidential campaign.[3] There's no limit on the amount of such donations so long as the money is used for party building, issue ads, or other independent campaigns. Those fall under the protection of the First Amendment. By October 1999, the Federal Election Commission was projecting that the major parties would raise at least $525 million in such "free speech" money, more than double the amount in 1996. Campaign spending is on track to top $3 billion for 2000, including $1 billion raised for congressional elections.[4]

Anyone yearning to reflect on the latest rendition of Law and Economics can reliably turn to the editorial page of the *Wall Street Journal,* where, for instance, in July 1999, these outspoken advocates of dollar-based democracy argued that those with "lots of money to throw into a contest" ought to do so with the goal that they might "alter the contest itself." Why? Because "this, of course, is precisely what the founders of the American system meant by a free society."[5]

In bowing out of her anticipated bid for a Senate seat in September 1999, Christine Todd Whitman, New Jersey's popular Republican governor, conceded that her decision was prompted by the prospect of raising funds to oppose potential challenger Jon Corzine, former chairman of Goldman Sachs, whose estimated $300 million in personal net worth instantly made him an electoral powerhouse despite being an admitted newcomer to politics. What possible credibility could New York's egocentric real estate developer Donald Trump have as a presidential candidate? Answer: a personal net worth that *Forbes* estimates at $1.6 billion ("The Donald" claims that it's closer to $4.5 billion). In today's merger of politics, money, and entertainment, his monetary worth is what makes him a player. Rich and clueless, but a player nevertheless.

The Roots of Money-Myopic Economics

It wasn't until I entered the congressional policymaking world in 1980 that the pervasiveness and the persuasiveness of today's Chicago-inspired Law and Economic model became clear to me. As a craftsman of federal pension law for seven years, I quickly found that our policymaking compass was routinely calibrated to the dictates of financial values. The phrase heard most frequently in committee debate was the need for a level playing field. The reason? So that financial capital could find its way in the world without the petty annoyances and vulgar distractions of public policy. Thus, for instance, because tax write-offs are allowed for the cost of employer-provided pensions, we now have $8 trillion-plus in the hands of pension trustees whose investment goals are limited to one goal: maximizing financial returns. Any tilting of the field for any other purpose remains a legislative no-no.[6]

The practical result of the Law and Economics movement was to dramatically narrow not only the boundaries of political debate but also the scope of policy options. That market-sanctifying model gradually forced to the periphery any doubters or naysayers as economic diagnostic creep became the rule and "economism" the official language of the faithful. Woe unto those who dared question whether the marketplace had exceeded its bounds. Or whether financial values had penetrated into domains where they did not belong. A political purgatory was reserved for those who challenged the anointed in their crusade to commoditize (and put a price tag on) all of creation. Amid that fervor, for anyone to suggest that ownership patterns might be less than optimal was viewed by some within the priesthood as a direct assault on the omniscience of The Market, certifying doubters as backsliders if not outright apostates. Ultimately, we were assured, "It" knows best. A clear victory for "It" was the 1986 passage of a Tax Reform Act in which we enshrined economism in a massive rewrite of the entire tax code (I was Senate Finance Committee counsel at the time). Bill Bradley claims the act as his primary legislative achievement (he was then a member of the Finance Committee). As of this writing, he's viewed as the liberal presidential candidate in today's version of the Democratic Party.

Although that effort eliminated some subsidies that no longer served their purpose (or whose lobbyists failed to prevail), it also marked the clear ascendancy of the market fundamentalists. Though their patron saint, Adam Smith, warned that markets make great servants but lousy masters (and, I argue, even worse religions), the Chicago clan remains united in their belief that the free-flowing forces of financial capital should be granted the final say. As a result, finance has gradually displaced policy (and even morality) as the currency of modern politics. Steadfast allegiance to this vision, I'm assured, provides a comfort that is best appreciated later, like that reassuring refrain from the old gospel song: "Further along we'll understand why." Meanwhile, the success of the Chicago elite's economic nostrums is reflected both in the distribution of wealth and income and in the impact on the environment. As the founders of this nation cautioned, we give shape to our institutions—and then they in turn shape us. We're both monkey and monkey grinder. That's how we came to the shape we're in.

Back from the Brink of Ideology

Democracy's turbulent history provides a painful reminder of the need to challenge any voice that claims universal validity for its values. Such grasping for power in a democracy can only *peacefully* be met by a more balanced analysis that combines respect for the narrow view with sensitivity to the much broader spectrum of values that comprises any well-functioning democracy. We've only just begun to understand how pervasively destructive are the trends set forth in earlier chapters. The devastation of these trends cuts a wide swath across every imaginable domain—social, fiscal, cultural, political, environmental. In combination, the results are stunning in scope and alarming in their implications.

The tortoise-like speed with which we're awakening to the source of the problem is easy to understand. In part it reflects the slow but steady pace at which today's finance-obsessed perspective has gradually gained influence in the policy arena. Also, it's difficult to evaluate the impact of that perspective when we've for so long lived it from the inside, steadfastly believing the market mantra that, yes, generating the best possible financial returns ensures the best possible results. Analysis is also hindered by the delay and sometimes the diffusion of the effects. Although many symptoms show up nationwide, others only touch us in ways that seem uniquely personal and even then may unfold quite slowly. In addition, our fierce independence—that true-grit loner lodged deep in America's John Wayne psyche—leads us to believe that the source of all our problems surely must lie within *us* instead of within the system. That confidence-sapping conclusion plays right into the hands of those who espouse the radical individualism that animates Law and Economics.

This chapter provides an overview of the human crises that our current economic model overlooks and our current leaders ignore. I also show that the root of our problems cannot be traced to a *single* factor, because the problems are blended in a stew of interwoven causes and conditions. Philosopher Buckminster Fuller cautioned that we avoid what he called "monological" thinking—the temptation to attribute cause to a single source. Yet although our problems have many sources, their common denominator is our use of a finance-myopic lens through which we evaluate our policy options. The temptation to view the full spectrum of life through that narrow prism explains why many of these emerging trends are dangerously antidemocratic and demonstrably unsustainable. Just as no illness arises in isolation, no remedy can be prescribed except in a broader context. Also, as you'll see, because none of these problems arose in a linear fashion, none can be solved except with a holistic response.

Crowding Out Caring

Imagine, for example, parents working, on average, an extra 4 $1/2$ weeks per year for the same or less pay as the work year steadily expanded since 1970.[7] That puts enormous pressure on the time, resources, and incentives for the supply of caring labor.[8] Studies indicate that parents spend 40 percent less time with their children today than they did thirty years ago.[9] Marvin Olasky, guru to the "compassionate conservatives," simplistically argues that the sole culprit is high taxes.[10] Yet according to the Bureau of Labor Statistics, the typical American now works 350 hours more per year than a typical highly taxed European. That's almost nine full weeks. And that fails to account for the time that goes unlogged as many companies do an end run around labor laws by engaging people as independent contractors to avoid paying time and a half for hours they work over 40 per week.[11] Many companies, such as software firms, now emphasize project work, with hurry-up cultures focused on completion dates to finish, say, the latest CD-ROM. It's not unusual to hear of software developers putting in 80- and even 90-hour weeks. "We have become our projects," cautions management adviser Tom Peters. Nor do these computations take into account time spent in steadily lengthening commutes. Here in Atlanta, the typical person now drives thirty-five miles per day, the highest commuter mileage of any city in the world.

So now we live in a nation learning to cope with the effects of a parenting deficit. We've long known that without enough care, children do not flourish. Without attention and stimulation, babies routinely languish, failing to reach their full potential. Without consistent nurturing from their families, kids underperform in school. How do we as a people recover from forgone parenting? What's the social cost of leaving children alone with today's television programming in a world where violence sells? Or with their choice of video games?

The high costs of outsourced parenting are only just now being tabulated. For instance, we know that young children bond with whoever is in their environment, regardless of whether it's a parent, a sibling, or a day-care provider. As a low-paid job, child care has an extraordinarily high turnover rate. We pay child-care workers less than we pay animal caretakers and parking-lot attendants. Thus, children experience a series of "bonding breaks" as they connect with one and then another in a string of typically part-time parent substitutes. Children who feel uncared for are more likely to grow up with an uncaring attitude ("No one cared for me"). Often that combines with a poorly developed conscience.[12] Upon hearing about two teenagers who killed their classmates and then themselves at Columbine High School in Littleton, Colorado, in April 1999, the first question a psychologist colleague asked was, "Were they raised in day care?"

The costs that accompany growing economic stress and financial insecurity are not always so apparent. For example, in 1999, the nation's three primary income security programs including Social Security, Medicare, and civil service pensions consumed $841 billion in federal tax revenues.[13] That's well before the first baby boomers begin to retire, and exludes 1999 medicare outlays of $143 billion. Meanwhile, Washington's General Accounting Office (GAO) found that the United States needs $112 billion to fix up the nation's dilapidated public schools. Forget about building any new ones; that's just to repair the old ones. There are relationships at work here that are easy to miss.

Consider this: A majority of our 42 million public school students cannot use computers, because, even if the nation's 87,000 public schools could afford them, most school buildings cannot accommodate them. Half lack adequate electrical wiring, while fully a third lack sufficient power. To force students into poorly equipped schools condemns them to a future of incapacity and mediocrity. There's no way we're going to sustain a high-tech, knowledge-based economy absent a high-quality education system.[14] Yet rather than prepare our children for the global information age, we endure rich-get-richer economic policies that ensure a crowding out of educational needs by the needs for income security.

As people catch on to today's economic reality, I anticipate outrage. Our current fiscal burden, with its huge and growing transfer payments, is akin to paying a budget-busting health-care bill for a makeshift medical procedure to remedy a condition that could have been prevented in the first place.

Unhealthy Societies

In *Unhealthy Societies: The Afflictions of Inequality*, Sussex University professor Richard Wilkinson documents inequality as a key psychosocial force that damages both physical and mental health.[15] We've known much of this for some time. Two decades ago, a study of 17,000 British civil servants found that the heart-attack fatality rate among clerks and messengers was four times that of more highly paid administrators. After weeding out such obvious explanations as differences in diet or smoking, it became clear that it was the intangible factors, such as control over one's life and a sense of security, that made the difference. Once income reaches a basic level, the standard of living becomes practically a nonfactor. British researchers also found that their largest gains in life expectancy came during the two world wars (among noncombatants), when income disparities were compressed as the need for national unity temporarily prevailed over the UK's traditional class divisions. Eighty percent of the most common causes of death, Wilkinson found, are 80 percent more likely to occur among blue- than white-collar workers.

Additional evidence comes from Japan, long known for its relatively small gap between top executives and the rank-and-file (17 to 1 versus our 419 to 1).[16] Japanese men, who are twice as likely to smoke as American men, not only live longer, but also have lower rates of lung cancer. The additional 3.6 years that Japanese men live compared to Americans (79.8 versus 76.2) equals the gain in male life expectancy that would be realized if heart attacks were eliminated here as a cause of death. Although other influences are also at work, Japan's wage-compression culture is widely regarded as a major contributing factor to a range of positive effects, including its social cohesion and low crime rate.

Research here supports that theme. Alongside widening economic disparities between whites and blacks in the United States, we also find widening disparities in the incidences of asthma, diabetes, major infectious diseases, and several forms of cancer. In a recent New York study, the rate of hospitalization for asthma was twenty-one times higher in the Bronx and Harlem than that of more affluent parts of New York City, with particularly high incidences among African American children.[17] The Atlanta-based Centers for Disease Control and Prevention report that from 1980 to 1994, the number of diabetes cases rose 33 percent among blacks. That's three times the increase among whites, mirroring the rise in cases of infectious diseases as well. Although the death rate from breast cancer fell 10 percent for all women from 1990 to 1995 (from 23.1 per 100,000 to 21), the higher rate for black women remained unchanged (27.5 per 100,000).[18]

Health Discrimination

Blacks also receive less, and worse, health care than whites. Thus, they are sicker than whites and die at about age seventy, six to seven years earlier than whites. A deadly mix of social and cultural factors, including limited education, poverty, poor diet, violence, and untreated disease, is also contributing.[19] Lower-income jobs among blacks also tend to insure greater exposure to toxic work environments. Research by the National Institute of Aging shows that blacks enjoy fifty-six years of reasonably good health, eight years fewer than whites and Hispanics. Although we've seen a significant nationwide decline in chronic disability and institutionalization for people sixty-five and older, "almost all the improvement is among whites," according to Kenneth G. Manton, director of the Center for Demographic Studies at Duke University.[20] The persistence of this race-based health gap has now stirred the search for explanations beyond the conventional one of disproportionately low income.

The increased risk of injury between high- and low-paying work also compounds wage inequality. Daniel Hamermesh, an economist at the University of Texas, identifies this difference in injury risk as a key reason that workers on the low end of the wage scale are falling even further behind. In 1979, the top quarter of wage earners lost 38 percent more days to on-the-job injuries than did workers in the bottom 25 percent. By 1995, the pattern had reversed, with low-wage earners losing 32 percent more days than high-wage earners. Hamermesh calculates that the change in injury rates alone magnifies the wage gap by as much as 30 percent. "Overall, workplace safety hasn't changed much," he says. "High-paid blue-collar workers with hazardous jobs have simply become low-paid blue-collar workers in hazardous jobs."[21]

Similarly, although 48 percent of workers have an employer-sponsored pension plan, less than 10 percent of those at the bottom can count on such benefits.[22] Health insurance coverage follows a similar pattern, as does access to paid holidays and vacations.

Other aspects of life as a hapless jobholder also imperil health. An MIT study found that depression at work is costing us $47 billion each year, roughly the same as the annual tab for heart disease. Our medical students are taught that the major predictors of sudden death from heart attacks are smoking and hypertension along with high cholesterol, diabetes, and family history. According to a University of Massachusetts study, there's another predictor that's even more reliable: job dissatisfaction. More people in our culture die on one particular day and at one particular time of the week: Monday at 9 A.M. We're the first generation in history to organize our work activities so that they take such a predictable human toll.[23] For low-income people, the first day of the month is often the most deadly. A study of more than 31 million computerized death certificates found that the combined death rate from substance abuse, suicide, accidents, and homicide jumps 14 percent during the first week of each month, compared with the last seven days of the previous month.[24] The research team from the University of California at San Diego suggests that this phenomenon is due to the fact that low-income people receive their benefit checks at the beginning of the month.

The Foundation of Health Care

A 1998 study of 282 U.S. metropolitan areas found that mortality rates are considerably more closely linked to relative income than to absolute income. High inequality, high mortality. Low inequality, low mortality. Ichiro Kawachi and Bruce Kennedy of Harvard's School of Public Health conclude that an erosion of trust or "social capital" underlies inequality's influence on health. That would be consistent with the better health found in old-fashioned immigrant cultures, which typically have a conspicuous closeness, as compared with the more individualistic lifestyle of the modern American community. In one telling example, a physician–sociologist team studied the health of an Italian-American town in Pennsylvania during the 1950s. Though its inhabitants smoked heavily and cooked with lard, they exhibited an unusually low incidence of heart disease. The neighborhoods were known for their collegiality, architecturally evidenced by friendly front porches, where neighbors would congregate and converse. During the 1960s, they became steadily more Americanized—individualistic and insular—building terraces behind their homes, where they would socialize more privately. Within a decade, their fatality rate from heart attacks was on a par with nearby towns.[25]

This is consistent with more recent research by Dr. Dean Ornish. In *Love and Survival*,[26] he points out that social isolation or a lack of friends accounts in one study of coronary patients for a threefold difference in the survival rate. Those with caring relationships live longer. They also develop stronger immune systems. Among the developed nations, Britain and the intensely individualistic United States have, by most accounts, both the highest economic disparity and the lowest life expectancy. That comes as a surprise to most Americans because our health-care tab now accounts for 15 percent of the GDP, putting the United States near the top in outlays and at the bottom in results. Wilkinson concludes that wide inequality is *itself* associated with poor health. His conclusion is based on a chain of reasoning that runs like this: A society that condones wide economic disparities evokes a culture preoccupied with material pleasures, money, and status. Those who cannot measure up develop a sense of inferiority and lower status, which triggers anxiety that quite literally eats away at people. As the anxiety becomes chronic, it releases stress hormones that impair the body's immune system. The impact on health is akin to rapid aging. These feelings "are so fundamental," Wilkinson notes, "it is reasonable to wonder whether the effects on the quality of life are not more important than the effects on the length of life." That's a health crisis. Yet not a word on the subject was heard during the 1993 national debate on health care.

Child Endangerment Economics

Those who challenge Wilkinson claim that material circumstances may play a larger role, particularly if one includes the impact of income-related differences on prenatal health care and parenting. Yet when Wilkinson's findings are paired with those by Harvard's Juliet Schor concerning the stressful lengthening of the work year, it means the typical American child now receives substantially less parenting from substantially more stressed parents who received for their extra work the same or less pay. Like Lewis Carroll's Red Queen, they run faster just to stay still. Less parenting and less pay, that's become the American way.

Although some argue that this is a healthy sign of people who believe in the work ethic and are now more self-actualized, the evidence suggests that it's more like being self-vaporized. Many people are groaning for relief, like workaholics in search of a moment of sobriety, while others are driven by rampant economic insecurity to prove their indispensability. Though some of life's experiences you may want to rush (a tooth extraction comes to mind), life itself may not be one of them. Peter Drucker tells the story of a young pianist who so impressed Johannes Brahms that he sent him to see his patron in Vienna. The patron turned the young pianist down, telling Brahms, "I have no interest in someone who plays the minute waltz in fifty-six seconds." Therein lies a lesson for our hurried times. Although certain problems require quick solutions and benefit from hurry-up, life is not one of them. That's why today's warp-speed economics feels so horrifically out of synch with our more natural rhythms.

Inequality also has a little-understood impact on early childhood development. The reasoning goes like this: Children who experience low social status have more aggressive interactions, even in their early years. On the home front, they tend to experience more personal trauma, often associated with heightened domestic conflict that typically accompanies household economic insecurity. They translate that confused mix of messages into feelings of personal insecurity, inadequacy, and inferiority. That results in low self-esteem along with a sense of personal defectiveness and vulnerability, triggering what psychologists call a shame-rage spiral, as they act out their feelings of being excluded and disrespected. Their personal experience is known as being "dissed" in those inner-city settings where this social pathology plays out in its most visible and violent form. Half the difference in societal violence, in social cohesion, and in life expectancy, Wilkinson found, correlates closely with economic inequality. If your family suffered financial difficulties when you were a child, by the age of twenty-three, you are more than twice as likely to be in prison if you're a man, and a lone parent if you're a woman. Homicide rates show a particularly strong correlation. You're also likely to be unemployed or earning below-average wages even ten years later. And to have fewer job qualifications.

Childhood poverty also has a long-term impact on physical and mental health. In Britain, where the number of children in poverty has tripled over the past 30 years, research confirms that poor children are more likely to have lower body weight and shorter height and are at greater risk of mental health problems as adults.

A powerful and perverse myth ("Never again!") surrounds the notion of childhood poverty, suggesting that hardship suffered by the young evokes a powerful determination *never again* to let their loved ones suffer the same deprivation. The research proves that the opposite is more typically the case.[27] The mystery is how anyone ever imagined that a poverty-plagued childhood, with its difficulties, deprivations, and insecurities, would equip people with the tools required to achieve prosperity.

Michele McGeoy, a young mother and Silicon Valley cyber-millionaire, asks that we reflect as parents on the lesson in fairness that we allow the current Congress to teach our kids. "Imagine four little girls eating apple pie. One girl cuts the pie into ten pieces and promptly takes nine of them for herself. The last three girls are left with a single piece. Most of us would be appalled by such behavior. We would chastise our children. Why accept that same behavior from our elected representatives?" An outspoken activist who vigorously opposed enactment of the rich-get-richer tax cut that Congress proposed in September 1999, she displays a Jeffersonian knack for putting the issue in proper context:

> I want my daughter to grow up safe and happy. I know I can't guarantee that safety and happiness. But I can improve the odds—by fighting anything that endangers my daughter's future well-being. This tax cut would be a giant step toward solidifying the unequal, unstable, unpredictable society that I fear so acutely. In a society increasingly polarized between the have-nots and the have-everythings, no children are safe.[28]

The threat to children's security (and to democracy) is also psychological. For instance, we've long known that the lack of self-esteem that accompanies economic insecurity weakens family and community ties—which in turn further weakens self-esteem in a self-reinforcing downward spiral. Psychological insecurity, in turn, plays directly into the hands of advertisers and their film images, in which "more" is portrayed as making you happier, hipper, slimmer, sexier. Consumption, in short, is the route to a new improved you. This attempt to satisfy primary needs with secondary sources casts us adrift—even at a very early age—in a sea of addictions that merchandisers are happy to feed. Of course, those secondary sources can never really satisfy, whereas consumption can easily become obsessive. Uprooted from families, homes, neighborhoods, communities, and even from nature with its reassuring cycles, people often feel lost, even bewildered, if not terrified. That's why a sense of restored connectedness—a new psychic context—plays such an important role in the recovery now required. As with most addictions, breaking through the denial is often the most difficult step.

Today's accelerating pace of change also takes its toll—on both children and adults. Three decades ago, futurist Alvin Toffler warned in *Future Shock* about the "dizzying disorientation brought on by the premature arrival of the future." He predicted societal breakdown if we didn't slow our pace. We didn't, and the effects are beginning to show. A 1986 poll confirmed his forecast, concluding that one of three Americans lives with daily stress, whereas six out of ten report great stress at least once or twice a week. We know that as much as 80 percent of all illness is initiated or aggravated by stress.[29] University of Maryland sociologist John Robinson found a steady racheting-up in hurriedness since 1965, when 25 percent of those surveyed reported that their lives were rushed all the time. That figure had risen to 28 percent by 1975 and to 32 percent by 1985. By 1992, Penn State researchers Geoffrey Godbey and Alan Graete put the figure at 38 percent, an ongoing trend chronicled in 1999 by chaos theorist James Gleick in *Faster: The Acceleration of Just About Everything*.[30]

Democracy and the Character of the Community

These crises are intimately interwoven. They refuse to be remedied with a little 1960s-style income redistribution. There's much more at work here. And more at stake. It has to do with the ways in which society distributes not just money but also power, status, dignity, security, and personal standing. In other words, it has to do with democracy. Although income is essential, that alone doesn't address the underlying indignity of being left out and left behind. What this research allows us to see is the invisible overlay of interwoven forces whose effects often take years to fully play out—and years more to be corrected. These few snapshots provide insight into why so many of our most troubling problems never seem to find a remedy. All too often we focus on the symptoms rather than the broader, more complex context from which they emerge. A genuine *living democracy* depends for its robustness on the constant interplay between our personal experience of democracy and our insistence that we have the economic relationships in place that are needed to evoke that experience.

Could it be that we now seek escape through consumption as a way to compensate for lives that have become ever more anxiety-ridden, deferential, and (it must be said) less free? With progress now measured by material acquisitions and economic indexes, I wonder how many of us are living lives of quiet desperation, our political confidence sapped of its vitality by a culture grounded no longer in the expansive spirit of democratic generosity but in the isolating confines of glorified and institutionalized self-interest.[31] If leisure and security are key attributes of affluence, why is it that in this rich country, so many of us are more harried and economically precarious? Little wonder that democracy is losing its vibrancy. Robust democracies depend on people willing to invest the time to become informed on issues, attend meetings, and participate in campaigns. That becomes ever more difficult with the steady expansion in working hours combined with the gnawing angst of scant financial resources and an economic model that assures us that the system itself is fine—the flaw lies in us.

A Growing Threat to the Pursuit of Happiness

Our political health has been put at risk by the steady widening in economic disparities. The wealth gap itself fosters nonparticipation in democracy. Therein may lie the most dangerous and disturbing of our many crises because as we construct our relationships in a democracy, those relationships *become* our democracy. In *Making Democracy Work*, Harvard professor Robert Putnam makes this point by contrasting the civic cultures of northern and southern Italy.[32] In the north, with its egalitarian tradition of cooperatives, he found a people who enjoy a cohesive and harmonious culture with high participation in civic and professional societies amid a high degree of shared prosperity. That contrasts sharply with the more hierarchical and inegalitarian south, with its economic concentration, far less civic participation, an entrenched Mafia, and, despite more police, a higher crime rate and more poverty.

His conclusion: It's naive to expect a "minimalist, light-touch government" absent a policy environment that promotes mutuality, solidarity, and horizontal bonds of reciprocity. The irony, he points out, is that it is the "amoral individualists" in the less civic south who clamor for sterner law enforcement. "Yet the vicious circle winds tighter still," he cautions, because "in the less civic regions even a heavy-handed government . . . is itself enfeebled by the uncivic social context. The very *character of the community* that leads citizens to demand stronger government makes it less likely that any government can be strong, at least if it remains democratic." In the absence of social solidarity and self-discipline, Putnam warns, hierarchy and force emerge as the only alternative to anarchy. That rings true. After all, it required the fascist leader Mussolini to jail the Mafia during World War II, only to have them released by the American liberators.

Again, the *nature of the community*, Putnam found, is as vital to happiness as personal circumstances such as family income and religious observance. In share-and-share-alike communities, people are predisposed to trust, to compromise, and to participate. Civic engagement, cooperation, and honesty are more common. Because citizens in the more civic regions enjoy the benefits of community, they are able to be more liberal. That makes sense. The word "community" comes from the Latin *com munere,* which means "to give among each other." "Happiness," Putnam concludes, "is living in a civic community." In the less civic, less egalitarian south, public affairs are the business of someone else—the politicians and the bosses, but not me. Political participation is triggered not by common purpose but by dependency or greed. Corruption is the norm. Compromise has negative connotations. Private piety stands in for public purpose. "Trapped in these interlocking vicious circles," Putnam notes, "nearly everyone feels powerless, exploited, and unhappy." That makes sense. "Humans are social," Harvard's Juliet Schor points out. "We judge our own situations very much in comparison to others around us. It is not surprising that people experience less stress, more peace of mind, and feel happier in an environment with more social cohesion and more equality."[33]

The Miniaturization of Community

Social commentator Francis Fukuyama chimes in on a similar note. He sees us conflicted as a nation. We want a sense of community, he found, along with the good things that flow from it, such as mutual recognition, participation, belonging, and identity. But we are increasingly distrustful of any authority, political or moral, that would constrain our freedom of choice (one of the key features of the information age is a radical increase in choice). In reconciling our desire for both community and autonomy, Fukuyama says that we find "a reduction in the radius of trust" and an accompanying "miniaturization of community," as people seek participation in smaller, more flexible groups and organizations whose loyalties overlap and where entry and exit entail relatively low costs.[34]

What I argue here is that a vibrant and balanced democracy requires an inclusive capitalism as its economic counterpart, combining greater financial autonomy with steadily shifting notions of community—in the workplace, where one lives, even through friendships and commercial relationships formed in cyberspace. On the one hand, it's comforting to know, as Fukuyama notes, that humans are *by nature* social creatures and that social order, once disrupted, tends to get remade. On the other hand, without some societal norms and rules of behavior, whether internalized or enforced by law, the character of the community can become highly undemocratic, as Putnam found. It's dangerously naive for us to expect democracy to sustain itself in an environment that grants such deference to the combined forces of unbridled individualism and the abstract values of finance. Putnam's and Fukuyama's insights into the character of democratic society bring to mind the tart response offered by Mahatma Gandhi when asked his appraisal of democracy in the West: "I think it would be a good idea."

Multiple Domains Now at Risk

One subtle by-product of the ascendancy of the financial model is the commodification of labor such that the social bond between employer and employee gradually becomes only an economic bond. Workers become just like any other factor of production. Whether responding to downsizing or to a call from a headhunter, people change jobs far more often than they used to. Yet game theorists confirm that trust, a key component of social capital, emerges as a function of the durability of relationships. So long as individuals meet one another often enough to have a stake in future encounters, they will begin to form pockets of cooperation. And once that happens, Robert Axelrod notes, "the gear wheels of social evolution have a ratchet."[35] Leave people connected to society with only a job in an environment where labor is viewed as simply another cost and its mobility a plus, and rest assured that you'll get just what we now have—restlessness, a sense of being out of place, a feeling of uprootedness, and a steady deterioration of civility.

The multidimensional impact that accompanies today's fast-widening economic disparities and fast-growing insecurity is oftentimes subtle, showing up in places you might least expect. For instance, research by ethnobotanist Paul Gary Nabhan uncovered evidence of an impact on the environment that only became apparent when a colleague discovered two county-by-county maps of the United States. The first map depicted the relative duration of human residency. The highlighted counties had unusually high turnover, with lots of people moving in and out—what economists call high labor mobility. The second map portrayed a high incidence of endangered species. When Nabhan placed one map over the other, he discovered a near perfect alignment.

That fits. When people move in and out a lot, there's less stewardship. Yet labor mobility is one of the key tenets of economic theory (advanced, ironically, by tenured professors) because the willingness of people to move restrains labor costs, boosting financial returns. If people remain connected to capitalism with a job as their sole source of economic security, rest assured they're likely to move. Economists figure that's a good thing. Yet Nabhan's research suggests that constantly churning mobility undervalues the important role played by a sense of place. And by a feeling of stability. There's a relationship here of which we're only dimly aware. How do we put a price on those aspects of our lives that we most value: conviviality, continuity, character, charity, relationships, remembrance, affection, family ties—and community? At what cost do we allow ourselves to be led hither and yon by financial signals that neglect the valuable in what we value? As Putnam's and Fukuyama's findings suggest, the very character of the community has value, constituting a key component of our social capital. Relationships count, yet today's economics has no way to measure them, and unless we can measure something, today's economic science won't concede that it exists.

Ownership connects people to place—to their homes and to their community. That's a key reason federal policy has long encouraged home ownership. Study after study has shown that home owners are more active in their communities than renters. They care more about the place—the politics, the schools, the appearance of the neighborhood, what's being financed with the local tax base, and so on. That's also why our tradition of sole proprietorships, particularly owner-operated retail businesses—grocery stores, lumber yards, shoe stores, and such—had a major stabilizing and democratizing influence on communities and on the nation. It was largely from their ranks that we drew our civic leaders.

Current ownership patterns—remote, concentrated, and often disconnected from the concerns of the community—endanger those civic roots. Or disrupt those roots, once planted. But, wow, is it ever great financially. Devastating to societal effectiveness, but swimmingly efficient. Just look at those *financial* results. The Dow Jones is up. Life *must* be good. End of analysis. End of discussion.

Sociopathic Policies

As a general rule, home owners cannot afford to retrofit for energy efficiency unless they stay put the five years or so it takes to recover their costs. Yet the Bureau of Labor Statistics found that in 1998 the average job duration was 3.6 years. That's down from 3.8 years in 1996. How do we put a price tag on forgone energy efficiency? Or forgone stewardship? What value should be put on unformed friendships? The research confirms what common sense suggests: There's high personal costs involved with moving. Anyone who's done it (and who hasn't?) knows that moving puts enormous wear and tear not only on physical and mental health but also on relationships and families. Combine a move with a layoff, and the stress factor multiplies. The Department of Labor reports that from 1995 through 1997, 8 million of us were pushed out of jobs involuntarily. That's one of every fifteen adult job holders. That's on top of the previous three-year period, when 8.4 million, one of every twelve, were laid off.[36]

The wholesale firing associated with "reengineering" boosted short-term profits and stock prices, along with the value of stock options held by those executives who eagerly embraced this latest management fad. Now widely viewed as a prescription that was both oversold and overbought, many of the staunchest proponents of reengineering, such as Michael Hammer and James Champy, who together wrote a manifesto of reengineering, have since acknowledged that much of it was an ill-advised, costly, and wrenching mistake.[37] It often caused long-term damage not only to the operations of the firm but also to its culture, leaving people feeling fearful, distrustful, and with a decidedly less productive attitude.[38] To my knowledge, no one has yet chronicled the social costs—the broken families, the personal bankruptcies, the uninsured family illnesses that went untreated, the college expenses that became unaffordable, the stress, the depression, the suicides, and the bewilderment and bereavement of children who now live with a single parent. There's no balance sheet on which the social costs of reengineering are tallied, despite their expensive and corrosive effect on individuals, families, communities, and civil society.

America's children, especially those in middle-quintile families, now grow up moving from suburb to suburb. Values suffer when you embrace the sort of accelerated, dislocating change that has become the hallmark of U.S. commerce. Neighbors often move virtually undetected in and out of interchangeable suburban backdrops, where cars slip in and out of automatic-door garages. There's seldom any need to step beyond your mailbox. Not only does the experience of a minimally connected, disposable world affect children, it transforms the very notion of family-in-community. Nationwide, one of every six children now takes Ritalin, an antidepressant. The number of preschoolers taking stimulants, antidepressants, and other psychiatric drugs arouse dramatically from 1991–1995.[39] The rate of suicide for those aged fifteen to twenty-four has tripled since 1960. More than 65 million antidepressant prescriptions were written in 1998—for Prozac, Zoloft, Paxil, Serzone, and Tofranil. Plus an unknown number for antipsychotics such as Haldol, Thorazine, Risperdal, Zyprexa, and Cloxaril. That leaves unchronicled the drugs bought from a dealer rather than a doctor. The abstraction, alienation, material acquisition, and mindless consumerism that now pass for community masks a much deeper malaise imbedded in a worldview that begets such a culture.[40] A steady buildup in the number of seemingly intractable social problems suggests it's time we strike out in a very new direction.

Lotteries and Lockups

Instead of a policy environment that promotes community and provides robust economic opportunities, we witness instead the sad travesty of legislative support for lottery opportunities. Lottery machines are almost as prevalent as cash registers in the thirty-eight states where they're allowed. Annual ticket sales now exceed $35 billion. Denied any reasonable chance to get ahead through legitimate means, our lowest-paid citizens flock to these scant-chance schemes like lemmings to a cliff. Fully 51 percent of lottery tickets are bought by just 5 percent of regular purchasers, who are mostly drawn from the nation's most down-on-their-luck households.

There has also been a seismic shift in the motivation behind gambling. In 1975, seven in ten told pollsters that they gamble for the excitement or challenge. Not anymore. Two-thirds now say they bet to win money, with African Americans more likely than any other group to offer that response.[41] Though states justify lotteries on the basis that they're voluntary and the proceeds are used to augment education, numerous studies show that they fail to increase the net amount spent on education.[42] In my home state of Georgia, where gambling was banned when I was a kid, the proceeds from lottery tickets sold largely to low-income blacks pay college tuition largely for middle-income whites. Paradoxically, the nationwide spread of legalized gambling mirrors the spread of what nowadays passes for conservatism.

The U.S. prison system is another example of the all-encompassing devastation wrought by rising inequality. In 1973, the United States had 350,000 people in prison nationwide. By 1998, that had soared to 1.8 million. Although some of the growth in the prison population is due to stricter law enforcement, tougher sentencing guidelines, and more restrictive parole procedures, the question remains: Why are our rates so dramatically out of line with those of other nations? Even our draconian "war on drugs" cannot fully account for the difference. As of the fall of 1999, 388,000 adults were behind bars for drug violations, compared with 52,000 in 1980. Something more is at work. The United States now has roughly 674 of its citizens in prison per 100,000, whereas the imprisonment rate throughout Europe is 60–100 per 100,000. Demographically, our fast-growing security-service industry employs people without property to guard the belongings of those *with* property—from those without property. Fittingly, the key construction industry to rival new prison construction as a growth area in the New Economy is that of the gated community.

Florida now spends more on corrections than on colleges. California soon will. In 1998, this bellwether westernmost state spent 9 percent of its budget on prisons as it responded to an eightfold increase in its prison population over the past two decades. The Rand Corporation projects that prison spending in California will top 16 percent of its budget by 2005. The state's prison guards were the largest single contributor to Governor Gray Davis's successful race for governor. With a national population one-fifth that of China, the United States may have a half-million more people in prison. In our minority communities, prison life has become so much a part of the culture—and is so often an improvement on street life—that it's called "three hots and a cot." That's the cultural fallout from a political decision to lock them up rather than lift them up. The stubbornness of these problems mandates a disturbing conclusion: We have become resigned to our inability to address national maladies in any substantive way. Rather than address the problems of our fast-growing underclass, we've focused our efforts instead on how best to live with the consequences.

It's useful to recall that democracy has as its goal a civic culture grounded in generous social relations, the vitality of human cooperation, and the rich diversity of human aspiration.[43] Yet even my recitation of those traditional goals now sounds somehow hackneyed, even quaint and simplistic, lacking as it does the hard edge now so common in discussions about our underclass. The challenge of living with and for others has long been a struggle in this most individualistic of all nations. Our extreme brand of individualism was particularly worrisome to Alexis de Tocqueville, who cautioned that the typical American might well become "shut up in the solitude of his own heart."

Today's democracy combines outward displays of material prosperity with fast-growing evidence of an inner spiritual poverty as we find ourselves coping with epidemic levels of alienation, anxiety, discontent, frustration, uncertainty, loneliness, and depression. We lose the right to be dismayed at sociopathic behavior among our youth when we mix a poorly developed conscience, rising economic insecurity, family stress, low self-esteem, an early introduction to drug use, and deteriorating civil cohesion with a culture that glorifies greed, consumption, self-interest, short-term-ism, and individualism while devaluing place, stability, the family, the community, and even the natural world in which all these ingredients are inescapably imbedded. The only surprise will be if we don't see a continuing rise in bizarre behavior. From the perspective of the risk imposed on democracy, the cost is best reckoned in terms of the loss of community, the bedrock on which all of civil society is built.

The commercial costs associated with this phenomenon can also be significant. Cost-conscious corporations often show a preference for singles and for employees without families. Children and other personal relationships can prove more expensive should employees relocate. Labor mobility is efficient and cost-effective. Relationships are not, at least not where a move may be in the offing. In combination, these forces make today's finance-myopic version of free enterprise the most revolutionary force ever unleashed in the human community. The effects are radical, ongoing, accelerating, and far from finished.

4

Is Today's Leadership Up To the Task?

Leaders see with the eyes of the whole nation,
Hear with the ears of the whole nation,
Think with the knowledge of the whole nation, and
Move with the strength of the whole nation.

—HUAINAN MASTERS

We've long known that the rich get richer. Everyone knows that. Most people figure it's a bit like the weather: Everyone talks about it, but no one can do anything about it. Today's leaders play on that popular misconception to avoid addressing the issue. Much as weather patterns influence the physical environment, wealth and income patterns affect the economic, social, and political environment. But unlike weather patterns, we can do something about wealth and income patterns.

Today's grotesque economic disparities flow largely from political decisions. That's a very different perspective from those who would have us view economic forces as a force of nature irresistible as the ocean tides. Highly concentrated wealth patterns aren't forces of nature; they're political choices. We can choose something quite different—*provided we're offered that choice*. This book is about framing that choice, and about educating a new corps of leaders committed to giving us that option. Outside of a very narrow range of issues, we haven't had a genuine political choice in this country for a very long time.

When Boomers Retire

We've only a very narrow window of opportunity to set in place the policy environment—the economic weather, if you will—to bring about this change. Otherwise, rapidly unfolding demographic pressures are poised to make our circumstances much worse. For instance, most of our 76 million baby boomers (born between 1946 and 1964) will probably live well into their eighties, and many into their nineties. Late twentieth-century advances in health care suggest life spans beyond even that.[1]

Some boomers are already beginning to retire. A decade from now, as the first of them turn sixty-five, they hope to make a smooth transition into retirement in the expectation that they will have enough assets set aside from which to draw a decent retirement income. They won't. At least one-third of them, and possibly as many as two-thirds, will be in quite poor financial shape.[2]

For the bulk of them, those funds simply will not be there. Guaranteed. And none of the proposals currently under discussion will get them there. Least likely of all are the ideas that generate the most attention, particularly those that rely on some version of incentivized savings such as Roth IRAs or Bill Clinton's proposed universal savings accounts.[3] Personal saving is not a feasible route to the accumulations required. That notoriously unworkable notion becomes steadily more nonsensical as we open our borders to foreign trade so that our workers find themselves adjusting to a wage standard affected by labor markets not only in Atlanta, Akron, and Austin but also in Budapest, Bangkok, and Bangladesh. The United Kingdom embraced open labor markets with a vengeance under the lash of Margaret Thatcher's Chicago-inspired leadership. The British now boast to the global business community that their workers are the lowest paid in Western Europe (while their child poverty rate soared to the highest in the developed world).

The Demopubs and the Republicrats have proposed very different but equally outlandish and unworkable proposals. Both are destined to make things even worse. Clinton proposed in his 1999 State of the Union address that 62 percent of projected budget surpluses be used to match personal savings invested in the stock market through universal savings accounts. There's far less there than meets the eye, even though he packaged it to sound like a government-sponsored 401(k) plan complete with a fetchingly patriotic title (USAs). Lost in the hype was that he proposed to match your personal savings with government bonds. In other words, excess tax revenues would be used to buy back government bonds, reducing government debt. Then new bonds would be issued to match your savings, *increasing* government debt—by as much as $1.2 trillion. Ask Gen-Xers what they think. For every dollar *you* put into USAs, *their* debt goes up a dollar, plus interest. Good thing Treasury Secretary Rubin beat it back to Wall Street before anyone caught on to that ruse.

The most prominent Republican proposal is suspect on its face because of the credentials of its chief proponent, Martin Feldstein, lead cheerleader for Reagan-Bush supply-side economics, the most virulent rich-get-richer scheme ever embraced by a democratically elected government. More on that in a moment. Feldstein proposes that budget surpluses be paid into personal retirement accounts in an amount equal to 2.3 percent of wages. Money managers would invest the funds. Three-quarters of any investment return would be used to fund social security benefits, whereas the rest would be yours to keep. Uncle Sam would insure that you receive at least as much as you're now promised under social security. If that sounds suspiciously like a free lunch, it is—except, of course, for Gen-Xers—who, again, would be obliged to make up any shortfall.

Rich-Get-Richer Retirement Policies

Both these proposals conveniently fail to mention two key facts. Under the Feldstein proposal, 2.3 percent of the nation's payroll totals more than $100 billion. That's $100 billion in tax revenues that Washington would invest in the stock market versus, say, in education or health care or infrastructure or environmental restoration or debt reduction. Think about it. If an additional $100 billion goes pouring onto Wall Street each year, who do you think will pocket the lion's share of the benefit as that money bids up stock prices? Does it strike anyone else as peculiar that the only way the Washington–Wall Street consensus can conceive to capitalize the boomers is by using tax revenues to pump up the wealth of those who've already pocketed the bulk of the benefit from history's longest stock market boom? Second, why is it that we're leaving *their* wealth holdings intact while everyone else struggles to dig out from under the impact of at least *ten* interrelated deficits that helped fuel that boom?

1. The accumulated budget deficits: $5,700 billion in 1999, up from $909 billion since 1980.[4]

2. A huge trade deficit ($2 trillion-plus), which sent $233.4 billion abroad in 1998 alone—money that foreigners have been willing to take for oil, cars, stereos, VCRs, and so on, and often then invest here in the stock market.

3. Our political choice to maintain an underfunded social security system. Unrealistically low labor costs boost stock prices while ensuring a larger social security deficit.

4. The fast-spreading use of options in lieu of salary to compensate even midlevel employees. The result is overstated profits and higher stock prices, since wages get charged against profits whereas stock options don't.[5]

5. A policy mix that supported record-low personal savings, ensuring that more consumption fueled equity values.

6. Record-breaking household debt for mortgages, car loans, and credit cards, fueled by the rate cuts of an accommodating Federal Reserve. These cuts worked their way into mortgage markets, in which home owners took on $1.5 trillion in new borrowing in 1998, nearly two-thirds of it refinancings that, in turn, fueled a spending boom (an average $15,000 per household).

7. The balance sheets of mortgage facilitators Fannie Mae and Freddie Mac expanded by $220 billion in 1998 versus $61 billion in 1997, ensuring another deficit should a downturn trigger Washington's as-yet untested guarantees underlying the government-backed mortgage market.

8. The steady growth in financial derivatives that protect individuals against risk by shifting that risk to the system as a whole. The fast-growing magnitude of unregulated leveraged derivatives financing exposes the global financial system to incalculable risks that expand each day.

9. Two decades of underinvestment in the nation's infrastructure, as even the most basic repairs and maintenance (for schools, bridges, public buildings, highways, etc.) were preempted by the fiscal priority given tax breaks for the well-to-do.

10. An environmental deficit resulting from duplicitous, environmentally insensitive bookkeeping.

The tenth deficit is perhaps the most disturbing and debilitating of them all. Examples of our misleading bookkeeping include counting as private income the consumption of nonrenewable coal, oil, and minerals along with the taxpayer-subsidized consumption of forests, fisheries, and other natural resources; subsidized agricultural practices that degrade soil fertility and deplete aquifers;[6] the failure to budget funds for cleanup costs (the decommissioning of nuclear weapons facilities alone could cost as much as $500 billion); the externalizing of environmental costs so that they show up instead as public health-care costs; the overinvestment in inefficient power generation alongside the underinvestment in even the most basic energy conservation measures (such as insulation, weather stripping, and building orientation); the failure to devote resources to develop alternative energy. And the list goes on.

Each of these ten deficits allowed a small minority to grow rich at the expense of the majority. Although the current economic model can compute the price of what was gained—particularly the astronomical value of private portfolios—it has yet to compute the costs incurred either by society or by the environment. Or the burden that future generations will bear. If a proper accounting were politically possible, any reasonable appraisal would conclude that a privileged few have prospered with the knowing complicity of elected policymakers, leading the nation to the brink of bankruptcy.

Retire-Poor Politics

For reasons that elude me, today's policymakers assume that boomers will be delighted to make do on social security benefits that now average $783 per month ($26.10 per day). Don't you believe it, particularly not once this generation realizes how policymakers rigged the system for so long for the benefit of so few, a little-understood phenomenon that I detail in the next few chapters.[7] A new crop of policymakers may be required to ensure that our wealth becomes more widely shared. The fiscal consequences of a misstep could be disastrous, both here and in other countries. Over the next twenty-five years, the number of persons of pensionable age (sixty-five and over) will grow by 70 million in the industrialized countries, according to the Organization for Economic Cooperation and Development (OECD). The UN projects that in 2050, a quarter of the developed world will be older than sixty-five. Working taxpayers worldwide presently outnumber pensioners by 3 to 1. By 2030, absent increases in retirement ages, this ratio could fall to 1.5 to 1 (as low as 2.1 to 1 in the United States). In Italy and other countries, it will drop to 1 to 1 or lower.[8] The longer we delay in capitalizing people, the worse the consequences.

On the other hand, a crucial issue yet to be addressed is the environmental implications of today's capital-accumulation model of economic security. For instance, what is the impact on the physical environment of generating sales of goods and services of sufficient magnitude that the value of the securities set aside for future retirees will be adequate to capitalize 76 million people, many of whom will need to live on that capital for twenty-five years or more? No one dares ask that most obvious of questions.

At least the developed world got rich before it got old. In the developing world, the trend is reversed. To avoid hard political choices (benefit cuts, tax increases), governments will be tempted to pile on debt. At a minimum, the increasing costs of supporting the elderly will divert resources that now go to the young. No country is prepared for this age wave. None. Asia stands to be particularly hard hit. In 1985, just 28 percent of the world's elderly lived in Asia; by 2025, its share will increase to 58 percent.

Japan also faces a huge challenge. In 1999, its pension liabilities totaled 107 percent of GDP, and its public debt 130 percent of GDP—plus a banking crisis that could involve up to $1 trillion in bad loans. In combination, that's the largest liability in the world—but with two key differences.[9] First, Japan's 21 million people over sixty-five claim average household savings of $207,000. Second, Japan's culture is one in which the care of seniors is more fully ingrained.[10] In *Management Challenges for the Twenty-First Century* (1999), Peter Drucker predicts that not only will demographic trends dominate the politics of developed countries for the next twenty to thirty years, the result could be that no developed country will enjoy stable politics or a strong government.[11]

How did we reach such an impasse? And why do none of our elected leaders offer plain talk and practical solutions? How could we in the United States, knowing that "demographics is destiny," devote the past two decades to the enactment of laws certain to redistribute wealth and income to the very richest—and yet *still* ignore wealth and income disparities as part of the public debate? If we hope to address these pending crises, we must discuss these issues openly because only through informed decision making can democracies *peacefully* change.

Educated into Ignorance

Perhaps no one talks about these matters because no one knows how to *think* about them. It's easy enough to complain about them. But then what? It's my belief that legislators, like the rest of us, have been educated into ignorance. We're particularly ignorant about those intangible, invisible forces known as finance. Though finance is woven into the very fabric of the United States (the Committee on Finance was among the first Senate committees established), it is the forces of finance that now divide and dominate us. How can we claim to have a genuinely free market when our rules encourage vast accumulations on one side while financial ruin typifies the other? That's hardly a system wired to reflect national priorities. Indeed, it offends our deepest democratic values in a profound way. Yet no one has proposed a sensible redesign. In all fairness to our leadership, it's enormously difficult to think about finance. As counsel to the Finance Committee, I have the advantage of firsthand knowledge of how intimately finance and politics are joined.[12] Let me offer one example.

When the Reagan-Bush era began in 1981 and Republicans took over leadership in the Senate, Bob Dole of Kansas took over as chair of the Finance Committee, ousting Russell Long, who had led the committee since the Great Society days of Lyndon Johnson. Calling himself a fiscal conservative, Dole quickly gaveled to enactment an $872 billion, *deficit-financed* tax cut known as supply-side economics, a key plank in the Reagan-Bush platform. Much of that legislation was designed to increase the supply of productive assets by allowing them to be written off (depreciated) more rapidly. The ownership impact was this: In 1982, the average wealth of the Forbes 400 was $200 million (the Dow was 777 in August 1982). By 1986, their average wealth topped $500 million. In other words, We the People got the mortgage (the deficits) while We-the-Well-to-Do got the house (the deficit-financed increase in the nation's supply of privately owned assets).[13]

I'm left with two possible conclusions, neither of them friendly to supply-siders. Either they didn't know what they were doing, so they shouldn't have done it. Or they *did* know what they were doing—which raises an even more disturbing question: *Why* did they do it? With total disregard for its quite predictable impact on ownership patterns, supply-side economics was more political syrup than economic science. Until picked as Reagan's running mate, George Bush ridiculed it as "voodoo economics."

From my perspective, certainly the political contributions that greased the enactment of supply-side economics boosted Dole's political ambition to become Senate majority leader, raising his national profile so that he could emerge a decade later as the Republican standard-bearer in the 1992 election. The only certain economic impact of supply-side economics was this: It made the rich far, far richer.

Adding insult to injury, those supply-side shenanigans were financed with our national credit card, using Uncle Sam's borrowing powers backed by our "full faith and credit" as provided for in the Constitution. To this day, no one talks about it. Certainly not Bob Dole, whom younger readers may best remember for his erectile-dysfunction commercials as a Viagra pitchman.

How can we expect people to be smart about finance when our leaders enact legislation that's so profoundly dumb, touting even the most unconscionable nonsense as common sense? And then pretend it never happened, its rich-get-richer consequences still denied. The "free cash flow" that supply-side tax cuts generated in the corporate sector helped kick off a boom in leveraged buyouts (LBOs), another greed-feeding phenomenon that dates from that era. The devastation that the 1980s "Decade of Greed" wrought on the democratic dream was not the result of some natural law; it stemmed directly from rule changes that were certain to benefit the wealthy and the financially sophisticated at the expense of everyone else.

Duke University history professor Larry Goodwyn concludes that historians will look back on this century "as the least creative political century of the last three." Certainly that's the case for the past twenty years. Broad-based prosperity—and the leisure that accompanies it—remains an achievable future that's long been promised yet longer still deferred. We can change that. But to do so requires that we break the mold of modern-day politics.

Unfortunately, the situation is poised to worsen following the October 1999 announcement that Columbia University economist Robert Mundell received the Nobel prize. Best known in Washington as an early apologist for supply-side economics, his nomination led allies like Jude Wanniski, former editorial writer for the *Wall Street Journal*, to declare the intention to "consolidate the supply-side revolution he began." Just when you think it's hard to see what more the rich would ask for, congressional Republicans proposed in 1999 a supply-side tax cut that reveals their clear intentions. Under the bill they sent to Clinton, the top 1 percent of income earners would receive 41.4 percent of the benefits for an average annual tax cut of

$46,389, while the bottom 60 percent would receive 8.5 percent for an average tax cut of $160. A person in the bottom 20 percent would take home an additional $24. And that omits the rich-get-richer impact of their proposed repeal of inheritance taxes.

Reinventing Democracy in the Capital Age

Let's cut to the chase. The issue here is about money and power. Global capital markets are now the world's eight-hundred-pound gorilla; they do pretty much as they please. Today's capital age is a lot like the nuclear age. You can't un-invent global capital markets any more than you can un-invent nuclear weapons. The question is what to do about them. Or in this case, how to make the world safe *from* financial capital while also making it safe *for* financial capital. Our finance practitioners are largely clueless about what's at stake other than maximizing their returns. Yet with both free-enterprise democracies and capital markets dramatically expanding their reach, it's essential we get the relationship between the two correct. Now that Soviet-style socialism is vanquished, this priceless but perishable opportunity cannot be allowed to slip away. Democracy has never faced such a combination of both risk and opportunity.

As with the Cold War, the challenge of the capital war is one of how best to control forces that could be our undoing. George Kennan, former U.S. ambassador to Moscow, advised in 1946 that the democratic West maintain a "patient but firm and vigilant containment" in its dealings with the Soviet Union. That provides a useful analogy. Much as the United States opted for containment as the way to control Soviet expansionism, we should take the lead in showing how to draw on the best features of global financial markets while containing the worst. We are poised to make one of the great strategic blunders of all time if we fail to restructure the rules of global capitalism when the attainment of a new level of peace and prosperity is so clearly within our reach. Yet to proceed abroad in a credible fashion, we must be clear about what sort of capitalism we meant to have here at home.

The Practical Pursuit of Happiness

To engage in that dialogue requires a civic maturity now badly stunted in a citizenry who devote, on the whole, more time in a single week to watching sitcoms than they spend in a year reflecting on the state of

their nation or of nature. Our national politics would be much enhanced—and the quality of our democracy much improved—by the
sincerity and authenticity of such a broad-ranging, heartfelt inquiry.
That would stand in particularly sharp contrast to the unspeakable superficiality of the current political debate. Democracy desperately
needs a presidential campaign that raises fundamental questions about
the obligations of U.S. leadership and the requirements of global citizenship. Yet no matter which way we turn, the compass of political
discourse points back to issues of financial capital—its impact, its ownership, and the signals to which it responds.

If we look to the history of the United States, it's difficult to identify a time when financial forces were more clearly in conflict with our
egalitarian democratic values. Goodwyn, an expert on turn-of-the-
century populism, writes about the natural link between the sensibilities of Thomas Jefferson and the agrarian populists who sought to
restore in their fellow citizens the capacity to have significant democratic aspirations. Goodwyn notes that somewhere along the way,
"the egalitarian current that was part of the nation's wellspring became not a constantly active source of ideas, but a curious backwater,
eddying somewhere outside both the conveyed historical heritage
and the mainstream of political thought."[14] The democratic impulse
has evaporated in the heat of an all-consuming, finance-focused individualism. Its few remaining eddies now surface not through visionary presidential candidates but through the occasional enthusiasms of
well-placed and powerful legislators.

Senator Russell Long's support for employee ownership is a classic
case. Though Long, like his father, had the capacity to think politically on a grand scale, one hallmark of a populist, he acted not as part
of a mass movement but as a solitary influential senator who used his
pivotal position to shepherd ESOPs into law.

For an aspiring democracy founded by property owners who limited the vote to property owners—initially to white, male property
owners—resolution of this ownership issue has been too long deferred. Even from the outset, it was covered over, consumed as part
of a larger debate about ends and means. For instance, in the pream-
ble to the Declaration of Independence, Thomas Jefferson adapted
Englishman John Locke's classic trilogy of life, liberty, and property
to read "Life, Liberty and the pursuit of Happiness." Looking back,
I believe that Locke may have had the better formulation. After all,
the practical pursuit of happiness has certain material preconditions.

The constitutional mandate is clear: The duty of a democracy is to actively advance the *general* welfare. Happiness is not an individual matter. The constitutional mandate suggests the need for a policy environment that encourages a *general* diffusion of the material means with which to pursue happiness.[15] Today's indifference about property patterns is a key barrier to that pursuit.

A child living in poverty is not enjoying a right to the pursuit of happiness. Yet one in five American children lives in poverty (one in four preschoolers). Undereducated or poorly educated youth are not enjoying a right to the pursuit of happiness when they are denied access to the skills, the resources, and, I believe, the attitudes and the outlook essential to cope successfully with life in an increasingly globalized economy. Yet our public school systems, with resources typically tied to local property values, ensure that the funding for affluent suburban schools is often three times that for inner-city neighborhoods, with their lower property values and denser populations. As a practical matter, that resource gap means that the gap in education is often now wider than before the landmark 1954 Supreme Court decision *(Brown vs. Board of Education)* overturning separate but ostensibly equal schooling and forcing school integration at Little Rock's Central High.[16] "It is the lot of the successful American politician," Edmund Wilson wrote in 1932, "to put a smiling face on the imperatives of property." To date, that's been the extent of our national policy on property patterns: a smiley face.

A Scant Chance at Happiness

Back when the federal government first became active in housing through the Federal Housing Administration Act of 1934 and then the GI Bill of 1944, almost all subsidized home mortgages were provided in heavily segregated suburbs. In 1960, not a single African American could be counted among the 82,000 residents of Long Island's famous Levittown housing tract. That was typical of the interpretation then given the general welfare (between 1930 and 1960, less than 1 percent of all mortgages went to black households). That practice continues four decades later, with blacks and Hispanics rejected for home mortgages twice as often as whites, regardless of income.[17] Black-owned small businesses are more than three times as likely as white-owned firms to have loan applications turned down, despite the same creditworthiness.[18] In 1999, the Department of

Agriculture finally gave its long-delayed assent to a class-action settlement to compensate black farmers who have complained for decades at being shut out of federal loan programs as a result of racism.[19]

Today there are 18,000 black farmers, down from 925,000 in 1920. Less than 1 percent of U.S. farmers are black, and they are abandoning farming at three times the rate of whites. Whites, with historically higher rates of home (and farm) ownership, benefited both directly and indirectly from this government-backed ownership policy as their access to equity helped make possible college educations, small businesses, and inheritances. Even Social Security contributed to inequality, because the original legislation exempted from coverage both farm and domestic work, areas that employed twice as many blacks as whites. As Yale sociologist Dalton Conley points out, that meant "any savings had to be spent during old age rather than being handed down to the next generation."[20] The result: In 1865, a few years after Lincoln freed the slaves, blacks owned 0.5 percent of the nation's net worth. In 1990, a quarter-century after passage of the nation's civil rights legislation, their net worth totaled just 1 percent—suggesting that neither wealth nor civil rights is trickling down.

In the biblical tradition, justice is viewed as liberation from oppression. The rhetoric of oppression is always the same, suggesting that some groups of people are less worthy—or at least not worthy in the same way as those generating the rhetoric. A ruse employed in the late 1990s by the make-racism-respectable crowd is an unusually ingenious attempt to deflect attention from these historic trends. They pointed to a test-score gap in which black students with parents earning over $70,000 averaged 144 SAT points less than white students at the same family income level. Their message: Lower intelligence among blacks accounts for the test-score "achievement gap." Thus, by implication, today's vast economic inequality is justified because *clearly,* blacks just can't cope in this knowledge-intensive era.

The truth is far different. And far more tragic. As Conley points out, if the test scores of black students are compared to those of white students *with the same family wealth,* the gap disappears. He urges that the race question be rephrased—"casting it in terms of stocks, bonds, business proprietorships, and real estate ownership rather than in terms of education and earnings." The solution, Conley argues, lies in policies "geared toward rectifying wealth differences." The best advantage you can have, he points out, "is having parents with wealth."

I'm not suggesting here that our democracy grant people rights. They already have those. What's missing is the means, the practical tools. As the nation's founders—property owners all—knew, that's what property provides. It's a means for pursuing happiness. Even now you hear politicians trot out that hackneyed line "It's not enough to give someone a fish, they also need a fishing rod and lessons in how to fish." A populist would point out that many people can't even get to the pond—there's a No Trespassing sign posted at the gate. A contemporary populist would suggest it's time we ask not only who owns the fishing rods but also who owns the pond and who owns the bank that holds the mortgage on the property.

The practical pursuit of happiness in a democracy requires an *activist* government sufficiently committed to its principles that it works to ensure broad-based property ownership. Today's candidates shrink from such fundamental concerns, recasting troublesome issues in trivial terms, forgetting that our government is meant to be as answerable to the claims of future generations as to those of the present. Today's one-dimensional focus on education and training is a classic example. Go get some skills so that you too can become a well-trained employee, working for someone *else* who owns. Compassionate capitalism, OK. Inclusive capitalism? No way.

Sentiments in this arena have always run strong. A libertarian web site proclaims that "property rights are human rights with respect to property." The power we've granted government to promote the general welfare suggests a duty to ensure that this nation's material wealth in the form of ownable property is diffused not partially but *generally*. That commonsense clarification could address a key flaw in a democracy whose vibrancy is now undermined by an increasingly troublesome economic divide. With the nation's happiness at stake and the future of democracy hanging in the balance, the need is for leaders willing to speak clearly and act decisively on this key issue.

Back from the Brink

For democratic capitalism to succeed in domains other than the financial, today's tightly pinched horizons of political possibility must be widened. That requires, in turn, that we reject the counsel of those who converted Adam Smith's limited theory about markets into an all-encompassing political ideology. Their single-minded, buttoned-down devotion to financial markets now saddles democracy with a doctrine not befitting a people who mean to live free and respect the natural world. Although the success of modern-day populism need not be built on the bodies of the Chicago-converted, it's clear that a more balanced economic model must quickly emerge if we hope to see today's out-of-control financial forces brought under democratic direction. It's not essential that the financial fundamentalists repent; they've too much invested in touting their flawed model for anyone to expect that. Yet their viselike grip on policymaking must relent, even if without a confession of fallibility. Their intellectual monopoly brought with it the same symptoms as those that accompany business monopolies, only instead of high prices and lousy products, we're forced to cope with bad ideas and lousy political candidates.

The power centered in financial capital—and in concentrated capital—is a force that no democracy has yet been able to bring under popular control. Communism proposed for that purpose a central party apparatus. That was a disaster, most clearly on display in the Soviet Union, where the Communist party spun wildly out of control, worsening the problem as it became clear that Marxism was a subterfuge for a profoundly antidemocratic and immensely corrupt regime. (The latest aphorism on the streets of Beijing is "As all are on the take, then let us take from all.") In market democracies, the massive modern state emerged as the non-Marxist alternative to radical laissez-faire. The government's countervailing power was meant to persuade us that the economic system was thereby rendered democratic. We were not fooled. The expense became horrendous while the bureaucracy became unbearably inefficient and frequently oppressive.

That brings us to our modern-day progressives, who promise to achieve the self-determination that democracy has long promised but never delivered. Yet for all they have promised, and it has been much (Bill Clinton and Al Gore hail from their camp), their shrunken vistas resulted in only apparent, not real, change as laissez-faire capitalism became marginally humanized but never truly democratized.[21] Critics claim that progressives have made things worse by pursuing an array of international agreements, including on-again/off-again support for the Multilateral Agreement on Investment (MAI) that would put the force of international treaty behind the unrestricted cross-border flow of funds. The MAI embodies the Chicago model's unspoken assumption that money knows best—no matter what local opinion might be. Looking back, it's clear that today's progressives offered only token accommodation rather than genuine inclusion. Democracy was the real loser, along with people's confidence in their ability to effect change. Though the progressives succeeded in the very narrow sense of generating a consensus to win back-to-back presidential elections (1992 and 1996), they failed to generate popular support, the only real sign of political success. Therein lies the political opportunity that this populist message is meant to tap.

Presidential Populism

I'm certain that financial forces can be harnessed to put this nation's economic well-being at the disposal of its people. And if *we* can do it, then so can any country. And we can show them how. To do so requires that this goal remain the focus of public policy both here and abroad over the next twenty years. That's because, absent revolutionary change, the evolutionary change I propose will take two decades to fully implement. Even though the present reality is quite raw, the promise is great. History suggests that we possess both the resources and the resourcefulness required if only we can get beyond today's confusions and delusions. If we embrace the challenge in a committed way, twenty years hence we will be able to look back with pride at the creation of a global capitalism that successfully supports humankind in its escape from poverty and its embrace, at last, of a life with dignity and with respect for the natural world.

Those leaders and hope-to-be leaders who refuse to step into this agenda with the commitment required to carry it to completion should not be considered serious candidates for public office. This nation is wealthy; it's only our policies that keep so many of us from realizing our affluence. I write this book so that those inclined to seek office might find both inspiration and ideas for their campaigns. For those interested in national elective office, I also offer a dollop of political advice offered me by Russell Long, who served thirty-eight years in the Senate, spanning the period from Harry Truman to George Bush. If someone were to campaign for the presidency on this program, Long advised, he or she might well get elected, provided the candidate knows how to talk about it and how to move people with the right combination of cool logic and heartfelt passion. Long's father, Huey, aspired to that office before his mysterious assassination.[22]

If a president then committed the requisite political capital to make this vision a reality, Long suggested, he or she could make enormous headway. A vigorous presidential campaign with these themes at the center is a key building block in mustering that political capital. Both this book and my previous one (*The Ownership Solution*) suggest components of a political platform meant to serve that purpose. Finally, Long asked, how could anyone who comes after such a president do anything other than agree to advance that agenda even further? That's what leadership is all about. That's also why we periodically hold presidential elections—hoping to evoke within the populace someone able to address the pressing needs of the time.

Democratic Finance

The reach of finance capitalism steadily broadened as the United States led the world in moving funds into the hands of money managers—banks, insurance companies, mutual funds, pension plans, foundations, university endowments, and the like. The U.S. portion of that institutional capital now tops $17,000 billion, the vast bulk of it managed on the basis of but one set of very narrow values—net present value (i.e., the value of an expected future stream of revenues).[23] The sheer magnitude of these funds suggests certain clear dangers, particularly because of their inability to include key aspects of the valuable in what they value. For instance, social cohesion, fiscal foresight, environmental sustainability—those values are simply too slippery and uncertain for financial analysis.

Physicist Hans Peter Durer, former president of the Max Planck Institute in Munich, offers a story to illustrate the limited range of values that plague financial analysis.[24] Imagine, he suggests, a fisherman who concludes that all fish are greater than two inches in length. How does he know? Because if he cannot catch it with a net, it's not a fish. To be certain, he also relies on a market test: No one wants to purchase a fish he cannot catch. What the fisherman neglects to mention is that his net is woven with two-inch holes.

It's time we recognize that because the measuring capacity of financial analysts is so very weak, their influence in democratic society should never be very strong. Though financial specialists proceed with great confidence from tree to tree, they often seem astonished when reminded that they operate in a forest. In fact, not only do they miss the forest, they miss most of the tree: its beauty, the cool shade it produces, the oxygen it generates, the songbirds it shelters. When they're in analyst mode, a tree becomes simply board feet. Author Steven Pinker offers a more sympathetic perspective: "We don't poke fun at the eagle for its clumsiness on the ground or fret that the eye is not very good at hearing, because we know that a design can excel at one challenge only by compromising at others."[25]

The thought process used in the realm of financial technology bears a keen resemblance to that used in biotechnology. To justify the design of living material that crosses biological boundaries, biotech reduces separate species to systems of information that can be reprogrammed into new biological combinations. Rather than think about the broader implications of creating transgenic species, it's easier to think only of the micro-reengineering of genetic codes and the re-patterning of bits of biological data. "Life becomes a code to be deciphered," notes biotech critic Jeremy Rifkin. "Eliminating structural boundaries and reducing all living entities to information provides the proper degree of desacralization for the bioengineering of life."[26] Even though a gene lacks all meaning except in the context in which it finds expression—and where it contributes to that context—genetic engineers view the gene in the most mechanistic sense. Borders recede into the background, so that there's no difference between the born and the made, creature and artifice, life and technology.

In a strikingly similar fashion, financial analysts likewise insulate themselves from the broader ramifications of their work, focusing instead on the minutiae of information found in financial flows and accounting conventions and in the reengineering of corporate capital structures. A merger or an acquisition becomes simply the re-patterning of bits of financial data and a reordering of the bookkeeping. Their interest lies only in how that information can be rearranged to enhance financial value. For both financial analysts and bioengineers, the perspective is stunningly narrow, mechanistic, insular, and, it must be said, ignorant and arrogant. Both choose to disregard the broader picture despite the clear implications.

The Populist Moment Is Now

My goal with this book is ambitious yet simple. My intention is to see us change the rules of capitalism such that we "peoplize" it by making it dramatically more inclusive. That's the only way I know to ensure that financial capital becomes subject to the countervailing forces of common sense. My intention is also to see the forces of corporate power and global finance brought under popular control, consistent with the values underlying a functioning democracy. The purpose here is not to look back or to blame policymakers for decades of profoundly bad judgment. There's evidence enough of that to bury both political parties. Instead it's about moving ahead by rolling up our political sleeves to create a democratic future that will make our descendants proud while preserving the environment for their descendants.

Our democracy's healthy skepticism has eroded into a corrosive cynicism, the legacy of two decades of movement without progress and of countless political promises that went unfulfilled. A long succession of mistakes makes for one staggeringly huge challenge. Much now is at stake. America's populist moment has long been pending. Its time, I suggest, is now. To ensure a democracy relevant to the demands of the twenty-first century, we must begin by democratizing our financial system. For far too long, we've been told that there's some greater calculus at work in the financial domain that, even though it doesn't work for us individually, somehow works for society as a whole. The problem, we're assured, lies not with the system but with us—if only we could grasp its superior logic or, by implication, if only we possessed the superior intellect of those who offer this suspect advice. To fully comprehend the illogic of that presumptuous stance, I turn in the next two chapters to an examination of the inner workings of finance. Chapter 7 then features a summary of ten key ingredients for a populist-inspired presidential platform.

5
Democratic Capitalism

Money should never be separated from values. Detached from values, it may indeed be the root of all evil. Linked effectively to social purpose it can be the root of opportunity.

—ROSABETH MOSS KANTER

There was a time when economic decisions were informed by conscience and made with sensitivity to the community. That was most clearly the case when elders were honored and close-knit communities were the rule rather than the exception. That richly textured, multiple-agenda decision making has gradually given way to a cool financial efficiency with but one set of values in mind: financial values. Modern-day capitalism now operates on the basis of "money on automatic." That's understandable now that more than $17 trillion resides in the hands of U.S. money managers hired and fired based on their ability to do but one thing: make *more* money.[1] Much of that money is just barely managed. As of mid-1999, Fidelity Investments had $765 billion invested in indexes that simply mimic the market by buying securities that match the market's overall performance. Barclay's Global Investors had $619 billion indexed, and Merrill Lynch & Company $501 billion.[2] Much like a preprogrammed machine unable to gauge its impact, this institutionalized, money-on-autopilot system—$1,875 billion indexed by just three firms—means that much economic decision making is now cut off from the foresight, the concern, and often even the simple common sense that reside uniquely with individuals and within their communities. The number of significant institutional investors in the United States is less than the number of members of today's presidential cabinet. Even though more voters than ever have a stake in ownership (however modest), popular control over the nation's commercial sector is growing steadily weaker as ever more deference is granted financial markets. That raises profound questions as to the legitimacy of the economic component of our present-day democracy.[3]

We're just awakening to the many flaws in the naive notion that money need only be accountable to itself. Adam Smith, the father of free enterprise, would be appalled at the way we've allowed money to run amok, converting the pursuit of financial returns into a secular idolatry. He envisioned not financial markets but an engaged humanity as the animating force through which the pursuit of private gain becomes a public virtue. Although global capital markets certainly display an uncanny capacity to seek out profitable investments worldwide, that search has left in its wake grotesque social inequities, oppressive political systems, and environmental tragedies. That's why, I suspect, Smith advocated a genuinely *self-designed* system operating through what he called "the invisible hand." Only a *people-based* system was, he felt, capable of reflecting the complexity of motivation, aspiration, and purpose that make humans so uniquely human. The eighteenth-century moral philosopher of considerable repute published his *Theory of Moral Sentiments* in 1759, which predates by seventeen years his more famous text, *The Wealth of Nations*. Both books make it clear that he favored a community-scale system based on *personal* decisions informed by what he called "human sympathies."

The notion of genuinely people-based, community-attuned control serves as the moral foundation of both markets and democracies. That's why markets defer to consumers, and democracies to their constituents. Democracies, in turn, are often characterized as marketplaces of ideas. Both are based on the commonsense notion that people should have an active voice in events that affect them. Today's remote-control, finance-dominant, globally attuned capitalism would strike Smith as an aberration, a freak of free enterprise. As we're now discovering, overreliance on that model often shows up as gains in financial efficiency at the cost of societal effectiveness and environmental sustainability.

Frances Moore Lappe, author of *Diet for a Small Planet* (1971), takes that analysis a step further, reporting on a debate with Milton Friedman, icon of the Chicago faithful. In response to his core argument that markets best serve freedom because they best respond to human choices, Lappe pointed out that "the market can only reflect human choices—and can therefore only serve human freedom—on one condition: that we all can make our choices felt in the market, and that requires a wide distribution of wealth and income. The concentration of wealth and income destroys the entire justification for the market." Further, she notes, markets don't respond to people or their rationale; they respond to people *with money*. Otherwise, "how can we explain a half billion people worldwide living in market economies and going hungry?"[4]

People-Free Free Enterprise

There's enormous irony at work here. That's because the component now most missing in this self-designed system is the *self*. Patterns of personal concern and personal responsibility are themselves an essential component of both free enterprise and democracy. Personal responsibility intensifies social creativity through the give-and-take of mutual interaction. That's the real motor of democracy.

For instance, although everyone may have a vote, a sickly 1 percent voter turnout is a very different democracy than a robust 95 percent turnout. Although private property rights, like voting rights, may be widespread, something is fundamentally amiss when the financial wealth of the top 1 percent exceeds that of the bottom 95 percent. For an avowed capitalist economy, that's a very sickly turnout. And for ensuring widespread responsibility, it's a disaster, as the endangered condition of our environment attests. Democracy needs new democratic channels—new means to ensure public accountability and new ways to evoke personal responsibility.

In the same way that you cannot take apart a cell and find its life force, both markets and democracies defy easy dissection. Their robustness will always remain a mystery, perhaps best known by their absence. Yet with a policy environment that evokes the proper breadth and depth of relationships, markets and democracies provide a container that can hold the human experience like no other system yet devised. Having worked in some thirty countries, I know it when I feel it. And also when I don't. Oftentimes, it makes me want to kiss the tarmac when my plane touches down on U.S. soil. Although we don't yet have it quite right, we've got it a lot less wrong than most.

What's overlooked in today's dollar-denominated market absolutism is what we all know intuitively: Not everything that counts can be counted, and not everything that can be counted counts. GDP rises regardless of whether funds change hands to find a cure for cancer, to pay the costs of O.J.'s murder trial, or to clean up an oil spill. Like a calculator missing a subtraction key, our economic measurements care only if cash changes hands, not whether genuine value has been created. GDP masquerades as mathematics when, in truth, it only scores transactions denominated in monetary terms—and every score is positive. Our national accounting system is good at identifying certain quantities; populism argues that democracy must embody certain qualities. Those qualities are determined by the relationships people have with those systems in which their lives are embedded.

Capitalism as a Conversation

One danger of today's disconnected capitalism is that it can quickly turn undemocratic. Many of the countries I've advised are in the midst of making the transition from state ownership to something else. What they discovered is that abolishing private property—the Marxist solution—simply doesn't work. Been there, done that. Yet if private property is an embedded feature of private enterprise, as it clearly is, the question remains: How do we best play to that strength? The answer lies not in the resolution of long-warring ideologies (Karl Marx versus Adam Smith) but in simple common sense. What's required is a fundamental reconfiguring of the economy's feedback loops, recognizing that peoplized property patterns are themselves a powerful societal tool for communication and for learning. Reduced to common principles, both markets and democracies are learning systems.

The Japanese capture the concept succinctly: All of us are smarter than any of us. The Chinese have a similar phrase: Anyone who rides on the knowledge of the many becomes wise. That's why sustainability requires democratic ownership patterns to ensure a genuinely democratic capitalism. Democracies must learn from everyone because they're meant to work for everyone. That's the "systems wisdom" embedded in their design. Markets need to follow this systems wisdom, too. Broad-based patterns of connectedness can help us better anticipate the future. We know from business settings that bottom-up organizations are more flexible and more resilient, a real plus in a globalized world, where ongoing adaptability is essential. That's also true for a political system that values personal freedom. Systems that lack designed-in "response-ability" either die or, to stay alive, make life difficult for those within them, as we saw in the Soviet Union.

Many of the most disturbing and unsustainable aspects of present-day capitalism are simply too remote in time or place to be measured in conventional financial terms. There's a huge and fast-growing gap between what financial markets claim to do *for* people and what they actually do *to* them. In his best-seller *Emotional Intelligence,* author Daniel Goleman offers a clue to the challenge of systems learning in the environment.[5] He points out that "the key to a *high group IQ* is social harmony. It is this ability to harmonize that, all other things being equal, will make one group especially talented, productive and successful, and another—with members whose talents and skills are equal in other regards—do poorly." He cites research from firms in which sustained growth and profits correlate closely with an environment of harmonious working relationships and "a strong sense of *psychological ownership* for the outcome of their work."

So the question remains: *How* do we smarten ourselves up so that financial forces no longer run roughshod over essential, nonfinancial domains? In short, how do we make capitalism democratic? Even more fundamentally, how do we evoke a free-enterprise democracy that generates harmony and accumulates memory from generation to generation so that we proceed with some semblance of wisdom? Disharmonious societies do not thrive. And smart systems prove themselves dumb unless their learning is preserved. The insights of one generation do not become the common sense of the next unless a way is found for one generation to converse with the next. Without education and the conversion of insights into law and common practice, hard-earned lessons are easily lost.

Toward a Peoplized Capitalism

What I propose here are methods to smarten up today's dumbed-down capitalism by building relationships with those who Adam Smith assumed from the outset would participate in the system's self-design. One thing we know for certain about systems: They can change dramatically by the amplification of just *one* element of feedback, as newly enfranchised democracies routinely discover, to their delight. Leave people disconnected, and they become discontented. Moreover, the system soon becomes dysfunctional.

The corporate entity consists solely of *relationships* both inside the firm (with shareholders, employees, managers, directors) and outside the firm (with customers, suppliers, regulators, etc.). The same holds true for democracy—it's a network of relationships. Though a democracy, like the corporation, may first be created on paper, it lives in those relationships. The challenge facing democracy is straightforward: How do we use property relationships more effectively and more creatively? How do we encourage ownership patterns that better tap our collective wisdom so that we improve both our economic and our political decision making? That has nothing to do with ideology; it's about using our common sense to design systems that learn better.

Ownership in a Globalized Marketplace

Imagine for a moment a single-economy world with freely mobile physical and financial capital. In such a world, pay differences between workers in different countries will steadily narrow as owners gravitate to locales with the most favorable wage rates. As the ongoing liberalization of the world economy makes developed countries richer while making many industrial and clerical workers within them worse off, who will gain the difference? Obviously it's those who own the capital.[6] What is globalization? Everyone is invited to a cookout—and you're the hot dog. And by the way, attendance is mandatory. The results are in. According to a survey by the WorldWatch Institute, Mexicans working for 2,200 U.S. multinationals in the *maquiladoras* area just south of the U.S. border are paid an average $1.67 per hour, while workers at those same factories on U.S. soil are paid $16.17. Though Americans are fond of their low-priced imports, this hollowing-out of the nation's manufacturing wage base shows up for producers as overcapacity and for workers as shrunken pay packages, displaced jobs, and fast-widening economic disparities.[7]

Think of it as neutron-bomb capitalism—leave the capitalism intact while killing off the customers. Cheaper products are terrific, but it's easy to forget that every producer requires a consumer. An abundant supply of productive power suggests the need for an abundant supply of consumer power. In systems science, that's known as "complementaries"—a nail implies a hammer, a car some gas. Those paired capacities are the essential yin and yang of economic robustness: Revenue-hungry producers require cash-flush consumers. Market demand evokes supply; supply requires market demand. We don't need supply-side theory alone. Nor demand-side (Keynes's specialty). We need a synthesis that ensures a balanced relationship between the two so that they work in tandem, like two sides of the same coin.[8]

If we save too much, we create the "paradox of thrift," as merchants are denied the sales revenues they need to pay workers, who need the income to buy the goods to keep the stores open and the workers paid. The high-saving Chinese now seek escape from this savings trap with a patriotic spending campaign that exhorts people to "love the country and consume." It's a paradox from which the high-saving Japanese may yet seek relief through a means long favored here: demand-stimulating defense spending.[9] "A worldwide shortage of aggregate demand has emerged as the world's premier macroeconomic malady," argues Princeton economist Alan Blinder, former vice chairman of the Federal Reserve Board.[10] Yet from the producer's side, it looks like worldwide overcapacity. "There is excess global capacity in almost every industry," complains Jack Welsh, chairman and CEO of General Electric.[11]

Overcapacity and underconsumption are two views of the same phenomenon. "No one has ever become very rich by saving their money," John D. Rockefeller advised. He might have added that even a rich nation can become poor if people save too much. If we can get the design right, successive sequences of investment and consumption will fuel both market dynamism and household capital accumulation. That, I suggest, is the most sensible route to a smaller government.

Democratic Capitalism:
A Campaign Promise Worth Voting For

Because both markets and democracies are learning systems, it's essential that every opportunity is taken to connect people to both systems so that both systems become smarter and more responsive. We know how to do that with democracies. Sort of. One person, one vote, was a good start. The question is how to get people to turn out at the polls. We know, for example, that although only 20 percent of the voting-age population has college degrees, they comprise more than 40 percent of those who vote in presidential primaries. Meanwhile, the already low participation of voters without a high school education has dropped by 50 percent since 1992. So that's today's democracy—a "sort of" democracy.

We're still learning how to smarten up both democracies and markets. To date, the market connection on which we've relied is jobs.

Governments worldwide are job-creation machines. That's because jobs have long been the currency of politics, a requirement enshrined in the Employment Act of 1946, enacted when Congress realized it was the war effort and not Roosevelt's New Deal that pulled us out of the Depression. Yet limiting economic connectedness to jobs alone has enormous drawbacks, including the temptation to maintain a huge defense budget as a full employment program, a temptation to which we have regularly given in for a full half-century. What's needed instead is a policy environment designed to encourage both jobs *and* ownership. Although jobs require ongoing education and training to steadily upgrade the nation's human capital, the missing piece has long been an ownership stake in the nation's labor-saving capital—which is fast becoming dramatically smarter (and saving more labor) with each new advance in our knowledge-intensive industries. Ensuring everyone an ownership relationship with income-producing capital could go a long way toward ensuring that the nation's income streams irrigate the economy with more genuinely democratic patterns of purchasing power.

Low voter turnout is the principal barrier to the realization of a genuinely democratic capitalism. Turnout in the midterm 1998 elections was 36 percent, the lowest since 1942, when millions of Americans were away at war. Among voters age eighteen to twenty-four, turnout was 15 percent (11 percent for eighteen and nineteen-year-olds). The lower two quintiles of the voting public are largely disenchanted with politics and, for the most part, politically dormant. That's understandable. They've yet to be offered a choice that would make any real difference in their lives. The 2000 presidential election asks them to validate a party-dominated, money-tainted process over which they've had little or no influence. Low voter turnout is best understood as a failure of political creativity. As a military leader, Colin Powell advised junior officers that when people no longer bring their problems to you, "it is for one of two reasons: either they think you can't solve their problems—or you don't care. Either is fatal to good leadership."[12]

Conscious Capitalism

We face a curious mismatch between our economic potential and our political will. On the one hand, less and less human effort is called for in the economic sphere to produce the goods and services that could open the vistas of broad-based leisure to our people. Meanwhile, ever more effort is needed to reinvigorate the political system so that this opportunity for leisure becomes a personal reality. Better yet may be the Australian practice of mandatory voting (either vote or pay a fine).[13] People need to know that the problem lies not with the capacity to produce abundance and leisure. That's already in place. What's missing is policymakers willing to insist that our abundance be broadly shared. The American voter has no idea that widespread prosperity is feasible. I'm certain it is. I also view this wider sharing as essential to the preservation of our democratic values. If we are to have democratic civil cohesion in a globalizing world, we must build a basic foundation of trust centered around our proven willingness to produce *and distribute* the abundance and the leisure of which we are capable. For that purpose, Election Day must become a national holiday with nationwide same-day voter registration so that it's easier for people to support candidates and policies that meet their needs.[14]

Civil cohesion is the source of our strength as a nation. Its absence can be devastating. That's why, when the Soviet Union collapsed, it collapsed so completely. It lacked the glue of open societies with their horrifically inefficient but delightfully effective mishmash of clubs, community groups, fraternities, lodges, sports leagues, and such, in which people form those personal relationships so essential to democratic robustness. All too often, the Soviet planners' clean, crisp, quantitative decisions displaced this human messiness. No wonder it didn't work. The humanity was sucked right out of it. We've seen this design flaw—a forced dehumanization—play itself out in other command economies as well—Cambodia, China, Vietnam, Cuba. My concern is that we may see this flaw emerging yet again through the extraordinary deference now granted financial signals, particularly when combined with the homage paid the bloodied tooth-and-nail of global competition. Unless these powerful forces are wired to serve some larger cooperative ends, democracy will continue, as now, to divide against itself.

Indeed, our already atrophied democracy may yet be torn apart by internal contradictions if we succumb to the insistent assurances of those who claim that finance capitalism will take care of itself—if only we'd grant financial forces a bit more freedom. We've passed this way before. In 1936, President Roosevelt warned that "the privileged princes of these new economic dynasties, thirsting for power, reach out for control over government itself. They created a new despotism and unwrapped it in the robes of legal sanctions."[15] Given the political forces aligned behind today's financial return-driven paradigm, modern-day populists need a shorthand phrase to describe the newest version of this very old phenomenon. I've pondered an array of phrases: financial fundamentalism (my favorite), financial fanaticism (too strong), financial fetishism (too clever), and finance fascism[16] (too accurate). I ask you: How might we best describe a system that insists on the ascendancy, even the moral authority, of such a very narrow bandwidth of values? How should we characterize a system that musters societal forces to enforce such a singular purpose? "The spirit of liberty," famous jurist Learned Hand advised, "is the spirit which is not too sure it is right." Today's finance zealots display no such humility. How should we characterize a political environment that insists on granting financial values not just a measure of well-deserved deference but instead command, even dominion?

My fear is that Divine Right has wormed its way back into the machinations of democracy as the divine right of capital markets.[17] That trend is accompanied by a financial feudalism that scours the globe, insistent that its tightly constricted values should take precedence over a broad swath of political, cultural, social, and even environmental values. To capture the danger and the illogic underlying that perspective, consider just this one paradox: In the midst of a worldwide stampede toward massive stock buybacks, what happens when a corporation repurchases *all* of its stock? To whom is it then accountable? Today's finance-ocracy is poised to become a parody of democracy, its values suggesting a need to amend Lincoln's memorable trilogy to read "that government of the capital markets, by the capital markets, for the capital markets shall not perish from the earth." How do we escape this alluring madness? The same way we jettisoned the insanity of Divine Right: We quit believing in it. And then we changed our laws and institutions to reflect that changed belief.

My intent here is not to disparage any particular devotee of today's finance ideology, but to serve notice of the extraordinarily dangerous forces they have unleashed in the world. Fully free capital flows may prove incompatible with the values of a fully free people.

6
Third-Way Capitalism

What self-centered men have torn down, other-centered men can build up.

—MARTIN LUTHER KING, JR.

When a people no longer trust themselves, they begin to depend on authority. That's a troubling symptom for a nation that aspires to remain a democracy. Of the many forms of political thievery I identify in these pages, that may be the worst because to rob a democratic people of their political self-confidence is to leave them with nothing on which to rebuild. Numerous surveys confirm that Americans now believe they are powerless. In overall matters of policy, only 7 percent say that government most often responds to the public's wishes. In stark contrast, interest groups and other lobbyists are named as most influential by 64 percent.[1] Most disturbing, however, is the remarkable passivity with which Americans have accepted their condition as somehow inevitable. Many now consider it their fate as capital markets and money-responsive politics have steadily grown in influence.

That impression is confirmed by the 2000 presidential race. By Labor Day 1999—a full year before presidential primaries used to begin—former President George Bush and his eldest son had worked their donor networks to raise $50 million barely ten weeks after announcing his candidacy. The amount was fully ten times the amount of the nearest Republican rival and twice that of Al Gore. With so many early state primaries now crammed into a narrow span of about six weeks, a heavily financed front-runner can overwhelm lesser-known candidates by saturating those markets (as they're now aptly called) with television, direct mail, and paid workers. Rather than getting to know a candidate, the original purpose of the primaries, voters instead get a political product, eerily akin to the rollout of a new breakfast cereal, complete with a memorable slogan and slick packaging.

That's why the vanity campaign of Steve ("Flat Tax") Forbes posed a credible effort in this money-dominated political era. He wrote a personal check for $37 million to fund his 1996 campaign and could have done that again in 2000 from the estimated $500 million-plus his daddy left him. A year before the 2000 election, Steve Forbes's public-relations firm, famous for repositioning Mrs. Paul's Fish Sticks, was test-marketing his packaging, recognizing the short shelf-life and limited consumer appeal of his single-issue message. Big money has become the political boss in a way that's arguably more corrupting than the political bosses of old, as evidenced by those corporate and Wall Street interests who successfully staged this year's Republican nomination—at least until John McCain's insurgency turned serious.[2] We're no longer constituents in need of genuine leadership; voters are now seen as political consumers in need of campaign salesmanship as these two parties of one persuasion muster funds to sell us on how they're different.[3]

Place and Politics

It's for good reason that *utopia* literally means "no place" because that's where capital markets operate—in financial cyberspace, which is both nowhere and everywhere at the same time. The reality of capital markets—like that of presidential politics—lies in the realm of the abstract, the invisible, and the intangible. Yet their impact is very real. Money markets, however, unlike politics, are notoriously unconcerned with any measure of value unless it shows up as financial value. Oddly enough, that narrow focus is routinely justified on the basis that financial markets—like presidential elections—thereby tap into the intelligence distributed throughout society. Markets, whether financial or political, are preferred over top-down, expert-engineered solutions or the guidance from an officious bureaucrat or a fickle ruler. Although that sounds terrific in theory, the uncomfortable truth is that financial capital has no loyalties, no allegiances, and certainly no commitments—not to person, place, or politics. Its only goal is to generate more of itself. I think of it as "sauntering" capital—from the French, *sans terre*, without land or home. The lack of allegiance makes these huge pools of capital enormously powerful yet profoundly immoral—precisely because they have no responsibility or obligation outside the very limited domain of finance.

Financial capital is inherently impatient. Idle funds are seen as a crime against capitalism. Unlike nature, the rules of capitalism don't allow for a fallow period. Capital is constantly on the lookout for its next ride into the future, certain always that the highest return is always for the best. For instance, much of today's abuse of nature can be traced to the time-compressed focus of financial capital. Crops force-fed with phosphates are made to fruit twice when they would more naturally flower but once, leeching lands of their nutrients while fouling streams and aquifers—all in the interest of generating ever-insistent financial returns.

The fact that genetically modified crops now override nature's time-designed wisdom suggests a social pathology reflecting the view that financial efficiency is the optimal trait for life. Over the past decade, we've converted the unthinkable into the debatable and then watched it become routine. Canadians now inject human growth genes into salmon to create super-salmon. We inject cold-resistant fish genes into tomatoes to make them survive the frost. Even the key objections against such engineering are time-related, as critics complain that the effects are unpredictable and irreversible.[4] Chemical pollutants operate on a contamination model; they dilute over time. Biological pollutants are very different; they involve organisms that can reproduce, mutate, and disseminate, creating what scientists call low-probability, high-consequence risks that may increase over time. In the meantime, though, life-as-technology boosts financial returns.

Bio-Politics

The bioethics committee at California-based Geron Corporation concluded in 1998 that it was OK to move ahead with human embryo cloning to produce replacement tissue for the mass market, provided the embryos were treated "with respect." Harvard professor Joseph Fletcher argues that "parahumans" might legitimately be fashioned for dangerous or demeaning jobs, through the use of female mammals (probably apes) to gestate hybrid "metahumans" to do low-grade work.[5] In a democracy, are these beings born or made? Are they kindred humans with rights or mere artifacts, more akin to a Coke can that you might kick in the gutter? In a fast-emerging scenario driven by the promise of huge financial returns, biotechnology may soon grant the well-to-do access to Genes R Us catalogs. In such a techno-eugenic era, those who can afford it could create more of themselves: smart, aggressive, accomplished, cynical. Eventually this could bring about the separation of the human species into what Chicago-style free-market advocate Lee Silver calls "the GenRich and the Naturals."[6] With lobbying from the biotech industry (Al Gore has a former Genentech executive on his senior staff), the government's 1985 ban on so-called germline engineering is now under review.[7]

Meanwhile, W. French Anderson, a biogenetic pioneer, is poised to begin a form of somatic therapy in 2002 with a high probability, he concedes, of "inadvertently" modifying the human germline. A large coalition of clergy declared such engineering "a fundamental threat to the preservation of the human species as we know it."

We stand on the brink of what could be the most portentous technological threshold in history. Yet it's not even a part of our democratic debate. What should we call it? I call this money-driven phenomenon "finance-eugenics." The result of blending money, politics, and biotechnology is all too obvious. For instance, under Clinton-Gore, the U.S. Department of Agriculture tried to implement a regulation in 1998 requiring that the definition of organic foods include genetically engineered foods. In a hopeful sign for democracy, popular opposition generated more letters of objection than any other regulation in the history of this nation. As with the values-free finance myopia that infects economics, the current focus in biotechnology leads in but one direction, which can only endanger democracy.

It is here that the debate between small versus big government often loses focus. The uncomfortable truth is simply this: Small government is no match for the relentless march of today's massive financial capital. Or for the global reach of technology, including biotechnology. To suggest otherwise is delusional. The relevant question is this: Can large government be democratic? It can, but not in a policy environment indifferent about patterns of capital ownership or about the values that underlie technology (the United States remains the global rogue as one of the few industrial nations not to ban human cloning). The power of financial capital, like political power, requires the countervailing power of local decision making. In a property-based economy, local decision making requires a component of broad-based localized ownership. That locale-specific input is precisely what Adam Smith had in mind with his advocacy of a self-designed system attuned to "human sympathies." As did the nation's Framers, with their support both for local control and for a strong federal government able to rise above narrow interests. They understood that it's only by working together collectively that we become free individually. The more relevant concern is big versus bad government. How can you tell? With good government, the center is a servant to the periphery, while the periphery is loyal to principles established by the center. Democracy is at risk because the periphery has atrophied while the center has become unprincipled (witness its uncritical, money-motivated embrace of biotechnology).

With the onslaught of global capital markets and their money-myopic principles, democracies must insist on an element of local financial control as a community-sensitive counterweight to the abusive power of the global money chase. Our current leadership has the lesson reversed. They bought into the notion that it's the duty of the United States to adapt to the needs of the global economy. That's nonsense. It's our duty to ensure that the global economy, including financial markets and emerging technologies, adapt to the needs of democracy. Ironically, financial markets are an outgrowth of democracy and of the security of property rights that accompany the spread of democracy. Property rights and democracy are inseparably paired. Properly peoplized, financial markets may someday emerge as an economic counterpart to democracy. But not with today's dysfunctional ownership patterns—concentrated, divisive, and disconnected. Instead our democratic dog is being wagged by its plutocratic tail while unprincipled leadership attunes its policies to Wall Street's financial values rather than to Main Street's commonsense human values.

"Big government" is needed to ensure that social space is preserved for small government—and for the people and the communities that constitute both. In other words, democracy with a small "d" can thrive only where Democracy (with a big "D") guarantees a supportive and protective framework. A strong national government is also required to address challenges that cut across interrelated domains—economic, social, and environmental. No institution representing less than the whole can take responsibility for issues best understood from the perspective of the whole. A centralized force is also essential to assure availability of the tools required for decentralized community-building and to ensure that we meet our obligation to intergenerational sustainability. To be effective, democracy must work at several different scales across both place and time. As we'll see in later chapters, it is for that reason that a coordinated international effort is required if we are to protect our democracy from the highly undemocratic forces of global finance. That's also why a *global* ban is required both for replicative human cloning and for human germline engineering. We must move quickly to protect all of life from the financial forces driving biotechnology and its assumption, as author Wendell Berry puts it, "that our knowledge will increase fast enough to outrace the bad consequences of the arrogant use of incomplete knowledge."[8]

Third-Way Capitalism

The Marxist-collectivist model has been rightly discredited. Marxism offers a telling lesson for what happens when ideology masquerades as economics. Ironically, today's radically individualist economic model delivers just the sort of inhumane results that could tempt people back into a collectivist mind-set. The search is on for a better way. To date, what we have instead is yet another ideology disguised as economics—only this time from the extreme political right rather than the left. In the ongoing search for a more hopeful path, the political rhetoric remains well ahead of the policy reality. In the early 1990s, we heard from Britain about the "stakeholder society." That vague concept came on the heels of our equally vague 1980s rhetoric touting "empowerment." Both are what I call wish words: Those who hear them *wish* they knew what the words mean. The stakeholder notion attracted enormous media attention as UK Labor Party leader Tony Blair positioned himself to replace Tory John Major as prime minister. When that notion was discarded because Blair never put any meat on its bare rhetorical bones, the so-called Third Way emerged to take its place. This latest, equally ambiguous phrase quickly made its way across the Atlantic, where its vacuity assured its warm embrace both by Al Gore and George W. Bush.

An early example of Third Wayism was Tony Blair's insistence that the Labor Party abandon its stance favoring public ownership. Soon thereafter, Blair was elected prime minister. By 1999, center-left governments had been elected in thirteen of fifteen West European nations, including Blair in Britain, Lionel Jospin in France, and Gerhard Schroder in Germany, where this policy is called *Neue Mitte* (New Middle). Though these developments suggest that we may yet see the emergence of a European Third Waydom, the signs to date are hardly hopeful. For instance, Blair's first major announcement from 10 Downing Street was his decision to grant Federal Reserve–like independence to Chancellor Gordon Brown, who oversees Britain's central bank. In other words, even among Third Wayers, financial values are given star billing in the constellation of democratic values. Similarly, in July 1999, Chancellor Schroder announced an agenda of Chicago-inspired changes designed to move his Social Democratic Party sharply right.[9] Frankly, absent a stance on ownership patterning, I find the Third Way a profoundly vacuous notion. In terms of ownership, a Third Way compared to what?

Third-Way politicians are winning, largely because they've succeeded in casting conservatives as simplistically antigovernment. Today's conservatives can't answer the most fundamental political question: What is government for? Third Wayers can supply an answer, albeit often only in the vaguest of terms and with prescriptions woefully lacking in specifics and agonizingly long on polemics. The four rhetorical balms of choice—opportunity, responsibility, community, and empowerment—are words you'll find mixed and matched in any Third Wayer's speech. "The truth is," notes *Policy Review* editor Tod Lindberg, "Third Way politicians are perfectly happy to have cast conservatives as an anti-government menace whose message for people who fall down is 'Get Up.'"[10]

American voters are ready for something new. We've grown weary of those who claim to want limited government while displaying disdain for government. We now find more resonance with Franklin Roosevelt's simple observation: "Better the occasional faults of a Government that lives in a spirit of charity than the constant omissions of a Government frozen in the ice of its own indifference." It didn't take us long to discover a revealing fact about today's perverse version of conservatism. Though our conservatives are delighted to belittle and disable government, even delegitimize and dismantle it, they're also happy to make government an arbiter of private morality. That's a key reason Newt Gingrich and his acolytes enjoyed so brief a day in the political sun: The populace quickly perceived their shadow and the dangerously one-dimensional nature of the democracy they espouse.

Both U.S. liberals and European social democrats have difficulty advancing their people-first agendas in an environment in which the money-first dictates of financial globalization are the economic reality. Former governor of New York, Mario Cuomo, correctly notes that although politicians may campaign in poetry, they must govern in prose. Global capital markets provide the harsh financial prose that requires advocates of social justice to find a new way.

Current circumstances in the United States can be considered Third-Way capitalism. Capitalism's first way was the "robber baron" era of the Industrial Revolution. The remarkable exclusivity of ownership that typified early industrialization provided Karl Marx all the excuse he needed to propose that private property be abolished and ownership transferred to the state. There it quickly become Second-Way state capitalism, replacing private-sector robber barons with public-sector robber bureaucrats. Although the second way was a profoundly stupid response, one can certainly sympathize with the stimulus. As earlier chapters indicate, the outline of today's Third-Way capitalism is crystal clear. Unfortunately, it looks suspiciously like the First Way. That's most clearly the case in Russia and in several other "in-transition" countries, where robber bureaucrats are emerging as the newly privatized and ownership-legitimized robber barons.

I suggest we reconsider our expectations for the spread of capitalism. Just what do we hope to get out of it? If it's only some form of what John Kenneth Galbraith calls democracy for the fortunate, then there's really not much for us to do. We can just continue to use our influence to open the borders of other countries to the free flow of goods and capital and let laissez-faire sort it out. But if we intend to enjoy the company of genuine democracies devoted to balancing an array of social values, then we must do with our financial and economic systems what governments worldwide are doing with their political systems: democratize them.

Out-of-Control Capitalism

What's needed is a new concept of capitalism, one that's politically neither left nor right—and certainly not centrist. The goal here is not some grand compromise. That's what unprincipled politicians do. The goal is to proceed more like nature. Nature doesn't compromise; it *optimizes.* "A pelican," biologist Peter Warshall reminds us, "is not a compromise between a seagull and a crow. It is the best possible pelican."[11] Our goal should be the best possible democracy. The notion of a genuine third way will fail unless it succeeds in finding new avenues for injecting democratic values into the realm of finance, optimizing the values of both democracy and capitalism.

Much of today's epidemic-level anxiety and stress stems from a widespread feeling of living in a system that's careening out of control. If today's fast-paced, fast-food world seems speeded up, that's understandable. Imagine $17 trillion-plus in the hands of U.S. money managers who are hired and fired based solely on their ability to generate *more* financial value. What is financial value? It's largely about generating revenue over relatively short periods. *Lots* of revenue. That requires selling stuff. *Lots* of stuff. And the quicker the better. That, in turn, puts a huge premium on advertising, branding, and persuading people that what it means to be human is to be a consumer. By compressing the space between a radio announcer's words, computer software—appropriately called "CASH"—allows broadcasters to schedule four to six more ads per hour.

We now spend more than $2 billion annually on advertising directed at children, over twenty times the amount spent ten years ago. Nationwide advertising expenditures for 1998 topped $200 billion, an 89 percent increase from 1980, or an average $1,987 per household. Drug companies spent almost $1.96 billion on consumer ads in 1999, up from $720 million in 1996. The typical American child spends 60 percent more time watching television each year than he or she spends in school—and sees between 20,000 and 40,000 commercials. At least 10,000 of those are food ads, mostly junk food and fast food. At six months of age, babies begin forming mental images of corporate logos and mascots. In a 1991 study, 91 percent of six-year-olds correctly associated Joe Camel with Camel cigarettes. Experts report that a lifetime customer may be worth $100,000 to a retailer.[12]

A consumption-centered society puts enormous stress on the environment (and on us) as more stuff is pulled through our consumption patterns en route to the landfill. And through us en route to the sewage treatment plant, the hospital, or the diet clinic. In December 1999, 20 percent of Americans qualified as obese, that is, at least 30 percent over their recommended weight (1999 saw 400,000 liposuction procedures in the United States). Worldwide, the number of overweight people now rivals the number of hungry, underfed people.[13] Our consumption, in turn, requires the support of steadily higher incomes and less time for pursuits unrelated to consumption. That's why we now see so many "downshifters"–people trading in their pursuit of money for a life as they choose more time and less income (estimates of the downshifting U.S. population range as high as 28 million).

If the economy feels to you soulless, no wonder. Driven by the dictates of finance, what was once the soulful art of "human sympathies" has become progressively more disconnected from human concerns. If today's "Chicago" system feels to you disconnected, it should, because it is. Disengaged, unconcerned, uncaring? That too. No wonder people feel alienated from a system that seems so unresponsive to their needs.

Third-Way Aspirations

Third Wayers have only the vaguest sense of what's amiss. They proudly proclaim their intention to replace top-down bureaucracies with an "enabling government" that pursues a bottom-up "empowerment agenda." Their rhetoric virtually soars with notions of how to "supplant class warfare with the politics of common aspiration." And how they intend to speak to "common values rather than narrow interests." And so on and on and on. . . . They acknowledge that an activist government is needed but that it must take a new shape and have a new focus. Yet while their embrace of what they call fundamentals (such as fiscal discipline and crime prevention) enjoys widespread resonance, they ignore plutocratic ownership patterns as a malady that continues to tear at the fabric of democratic society. Perhaps that's for fear of being branded as too far to the political left. After all, the last person to question ownership patterns was Karl Marx, who failed miserably in crafting a remedy. Or perhaps it's for fear of being branded as too far to the political right. After all, the last politician to advocate a more participatory capitalism was Margaret Thatcher, who also failed miserably. Or perhaps there's simply a residual reluctance to raise an issue as personal as what people own, particularly when any mention of another's patrimony is often viewed as impolite, even impolitic.

Nevertheless, any *credible* Third-Way policy must include a feasible stance on ownership, including a program directed at evoking an economy better wired to reflect *your* views and incorporate *your* values. That's what democracies are supposed to do. Markets too. That's why we enshrined the notion of self-correcting systems in both politics and economics. It's just that we still haven't figured out the wiring. To the extent that components of ownership can be used to construct a more robust web of personal and community relationships, that too is progress in the spirit of the Third Way.

For instance, as part of a strategy begun to combat rampant graffiti, the City of Philadelphia sponsored a mural-painting project, enlisting the help of local artists to beautify graffiti-blighted walls, abandoned buildings, and other public spaces with brightly colored paintings of landscapes, sports scenes, even fantasies. In each case, artists and the city work with local residents to select a theme. For instance, one wall features a two-story-high photorealistic painting of Julius Erving ("Dr. J"), legendary star of the Philadelphia 76ers basketball team.

After an incidence of racial violence, residents of another neighborhood opted for a wall (approximately twenty by fifty feet) depicting a series of intermingled hands of different skin-colored hues. Other structures feature flower gardens. Or fanciful imagery. Each is distinctive in its own way. With more than 1,700 murals now scattered around the city (and graffiti largely banished), what began as a mid-1980s beautification campaign for the City of Brotherly Love has since matured into a distinctive contribution to the personality of one of our oldest and most historically significant cities. What has that to do with sharing our wealth? A significant portion of the wealth of any community is its neighborhoods, including the pride that people take in where they live. This "Third-Way" effort enabled neighborhood residents to reclaim ownership of public space, a critical component in the creation and preservation of social capital.

Back when farmland was owned by those who worked it, it was said that the best fertilizer any acreage could have is the feet of its owner. We're slowly beginning to realize that ownership, like finance, has become too remote, detached, and indifferent when what's needed are owners who have some presence and proximity to the work being done. The starkly clean efficiency of capital markets needs to be muddied up with the complex mix of human motivations, aspirations, and values that make humans so uniquely human—and democracies so uniquely democratic. Some calculated inefficiency—of the same sort that's designed into the checks and balances of democracy—would go a long way toward injecting the self back into the self-correcting design of free enterprise. "Freedom," Dr. Martin Luther King, Jr., rightly observed, "has always been an expensive thing." A policy mix that ensures a component of up-close, personal, community-sensitive ownership would offer a bona fide political alternative. *That* would be a genuine Third Way. The Third Way has the potential to become the most important political development of this generation. However, it also has the potential to be rightly dismissed as yet another sorry spurt of starry-eyed, fuzzy-headed rhetoric.

Third-Way Banking

Our agrarian history offers a disturbing precedent for Third Wayers to ponder, illustrating what needs to be done to transform financial capital into a democratizing force. One of historical populism's great political ironies dates from the turn of the last century and the attempt by farmers to wrest control of their personal destiny from the financial forces that dominated an era when land was the primary form of productive capital. A quick review also suggests why that troubled period marks the last time events evoked a populist movement. Soon after the gold standard was legislated into law in 1901, the United States experienced the Panic of 1907. The financial community, led by financier J. P. Morgan, saw that a more flexible currency was required to ensure adequate financial capital during each autumn's harvest, when the funds required to bring crops to market created nationwide liquidity shortages. That seasonal demand also meant competition for the funds required for ongoing industrialization, a key Morgan concern. Thus, the 1912 report of the National Monetary Commission proposed a system that could better respond to the nation's credit needs, including the needs of farmers. What initially emerged were the twelve branch banks of the Federal Reserve System, meant to meet regionally sensitive liquidity needs. When wheat farmers in Missouri, tobacco farmers in Virginia, and cotton farmers in Georgia needed funds, the Fed stood ready to ensure availability. Its branch locations (such as St. Louis, Richmond, Atlanta, Chicago, Cleveland, Kansas City, Minneapolis, Dallas, and Denver) reflect the original goal of meeting the seasonal credit needs of an agrarian age. Mirroring the nation's political make-up at the time, eight of the twelve original Federal Reserve Banks (all still operational) were east of the Mississippi.

In operation, however, the creation of a central bank eased access to funds not only for harvest purposes but also for the nation's larger farmers, who lost no time in tapping that expanded credit to buy out small-acreage farms. It was not until much later, with passage of the farm loan acts of Roosevelt's New Deal era, that the needs of the family farm were addressed. By then, however, most small farmers had been forced into tenant status by large farming interests whose enhanced access to credit enabled them to acquire ever more land at the expense of small holders. In terms of ownership patterns, agribusiness began to emerge within a decade after Washington offered a credit system envisioned as a way to assist the small farmer.

Contrary to modern accounts, the centralization of farm ownership was not due to the economies of scale associated with large landholdings. Large-scale corporate farming would only prove its "efficiency" much later. The Fed-facilitated access to credit led to the loss of economic autonomy for millions of Americans. The result not only marginalized huge numbers of previously self-sufficient families, but also provided a ready labor pool anxious to leave their tenuous status on the land and make their way to industrial jobs in the city—where they would also be denied a chance to own.

Although the transition from a locally based agrarian economy to a national industrial one was enormously turbulent and troublesome, today's ongoing transition—from national to global and from an industrial age to an information age—promises to be even more so.[14] As with the earlier transition, the ownership-pattern implications of today's transition remain a subject outside the sphere of public debate. That's a huge mistake. We need only recall that this earlier transition, distinguished as well by profound political ineptitude in providing a policy environment appropriate to the times, produced not only the Great Depression but also Hitler's Germany, Mussolini's Italy, and Stalin's Russia.

Consolidated Credit

Established in 1913, the same year that J. P. Morgan died, the Federal Reserve soon abandoned the notion of regionally responsive, seasonally sensitive banking. By 1935, Franklin Roosevelt had approved a consolidated credit system, with monetary authority centralized in the Washington-based Federal Open Market Committee, which would make credit decisions based on the *national* need to pull us out of the Depression. That nationwide focus remains intact. As with the original legislation, access to credit continued to favor those with collateral and financial sophistication. As a result, concentrated ownership soon became the hallmark of American commerce in both agriculture and industry. The rest, as they say, is history. Democracy's ownership pattern was cast, with support from a publicly chartered banking system that remains indifferent to how its operations impact ownership patterns.

Commercial banking, though still important, is being pushed aside—some might say eclipsed—by the access to loan funds through capital markets. Rather than provide an IOU to a commercial bank, companies find they can sell their IOUs directly in the marketplace, resorting to "commercial paper" (or corporate bonds) to raise funds. So now we have two parallel systems for accessing capital: banks and capital markets. The difference narrows more each day as banks bundle their loans into securities for sale in capital markets. Both suffer from the same practical shortcoming: Credit remains very strictly allocated—to those with collateral (and a feasible business plan). Try borrowing money without it.[15] That's a key reason that "the rich get richer." That financial reality also makes suspect any deficit-reduction or economic empowerment plan based simply on the notion that it will result in lower interest rates. For whom? Another more subtle set of forces must also be understood if one is to grasp just why ownership patterns have been so exclusive for so long: that's due to today's "closed" system of finance, the least understood element of free enterprise that puts democracy at risk.

Opening Democracy's Closed System of Finance

The very purpose of finance is to acquire assets before you possess the funds to pay for them. With access to credit, income-producing assets can generally pay for themselves out of the earnings they generate. That's a fact well known to the well-to-do and to the financially sophisticated. This "self-financing" logic must be more widely applied if ever we hope to have a genuinely democratic capitalism. Here I describe corporate finance in a way that's demystified and de-jargonized, and in terms the layperson can understand.

We know that capitalism routinely expands without expanding the ranks of those called capitalists. That's because firms finance themselves within a tightly closed system. Thus far, we don't have a capitalism designed to create capitalists; it's only designed to finance capital. Democracy requires a capitalism that does both. Here's how the closed system works. There are just two sources of funds for any firm: (1) those it generates *externally*—through debt (borrowed funds) and equity (invested funds), and (2) those it generates *internally*—by reinvesting its earnings, plus what it sets aside as depreciation reserves. Depreciation reserves are the funds for which the tax law allows a write-off to replace outmoded or worn-out equipment, machinery, buildings, and such. Economists refer to those internally generated funds as "business savings" (reinvested earnings and depreciation) because the funds are invested rather than spent.

Let's take one source of funds at a time to see what's at work here, looking first at external funds—debt and equity. Access to borrowed funds (debt) is limited to those with collateral. That makes sense. If you put up the collateral, you keep anything financed with the credit you secure. That's why debt routinely finances new capital yet seldom creates new capitalists. What about sales of new equities? They don't amount to much. Not since the days of J. P. Morgan have new equities amounted to more than 3–5 percent of the funds that firms raise each year. That includes today. Even with the high-profile media coverage given initial public offerings (IPOs) of Internet stocks, new equities remain a very small blip on the capital-raising radar screen. Plus, most are bought by people with discretionary funds and financial sophistication. In addition, current shareholders often have preemptive rights, which requires that any newly issued shares first be offered to them. The result: Neither source of external funds—neither debt nor equity—creates many new owners.

What about internally generated funds—reinvested earnings and depreciation reserves? A firm's earnings are reinvested for those to whom the firm belongs. That's straightforward. And the tax law says you can't claim depreciation until an asset is "placed in service." Because depreciable assets are placed in service by current owners, they claim the allowable tax write-offs. The subtle aspect here is the nature of those reserves. As a general rule, external funds (debt and equity) generate 25 percent of total funds, whereas internal funds comprise the balance. Of the 75 percent of funds generated internally, 90 percent are due to depreciation. That's important to understand because depreciation exemplifies the very concept of private property in a free-enterprise economy. In an *income tax* system, before you compute taxable income, you must first allow the taxpayer a chance to recover the cost of the property used to generate that income. Otherwise, you're taxing not the income but the property that generated the income. That reflects the private-property concept underlying depreciation. Ninety percent of 75 percent is 67 percent. Thus, two-thirds of the funds used to finance our private-property system are *embedded in the very concept of private property.* Those funds "show up" as tax write-offs. That's also why credit is so strictly allocated: those with access to depreciation write-offs can shelter their income from tax, using it instead to pay for new, improved income-producing assets. In practice, depreciation allows you to use write-offs on *today's* technology to purchase *tomorrow's* technology, a key reason ownership patterns have historically remained so very concentrated.

Many of America's rich became fabulously rich by using this closed system to acquire income-producing assets on terms with which the assets pay for themselves. That commonplace "closed system" business practice is the hallmark of private-property economies world-wide. Left to operate on its own, it locks in a self-reinforcing, wealth-concentrating inevitability that undermines democracies by creating plutocracies. Yet the financial logic that fuels today's exclusive system could provide a powerful way to redirect financial know-how into radically inclusive patterns of economic participation. Certainly the nation's fiscal foresight would be much improved by connecting more people directly to their economy's income-producing inputs.

Today's economic model optimizes only one part of an economic system—say, the financing—against only one element in isolation—such as bringing new productive assets on-line. What's needed is to *optimize the whole system for multiple purposes*—enhancing productive output while also enhancing the broad-based capacity to consume or to save.[15] That's the way to realize multiple benefits from a single outlay while also advancing "fiscal efficiency" as more people become financially self-sufficient through the day-to-day operations of the nation's financial technology. In truth, if those two elements–investment and income—are not working together, they'll tend to work against each other, as they do now. With the appropriate financial linkages, the economy could create things to consume at the same time that it creates consumers with the financial means to buy them. To neglect consumption patterns while financing ownership patterns is like installing pumps with no concern for the piping. If we want market mechanisms to broadly irrigate the economy with purchasing power, we can't afford to be indifferent about our property patterns.

The magnitude of today's transfer payments and the fiscal drag they represent is symptomatic of enormous systemwide inefficiency. Whole-system optimization would reflect far better foresight. Our economic forecasters are remarkably adept at predicting every year how much capital financing we'll have nationwide ($931.6 billion in nonresidential plant and equipment for 1998).[16] We need to match that forecasting ability to better "backcasting" to determine the ownership pattern that best advances fiscal sustainability and then design a financial incentive structure to get us there. To do anything less is fiscally irresponsible—akin to constantly saving drowning people instead of sending someone upstream to figure out who keeps pushing them in. The emerging demographics are clear; what's required is a functioning democracy to address those foreseeable needs.

Corporate Democratization

It's both financially inefficient and politically dangerous for a democracy to allow private property and the corporate entity *to work so well for so very few*. Keep in mind that the corporation is designed to be immortal. Though its owners may change, it has a life independent of those who may own its shares at any particular moment. For an actively traded company, ownership can change dramatically every day. For instance, the average time that shareholders held Amazon.com in 1998 was seven days. More than three-quarters of a billion shares traded daily on the New York Stock Exchange in 1999 (an average 809.2 million per day), up 21 percent. About 160 billion shares changed hands in 1997 on the various exchanges, up 27 percent from the previous year. Ownership of a corporation can shift every few minutes, as public-company "ownership" (more like a betting slip) is auctioned every day.

The word "corporation" (from *corpus*) comes from the same word as "body" or "corpse." The corporation is essentially a lifeless entity, a legal agreement evidenced by a charter and by-laws memorialized on paper. It's then animated by those who connect with it, by the financial forces that flow through it, and by the managers who run it. Since 1886, the Supreme Court has treated the corporation as a natural person under the Constitution *(Santa Clara County vs. Southern Pacific Railroad)*. The essential lifeblood of this "person" is the revenues on which it constantly renews itself, and on which its value to shareholders is largely determined. In that sense, a corporation–like a democracy—is a constant work in progress. Shareholders jump in and out; revenues ebb and flow; products and processes shift with the markets. Yet the *corpus* of successful companies endures, immortal in the same way that democracies endure though the citizens who comprise them constantly change.

Just as water flows through a whirlpool and creates the whirlpool at the same time, the corporate body rapidly loses its vitality if its nutrients—its energizing revenues—grind to too slow a pace. Depreciation provides an essential financial nutrient for companies that rely on income-producing property for their success, allowing them to use revenue-preserving tax write-offs to fund the firm's renewal, replacement, and regeneration. It's important to remember that those tax write-offs trace their source to the need to protect and regenerate private property. In the same sense that *nature* means "endless birth," depreciation is part of our private-property system's very nature, enabling it to give financial birth to successive generations of technology—each of which gets sucked into a democracy-threatening vortex of exclusion and economic privilege. That suggests the pivotal role that property plays in the workings of finance capitalism. Any attempt to devise a New Economy—whether a Third Way or otherwise—must address the central role of property in all things economic.

The Transgenerational Democratic Corporation

I'm not the same person I was yesterday. Part of me has changed. Nor will I be the same person when I wrote this as when you read it. Like the corporate entity, I'm in a constant state of renewal and regeneration. Within that mix of ingredients called "me" is a small voice that tells me I have obligations not only to myself but also to those not present, including those who comprise generations yet to come. The corporation should have similar obligations. Indeed, more so because of its legally recognized immortality. Its legally sanctioned, transgenerational status implies that it *must* operate in a sustainable fashion. For equity and sustainability to have any chance at all, it's essential that the corporation escape the prison of its short-term financial conditioning and become attuned to the personal, the democratic, the sustainable, the local, and the long-term. That becomes ever more clearly the case now that such substantial amounts of stock are held by pension plans (48 percent of our $17 trillion-plus in institutional capital). Because pension obligations don't mature until well into the future as pensioners retire, those funds must be invested with an eye to circumstances that will not unfold until well in the future. Accordingly, pension trustees must limit their investments to firms that show genuine concern for the future. As trustees of funds pledged to intergenerational purposes, how could they prudently invest otherwise?[17]

The corporate entity is periodically required to adapt to the evolving demands of democracy. First allowed under royal charter, the modern corporation originated as a way to organize costly expeditions funded from the public purse, such as the East India Company, the official trading arm of the British Empire. Although the colonialists declared their independence from King George, it was the royal charter corporations that raised the armies, suppressed dissent, and imposed taxes. For this reason, when the thirteen original colonies convened, they insisted that corporations be chartered only by the states. The corporation has since emerged as the dominant player on the global stage, eclipsing all but the largest nation-state in size, scope, and power. That very new development mandates that the centuries-old organizational logic of corporations be revisited—not only in light of new knowledge about environmental sustainability, but also in terms of what its operations mean for the health of free-enterprise democracies. In my experience, discussing such matters with money managers is like a school of fish discussing the possible existence of the sea. They are so absorbed in the cross-border ebb and flow of funds that they simply cannot see beyond the narrow confines of their craft. They have a very simple mission and absent rules to the contrary, they're not about to have their world muddied up by any goal other than making money.

The answer, I suggest, lies in realizing that the corporation—as a creature of property—becomes a new entity every day. Like the wet-ness that never leaves water, shareholders never leave the corporation, though their identities may well change. In the same sense that you can never step in the same river twice, the corporation remains while its shareholder base is constantly in flux. The challenge lies in how best to animate that lifeless *corpus* with values that can supplement the financial values by which it is presently so enraptured. International regulation is one route, though a challenging one in a world with 187 member-states of the UN. Yet the corporate entity's perspective needs to be broadened and its timeframe extended if it is to retain its legitimacy in countries that consider themselves demo-cratic. Corporate depreciation may offer an access point, linking its al-lowance to requirements that the firm's ownership become more broadly peoplized and localized. That would help inject into corpo-rate decision making a broader range of values.

By conventional financial criteria, institutional capital should already be turning sharply in this direction. Yet it isn't. For instance, 1998 marked the fifth consecutive year that the Employee Ownership Index outperformed the majority of stock market averages, including both the Dow Jones Industrial Average and the Standard & Poor's 500.[18]

The Moral Foundation of Democratic Ownership

Many people think the rich are smarter. Or somehow more deserv-ing. Their accumulations are not only praiseworthy, but a sign of moral achievement as well. The poor, on the other hand, suffer from an ill-defined character-deficit disorder. Or poverty is seen as a sign of divine disfavor, reflecting some unknown moral transgression. Surely it must be them and not the system that's out of whack. If you suffer from these common delusions, I urge you to read this chapter again. And think again. Although it's certainly true that a measure of hard work and creativity accompanies successful businesses (nineteen of 1999's new entrants on the Forbes 400 are Internet entrepreneurs, including several new Web Master billionaires), it's also important to keep that in perspective, given the practical financial realities and the undeniably plutocratic results of modern-day finance. Continued capital accumulation is the certain legacy of inclusion in today's closed system. For instance, 149 members of the Forbes 400 inherited some or all of their wealth. Their average net worth is $2.5 billion, whereas the average net worth of the 251 self-made members of the Forbes 400 is $2.7 billion. Regardless of how they came by their wealth, the average Forbes 400 member tallied an *increase* of $1.6 billion from 1989 to 1999—$160 million per year. What about those left out? There's a folk saying here in the South that sums up their dilemma: "Play the cards fair, Billy Bob, 'cause I know what I dealt you." The one-year, $125 million *increase* in wealth required for inclusion on the 1999 Forbes 400 list ($625 million in 1999 versus $500 million in 1998) would take a minimum-wage worker 12,136 years to earn.

Throughout this book, I describe how policymakers regularly change the rules that govern the workings of the so-called laws of economics. There's no more dramatic example than in 1981: With the enactment of Reagan-Bush supply-side economics, companies were allowed to write off their assets much more rapidly. For instance, a commercial office building constructed in 1980 could be written off over forty-five years, whereas the cost of one built in 1982 could be recovered in just fifteen years. That was the political impetus behind all those high-rise office towers that sprang up across the nation in the mid–1980s, all in the name of free enterprise (even though supply-side incentives were 100-percent deficit-financed).

The magnitude of the sums involved is stunning. Corporate-claimed depreciation from 1982 to 1987 totaled $1,650 billion. It staggers the imagination to think that no one bothered to ask about the ownership impact of that deficit-financed stimulus. Didn't anyone care *who* would be supplied with supply-side economics?

Now you have a road map for how the rich get richer. And a sense of the practical financial challenges facing anyone interested in a Third Ownership Way. Everyone understands intuitively what's going on. Them what has, gets. But precious few understand either why or how. There's no smoke and mirrors here, just the steady workings of very conventional finance dependent on an accommodating policy environment. Exclusion is not a trait hard-wired into the DNA of capitalism. It's just a very bad habit held in place by policymakers who choose to leave it that way. Inclusion is a matter of design; we must choose it. And insist on it. The so-called "laws" of economics are downstream of politics. The rules governing private property are a political choice. If you don't believe me, ask the Russians about 1917. Or the Chinese about 1949, or the Cubans about 1956. Better yet, ask any American real estate developer about the building binge in the 1980s. Or ask any of the ninety-five countries that the World Bank identifies as now busily unwinding unworkable systems of state ownership—adopted as a reaction to formerly unworkable patterns of private ownership. Both the patterns and the privileges of private property remain dependent on the public's discretion. Property patterns are not some *thing* that appears in nature; they're collectively and culturally determined. Today's design is profoundly undemocratic and demonstrably unsustainable—yet no one even talks about it.

For most readers, this is all very new—the ability to see a financial system that was previously invisible. The question is how long will it take for a critical mass of us to see the obvious? Our individual liberty may well depend on our willingness to redesign the powers and privileges granted private property. By making visible those laws, rules, and customs that lie behind today's plutocratic patterns, I hope you can see why you've been left out. With that understanding, you can make wiser political decisions. Once you understand how a system works, you no longer have to remain a passive observer or a witless victim. Property can be designed to operate in a far more inclusive way. As Supreme Court Justice Oliver Wendell Holmes argued in a 1905 court opinion: "A constitution is not intended to embody a particular economic theory." As practical Americans, we must turn our attention to how we can ownerize capitalism in a more sensible way. Never mind economic theory; common sense will do just fine.

Democracy and Scale

It gets scary if we consider the multidimensional impact on democracy that accompanies the lack of inclusive finance. Today's combination of closed-system financing and easy access to capital markets makes for a very heady brew, in terms of ownership patterning. In

1997, the United States saw $1,000 billion in corporate mergers and acquisitions. In 1998, the total was $1,600 billion, whereas 1999 topped $1,750 billion ($3,440 billion worldwide). We've seen conglomerates formed before, during the go-go years of the 1970s. But back then, the goal was to gain stability by diversifying risk, spreading investments over several industries. Today's goal is to dominate one, or a few, fields. Never before have we seen anything remotely like this, and never before with such a global sweep. The pace continues to quicken. During the twelve years of the Reagan-Bush administration, there were 85,064 mergers, valued at more than $3.5 trillion, according to the Securities Data Company. After nearly seven years of the Clinton-Gore administration, there had already been 166,310 deals, valued at more than $9.8 trillion. Even the major law firms are merging to better serve the frenzy. In July 1999, London's huge Clifford Chance merged with New York's old-line Rogers & Wells. Why? "Because we want to do the best deals for our clients," says Keith Clark, senior partner at Clifford Chance.[19] He also announced the firm's intention to push forward with plans to merge with Germany's third-largest law firm. The combined firm will have 2,700 lawyers in thirty offices worldwide, earning more than $1 billion in annual fees.

My attempt to identify operational reasons for today's megaconsolidations came up with a very short list (see below). Rather than consolidate, high-tech companies routinely find that their best innovations come from collaborations and project-focused relationships across traditional corporate borders. So what's behind this megamerger boom? One key impetus is identical to what motivated the reengineering craze: access by corporate executives to huge portfolios of stock options. For instance, on the day that the merger was announced between Citicorp and Travelers Group, Citicorp CEO John Reed saw the value of his stock options rise by $67 million, while Travelers CEO Sanford Weill added $248 million to his personal portfolio.[20] Not a bad day's work.[21] In October 1999, a few days after Congress agreed to repeal legislation prohibiting the merger of bankers, brokers, and insurers, recently retired Treasury Secretary Robert Rubin, the legislation's most vocal proponent, joined Reed and Weill to form Citigroup's three-member office of the chairman.[22]

Entire industries are beginning to work as if they were one company. There's a certain enhanced efficiency that accompanies consolidation; less headquarters personnel are needed if you have only one headquarters. It's also easy enough to generate one-time savings by consolidating overlapping operations and eliminating redundant employees. When Chase and Chemical Bank merged, they no longer required two accounting departments or neighborhood branches near one another. Cost savings were estimated at $1.7 billion, or 20 percent of the combined premerger value. Some ongoing savings may even accompany the integration of certain activities such as research or procurement. That's what they discovered at Boeing-McDonnell Douglas. Does this require that these firms operate under a common ownership umbrella? Or that their top employees be provided option packages enabling them to pocket a substantial portion of the savings? Not at all. Indeed, if you judge the merits of consolidation by the practicalities of economy of scale, it's clear that these behemoths should remain small. Quite small. As a general rule, *operational* efficiencies (versus organizational efficiencies) begin to decline once firm size creeps much above 300–500 employees per work site, with some rare exceptions for capital-intensive endeavors such as aluminum smelting and auto assembly.[23] The Internet means that technology companies, which typically benefit from economies of scale, can pass on those benefits in a way that allows firms to stay small without suffering from the disadvantages of being small.

Because operating through alliances takes more time and more human interaction, it looks less efficient. Negotiations are often ongoing, whereas a merger or an acquisition is easier to negotiate and quicker to implement, and with it, change can be mandated from above.[24] Alliances operate more in the spirit of partnership, whereas mergers and acquisitions allow dominance by one party.

Today's doctrinaire corporate giantism runs directly contrary to the organizational insights offered by *Lean Thinking* authors James Womack and Daniel Jones, who found that large-scale production facilities and equipment are often the key to *in*efficiency and *un*competitiveness.[25] The optimum, they say, is to match the scale to the precise needs of the whole system.

Sewage treatment offers a classic example. Though a huge sewage-treatment facility may capture on-site economies of scale when considered in isolation, the scale of the *whole system* is hugely inefficient because of the additional investment in pipes and pumps to service a larger area (often 90 percent of the costs). The most cost-effective sewage system is often one with local or even on-site solutions using biological rather than chemical treatment.

My sewage-treatment example is not meant as a "small is beautiful" lecture; the question is one of appropriate scale. You don't run an aluminum smelter with windmills or heat your home with a nuclear reactor, as *Small Is Beautiful* philosopher Fritz Schumacher pointed out in the 1970s. Yet a democracy must concern itself with matters of scale—as must ecologically sound development. For instance, Amory Lovins at the Rocky Mountain Institute found that some seventy-five effects of scale typically make decentralized power sources tenfold more valuable than traditionally supposed. "That's enough," he insists, "to make even solar cells cost-effective, *now*, in most applications."[26]

There's another impact of giantism, too, that has to do with the impact of scale on civil society. For instance, democracies have long relied on committed leadership in both the public and the private sectors. Business and professional leaders often become our public officials, whether it's the local lawyer running for Congress or the owner of the corner drugstore becoming justice of the peace. Often they move seamlessly from one domain to the other and back again. But consider for a moment the impact, say, on Minneapolis when Grand Met, a British conglomerate, acquired Pillsbury in 1989. Although some may complain about the downside of a single family owning so much, the Pillsbury clan did reside in their community as involved corporate citizens, participating in civic life and contributing, financially and otherwise, to make Minneapolis the attractive and livable city that it is.

What now of Minneapolis? Where do the loyalties of Grand Met's managers lie? In Minneapolis? Or is their eye on a career track in a British conglomerate? Are their interests anchored locally, or are they more interested in their stock options in a UK parent company? What happens to Minneapolis in that mix? And to the civic leadership on which robust democracies depend? What now for Detroit since Daimler acquired Chrysler? Or for San Francisco since Charlotte-based NationsBank acquired Bank of America? Has civic leadership also been sucked into the abstract and disconnected world of financial cyberspace? Is there any limit to the values we're willing to forego in the name of financial values? Is the soul of democracy being sacrificed for some greater financial good? Is this to be the Third Way?

7

Peoplizing Ownership

Laws should be like clothes. They should be made to fit the people they are meant to serve.

—CLARENCE DARROW

So what's to be done? If broad-based ownership is the relationship required to put things right, how do we get from here to there? There are ten primary recipes with which I'm familiar. Any one in isolation will be only modestly effective. But combine them, mix thoroughly with a sustained policy push, and spice generously with moral suasion from populist-inspired leadership, and enormous progress could be made if cooked constantly during just one presidential term. Extraordinary strides could be made in two terms, setting the nation's course in a new and far more hopeful direction. If these initiatives are not enough—as they may not be—then we must resort to stronger medicine to cure this illness. I turn to that plan in Part 4, Share Our Wealth.

Here I suggest not only new institutional incentives, but also a half dozen or so new "ownerization" forms through which those incentives could operate. I will discuss first two of the ten general categories of initiatives—tax policy and government contracts—because they are developed in more detail in my earlier book, *The Ownership Solution* (1998). I describe each initiative as though it were part of a populist presidential candidate's platform for a thematic legislative push during the new administration's First Hundred Days. I also offer examples of how policy-makers often work the system to their personal advantage. And I show why inclusive financing techniques are an essential supplement to personal savings as a national capital accumulation strategy.

Tax Policy

Russell Long once advised me that with the proper mix of tax incentives, you could make water run uphill, a feat that he and Chicago-area legislators reportedly once accomplished with the help of the Army Corps of Engineers. As chairman of the tax-writing Senate Finance Committee (1965–1981), he knew firsthand what tax policy could do. Anywhere that tax policy affects finance (and believe me, that's everywhere), there's an opportunity to encourage business behavior more consistent with democracy and sustainability.

One area of current interest is inheritance taxes. Although repeal sounds terrific when justified on behalf of a small business owner or the family farmer, the reforms proposed reach well into the ranks of the superrich. The $792 billion tax cut that Congress proposed in the summer of 1999 would have phased out the estate tax entirely. On the Forbes 400 list for 1999 are 149 people who inherited some or all of their wealth (average net worth: $2.5 billion). Considering that the 1997–1999 period saw an average increase in wealth of $940 million for those on the list, those 149 heirs saw their wealth *expand* $140 billion over just twenty-four months. That's quite a farm.

Candidate George W. Bush proposes to phase out the inheritance tax by 2009, making good on Ronald Reagan's proposal for economic equality "to end the inheritance tax for rich and poor alike." Franklin D. Roosevelt put in perspective the implications for democracy when commenting on unlimited intergenerational wealth transfers sixty-five years ago: "Inherited economic power is as inconsistent with the ideals of this generation as inherited political power was inconsistent with the ideals of the generation which established our Government." Oddly enough, it took a billionaire (Donald Trump) to suggest the obvious: a wealth tax. Dubbed "The People's Billionaire" by the *New York Daily News,* he proposed in December 1999 a one-time levy of 14.25 percent on personal net worth of $10 million or more, with the proceeds dedicated to debt reduction.

The marriage of democracy and taxes is an uneasy one. The question has long been one of how to write the rules in a way that supports rather than undermines democratic values. A populist administration would propose a panoply of ways to ensure that tax policy steadily expands ownership, whether it's allowing lower tax rates or faster depreciation for ownership-sharing companies. Or encouraging banks to make loans that broaden ownership. Or urging that companies be sold in a way that expands ownership. Or favoring mergers and acquisitions that include ownership-broadening over those that don't. Or capital gain tax incentives.[1] Anywhere there's a financial transaction, tax policy plays a role in the emerging ownership pattern. The question should become why *not* favor broad-based capital accumulation? The exception should be the policy that remains neutral.

Computers operate with a two-word lexicon of 0 and 1 to communicate with each other in a binary language. It's either one or the other. Tax policy can either concentrate ownership or spread it out. Exclude or include. It's just that simple. At present, we defer to the so-called "level playing field" typified by the highly exclusive closed system of finance. Given today's horrifically uneven playing field, the rules of the game must be rewritten to reflect three populist tax policy principles: inclusion, inclusion, and inclusion. There's no such thing as *not* making a choice here. Choosing to do nothing ensures even more concentrated ownership. Until the system is rewired, that's the certain result. The nation's largest single use of tax revenues is for income transfer payments—the fastest-growing component of the federal budget and notoriously the most difficult to control. Any sensible tax policy would anticipate those needs by encouraging widespread economic self-sufficiency.[2] Or we can continue to finance our future like total fools.

During the First Hundred Days, a populist tax policy environment would encourage the private sector to embrace a more democratic ethic by constantly expanding ownership and by embracing environmentally sustainable practices. For instance, Washington currently collects a federal fuels tax based on the quantity of fuel used rather than its quality. Yet we've long known the environmental culprit: carbon content. Properly targeted, the fuels tax could stimulate the entrepreneurial drive and market competition required to catalyze the shift to cleaner fuels. Similarly, tax policy should turn its attention to how buildings, major consumers of hydrocarbons, can be made more energy efficient. Small changes made now can have huge long-term payoffs. Tax policy is a signaling system. Today's signals reward stupid, unsustainable behavior.

Resource-Sensitive Tax Policy

Tax policy should encourage market innovation in industries producing consumer durables. Nylon carpeting, for instance, requires

20,000 years to break down in our already overfull landfills. Although we may not live forever, our trash just might. Today's tax policy encourages extraction, production, consumption, and disposal ("take, make, waste")—with little concern either for nature or for how the product ends up back in nature. We pretend that natural resources mysteriously appear (enter nature, stage left), where they're crafted into consumable goods—and then just as mysteriously disappear (exit waste, stage right).[3] Despite the world's most sophisticated accounting system, we count as income the liquidation of our natural resources and score as cost-less their disposal. We treat nature as essentially free; we mis-price our resources, reward waste, and then impose costs on future generations who have no say in the matter. Oftentimes, even ecological common sense is forced to "show up" as a noncompetitive business practice.

Tax policy should help us get ahead of history by pricing resources now so we *use* less, rather than later, when we *have* less and have more of a mess to clean up. Taxes, like subsidies, are a feedback loop. Taxes signal us to use less; subsidies tell us to use more—whether it's subsidies paid to tobacco growers, the under-pricing of irrigation water, the Forest Service selling sixty-five-foot lodgepole pines for $2 each, or taxes we choose *not* to levy on hydrocarbon use. Landfill taxes in Denmark increased the reuse of construction materials from 12 percent to 82 percent. That compares to our 4 percent reuse rate in the United States, where from 15 percent to 40 percent of landfill is construction debris. Holland used a green tax to cut its heavy-metal leakage by 97 percent since 1976. Taxes tilt the playing field. That much we know. That's unavoidable. The question is whether tax policy is designed to end today's illusion of cheap, abundant natural resources while labor (heavily taxed) appears quite dear. At present, we've got our signaling backward.

Over time (two decades is optimal), today's capital investments could be replaced within a tax policy environment that steadily lowers the rate of tax on labor while steadily shifting it to resource-gobbling equipment, machinery, buildings, fuels, and such. Right now, our tax policy contradicts our full-employment policy. By keeping the market price of labor high vis-à-vis other inputs (such as fossil fuels), we encourage the use of natural capital and discourage the use of human capital. That's dumb when what's most needed is labor's input to help with resource saving and resource restoration.

Tax policy can also encourage a more workable income distribution. Although a complex mix of factors influences income distribution—

including policies on education, trade, and civil rights—we've relied largely on the minimum wage, public education, and progressive tax rates as the means for raising incomes that market forces keep low. Recognizing the inadequacy of federal minimum-wage laws, at least forty cities and counties in seventeen states have enacted living-wage ordinances. Examples include Baltimore, Chicago, Durham, Los Angeles, Milwaukee, and Tucson. There's long been talk of a "maximum wage," which would deny tax write-offs to companies that, for instance, pay their executives more than twenty-five times what their typical worker takes home.[4] As with resource-use taxation, we should relieve taxes on what we consider "goods" such as jobs (less payroll taxes) and shift them to "bads"—practices that are inequitable or unsustainable or that undermine democracy. For instance, companies could be denied a tax deduction for the expense of using print, radio, or television advertising unless they utilize media outlets that also carry free political advertising. That could help address the stalemate in campaign finance reform, at least to the extent that the funds are used to buy media. Or the deduction could be disallowed if the media fail to pass a screen for broad-based ownership (for instance, 58 of Canada's 104 newspapers are owned by a single person). Democracy converses with itself through the media. If forced to choose between a free press and a freely elected government, Jefferson opted for the former. A democracy's tax policy can ill afford to be indifferent on either the ownership or the utilization of the media.

Government Contracts

Government contracting has long been a way for the politically well connected to tap the public till. Ask Ross Perot, the alleged populist who ran for president in 1992 and again in 1996 on the platform of a smaller, less debt-ridden government. What's the largest part of government? Social Security. How did Perot make his billions? Initially from government contracts for Social Security administrative services performed by his firm, Electronic Data Systems (EDS). He could have financed EDS so that it became broadly owned (incentives were available for that purpose). He refused. Instead, he's standing around with $3.8 billion whining about the big government that put that money in his jeans. Hardly a populist. Populists are people like Bob Thompson, who sold his Michigan-based road-building company for $422 million in 1999 and shared $128 million of the proceeds with his 550 employees, creating some eighty millionaires. He plans on giving away much of the rest. Unlike Perot, he tempered his greed with gratitude for those who helped him make it. "There is need," Thompson argues, "and then there is greed. We all need certain basic comforts, and beyond that it becomes ridiculous."

Where should we look for the next taxpayer-financed "Boss" Perot? Check out the high-tech wealth accumulations due to federal, state, and local government purchases of information technology and related services (governments' primary product is information). As a taxpayer, how many Dell computers and how much Microsoft software did you pay for? How much of their original research did you fund through NASA and the Department of Defense? How much taxpayer money was used to aggressively enforce antidumping laws in semiconductors (though not in steel)? In 1998, Washington quietly approved the largest public works bill since the New Deal, a $217 billion transportation bill. Uncle Sam is offering $162 billion over the next five years for building, maintaining, and expanding roads. Keep a close eye on who gets those contracts. Then match those contracts against lists of campaign contributors. I've seen all this before, like pickpockets at a fair. As Senate Finance Committee counsel, I sat through Bob Dole's $872 billion tax-cut giveaway in 1981, where I was lobbied by the best of the best. It quickly became apparent that the most cost-effective expenditure any corporation could make was to hire a lobbyist to line up at the trough.

That's why I groan whenever someone argues we need publicly financed federal elections. Most of them already are; you just can't see it. After your tax dollars flow to Washington, a sizable portion flows back out as government contracts, industry-specific tax breaks, sector-specific subsidies—mining, timber, tobacco, sugar, peanuts, shipbuilding, ranching, and so forth. Part of that outflow finds its way back to Washington as campaign contributions. None dare call it graft. Now it's called the "power of the incumbent."

In an award-winning 1998 exposé, *Time* identified $125 billion a year that's doled out in corporate welfare on various subsidies, tax abatements, and below-market financing. In truth the figure may be closer to $1.5 trillion by the time you include below-market leases to ski resorts, bargain sales of minerals on public lands, irrigation subsidies, and bailouts for corrupt savings and loan operators (more than $30 billion per year). One of my favorites is the U.S. Forest Service, which had built 377,976 miles of logging roads by mid-1999, more than eight times the length of the entire interstate highway system.

During the summer of 1999, the Republicans quietly created an elite donors club (Team $1 Million), whose corporate and individual members are expected to contribute $250,000 a year, or $1 million every four years.[5] Democrats have a similar program (Leadership 2000). Both provide an experienced staff member to arrange for donors' access to policymakers. Flush with funds early on, the Bush campaign decided in June 1999 to refuse $16.5 million in federal matching funds for the presidential primaries, exempting the Republican candidate from the overall $40 million spending limit on those who accept public financing.

Many voters wonder if elections have become auctions. It's easy to imagine a Chicago-schooled economist arguing that's what they should be. In today's money-drenched democracy, it's instructive that of the top ten donor zip codes, five run up the posh East Side of Manhattan, where Wall Street's elite reside.[6] Elected officials are the only people in the world who walk up to strangers, ask them for hundreds of thousands of dollars, and then expect us to believe that the money has no effect, achieving what Congressman Barney Frank calls a state of "perfect ingratitude."

It's difficult to know how to characterize a system that allows donors to give unlimited amounts to those who craft policies that enrich those donors. Perhaps a "donor-ocracy"? Until we find a way to reclaim self-government, it can't rightly be called a democracy. Former Senators George Mitchell and Bill Bradley point to the growing role of money in politics as a key reason that they retired from the Senate. Former Senator Tim Wirth of Colorado recalls spending more than 50 percent of his time raising money, increasing to 80 percent in the year he ran. In the summer of 1999, Clinton chief fundraiser Terry McAuliffe placed with Bankers Trust $1.35 million in cash, an amount equal to the Clinton's mortgage on a New York home. The deposit (since withdrawn) was intended to serve as collateral with the lender should the Clintons be unable to make their mortgage payments.[7] The White House counsel's office deemed it not a gift, because it couldn't be precisely quantified, a mathematics apparently unique to those inside the beltway, where even when something is given, nothing is received.[8] In today's incestuous web of money-lubricated interests, it should come as no surprise that the interests of the donor class often receive more attention than those issues of concern to what remains of the middle class. Before continuing with our list, let's take a closer look at two high-profile beneficiaries of the current system: Dubya and Al Gore.

Relationships and Riches

The public financing of private wealth accumulation operates in a variety of nonobvious ways, most known only to insiders, particularly those positioned to massage that permeable barrier between politics and finance. For instance, as governor of Texas, Dubya saw the value of his stake in the Texas Rangers baseball team rise to more than $15 million from his $500,000 investment after taxpayers approved a sales tax increase to cover $135 million of the estimated $190 million cost of a new stadium for the so-so club. In return for putting up only 1.8 percent of the funds, he was given a 10 percent stake when the club was acquired in 1989 for $86 million (he later boosted his 1989 ante by $106,000). Others ponied up the balance while naming Bush a managing general partner, assuring him a series of media appearances as he ramped up his run for the governor's mansion. When his bid for the team did not quite make the grade, it got a friendly nudge from Baseball Commissioner Peter Ueberroth, who stepped in to broker a deal with Fort Worth financier Richard Rainwater, who was asked to join the deal "out of respect" for the president.[9]

The president's boy borrowed the $500,000 from a Midland bank where he'd been named a cameo director three years earlier, pledging his Rangers stock as collateral. The loan was repaid in June 1990, six months after his tiny oil company (with no experience either overseas or in offshore drilling) signed a lucrative offshore oil exploration deal with the government of Bahrain in the Persian Gulf. Bush, a director, sold his stake at $4 per share, pocketing $848,560 and repaying his loan. After the company reported huge losses, the stock nosedived, soon losing 75 percent of its value and finishing the year at a little over $1 per share. Bush was ultimately cleared of insider-trading charges, successfully claiming that the proper disclosure form had been lost (the SEC general counsel at the time was the same Texas attorney who had handled the sale of the Rangers team in 1989). When Bush's oil company, Harken, almost went bust, a Saudi investor injected enough cash to keep it afloat, taking a 17 percent stake and gaining his representative a seat on the board. By August 1990, the investor was dining at the White House and discussing Middle East policy with Dubya's dad.

Dubya is hardly the first politico to benefit from his connections. Lyndon and Lady Bird Johnson grew rich through LBJ's deft corralling of broadcast licenses. Huey Long was known for his offshore oil leases in Louisiana's Win-or-Lose Oil Company, later acquired by

Texaco. And Al Gore, Jr. has his above-market zinc mine royalties from farm property acquired by his father with help from Armand Hammer, the late chairman of Occidental Petroleum and a Washington deal-maker.

Hammer is best remembered for lying to the FBI and a Senate committee about giving $54,000 in laundered hundred-dollar bills to Nixon fund-raiser Maurice Stans for use in the Watergate coverup (Hammer was the young Gore's guest at Reagan's 1981 inauguration).[10] In 1950, Hammer made then-Representative Al Gore, Sr., a partner in a Tennessee cattle-breeding business, an arrangement well known to a curious FBI director, J. Edgar Hoover, who knew of Hammer's lucrative business ties with the Soviets and his close relationship with their leaders. (Lenin reportedly told Stalin that Hammer was a "path leading to the American business world, and this path should be made use of in every way.")

In 1992, a *Washington Post* investigative reporter found that profits from the cattle-breeding operation enabled the senior Gore and his family to reside in a luxury suite atop the exclusive Fairfax Hotel, one of the most sumptuous of digs along Washington's elegant Embassy Row. Reporter Charles Babcock suggests that in return for the elegant accommodations, Gore performed various services for Hammer, including fending off the FBI while Al Junior completed his education at Washington's very preppy (and very expensive) St. Alban's School before trundling off to Harvard, graduating with nary a student loan. Throughout, the investigator suggests, political favor-seekers were steady purchasers of some of Tennessee's most expensive cattle. When Senator Gore Senior lost his 1970 reelection bid, Hammer put him on Occidental's board and named him chairman of an Occidental subsidiary, posts that would bring him more than $500,000 per year. Within a year of that subsidiary acquiring a Tennessee zinc mine property from a widow in 1972, the elder Gore bought it and sold it to his son. The original $227-per-acre annual payment by Occidental was reportedly 7.5 times the going rate of $30 per acre that Hammer's company had been paying locally only a few years before. Until 1985, Babcock notes, Occidental paid Gore Junior "190,000 for the lease without mining under the property because it never built a mine in the area."

I pick on these two because they are presently so very visible. Rest assured, Dubya is not the first politician to pocket taxpayer-subsidized wealth generated through community pride in professional sports teams. Between 1980 and 1990, U.S. cities spent $1.5 billion to build or renovate stadiums. The tab for the 1990s tops $11 billion.[11] Bush sold his Rangers' stake in 1999 for a tidy $14.9 million profit, more than the salaries of Mark McGuire and Sammy Sosa, combined. Like the fellow who was born on third base and thinks he hit a triple, he quickly parlayed that bonanza into a strategy for buffing up his Texas image of frontier individualism, buying a 1,550-acre, $1.3 million ranch. Critics can rightly ask just who was it, really, who paid for that ranch?

We know something about who pays for sports stadiums. Ticket prices rise an average 35 percent when a team moves into a new park, typically with less general seating availability, as teams sell more of their seats to season ticket holders, mainly corporations. Corporate sponsors don't come free. Detroit's successor to famous Tiger Stadium is now Comerica Park, the latest of more than twenty stadiums to sell their name to the highest corporate bidder. Or, in the case of Atlanta (my hometown), to give yet another boost to the team owner's ego, as Turner Field became home to the Braves. In Seattle, city voters said no to the approval of municipal bonds to finance a new stadium (Safeco Field). That didn't matter. New taxes paid the freight instead—on restaurants, bars, rental cars, and stadium admissions. The final cost: $517 million. Adjusted for inflation, the income of season ticket holders nationwide was one-third higher in the mid-1990s than in the early 1970s, steadily converting the national pastime from a game for everyone to a pursuit for the suits.[12]

Rewiring Political Largesse

Anywhere public policy has an impact on private capital accumulation, why *shouldn't* we encourage broad-based rather than narrow-based ownership? Government licensing offers a clear opportunity (airport gates, broadcast licenses, etc.). Instead, broadcasters recently received *free* digital TV licenses worth as much as $70 billion if they had been sold on the open market, according to the Federal Communications Commission, a giveaway that *Business Week* ridiculed as "ludicrous" and a "freebie." In truth, the gift wasn't quite free; Common Cause, a nonprofit organization focusing on campaign finance reform, documents that broadcasters contributed nearly $5 million in soft money political contributions from 1991 to 1997. That's what I mean about cost-effective corporate spending— $5 million in contributions begat $70 billion. How much is $70 billion? That's three-fifths of the $115 billion of your tax dollars that Al

Gore, Jr., promises to spend on education if elected. That's enough to construct 14,000 new elementary schools at $5 million apiece or to renovate and run each of our 368 national parks until 2018.

Ownership-sharing conditions should be imposed wherever private access is allowed to natural resources on public lands (for mining, oil drilling, logging, etc.). During the First Hundred Days of my proposed populist president's administration, a comprehensive survey will identify government procurement and contract policies that can be retooled to promote widespread ownership and environmental sustainability. Whenever public policy is converted to private gain, a broad base of Americans should share in that gain.

That principle could be extended to transactions that originate well beyond our borders. For instance, with the expansion of the North American Treaty Organization (NATO) to include Hungary, Poland, and the Czech Republic, U.S. contractors are lining up to sell military and other equipment not only to NATO commands but also to a newly militarized European Union. The General Services Administration maintains a list of approved merchandise, allowing government purchasing officers to order everything from wireless communications gear to fighter jets.[13] That list should be screened to ensure broad-based ownership in those companies.

These first two means for capitalizing Americans are obvious, though apparently not sufficiently obvious that anyone has yet proposed them. Revenues collected by Washington and passed along to private business are a veritable Mississippi River of ownership-enhancing revenues. Indifference about the resulting ownership patterns is fiscally irresponsible, elitist, antidemocratic, and demonstrably corrupting. Even where we charge companies a royalty on resources taken from federal lands, we do a lousy job of ensuring compliance. Eighteen oil companies drilling on federal land agreed in 1999 to pay an astounding $5 billion to settle lawsuits brought by state governments when their underpayment was discovered.[14] Those royalties are earmarked by the Treasury Department for environmental and historic preservation projects plus payments to twenty-four states, many of which use the money for education. That will give you some idea of whom they were ripping off.

Financing Techniques

Finance is fueled by a supportive policy environment. Study the Forbes 400 list ([www.forbes.com]) and note how many are financial engineers, particularly those who entered the list during the 1980s era of the leveraged buyout (69 of the 1999 members derive their wealth from finance and investments).[15] That's not brain surgery they're doing. They're applying the routine business logic of self-financing to enrich themselves—turning work directly into money, often without the messy need to produce anything—cars, computers, clothes. Why make things when you can just make money? Any legislator should be turned out of office who fails to insist that our most common financial technologies be put to work for the common good. Why should the financial benefits that flow from this nation's everyday commercial practices be monopolized by the financially sophisticated? We've had some success in tapping these technologies with employee stock ownership plans. At United Airlines, for example, tax-favored ESOP financing enabled employees to acquire a majority stake in the company, pledging a portion of the company's future earnings to repay $4.9 billion in acquisition debt, with those earnings enhanced by "investment bargaining" (six years of pay concessions). Most any company can be acquired with borrowed funds. The challenge lies in persuading someone to lend the funds. Though federal ESOP legislation has been only modestly helpful, it has shown what's possible with widespread self-financing.

In the late 1990s, the United States imported a new system of finance from Bangladesh, one of the poorest of countries. Faced with a famine and abject poverty in the 1970s, economist Muhammad Yunus founded what has since become a nationwide banking system dedicated to making small loans, largely to low-income female entrepreneurs—people whom conventional banks considered not creditworthy. With a "microcredit" repayment rate better than that of traditional banks, Yunus argues that "the real question is whether banks are people worthy." Among the many remarkable results tallied by the Grameen (Rural) Bank, he found that child mortality is 34 percent lower in households with access to microcredit financing. An international movement is now under way to extend microcredit to 100 million people by 2005. Some of those people reside in the United States, including jewelry craftsmen in Albuquerque and furniture makers in California. There's a lesson to be learned when one of the poorest countries exports its banking practices to the world's richest capitalist nation. "My fondest dream," Yunus notes, "is that some day our next generations, our children and grandchildren, will go to museums to see what poverty was like because there will no longer be any on this planet."

Occasionally we acknowledge shortcomings in the financial system, though typically without taking steps to remedy them. For instance, Congress passed the Community Reinvestment Act (CRA) in 1977 to reverse widespread bank redlining in low-income and minority neighborhoods. The banking community made very few commitments under the act for two decades, until the merger boom of the late 1990s. Because the CRA's muscle comes into play when banks need regulatory approval, government regulators and activist groups used that opening to expand CRA commitments from $1.25 billion in 1988 to almost $696 billion in 1998. For instance, the megamerger of NationsBank and Bank of America evoked a commitment to target $350 billion to poor communities over the next decade.[16] CRA opponents are understandably upset at the extortion implications of how the legislation operates, whereas supporters rightfully fret that the policy is not yet genuinely embedded in the financial system.

More financial continuity is required. For instance, institutional investors could use their bank equity holdings to influence lending that not only revives communities but also spreads ownership and advances stability. Because of our fractional reserve banking system, in which federal law requires that banks keep cash on hand equal to only 8 percent of their loans outstanding, every dollar of fresh bank equity creates a huge multiplier effect. Imagine, for example, if institutional investors were to make "owner-eco" equity investments in banks nationwide, on the condition that banks show a preference for locally owned businesses in companies with commitments to operate in an ecologically sound fashion. A mix of federal and state policies could nudge money managers to embrace this peoplization/localization investment strategy.

Personal Savings

Household saving as the route to riches is both the most prevalent policy and the least workable—unless you're a Michael Jordan, Tiger Woods, or Mark McGwire. That strategy also works reasonably well for the top fifth of the nation's income earners, primarily the fortunate 20 percent with college or postgraduate degrees (known as "knowledge workers"). However, we should reject any candidate for political office who proposes to leave people dependent for their economic security on savings from their labor. No matter how that outdated policy is dressed up, it remains old wine in new wineskins, a half-pint solution to a gallon-sized challenge.

Let me make just four obvious points. First, we've been waiting more than a century for people to save their way to significant capital accumulation with the earnings from their labor. It hasn't happened yet. And it won't. Insanity, I'm advised, is doing the same thing over and over again and expecting a different result.

Second, free trade makes this strategy steadily less viable as wage incomes are constrained by a growing need to compete against labor rates worldwide. After adjusting for inflation, the average American worker was making less in 1998 than in the mid-1970s, a period when productivity soared 33 percent.

Third, personal saving rates are now negative. Yet notice how investment continues, despite the economists' plea that we need more household savings to generate job-creating investment. Hogwash. As I show in Chapter 6, it's not personal savings but business savings that have long been the dominant source of investment funds. The issue is not how to boost your savings but how to transform business savings (depreciation and reinvested earnings) into broad-based capital accumulation.

That leads to the fourth reason that this simplistic solution is so far off the mark. It's difficult to keep personal savings at work in a community when ownership resides outside the community, a bit like expecting to retain body heat while wearing your pajamas outdoors in the winter. For instance, mortgage interest payments typically flow out of the community, particularly now that financial consolidation has converted most mortgage companies into national concerns. With those payments accounting for a steadily higher portion of household budgets (and low down payments ensuring a higher component of interest charges in each payment), financial outflow has soared. This "community leakage" also accompanies the spread of megaretailers such as Wal-Mart, Toys "R" Us, and the Home Depot (850 stores in four countries). Savings invested in such stores generate attractive short-term returns only to ensure a perpetual outflow of local consumer dollars. How do you think the five heirs of the late Sam Walton, owner of Wal-Mart, accumulated $80 billion?

To live in a community whose savings and consumer dollars are hemorrhaging elsewhere, residents must work more than necessary. That need has grown alongside the outrageous skimming of corporate financial value by top executives. Any sensible policy environment would link local savings to incentives ensuring a component of broad-based local ownership. The Winnipeg-based Crocus Investment Fund has attracted US$100 million-plus in local savings that Manitobans invest in community-targeted venture capital, largely to facilitate start-up businesses. Working with banks, communities could expand that concept to fund the local acquisition of retail businesses as an alternative to the dominance of national chains. While most venture capital generates one job for every $30,000 invested, Crocus requires only $15,000. The fund also encourages employee ownership, both at the outset and when Crocus exits its investment. It gets cold in Canada; Manitobans know better than to go outdoors in their financial pajamas.

New Ownership Opportunities

We must quickly become more creative about how we finance the future and how we expand the edges of the corporation to include more stakeholders as shareholders, transforming outsiders into insiders. Dee Hock, founder and CEO emeritus of Visa International, captures the challenge of marrying our very old notions of ownership to today's very new organizational realities:

> We are in an unprecedented moment in time when the capacity to receive, store, utilize, transform and transmit information has completely escaped the boundaries of all existing forms of organization—nation states, cities, corporations, churches, families, communities. . . . It is transcending and enfolding them into new, much more complex and diverse systems and entities, the shape of which is only dimly perceived. Today, we don't know where business begins or ends—what the distinction is between supplier, manufacturer, distributor, retailer, consumer and banker, or if those concepts are even useful in thinking about it. We don't know what the functional boundaries of a nation state really are. The distinctions between races, cultures and beliefs are increasingly blurred. Old concepts of organization are dissolving before our eyes and we grow desperate trying to make new societal realities conform to old notions of organization. In all of recorded history, that has never worked and it won't work this time either.[17]

Below are descriptions of several promising ownerization notions designed to reflect new societal realities. An ecologist might liken these to wetlands—those hyperproductive boundaries between land and water that have attracted human settlements for centuries.[18] I like to think of them as new information-rich relationships with intrinsic value, much like the nutrient-rich biodiversity found in wetlands. To visualize what's going on here—and to stimulate your own creativity about what's possible—keep in mind that the domain of finance is totally metaphorical and those metaphors are based on water imagery: liquidity, cash flow, sunk costs, pooled assets, rising tide, trickle-down. Even "leverage" has its counterpart in hydraulics. Before describing five more ownership-expanding initiatives, I offer below eight specific forms through which these ownership initiatives could do their work:

Customer Stock Ownership Plan

If you live in an investor-owned utility district, you have added to each month's bill a financial return for an investor who may well live abroad. You could reside in that utility district for a hundred years and continue to pay that return to someone else who lives somewhere else. Why not, over time, convert some component of that ownership into customer equity? That's a CSOP (customer stock ownership plan). The next time your utility needs debt financing, why not use debt that converts to customer equity at maturity? The next time it needs equity financing, how about using dynamic (versus static) property rights, so that investor cash becomes customer equity once a minimum agreed-to return has been paid and the investors have recovered their funds.

We insisted on such *dynamic* ownership early on in our history. After investors (typically Europeans) recouped their investment and earned an agreed-to return, they were required to turn over the facility—usually a toll road or a canal. A similar time-limited notion governs the property rights of patents. Infrastructure development is commonly organized as BOOT (Build-Own-Operate-Transfer) projects. Australia's Sydney Harbor Tunnel is being built on a BOOT basis. Water treatment plants are common BOOT transactions. Why grant investors a permanent ownership stake when they've invested their money based on short-term computations? Why ensure a perpetual drain of financial resources *out* of your community? Why not gradually phase out outsider ownership? Where does the company end and the customer begin? Where does the financing end and your bill-paying begin? Where should bill-paying end and capital accumulation begin?

General Stock Ownership Corporations and Citizen Funds

Under the leadership of Republican governor Jay Hammond, the state of Alaska established in 1977 the Alaska Permanent Fund in which each Alaska resident has a nontransferable stake. When oil from state-owned lands is sold, a portion of the state's royalty income is reinvested broadly, with investment returns paid each year to individual Alaskans, who now number about 575,000. More than $7 billion has since been paid on a 1999 principal exceeding $26 billion. The 1999 dividend was $1,769.84. A family of five collected $8,849. Families who have reinvested their money since the dividends began to flow in 1982 are now sitting on a nest egg of about $100,000. In a September 1999 referendum, Alaskans were asked to sacrifice some of their dividends to close a $700 million hole in the state budget. More than four-fifths (83 percent) of voters said no. Those dividend payments, more than $1 billion in 1999, now exceed the state's oil industry payroll.

Under federal law at the time, Alaska could have formed instead a tax-exempt company to hold title to the oil royalties, provided each resident owned at least one (but no more than ten) transferable shares and provided the company paid out 90 percent of its earnings each year. That's called a general stock ownership corporation (GSOC). A GSOC is particularly well suited for ownerizing and democratizing assets for those who share a common geography or history, as every culture does. Through a variety of settlements reaching back to the nineteenth century, Native Americans gained ownership of what are often vast and valuable lands rich in natural resources, including minerals, petrochemicals, timber, and water. In Montana, for instance, the Crow reservation has coal reserves reportedly valued at $26 billion ($3.3 million per person). One of the key challenges facing Native Americans lies in designing a commercial structure that equitably benefits all those in whose tribal name these settlements were reached.

In North America, for example, a confederation of tribes could band together, using a GSOC to ownerize the entire Native American population, including a pledge to capitalize the GSOC with any natural resources thereafter developed on Native American land. Ownership of the casinos now operating on Indian lands could be restructured as GSOCs in which every tribal member owns a stake. Similar capitalization strategies could be used abroad by, for instance,

Trinidadians using a GSOC to develop what may be as much as 75 billion cubic feet of recently discovered natural gas. The people living around the Caspian Sea could use a GSOC to develop a stake in the estimated 200 billion-plus barrels of oil lying under that hugely volatile and poverty-stricken region. Or to "indigenize" the ownership of pipelines proposed to bring that oil to market.

Shopper Stock Ownership Plan

In Atlanta, Joel Shapiro is launching OWNERShop.com to sell consumer nonperishables—diapers, dog food, detergent, and such. Rather than offering customers a $5 rebate on each $100 purchase, the company offers instead $5 of stock. Once the initial stock issue is fully subscribed, more stock will be issued at the new value. And then again and again, in perpetuity. Figuring anyone would be foolish to spend his or her purchasing dollars elsewhere, the founders are using ownership to lock in long-term relationships with their customers. OWNERShop.com also accepts food stamps, providing a way for Washington to capitalize low-income households through their food purchases. Where the cash flows, ownership grows. As a policy matter, why should taxpayers subsidize food purchases that *don't* capitalize those in need? Where does the company end and the customer begin? Where do poverty programs end and capitalization policies begin?

The next obvious policy question is this: Why should taxpayers use shippers (UPS, FedEx, etc.) to transport those nonperishables unless those firms also offer a similar ownership-expanding capital structure? For that matter, why should taxpayers reimburse government travel unless civil servants use airlines, hotels, and rental car companies that are broadly owned? Or food-service or vehicle-maintenance companies? If the goal of capitalism is to capitalize, why shouldn't every revenue stream be viewed as a potential source to create more capitalists?[19]

What if each time you approached a cashier, you knew that your purchases might gain you another few small slivers of stock, depending on which company's products you choose? And depending on which store you choose to patronize? With today's information technology, equity purchases could be embedded in product purchases. VISA International now clears more credit-card transactions in a week than the Federal Reserve clears checks in a year. It's no longer a question of available technology but of organizational and institutional reform. In a nation of consumers, not savers, it's fast becoming essential that households become capitalized through their consumption expenditures. Imagine, too, how your interaction with cashiers might change, with their role now expanded, upgraded, and dignified to become investment counselors ("Did you consider brand X—they've a new customer-equity offering this week?"). With a shopper's stock ownership plan, the line between consumption and investment is blurred. And no longer must a commercial transaction be separate from sharing human dignity.

Blue Fish Clothing raised $4 million in 1996 from a stock offering directed largely to its distributors and retailers. Its customer-targeted announcements were shaped like pastel fish attached as hangtags to their clothing. Several wineries and breweries have raised capital from their regular customers. Similar affinity-group offerings have been used by socially responsible mutual funds—beginning with the anti-apartheid "screening" of investments in South Africa and, since then, the maturing into an amazing array of investor choices. Zap Power Systems (for "zero air pollution") successfully targeted an offering to its local community around Sebastopol, California, by generating local news coverage and holding open houses at its plant, where it offered free rides on its electric bikes. Changes to federal law enacted in 1999 allow banks to underwrite such offerings and provide interim financing. There's even been a successful offering targeted to a subculture of believers in homeopathy. Several Internet companies have given away free shares, including Monsterbook, a phone-book-like directory of Internet business sites. They understand that relationships count. Dozens of socially responsible investment funds now recognize that educated consumers prefer to invest in (and buy from) companies that aren't causing harm. With on-line trading emerging as what may become the norm, doubtless we'll soon see services offering embedded metrics that rate investments based on a broad range of standards for equity and sustainability.

Related Enterprise Share Ownership Plan

At Jamaica Broilers, a chicken-processing firm in Kingston, the company turned to a bank for funds to repurchase the shares of a U.S. investor. The question then became what to do with the shares. In the usual case, the shares would be retired, making current shareholders richer. The company's senior management decided instead to share the prosperity as a way to demonstrate their Christian commitment to their community. To do so, the company borrowed a bit more money with which they upgraded the chicken-growing facilities of some three hundred independent farmers, ensuring that the firm was supplied by motivated owners raising chickens with uniform sanitation and uniform feeding. They also helped fifteen small trucking companies upgrade their fleets (of three to four trucks each), ensuring uniform sanitation, reliable refrigeration, and on-time delivery. Though the loans were repaid largely with the company's earnings ("productive assets can pay for themselves"), they also adopted a modest payroll deduction system along with an invoice deduction system for their suppliers and distributors. Working with Prime Minister Michael Manley, I advised on the crafting of legislation meant to encourage more such RESOPs (related enterprise share ownership plans).

While working in Morocco, I found a dairy that a similar strategy in almost identical circumstances, using repurchased shares to create ownership both by employees and by the farmers who provide milk to the dairy. Where does the processing company end and supply and distribution begin? Where does invoicing end and investing begin? Where does the workplace end and religion begin?

Employee Common Ownership Plan

At Scotland's Tullis Russell paper company, 70 percent of the firm's shares reside in a trust, locking in a perpetual job-creating stake for the community and for the firm's 1,200 employees. The balance of the shares are owned by employees. Half the company's profits are credited to employees' accounts, whereas another portion is used to purchase the shares of departing employees. That ensures the shares are liquid while the company recycles repurchased shares to both new and old employees: That rewards long-term employees and encourages everyone to keep a sharp eye on profits.

Such ownerization hybrids provide a useful guide for our struggling health-care industry in its ongoing search for an organizational form that can attract and retain professional caregivers while also operating on a cost-effective basis in a sector constantly in need of new capital. In the case of health care, an employee common ownership plan (ECOP) could blur the traditional lines between altruism and profit making, meeting both the firm's need for ongoing investment and the employees' need for capital accumulation while fusing capitalism and caring.

Depositor Share Ownership Plan

In Australia, New Zealand, and Pakistan, depositors own a significant stake in banks holding their deposits, an ownership structure I call a DSOP (depositor share ownership plan). In 1983, California Federal Bank (Cal Fed) sold $45 million of its shares in forty-five days through an offering to its customers.[20] Imagine borrowing money from a bank (or using their credit card) knowing that you're paying interest to yourself. There's now a credit card available with which you can borrow against the balance in your 401(k) plan and pay yourself interest—at far lower rates than conventional credit cards. In a DSOP, the line blurs between debtor and creditor.

Innovator Stock Ownership Plan

Mark White, a Mexico City systems consultant, suggests that innovation be stimulated with ISOPs (Innovator Stock Ownership Plans). Just as no good idea has only one parent, few innovations can be laid at the feet of a single inventor. He suggests a system in which those who contribute to innovation be credited with equity according to the relative significance of their contribution.[21]

CIA Stock Ownership Plan?

In September 1999, the Central Intelligence Agency (CIA) announced its plans to start a $150 million venture capital firm to keep abreast of fast-paced technological change by funding innovators able to meet their need for smarter CIA search engines, better ways to visualize data, and tighter security for Web surfers. The venture is called "In-Q-It"—combining intelligence with IT (information technology). "Q" is the code name used by the high-tech wizard in James Bond movies. The agency remains mum on its ownership strategy.

The Future of Ownerization

In time, such ownerization technologies will overlap, combine, and intersect so that relationships themselves become the foundation around which corporate capital structures are designed. Nature does that naturally, using blurred boundaries to avoid abrupt interfaces where weaknesses tend to emerge. Farsighted corporate leaders see the potential for these ownership plans already. Don't be surprised if we see specialty credit and debit cards that allocate bits of vendor equity to regular customers as a way to enhance customer loyalty. Savvy consultants are discovering that they can develop a varied portfolio by attracting diverse clients with fees paid partly as client-company shares and share options. In that relationship, the difference between consultant and client is blurred, as is the difference between consulting and investing, and between short-term consulting and long-term client commitment.

The Canadian firm of Golder Associates typifies the sort of virtual company that will become increasingly common in the knowledge economy. Founded in 1960, this firm of consulting engineers with 1,700 employee-owners operates in more than seventy locations worldwide yet maintains low managerial overhead with no central headquarters and a nine-member management team that convenes electronically over three continents. Its whereabouts are both nowhere and everywhere, exemplifying cyberspace's reverse rendering of the real estate maxim: no location, no location, no location.[22]

All well and good, you might say, but we don't have any progressive businesses around here, much less corporate visionaries willing to be creative with capital structures. And, besides, you might add, we don't have any oil to own. Perhaps so, but you could accumulate capital by requiring that people pay for the harm caused by its use. In shifting our focus back to legislative initiatives, the next section explains how emerging ownerization designs can also be used to address environmental issues of growing concern: air quality, global warming, and the depletion of the ozone layer. And, in the process, create a newly ownable asset to capitalize our undercapitalized population.

New Assets to Be Owned

Chronic environmental degradation, today's silent emergency, threatens people worldwide and, according to the UN, undercuts the livelihoods of at least a half-billion people.[23] The quality of the gaseous bubble surrounding the earth is crucial to the quality of life on earth, yet our overuse of fossil fuels has put that commons at risk. In the United States alone, we combust 9 million barrels of oil each day. That's 570 gallons per person each year. The United States spews 1.5 billion tons of carbon into the air every twelve months, 6 tons for every man, woman, and child (33 pounds per person each day). That's one-quarter of worldwide emissions. What's the effect? Although scientists have not unequivocally proven it, most believe that numerous climatological disasters of the late twentieth century have some connection to the air pollution produced by humans. The tropical world was hit by a "once-in-a-century" El Niño in 1997–1998, and a "once-in-a-century" hurricane devastated Nicaragua and Honduras in 1998. During 1998, almost sixty countries suffered severe flooding while forty-five recorded severe droughts. Record-breaking rains devastated vast areas of China and, aided by a vast headlands denuded of trees by clear-cut logging, inundated more than 60 million acres and displaced 233 million people. November 1999 saw a "once-in-a-century" flood devastate Vietnam and a once-in-a-century cyclone rip through India, while December witnessed a once-in-a-century flood that killed 50,000 in Venezuela and a once-in-a-century windstorm swept across vast sections of westernmost Europe. The increasing frequency and severity of these disasters has led some to argue that the developing world should seek reparations for the weather-related repercussions of energy use in the developed world. A report by Christian Aid argues that far from being in debt to rich countries, the world's poorest nations are owed hundreds of billions of dollars as a result of the disproportionate amount of environmental damage that we in the richer countries inflict on the planet.[24]

The sky may already have surpassed its absorptive capacity for acid-brewing sulfur, ozone-eating chlorine, and heat-trapping carbon dioxide. Oil is no longer in short supply; sky is. Yet because the atmosphere has no owner, it's treated like a common sewer—free and available for unlimited dumping. That keeps energy prices low because when you buy gas at the pump, there's nothing factored into the price for your use of the atmosphere.[25] The demand for skyborne carbon storage is the flip side of our demand for fossil fuels. We pay for the oil because we assign property rights to its use. We don't pay for the air to hold combusted residues, because only recently have we learned that atmospheric capacity is scarce. Property laws are a traditional way to allow owners of scarce things to charge other people for their use. That approach could be utilized to charge for use of the atmosphere much the same as for land use. What's required is that we create atmospheric property rights and then assign them to owners. There lies both opportunity and danger.

A study by DRI/McGraw-Hill put the value of U.S. carbon-absorption capacity at hundreds of billions of dollars per year. The value of the sky rises as emission limits are lowered because of the scarcity factor (people will pay more to use a limited resource), thereby aligning interests in conservation and income. This is where an Alaska Permanent Fund or GSOC-like model could be put to good use, creating a property right in which everyone in the nation is made a beneficiary ("Sky Trust" is proposed as the title).[26] In short, this approach suggests that one way to preserve the atmosphere is to treat it as property and price it. If hydrocarbon consumers pay not only for goods but also for "bads," then atmospheric scarcity would be factored into the price of fossil fuels. That extra cost would become income to those who own a stake in this newly created property right.

One key challenge here lies in ensuring that the "carbon club" (the oil companies) do not succeed in their effort to claim this property right for themselves. Under the Clean Air Act of 1990, coal-burning companies can trade sulfur emission permits among one another, allowing the industry as a whole to find the cheapest way to reduce overall emissions. Those permits now trade at the Chicago Board of Trade alongside grains and pork bellies. What has happened with sulfur could now happen with carbon and other gases (sulfur emissions are only 9 million tons a year). Though it beggars belief, some oil producers argue that they should be given these new property rights, *based on their past emissions*, and that we should buy those rights back from them at their price. If they get away with it (they're very heavy campaign contributors), you would pay them twice—both for their pollutant and again for their permission to pollute. Surely that must qualify for the lobbyist chutzpah award of the century.

The sums involved make this a major issue, particularly when the search is on for new ways to capitalize our population. Other plans to capitalize the population include Bill Clinton's universal savings accounts (at a cost of $700 billion over fifteen years), Senator Bob Kerrey's Kid Save Account ($250 billion over fifteen years, funded by social security taxes), and authors Bruce Ackerman and Ann Alstott's proposal for a 2 percent wealth tax to fund a nest egg of $80,000 for each citizen on his or her twenty-first birthday.

Though the Sky Trust too proposes to create a nest egg, the funding is quite different. The idea here is to create a *new* capital asset by ensuring that energy users pay for their pollution. Projections suggest that the proceeds could exceed $1 trillion over the next fifteen years, more than the Clinton and the Kerrey plans combined. Plus the revenue wouldn't depend on iffy budget surpluses, transfers from social security, or wealth taxes. Instead, it would rely on the idea of personal property rights created from the commons (the atmosphere) and as-signed individually to those with a stake in it. Also, unlike a tax on pollution, which would create a drag on the economy, the Sky Trust relies on the concept of user fees (which would raise energy prices) but with those fees disbursed as taxable income for people to spend as they wish, bypassing the Treasury.[27] Rather than an economic drag, the effect should be to reduce the use of pollutants while simultane-ously stimulating either consumption or saving. If we shift taxes to what we want less of (pollution), we could begin to relieve taxes on what we want more of—such as jobs (the social security payroll tax is the largest tax most people pay). Dividends due children could be put in an education trust account, relieving some of the fiscal burden of education costs.

This provides a simplistic account of a complex and multilayered subject. Today's pollution and climate crisis threatens not only the United States and other developed countries (the key polluters) but also developing countries who are mindful that although the richest one-fifth of the world consumes 58 percent of total energy, the poor-est 20 percent consume less than 4 percent. The Third World can be expected to resist any restraint on their development linked to a re-pricing of energy, or due to any system that enables rich countries to buy their way out of commitments to clean up the air they pollute.[28] In June 1999, in response to the UK government's announced in-tention to impose a "climate-change levy," the Confederation of British Industry agreed to design an emissions trading scheme in con-junction with thirty top UK companies.[29] During the First Hundred Days of my proposed populist president's administration, an interna-tional task force would convene to craft a U.S.-led strategy to address climate change. In addition, legislation imposing a climate-change levy would be introduced to stimulate the creation of an alternative scheme for limiting emissions in a way that is fair to all concerned.

Capitalizing Common Sense

The failure to properly price energy use has long kept alternative en-ergy out of the marketplace or left it dependent on tax incentives whose renewal is subject to the shifting whims of Congress. That's why I urge that a portion of Sky Trust proceeds be used to encour-age alternatives.

Wind energy, for instance, has enormous potential as does solar (annual growth in the sale of photovoltaics exceeded 70 percent in the late 1990s). The Department of Energy found that seven of the ten states ranked highest for wind energy potential are in the Midwest—the Dakotas, Kansas, Nebraska, Oklahoma, Minnesota, and Iowa. The Dakotas and Texas alone have sufficient wind resources to provide electricity for the entire nation, with Texas having a possible revenue of $30 billion a year.[30] Wind farms now dot the Corn Belt, with 200-foot lattice towers, each weighing fifty-seven tons and topped with a plane-fuselage-sized housing to which are attached three 80-foot-long fiberglass blades that turn one revolution every two to three seconds. The kilowatt-hour cost of wind energy has fallen by 90 percent just since 1980, from forty cents to between four and five cents, closing in on the roughly two cents per kilowatt-hour now charged by natural gas power plants. Worldwide, only 10,000 megawatts of wind power are replacing conventional fuel. That's enough electricity to meet the needs of 3 million households. About one-quarter of that is generated in the United States. Though the Department of Energy announced in June 1999 a goal of putting 10,000 megawatts on line by 2010, the First Hundred Days will include a New Deal–scale effort with the goal of putting 100,000 megawatts on line within eight years of the election of a populist president, enough to meet the needs of 30 million households.

To give you some idea of the potential, the 259 turbines near Storm Lake, Iowa, eighty miles east of the South Dakota border, generate 193 megawatts of power, enough to serve 72,000 households. The turbines are spread along a track seventeen miles long and eight miles wide. To generate that amount of electricity with coal would require the energy-intensive mining and transport of 300,000 tons of coal each year. Burning that coal would generate 502,000 tons of carbon dioxide and 2,600 tons of sulfur dioxide.

One of the most natural locations for a large component of this extensive wind farm would be the rise that runs along the watershed divide between the Missouri and the Mississippi rivers, where the wind conditions are particularly favorable (a reasonably consistent eighteen miles per hour). This project could be financed within the same Sky Trust GSOC, applying a portion of emissions-rights revenues as the equity capital, creating a multiplier effect that could be used to fund solar energy as well.[31] As these alternative energy sources ramp up to capacity, additional fiscal savings should kick in as we phase out the perverse subsidies that presently encourage resource inefficiency and consumption rather than resource productivity and conservation.

Though wind-power developers were initially worried at the reception these space-age contraptions would receive in the Midwest, the Storm Lake project confirmed again that farmers, as the nation's *genuine* conservatives, are great stewards. This project appeals both to their environmental common sense and to their good business sense— along with their innate inventiveness. An encouraging historical cycle is at work here. The Midwest provided much of the agricultural surplus that fueled both the Industrial Revolution and the nation's expansion westward. Now America's heartland may be poised again to play a crucial role at a critical point in the nation's development.

Restoring Sanity to Water Use

An aquifer-depletion levy will also be introduced during the First Hundred Days, with the goal of developing an alternative to the current system, whereby, for example, the vast Ogallala aquifer, stretching from Canada to Mexico, is now projected to last only another two decades. At present, the nation's freshwater supply is priced as though it were infinite in supply and replenishable at will. It is neither.

Though the Ogallala aquifer recharges at a rate of less than one-half inch per year, by 1990 it was being drawn down at a rate of three to ten feet per year. Among its other uses, the aquifer provides water to grow the grain for fattening up 40 percent of the nation's feedlot cattle. To produce a single hamburger requires at least 210 gallons of water, along with 1.75 pounds of livestock feed, which generates 12 pounds of feces and other organic pollutants.[32] Yet McDonald's can sell two double cheeseburgers for a deceptively priced $2 and still make a tidy profit. For a nation that prides itself on intelligent markets, that's profoundly dumb and demonstrably unsustainable. Vegetarians are correct that "the personal is political," urging that we eat lower on the food chain, growing more grain for our consumption and less for our cattle.

The number of people living in water-stressed countries is projected to climb from 470 million to 3 billion by 2025.[33] Many countries lack a coherent national water policy, including the United States. Most countries irrigate with little concern for depletion, and there are few international agreements on sharing water from rivers and lakes that cross international borders. The water wars are now beginning. In November 1999 Canadian Foreign Minister Lloyd Axworthy announced Canada's intention to place a ban on bulk water removals from all Canada's major watersheds. The U.S.-Canadian border, the longest in the world, includes more than three hundred lakes (including the Great Lakes) and rivers that either form, cross, or straddle the border. Canada's approach recognizes that water should be regulated in its natural state, before it has become a commercial good or a salable commodity with trade implications if, for instance, the ban was directed at water exports.

The Sri Lanka–based International Water Management Institute projects that a third of the world's population will experience severe water shortages within the next twenty-five years. The United Nations Environmental Program (UNEP) predicts that the number of people without access to safe drinking water will jump from 1.3 billion today to 2.3 billion by 2025 unless governments take faster action to address water shortages.[34]

For those who question whether we should do a better job of pricing (and policing) air and water, imagine for a moment what you would be willing to pay if you ran out of either. Until recently, that was not considered a possibility. That the idea is even *thinkable* suggests the need for a very new pricing paradigm for both. Amazingly, we've managed to endanger the entire 330 million cubic miles of water that circulate near the surface of the earth. Today's radical laissez-faire model is radically dysfunctional when it comes to the environment. Governments must evoke more appropriate markets if markets are to work. Either that or coordinate regulation on a worldwide basis. Inaction only ensures more environmental anomalies, such as Coke's annual sale of more than 10 billion plastic bottles that are not made from recycled or recyclable material. Such insanity must cease.

Fiscal-Foresight Pension Investment Practices

Another key capitalization strategy may require a lawsuit. Having crafted federal pension law for seven years, I suggest it's time Washington enforced the nation's pension fiduciary law.

Allow me to explain. Pension trustees' obligations do not mature for ten to twenty years, because that's when pensioners retire. For this reason, trustees cannot be indifferent about the ownership environment into which their beneficiaries retire, because pension payments lose all meaning absent a stable financial environment. A high rate of inflation, for example, is devastating to a pensioner living on a fixed income. Yet that's what we may soon face if we don't very quickly capitalize our 76 million baby boomers. Leave voters impecunious and the ballot box becomes a tempting way to access income.

Wal-Mart offers a case in point. The multinational chain of home-improvement stores looks like a great investment, using traditional Wall Street accounting. Its rapid expansion regularly generated double-digit returns for a decade or more. But pension money is not traditional investment capital. Because its obligations are deferred and intergenerational, a higher standard of prudence is required. Consider this: If pensioners retired today, would they be better off retiring into a fiscal environment in which the five heirs of one Arkansas businessman have accumulated $80 billion (Forbes 400 1999 estimate)? Or an environment in which 400,000 families have accumulated $200,000 each (Wal-Mart has 850,000 employees)? This is not to suggest some sullen egalitarianism. Not at all. It does, however, suggest that *indifference* on this key point is a gross breach of fiduciary duty requiring the removal of those trustees. During the First Hundred Days, a populist attorney general would file suit charging precisely that. The fact that other fiduciaries were similarly imprudent should not forgive this clear lack of compliance with the law's intent.

The effect of such a lawsuit, the nation's first multitrillion-dollar litigation, could galvanize the investment community by awakening them to an intergenerational obligation long unmet under current law. Pension plans hold almost half of today's $17 trillion-plus in institutionalized assets. Every dollar of that money was put aside with the help of federal and state tax incentives. Every cent has grown tax-free ever since. There's a huge public investment underlying these funds—an investment in a sound future. It boggles the mind that fiduciaries would allow those funds to be used to create multibillionaires. The best thing that pension trustees could do with funds entrusted to their care is ensure that competitive financial returns are coordinated with investment practices that steadily broaden the nation's base of self-sufficient households. Anything less puts at risk the very benefits they're required by law to protect. This lawsuit should include several related causes of action. For example, the attorney general should challenge whether pension trustees can prudently endorse a merger or an acquisition with no concern either for the resulting ownership pattern or for the location of those owners—here or abroad. Similarly, trustee acquiescence to the steady racheting-up of executive compensation is also a breach of their fiduciary obligation, allowing executive pay (excluding options) to soar to 419 times that of the typical employee. That's up from an already astounding 120-to-1 ratio in 1990 and a 42-to-1 ratio in 1980.[35] Pension fiduciaries should be given an opportunity to explain why they failed to actively oppose a managerial environment that allowed a single Coca-

Cola employee (i.e., chief executive Roberto Goizueta) to walk away with over $1 billion in stock grants (Warren Buffett's Berkshire Hathaway is Coke's largest shareholder). Or why a single Disney employee (CEO Michael Eisner) continues to succeed in equity raids on his employer that stand to net him more than $1 billion.

Where were the fiduciaries in April 1999 when Aetna bought U.S. Healthcare and a single employee, CEO Leonard Abramson, was paid $900 million in cash and stock along with a $25 million Gulfstream jet and $2 million a year in operating expenses?[36] Or when $700 million was pocketed (thus far) by Sanford Weill, a Travelers Group employee now working for Citigroup? Did fiduciaries sign off on the $470 million that Sprint employee William Esrey realized when his golden parachute opened as MCI Worldcom acquired Sprint in October 1999 and he was let go?[37] Or the $410 million in stock options plus $9.8 million in severance pay that Compaq Computers employee Eckhard Pfeiffer took with him when he was forced to resign in April 1999 because of his *subpar performance*?[38] Or the $100 million that Bankers Trust employee Frank Newman pocketed after orchestrating a merger with Deutsche Bank just three years after quitting his job at the U.S. Treasury? Where were the pension fiduciaries when, as pay expert Graef Crystal reports, boards of directors nationwide became 60 percent staffed by CEOs, thereby ensuring a steady racheting-up of CEO pay in this mutual back-scratching exercise called "comparable" compensation? Where was the oversight when these emperors of entitlement abused their leadership to siphon off hundreds of millions, even billions, of dollars in shareholder value?

It's an outrage that fiduciaries would allow executive pay to degenerate into a boondoggle that rewards mediocrity and cronyism. In effect, their lack of oversight has allowed unchecked avarice and managerial abuse to undermine the health of companies, the well-being of employees, the interests of other shareholders, the welfare of pensioners, the soundness of our tax system, the stability of communities, and the viability of democracy as they created a corporate caste system. Recovery of those funds should be sought.

This suit has the potential to "democratize" almost half the nation's institutionalized capital while also reversing the plutocratization of our management corps. A populist administration would serve notice that no employee in a free-enterprise democracy is worth thousands of times another, not even one who proves successful at generating extraordinary finance-calibrated value. No

change in law is required to pursue this lawsuit, just rational and vigorous enforcement of existing law. With senior executives now laying
claim to an astounding 13 percent of the equity in America's major
firms, it's self-evident that trustees have allowed matters to spin completely out of control.[39] The removal of these trustees should be
sought and personal liability pursued. To fail to pursue such a lawsuit
would concede that a democracy has no power over the financial
realm. And it suggests that once these tax-favored funds are put into
the capital markets, we've no choice about how they're utilized.
Both notions are asinine.

Defendants in this case should be drawn from the ranks of *all* those
fiduciaries who stood by while trends in economic disparity dramatically worsened, much to the detriment of future retirees whose interests they were obliged to tend. Trustees of the major public-sector pension plans should be included (California, New York, etc.). Both past
and current state comptrollers, typically elected officials, should also be
named defendants. That will provide them an opportunity to explain to
voters why their taxpayer funds were invested to create billionaires and
multibillionaires. Several of the large private-sector trustees should also
be named defendants, particularly those that have taken a leadership
role in setting today's financial community standards as investment
managers and trustees. Obvious candidates include Boston-based State
Street Bank (managing $600 billion and a trustee of $5.8 trillion) and
TIAA-CREF, the teacher's annuity program, with $270 billion under
management as of mid-1999. Last, the lawsuit should include the
trustees of at least one large union-sponsored multiemployer plan.
Union leaders should explain why a portion of their members' hourly
wages were put to work creating multibillionaires in Arkansas (the
Waltons). This suit will be joined by the various attorneys general of
the states in which these fiduciaries operate. By investing in a way that
ensured a mismatch of ownership patterns and demographic needs,
these trustees ensured a financial future that is poised to devastate not
only the federal budget but state budgets as well.

The implications of such intergenerational investment obligations
need not stop with prudent ownership patterning. For instance, a
corporate tax deduction is allowed for business expenses paid to insurance companies—for health, life, and casualty coverage, and so
forth. Worldwide, insurance companies are far larger than the "carbon club" companies (oil and coal). A sane and sustainable policy environment would do the obvious: encourage insurance companies to
make energy-saving investments—both to reduce insurance risks and

to boost long-term investment returns in an area that requires long-term capital. For instance, insurance companies hold huge portfolios of commercial properties that could profitably be retrofitted with energy-saving upgrades. Insurance companies are slowly awakening to this linkage, particularly now that they find themselves making record payouts for climate-related property and casualty claims.

An Ownership-Pattern-Sensitive Policy Environment

Ownership patterns must quickly become a central concern of policymaking. It's astounding (suspicious, some might say) how little thought has been given to the role that property patterns could play in the world's foremost private property economy. Instead, policymakers steadfastly focus on jobs alone. For instance, none of our econometric forecasters have yet considered what the impact of broad-based ownership might be, say, on our future need for income transfer payments. Yet that's the largest, most intractable component of the federal budget. What gives here? How could that possibly be overlooked?

We live in a time of profound policy confusion, and nowhere more so than in economics. We now know that economics is just one of many domains (politics, society, culture, the environment) nested inside one another, like so many Chinese boxes or Russian dolls. It's impossible for policymakers to affect one without affecting them all. Any attempt to solve problems in isolation, with no concern for how that solution may impact the whole system, is a notoriously effective way to generate unintended consequences (witness the financial return myopia of pension fiduciaries). Whole-systems analysis recognizes that sustainable solutions emerge only when problems are viewed as interconnected and intergenerational rather than isolated or frozen in time. Yet economic science remains steadfastly aloof, secure in its pigeonholed subspecialties and intellectually isolated in its comfortably abstract cocoon. Its practitioners seem content to spin out empty subtleties and obscure irrelevancies, unwilling to consider real social problems or to acknowledge that their craft has been corrupted to benefit the few at the expense of most everyone else while harming the environment as well.[40] Rather than address real-world problems, these theorists puzzle over why what works in practice can't possibly work in theory.

Theory determines the questions we ask, the problems we perceive, the patterns we recognize, the range of solutions we consider, and the actions we take. When theory fails to match the problem, it's at best delusional and at worst dangerous. That's particularly the case where theory ignores the very context (private property) within which the real economy operates. Yet Law and Economics theorists do just that, perverting economic science—the dominant voice of authority in our finance-obsessed culture—to advance policies that endanger the democratic foundation of free enterprise. Their determination to engineer the information age not for leisure but for employment brings to mind Aldous Huxley's observation in *Brave New World* in which genetically engineered humans don't protest that their lives are devoted to commercial and industrial purposes because they are designed "to love their servitude."

Even the concept of ownership needs to be rethought in these knowledge-intensive times. "When the assets of an enterprise are primarily its people," Charles Handy notes, "it is time to rethink what it means to say that those who finance the enterprise can in any sensible way 'own' those assets."[41] We can add to that philosophical quandary the displacement of many corporations' hands-on proprietors by remote, return-seeking investors. Yet even there the notion of ownership is flawed because those investors typically put their money not in the company but in the secondary stock market. And often "investors" no longer means people but institutions. Their money never goes anywhere near the company. Nor, typically, do they. Ownership simply provides a means to place a bet on the stock market. That's not to disparage ownership in publicly traded firms. However, it's essential that we recognize what ownership has become as we consider how best to "re-ownerize" free enterprise. The reality of today's capitalism is that the large, publicly traded firm is now a socialized, capital-marketized institution whose owners are now speculators dispersed to the four winds. Control, a key component of ownership, has shifted into the hands of an elite corps of professional managers and directors who, in turn, take their signals from financial markets.

Business Week reports that stock volatility is at an all-time high. Some 76 percent of the shares of the typical listed company turned over in 1998. That's up from 46 percent in 1990 and only 12 percent in 1960.[42] Day traders (please don't call them investors) may hold their positions for only a few moments. Most have little idea of the real-world businesses represented by the constantly shifting stock charts that flit across their computer screens.[43] Capital has become increasingly impatient as some companies see their entire float (all the shares minus those held by insiders) change hands as much as fifty times a year. At Priceline.com, typical shareholders held on to their shares for four days. At DoubleClick, it was five days. At Yahoo! eight days. That makes Dell Computers look stable, with an average shareholder duration of 3.7 months.

The implications for sustainability are profound. As ownership becomes ever more abstract and ephemeral, investor impatience signals managers whose short-term perspective, in turn, may be reinforced by the stock-market-determined value of their options. Today's churn factor aligns financial signals with expediency and short-term-ism, undermining a company's ability to stick to what may be a difficult but necessary course (such as converting to sustainable production practices). If the market turns, this built-in volatility could trigger a financial rout, even a full-scale collapse, regardless of the underlying merits of the company or the real-world practicality of the course it has undertaken.

Monetary Policy

Other key policy domains also exhibit a curious blind spot on the sensitive subject of ownership patterns, including monetary policy managed by the Federal Reserve. Initially established to ensure the nation's financial stability and stimulate the economy, that twofold mission remains fundamentally unchanged. Compared with a time when money was linked to gold reserves, a modern economy can no more run out of money (more accurately, credit) than it can run out of inches, quarts, or pounds. That's because money no longer has any linkage to a commodity-based measure of value, such as precious metals. It's now best viewed as an obscure but powerful social tool that operates in ways precious few fully understand. As we saw earlier, commercial credit is quite strictly allocated—to those with collateral. The Federal Reserve (the Fed), in turn, operates to ensure that its member banks never run short of growth-stimulating credit as long as price stability is maintained. Does that mean that the Fed, a quasi-public agency, ensures that those with collateral and a feasible business plan never run short of money? That's the practical effect. Those with collateral at their disposal, plus those with keen financial sophistication, are pretty much assured access to the Fed's money-creation capacity, even if the credit is used for financial speculation. Doubtless that will sound to some like a conspiracy. Monetary policy has long attracted conspiracy theorists. The truth is far less interesting. I've worked behind the scenes in Washington, in investment banking, in law and consulting firms, and with international financial institutions, such as the World Bank. I've not yet found a conspiracy, though I detect a shared "Chicago" mind-set whose results make policy look like a conspiracy.

The United States is fortunate in never yet having a Federal Reserve chairman who wasn't well-meaning and competent. Yet nor have we had a chairman, no matter by whom appointed, whose policies were not indifferent to the impact of central banking on economic disparities. That's simply not a component of the Fed's legislatively determined mission, at least *not yet*. Although the Fed is charged with a few economic development obligations (civil rights, consumer protection, community reinvestment, and such), federal law spells out its principal goals as maximum employment, stable prices, and moderate long-term interest rates. Its insensitivity to ownership patterning is not the result of some nefarious plot hatched by the Rothschilds, the Rosicrucians, the Rotarians, and the Rolling Stones—or whatever the latest bizarre conspiracy theory may change. Nevertheless, monetary policy, too, needs a thorough checkup to ensure that it works in support of a nationwide capitalization strategy that will ramp up during the First Hundred Days.

Who knows, perhaps we'll decide to return to a more regionally responsive money-creation system, much as we had until FDR centralized Fed decision making in Washington, shifting the emphasis to national economic development as we focused on recovery from a devastating deflation and depression. During the Fed's early years, the Atlanta branch was particularly active, using its autonomy to combat the South's dependence on "King Cotton" and its single-crop economy. Though now but a distant memory, the Fed's regional activism and targeted lending symbolize the responsiveness to economic conditions that remain central to the Fed's policy mission.[44] Its history of aggressive intervention is evidence of a long history of democracy's innate populism as our citizens seek control of market conditions, behaviors, and outcomes to turn them to democratic ends. For instance, for more than two decades, the Fed made direct business loans, including lending working capital to nonfinancial firms. Certainly the voting public needs to insist that the Fed put an end to the use of the banking system for gambling purposes, as we found with the September 1998 collapse of $125 billion in leveraged financial-derivatives trading by investors in Long Term Capital Management, a Connecticut-based investment fund, discussed in a later chapter.

Mechanistic Money

It's not well understood that our national currency (Federal Reserve notes) starts its life as a public asset. That's because borrowing, whether by the private sector or by Uncle Sam, is the only means we have for creating money. Only private borrowing (or public spending in excess of tax receipts) can trigger an increase in the money supply. The best path to long-term price stability lies in ensuring that any credit expansion serves to capitalize households in sufficient quantities that they'll not be tempted to pressure Congress for more budget-busting transfer payments. At present, Fed policy operates with a highly mechanistic model—as befits the dominant mode of thinking at its founding in 1913. If the Fed's governors can just succeed in maintaining price stability over here, then it will meet all its goals over there. That's the current reductionist-style thinking. Indeed, Fed insiders will tell you (as they've told me) that to stray beyond that very narrow focus would force them to consider issues well outside their specialized expertise as central bankers and push them into areas dealing with social structure. Yet, as modern systems science confirms, no component of a structure stands alone; all components are inescapably interrelated.

It's difficult for me to take seriously the Fed's inflation-fighting strategy when we can see monetary policy blithely operating behind the scenes in support of a rich-get-richer process that ensures us a profoundly undercapitalized baby boomer generation. The emerging demographics are destined to put untold political pressure on the nation's fiscal condition, a key determinant of price stability, as the boomers realize that they can't make ends meet without more government assistance. That makes the Fed's indifference irresponsible, even reckless, and contrary to its stated goal of anticipating and preventing wide-scale systemic disruptions.[45] This anomaly would be addressed by my proposed populist president in the First Hundred Days.

Economic Concentration

Antitrust policy offers another potentially powerful forum to encourage a more democratic capitalism. I don't mean just the average run-of-the-mill monopolies that now operate without scrutiny, reprimand, or remedy, such as the "Fortress Hub" airlines that routinely gouge travelers on routes where there's little competition. Here in Atlanta, where Delta accounts for 78 percent of the seats sold, I can travel round-trip to Tokyo for less than I can fly to nearby Winston-Salem, North Carolina, on a walk-up fare. Other flyers share similar horror stories, including those traveling American Airlines out of Dallas–Fort Worth (69.5 percent of seats sold), Continental's hub in Houston (79 percent), Northwest in Minneapolis (80.5 percent) and U.S. Air out of Pittsburgh (87.6 percent).[46] Monopolistic practices are often, though not always, wed to monopolistic ownership patterns. Monopolistic firms could be broken up in a way that fosters widespread ownership, particularly among employees, suppliers, distributors, even competitors, customers, and others who make up the web of a company's many relationships.

Microsoft, for instance, could be required to sell its key components and to break up the operating-system company into several equal-sized firms. Although it will be tempting to impose a conduct remedy akin to "Go out and sin no more," the only remedy consistent with the antitrust ethic is a structural one that not only breaks up the monopoly but also reallocates wealth wrongly accumulated by Microsoft's monopolists. Although highly punitive treble damages are often imposed in civil cases where a dollar amount can be estimated, I suggest instead that Microsoft's components be sold for one-third their appraised value, with major shareholders required to accept in payment a no-interest note, with the principal paid solely from future sales. That may be unduly generous as it would allow the monopolists to retain a huge component of their monopoly-generated wealth. They could also recover the balance to the extent that the successor companies can do well in a genuinely competitive market. As of this writing, it appears we're likely to see instead an opinion far more friendly to markets than to democracy. For instance, as of this writing, federal Judge Richard Posner had been appointed mediator in the Microsoft case. A law professor at the University of Chicago and a notoriously outspoken advocate in the Law and Economics cabal, he once famously suggested that the adoption system might be much improved if we allowed babies to be sold.

New antitrust rules are required to ensure that democratic ownership patterns emerge as a matter of course. Antitrust enforcement must become more proactive, better attuned to both structure and conduct. As mentioned earlier, few components of corporate consolidation could not be achieved instead with cooperation among independent firms. Policymakers in both the public and the private sector should look for leverage points to unwind today's democracy-threatening megamergers, replacing them with agreements among separate operating units while fostering within these units more peoplized and localized ownership. Rest assured, the same financial engineers who put these mergers together would happily take them apart, gleefully collecting yet another round of fees in the process. As this unwinding proceeds, doubtless we'll see academics and management consultants concoct yet another round of elegant theories assuring us that small, local, speedy, nimble, responsive, and culturally aware is an improvement over large, remote, slow, inflexible, insensitive, and culturally out to lunch.

Antitrust theory also needs to be rethought in light of new insights into such shopworn economic concepts as diminishing returns. Diminishing returns assume *negative* feedback loops. Twice the fertilizer doesn't double the yield. The third candy bar doesn't taste as good as the first. The more you do of something, the less profitable or tasty it becomes. That was the old economics.

In the New Economy, we know that *positive* feedback loops are also possible, in which the feedback amplifies the effect, along with *increasing* returns, an idea developed by Stanford economist Brian Arthur. A classic example is the mid-1970s videotape competition between Betamax and VHS in which VHS won. Betamax is now locked out. Success to the successful, the technological equivalent of "them what has, gets." Likewise the standard QWERTY keyboard layout on the typewriter. Invented in 1873 as a way to slow down typists, its technical standard has since created a lock-in. Fax machines illustrate a classic way that increasing returns accompany certain technologies. One fax machine isn't much use. Add another and I've someone with whom I can exchange faxes. Now there are millions of fax machines worldwide. The same principle operates with e-mail (Americans now send 122 billion e-mails annually, according to Jupiter Communications).

As technology becomes more dominant and more global, technical standards become steadily more important. That gives an advantage to the gatekeepers.[47] For antitrust purposes, invention has now become the mother of necessity. The rules lag well behind the reality.

Gateway Monopolies

In today's high-tech, high-touch, highly connected world, it should come as no surprise that we're now reaping the financial whirlwind that accompanies technological lock-ins with their highly lucrative positive feedback loops. Microsoft's market-dominant Windows software is only the most obvious of many examples of gateway technologies that reap enormous monopoly profits—along with the financial muscle to bully or buy out potential competitors. Federal District Court Judge Thomas Penfield Jackson found this to be the case in his blunt November 1999 "findings of fact" in the government's antitrust suit against Microsoft.[48]

It's essential that antitrust—both theory and practice—catch up with the real-world economics of an increasingly networked world. Kevin Kelly captures the challenge in his systems-savvy book *New Rules for the New Economy*: "As the number of nodes in a network increases arithmetically, the value of the network increases exponentially."[49] Like a gardener pulling the sprouts of plants known to be harmful, we need to uproot foreseeable monopolies in their infancy. That's because there's far more policy leverage available in reducing the gain around a positive loop (i.e., anticipating and slowing the growth of a technological lock-in) than in strengthening negative loops (such as by hindsight-oriented antitrust enforcement). By the government's own admission, its Microsoft proceedings, commenced in 1994 (with a consent decree), could drag on with appeals until at least 2002, allowing Bill Gates to increase his lock-in monopoly wealth to some multiple of the staggering $130 billion that his personally held Microsoft shares were worth in December 1999.[50] Indeed, it's possible that the legal remedies may be irrelevant by the time all legal challenges are resolved, given the pace of change in the software industry. The monopolists can take their fortune on to their next venture.

At the very least, a more farsighted, ownership-pattern-sensitive policy environment should ensure that more people associated with emerging lock-ins share in the increasing returns. Rather than waiting until those firms grow unduly market-dominant and their owners anti-democratically wealthy, we need a policy environment that slows the out-of-control positive feedback loops that typify high-tech monopolies. Or at least disburses their benefits more broadly, retroactively if necessary. As Donella Meadows, systems theorist and Dartmouth professor, puts it, "It's the same as slowing the car when you're driving too fast, rather than calling for more responsive brakes or technical advances in steering."[51]

One of the most troublesome areas on the immediate antitrust horizon is biotechnology, including gene technology, the very source code of life itself. The precise sequence of DNA in all 100,000 genes in the human body will be completed by the spring of 2001; a rough draft by spring 2000.[52] If successful, the identification of these patterns of information may enable health care to shift from the current model of detect-and-treat to one of predict-and-prevent, with therapies aimed at the genetic roots of illnesses such as cancer and heart disease. That leads some experts to predict that this new science may make it possible for a child born today to live 140 or more years (another good reason to get our life-cycle capitalization policies right).[53]

Is there to be a commercial gatekeeper for the biopharmaceutical industry, reaping biotech lock-in profits by vending their portfolio of genetic patents in the marketplace? Or will this information remain in the public domain for the common good, as the National Institutes of Health hope will be the case? Those in the know concede that they hope to apply Moore's law to biology—a reference to the observation that computer processing power doubles every eighteen months. Similar exponential growth may be available in this new high-tech biological domain. At the cellular level, science may well conclude that it is the information in genetic coding that really counts and that humans are just a very specific pattern of information unfolding over time. This complex interplay of science, ethics, economics, and theology provides the backdrop against which new horizons in antitrust policy will emerge.

Biotech Lock-Ins

In mid-December 1999, a class-action antitrust suit was filed accusing Monsanto of operating at the hub of a global conspiracy, of rushing genetically engineered seeds to market without properly testing them, and of forming an international cartel that conspires to control the world's market in corn and soybean seeds. A third of the nation's corn crop and 55 percent of our soybeans have already been genetically modified, with implications that are, at best, dimly understood in what can only be described as the largest human experiment in the history of science. Thus far we've been denied even the informed consent that democracy demands as genetically modified organisms have spread unannounced throughout our food supply. Indeed, Monsanto bragged that its rollout of genetically modified crops has been the most "successful launch of any technology in agriculture, including the plow." British biophysicist Mae Wan Ho counters the appraisal, characterizing the current state of biotech as "crude, unreliable, uncontrollable, unpredictable, inherently hazardous and guided by a paradigm that is flawed, out of date and in conflict with the scientific findings themselves."[54]

Biotech companies are now accused of attempting to control the spread of technology by patenting genetically engineered seeds and then leasing them to farmers, requiring growers to sign a licensing agreement. This arrangement would eliminate the age-old role of farmers as breeders and managers of genetic resources. Genetically modified seed varieties often carry traits that necessitate the use of one or more agrochemicals, enabling an agribusiness company to integrate the sale of seed and several other products (fertilizer, pesticides, herbicides), without which the patented seeds fail to function optimally. By controlling ownership of the seed itself, patent-holding companies gain substantial control over the entire farming process. Fearful that these developments reduce them to "renters of proprietary germplasm" who provide little more than land and labor to agribusiness, the Rural Advancement Foundation International charges that farmers would be reduced to little more than "bio-serfs."

Facing a fast-mounting commercial and political backlash along with a public-relations nightmare, Monsanto announced in October 1999 that it would not market sterile "suicide" seeds though it will continue research.[55] Despite this announcement by Monsanto (nicknamed "Mutanto" by critics), enormous doubts about the safety of U.S. crops persist. U.S. corn exports to the European Union reportedly dropped 96 percent in a single year; one giant processor announced that it would pay extra for non-genetically-modified soybeans; and Deutsche Bank, the largest European bank, urged investors to sell Monsanto shares.

Gateway Finance

Banking is arguably the economy's most powerful gateway monopoly. The nation's power to create money has been largely delegated to privately owned companies (i.e., banks). Because our fractional reserve system allows banks to lend out roughly twelve times the amount they have on deposit, populists must keep a close eye on the role that banks play in three realms: (1) locking in today's ownership patterns, (2) generating financial signals that affect sustainability, and (3) allocating economic risk and reward. That's particularly the case since the October 1999 political accord repealing Depression-era

Glass-Steagall rules that had long restricted the banking, securities, and insurance industries from expanding into one another's domains. Passage was reportedly lubricated by more than $300 million in Wall Street political contributions during 1997 and 1998.[56] As with all policy matters nowadays, this repeal also rode in on the Chicago logic of enhanced competitiveness abroad and expanded efficiency here at home. Never mind that it set the stage to inflate the stock market bubble with even more air while ensuring vast new concentrations of wealth and power in the financial sector.

A mid-1990s study by McKinsey and Company found that the financial assets of OECD (Organization for Economic Cooperation and Development) countries have grown two to three times as fast as their underlying economies since 1980. That's one reason returns in the financial sector outstripped other industry categories during this period. Firms that produce real goods and services (wages, profits, jobs, living standards) had to compete for investment capital against the more abstract world of financial markets, with its ever-expanding array of securities, options, warrants, derivatives and such.[57] That financial competition also forces "real-world" executives to embrace such profit-boosting gambits as layoff-intensive reengineering and natural-resource depletion along with cutbacks in key expenses such as training, research, and environmental cleanup.

The externalization of environmental costs looks reasonable in that finance-calibrated context as does currying political favor for subsidies, tax abatements, government contracts, and bailouts. Refuse to play along, and a corporate raider may show up—unless institutional investors force you out first. After depleting real wealth to boost financial wealth, this hollow prosperity is then pledged as the inflated collateral for another round of borrowing. Thus the Wall Street feeding frenzy in which money-denominated capital spirals ever upward while all other forms of capital—natural, institutional, and social—are either stagnant or in decline.[58] History suggests that Washington will step in when this leveraged bubble bursts, bailing out the banks that—once again—will be viewed as "too big to fail," leaving taxpayers—once again—to pick up the tab. Only this time the tab will be for larger and much more politically well connected financial behemoths run by executives whose personal portfolios (just coincidentally) will also be preserved in the inevitable bailout. No one dares characterize this predictable process as thievery on the grandest possible scale. At least *not yet*.

Concentration and Community

The level of economic concentration that we now tolerate is stagger-ing. And it's increasing at an ever-accelerating pace. Wal-Mart alone, with 3,983 outlets and $138 billion in 1999 sales, accounts for 6 percent of national retail spending. The Home Depot and Lowe's now account for one-quarter of all hardware sales. Rite Aid, Walgreens, and CVS dominate what were once community pharma-cies, with a combined 9,000 stores and $37 billion in revenues. Independent bookstores saw their market share plummet from 58 percent in 1972 to just 17 percent in 1999, as Borders Books and Barnes & Noble surged to take 45 percent of the market. According to research at the State University of Iowa, between 1983 and 1993 alone, Wal-Mart's expansion caused the collapse of an estimated 7,326 businesses, mostly in the hardware, grocery, and clothing ar-eas through "retail cannibalism." The wave of cross-border megamergers in the late 1990s is fast concentrating economic power in megacorporations—at the risk of eroding competition while un-dermining other key values. By 1998, the top ten companies in pes-ticides controlled 85 percent of a $31 billion market, whereas the top ten companies in telecommunications controlled 86 percent of a $262 billion global market.

Just a handful of companies (including Monsanto, DuPont, and Novartis) are striving to control 90 percent of the germ plasm that provides the world with 90 percent of its caloric intake.[59] Of the top six domestic merger and acquisition deals of all time, five (Exxon-Mobil, Travelers Group–Citicorp, SBC Communications–Ameritech, Bell Atlantic–GTE, and AT&T–Tele-Communications, Inc.) were announced in 1998 in transactions that totaled $372.6 billion, for an average $74.5 billion each. The sixth—MCI Worldcom's proposed acquisition of Sprint in October 1999—totals $108 billion. As of this writing, several far larger mergers were already under discussion.

Even in the politically sensitive arena of the media, for which con-centration has profound implications for public debate, the focus is not on the needs of democracy but on the market and *its* need for fi-nancial synergy to meet the pressures of global competition. Relying on Chicago-inspired ideology, the Federal Trade Commission contin-ues to steadily loosen its rules on ownership concentration in the me-dia—all in the name of market competition with no concern for the relationship between media ownership and democracy.[60]

The Exxon-Mobil merger ($138 billion in combined assets) put back together two large pieces of the old Rockefeller oil empire that was split into thirty-four companies in 1911. In approving the combination, the FCC focused solely on its impact on citizens *as consumers*. Yet sheer size in itself is a concern, particularly where these global Goliaths work their influence on governments. Exxon-Mobil is now larger than many of the oil-producing countries with which it negotiates.

Citigroup, NationsBank-BankAmerica, and other financial giants may, in effect, be beyond the law as a result of their deep-pocket capacity to hire sophisticated teams of lawyers to stymie prosecution (and pursue legislation) and their capacity to absorb even huge fines as simply another annoying cost of doing business. Cross-border corporate giantism raises another obvious concern for democracy: How does a nation-state govern itself when its commercial entities are both gargantuan and global?

In the information age, the next antitrust challenge may emerge through the shift to more Web-centric computing in the form of "application service providers" through which consumers access on-line software and other services. That could mean sub-$600 personal computers that may eventually use an alternative to Microsoft Windows or tap into an on-line operating system. In 1999, the leading Internet empire-builder is Masayoshi Son, an American-educated Korean/Chinese entrepreneur who lives in Tokyo.[61] Judging from Internet advertising patterns, major players are already staking out their lock-in turf in cyberspace, with only ten companies accounting for 70 percent of the fledgling $1.9 billion in 1998 ad revenues.[62] On-line alliances may soon emerge as a new area for antitrust concern such as drugstore giant CVS agreeing in October 1999 to link its Internet site with pharmaceutical colossus Merck & Co. and Merck's managed-care unit, which administers prescription benefits for 51 million people.[63]

Donella Meadows's car metaphor may apply more generally as well. For example, many people feel that the current pace of change is destabilizing, disorienting, and stressful. Yet the financial demands of institutionalized capital are not to be denied. The most promising way to slow the pace is with a policy environment that favors economic relationships in which financial returns become less dominant in their influence. Many people would happily ease back a bit on the gas pedal in order to feel a bit more in control of their lives (69 percent of us say we'd like to live a more relaxed life).[64] But first we need an economic environment that gains us some element of economic security and personal control. At present, many people feel like they're being driven rather than driving. Forty-two percent of us report that we feel "used up" by the end of the day.[65] Putting aside the implications for personal and family health, that's a dangerously antidemocratic condition (i.e., to feel at the mercy of the system). In a system driven by finance, high-tech advance, and a need for steadily increasing financial returns, people need a new perspective from which to insist on new goals. To stretch the metaphor, they need a system that puts them in the driver's seat. That's what democracies and markets are supposed to do—and currently don't.

A Game of Our Own Choosing

As the world's dominant democracy, the United States must take the lead in addressing the worldwide implications of this marriage of globalization and corporate giantism. The trillion-dollar enterprise is already emerging in telecommunications and aerospace. For instance, it's clear that the transatlantic merger of defense contractors is inevitable, something both Europe and America have long resisted. Yet the recent integration of financial, technological, and military power is certain to accrue largely to the benefit of U.S. firms.

That's particularly the case after the demonstration in Kosovo of our high-tech advances in military might. Indeed, the Chinese charged that the real reason we were there was to field-test and showcase our latest in lethal know-how. The world watched as we launched bombers lazily into the sky over Missouri, refueled them en route to a precision-bombing raid in central Europe, and then brought our pilots safely back home for dinner with their families thirty-two hours later. The question is no longer whether we have that power; the issue is how it will be used and who will harvest the economic benefit. It's easy to see why other nations might worry that we mean to hog the road as our unrestrained financial triumphalism fuels growing mistrust and resistance.

They have good reason to worry. Look around. Just what is it we're offering? We've proven our willingness to sacrifice even our concept of community to the abstract values of financial efficiency. For instance, as we've embraced the financial logic of national chains, our landscape has become world famous for its stark uniformity. Formula-tested marketing brings with it a formula-tested blandness of architectural style that exudes cost efficiency, often at the cost of taste and diversity, while the product-identification demands of global branding insure a sterile similarity. Drive down any urban street in the United States, and you see virtually the same mix of stores, strip malls, and fast-food outlets. You could be anywhere. Because retail spending in any community is a relatively fixed pie, an economic crowding-out of smaller retailers is assured as a town's sole proprietors close their doors in deference to competition from the retail giants. Business failures then leave communities looking forlorn. Meanwhile, residents drive longer distances for even the most basic of necessities as megaretailers often locate on the outskirts of town, where land is cheaper, zoning is less restrictive, and revenues from other nearby towns may be siphoned off as well.[66]

Absentee ownership, corporate giantism, economic concentration, consumption-driven cultures, and fast-widening social disparities travel together in today's hyper-standardized global commerce, along with a lack of any real commitment to communities from which profits flow in only one direction: out. Even the dignity of dying is being commoditized, commercialized, and conglomeratized as national mortuary chains displace the personal with the profitable.

Invisible ecological dangers also lurk beneath this veneer of retail efficiency and its embrace of an all-encompassing uniformity. For instance, over the past few years, most family-owned seed companies have been acquired by agrochemical conglomerates (ten seed companies now account for 38 percent of commercial seed trade worldwide). That ownership pattern, combined with the movement of national chains toward standard genetic seed varieties (to service nationwide markets), has resulted in an 84 percent loss in regionally adapted garden seeds just since 1984.[67] Of the reliable cultivated food plants grown in 1900, 97 percent are no longer available. We see similarly rapid declines in local traditions, values, arts, and small-scale economic lifestyles.

The ongoing "Arkansas-ization of America" has three benefits: lower prices (the consumer ideal), plus broader selection (at least for some things), and financial results that reflect the Wall Street ideal. Look at those returns! That's the alluring "content" of giantism. The context is far less attractive. For example, these corporate behemoths are notorious for their reliance not on local services but on out-of-state suppliers for support services such as printing and banking. Arkansas is famous for its two megawealthy families: the Walton's of

Wal-Mart fame and the lesser known Tyson's, the nation's largest purveyor of processed poultry. Although small pockets of affluence can be found scattered throughout the state, much of Arkansas is struggling. In that sense, Arkansas reflects the United States, its economy a microcosm of the rewards that flow to a few when entrepreneurial drive is coupled with raw financial (and political) power, assuring yachts and limousines for a few alongside a humdrum existence for most everyone else.

Not only does Arkansas provide a poor model for emulation elsewhere in this country, other nations are slowly awakening to the many untabulated costs of our highly touted finance- and efficiency-driven model. They are also growing rightfully wary as they see us use our economic and diplomatic clout to press for a new world order that would spread this democracy-endangering model worldwide. Yet this is precisely the model that's fast emerging, as Cyrus Freidheim, vice chairman of Booz-Allen & Hamilton, documents in *The Trillion-Dollar Enterprise*. He predicts that megacorporations and immense cross-border alliances will soon dominate not only telecommunications and aerospace but also automotive, banking, energy, commercial aviation, pharmaceuticals, accounting, primary metals, and computer hardware and software.[68] That's likely to be followed by what he calls a "next wave" of companies in biotechnology, electronics, machinery, apparel, textiles, chemicals, paper, wood products, and food. Following fast on their heels will be companies in construction, glass, hotels, publishing, health care, retailing, and advertising. That covers pretty much everything.

Globalization mandates that we answer a fundamental question: What's the business of democracy? What "product" do we aim to produce? At the very least, antitrust efforts must be coordinated on a global basis and expanded to include an appraisal of monopolistic ownership patterns as well. For years, researchers have compared the size of our largest firms with the economies of countries worldwide. Now we can compare individuals with entire countries. For instance, the October 1999 combined wealth of Sam Walton's five heirs and Microsoft's top three founders totals $233 billion, more than the GDP of Sweden, the world's twentieth largest economy. Warren Buffett has a net worth equivalent to the GDP of Kuwait, a nation we went to war to defend. Microsoft cofounder Paul Allen has a net worth equal to the GDP of the United Arab Emirates. The UN Development Program captures a slice of today's democratic dilemma:

The global economic system tells us to hurry up. It tells us all to worry about our speed. But it does not tell us how long the race will last—or what the best long-term strategy is. And it does not tell us how victory will be defined. If we are going to compete, let it be a game of our own choosing. That, in a nutshell, is the challenge of the new global order: how to define a world economy that preserves the advantages of market competition but establishes strict limits and rules that prevent competition from taking a destructive turn.[69]

It is to the resolution of those challenging issues that we turn in the next section.

PART TWO

Reclaiming Global Leadership

8
From Containment to Community

Economic inequality, especially that between developed and developing nations, remains the greatest source of suffering on this planet.

—HIS HOLINESS THE DALAI LAMA (1999)

No one has yet articulated a persuasive democratic vision for this globalized age. Nor has anyone suggested a coherent and credible program for democracy to cope with globalization. Yet those remain at the heart of all conversations concerning the post–Cold War era. We can deal with it or we can continue to deny it, but the need remains. For instance, huge accountability issues surround the fact that, of the world's hundred largest economic entities, half are corporations. Yet the political community has steered well clear of grappling with even such basic issues as who governs these corporations— and *for whom*—deferring instead to global capital markets. Many of these entities are global freeloaders content to operate with the support of national infrastructures, relying on deceptively priced energy and showing little or no concern for social or environmental costs while insisting on international norms that allow them uninhibited access to markets worldwide. Along with corporate giantism comes giant-sized personal fortunes of a magnitude unlike anything ever before seen. All this makes for a far more complex foreign policy environment, including the sensitive issue of just where the line should be drawn between private- and public-sector decision making. As a superpower, the United States has been so long focused on a common threat that it's now floundering for lack of a common goal. Absent either goals or a strategy, there is only drift.

Economic inequality has long been capitalism's geopolitical Achilles heel, and concentrated ownership its most common feature. Without reform, instability is assured in a world that is simultaneously being knit closer together—by markets, technology, information, and telecommunications—while being split apart socially and economically. Today's fast-emerging conflict between property rights and the human rights of the global citizenry must be addressed, particularly in today's finance-dominated environment with its steady blurring of the divide between political and commercial interests.

During the First Hundred Days of my proposed populist administration, U.S. intelligence-gathering agencies would commence the first-ever global ownership survey. The initial overview should take no more than a year. By combining high-resolution satellite photography with an analysis of land, shareholder, and business registries worlwide, a rough profile of property patterns can be compiled, absent gaps where ownership remains unclear or in flux, such as China or Cuba, or where ownership is obscure or hidden, as is often the case in the United States.[1] A global survey is essential if we hope to muster the international cooperation required to advance the spread of robust and sustainable free-enterprise democracies. If, as I suspect, plutocratic ownership patterning is the global norm, that information must be taken into account when evaluating the impact of international agreements in the economic sphere.

Forgone Opportunities

In the course of defending our private-property system and the democratic values that underlie it, U.S. taxpayers invested $12.7 trillion in military expenditures during the four decades of the Cold War (1948–1989). Now that a full decade has passed since the fall of the Berlin Wall, what's the result? How is our half-century investment paying off? We don't know. In fact, we've yet to identify an agreed-to benchmark for measuring either success *or* failure. Instead, a curious laissez-faire absolutism squelches any effort to describe just what sort of free enterprise we mean to have. Or even *whose* free enterprise we propose for it to be. In this section I describe the free enterprise I believe a democracy is obliged to leave for its descendants. Without such standards—even if rudimentary—we have no way to know whether we're making progress in reaching our goals.

In much the same way that voter turnout speaks volumes about the robustness of democracy, a capital-ownership survey would tell us much about the robustness of capitalism. It will also reveal the challenges facing democracy's continued advance. For example, we devoted substantial resources assisting Russia with its troubled transition. Yet a survey of ownership patterns will confirm that grotesque inequity and massive corruption undermine genuine progress, particularly in key sectors such as natural resources and finance, where the potential for cheating was greatest. In the wake of a full decade of reform, we find widespread abject poverty alongside the smoldering potential for instability in an oligarchy-ruled, crony-capitalist state. An ownership survey would help the Russian people identify those who took advantage of the transition so that corrective measures might be crafted.

We have already missed a full half-century of opportunities to use ownership patterns as a tool for advancing democratic and sustainable development. If only our international aid efforts had been sensitive to their impact on ownership, things might by now be far different in developing countries. For instance, practically every construction project funded by the World Bank Group since its inception—dams, levees, canals, power plants, roads, buildings, irrigation projects—involved contracts with private companies paid with loans guaranteed by local governments (the bank's official name remains the International Bank for Reconstruction and Development). What sort of ownership patterns emerged from a half-century of subsidized borrowing for reconstruction and development? Who was capitalized with that capital? To admit we don't know suggests that we don't care. How could that be? How could ownership patterns be irrelevant to development? If our intelligence sources can identify terrorist cells worldwide, as they claim, surely they can compile a global wealth registry.[2] Our very willingness to sponsor such an effort would acknowledgeof key social justice issues that undermine stability and motivate terrorism.

Needed: The Spotlight of Global Scrutiny

We also need an ownership counterpart to the Geneva-based International Labor Organization (ILO), an agency of the UN. Though labor leaders see the ILO as toothless and underfinanced, the organization has had a positive impact on working conditions worldwide. That's not because it has any legislative powers, but because this 174-nation body shines the spotlight of public awareness on unfair and abusive labor practices and presses for international treaties to ban them.

An analogous effort could highlight unfair and abusive *ownership* practices. International accords could identify the worst cases. It's impossible to imagine, for instance, that we would have continued our support of Indonesia's Suharto regime if we had known then, as we know now, and as the Central Intelligence Agency (CIA) knew all along, that the Suharto family abused our backing to accumulate $35 billion in personal wealth, according to CIA estimates.[3] Following the standard prescription of the International Monetary Fund (IMF), the Indonesians formed a financial restructuring agency in 1999 mandating that the nation's crony capitalists cough up $23 billion owed to various banks. If they fail, the companies will be sold and the proceeds applied to reduce the IMF's $40 billion rescue loan. Who would then become the owners? Largely foreign investors. From an ownership-pattern perspective, this common IMF strategy ensures that Indonesians will exchange a domestic plutocratic elite for a foreign one—utilizing as the catalyst the IMF's stamp of approval and drawing on state-subsidized credit.[4] Absent a sensible stance on the need to reform ownership patterns, the old oligarchs often return, even in countries in which corruption is most rife and the gains so clearly ill gotten, as is now happening in Indonesia, the Philippines, and elsewhere.[5]

There's much that governments could do to improve ownership patterns. For example, in June 1999, President Clinton issued an executive order forbidding government agencies to buy products made with forced child labor. Agencies must consult an approved list before purchasing, while government contractors must certify that child labor is not involved. Similar screening could ensure that unconscionable ownership practices are not unwittingly supported by U.S. taxpayers. Both aid and trade have a notorious history of callous indifference on this critical subject, whether it be support for the excesses of the shah of Iran or for the kleptocratic Marcos regime, in which Imelda Marcos, former Philippine first lady, acknowledges that her family pocketed $12.5 billion.[6] That counterproductive, democracy-damaging indifference continues to permeate U.S. foreign policy.

In the early 1990s, for example, *Forbes* reported that Mexico's Salinas regime created twenty-eight billionaires in the course of privatizing its banking sector. When those banks got into difficulty, the United States led a $47 billion bailout, which Robert Rubin, then secretary of the treasury, proclaimed a success because the U.S.

Treasury pocketed some interest payments when the loans were re-paid. The sensitive issue of who pocketed the ownership was never raised. That curious oversight undercuts all three of the stated reasons for foreign assistance: the spread of democracy, the alleviation of poverty, and the creation of conditions helpful to development. Yet Mexico's choice of privatization methods was made in close consulta-tion with our treasury and implemented on the advice of U.S.-schooled Mexican officials. This in a country in which thirty-seven families have long owned at least 40 percent of the economy and, by the government's own admission, 40 million of its 98 million people live in poverty, 26 million of those in extreme poverty.

Induced Transparency

From 1995 to 1999, U.S.-led financial rescues entailed $230 billion in just six countries: Mexico, Thailand, Indonesia, South Korea, Russia, and Brazil. What's been the impact on ownership patterns? We don't know. What we do know is that information alone has power. Ownership-pattern transparency offers a promising new means for stimulating democratic debate on a sensitive subject that has long worked a corrosive influence in democracies worldwide.

Transparency alone can help. For example, in 1986 the U.S. gov-ernment required that factories report their emissions of hazardous air pollutants. Though there was no law requiring their reduction, emissions declined 40 percent by 1990. One chemical company on the widely publicized Dirty Dozen cut its emissions by 90 percent just to get off the list. As arms negotiators discovered long ago, trans-parency is itself stabilizing. In the case of ownership, it would be re-assuring for the populace to know that the well-to-do are speaking openly about their holdings and are willing to engage in dialogue about policy alternatives. Today's secrecy is inherently suspect. Democracies can't change what they don't know needs changing. Information itself can have an effect. For instance, in a subdivision of identical homes, electrical meters were installed in the basement in some homes and in the front hall of others, where residents could see their meter constantly turning. In those houses with the meter in the hall, electricity consumption was 30 percent lower.

With ownership patterns, the missing ingredient is not only infor-mation but also some indication of why the information matters. Change will come more rapidly—and move naturally—as we point out the many anomalies and drawbacks of our current capitalism—a key purpose of this book.

We know, for instance, that organized crime grosses an estimated $1.5 trillion a year, rivaling multinational corporations as a presence in the global economy.[7] A global survey could tell us what those criminals own, and where. Perhaps Steve Forbes could publish an annual *Felons 400*. Criminal syndicates now have the power to corrupt politics, commerce, and law enforcement worldwide, yet there's no coordinated effort to identify their ill-gotten gains. That deficiency undermines the best-known law enforcement remedy: seizure of their assets.

Improved transparency could also help ferret out political corruption. With access to better information on ownership patterns, financial muckraking could emerge as a new journalistic genre, taking its place alongside political muckraking as a source of insight, intrigue, and media-induced reform.

One of the most cost-effective, democracy-inducing activities that the international community could support would be rewards for ownership-pattern whistle-blowers. Generous financial incentives could be coupled with offers of political asylum to induce the release of information from those in the know (accountants, secretaries, lawyers) who reside in tax-haven countries. That could prove a powerful way to expose criminal accounts and reveal the riches of tax-evaders and the politically corrupt.[8] I suggest that this internationally coordinated effort be called the Induced Transparency Program. International stability and the rule of law so essential to the spread of democracy would be much improved with greater doses of the sunshine that Supreme Court Justice Louis D. Brandeis called "the best disinfectant."

Global Norms

The Isle of Man, off the British coast, is one of several thriving havens for those who seek a shield against taxes, regulations, or the rule of law. With a population of 72,000, the island has a corporate registry that boasts 42,000 companies, mostly empty shells. That's well ahead of rival English Channel tax havens on the Isles of Jersey and Guernsey and the tiny island of Sark. Other infamous tax asylums for the well-to-do include Cyprus, Gibraltar, Luxembourg, Liechtenstein, Panama, and many countries that dot the eastern Caribbean.[9] And let's not forget the ever-so-sophisticated Swiss who, embarrassed at late 1990s revelations of their Holocaust profiteering during World War II, grudgingly yielded to international pressure to open their books to authorities under limited conditions. In this global race to the bottom, these crook-catering enclaves welcome everyone, their competitive edge determined by the extent of their officially enforced secrecy.

From drug lords to reclusive billionaires, Russian oligarchs to petty swindlers, and from high-rolling financial entrepreneurs (Long Term Capital Management was chartered in the Caymans) to outlaw banks (likewise the infamous Bank of Credit and Commerce International), these outlaw outposts offer the wealthy what those in the know realized long ago: Taxes are optional. Media mogul Rupert Murdoch openly boasts how his advisers shuttle his complex financial transactions through tax-haven shell companies to keep this multibillionaire's worldwide tax rate well under 10 percent. That, in turn, provides him a competitive edge as he scurries about the globe in what appears to be an ongoing attempt to monopolize entire segments of the worldwide media. His decision to swing the London *Sun* (3.5 million daily circulation) behind Tony Blair is widely regarded as one of the main reasons for New Labor's electoral success. Of course, Murdoch and others of his ilk are happy to take full advantage of the benefits offered in countries where their money is made, including making extensive use of the infrastructure—courts, highways, airports, telecommunications, an educated workforce, and so forth. They just can't be bothered to pay any of the costs. As Murdoch candidly puts it: "Isn't that one of the advantages of being global?"

Without transparency, the international community will necessarily operate somewhat blind as it turns its attention to the crafting of norms of civilized and sustainable ownership-pattern behavior. At the outset, the best way to nudge the system toward the tolerable is to address those developments that are clearly intolerable. By focusing first on chicanery, corruption, and criminality, this initiative will gain an immediate advantage over its inevitable critics, including those Law and Economics ideologues who routinely trot out their lame laissez-faire party line even in the most egregious of circumstances. There's a very simple reason why no one defends global ownership patterns: They are indefensible. Yet no leader has yet dared engage either in articulating the problem or in seeking a solution. Even though we may pay a disproportionate share of the costs of advancing such minimal norms, that role naturally falls to the United States as the leading proponent of global free enterprise. That also means that our capitalists, including our institutional investors, will need to rethink their investment practices. Their indifference on the sensitive subject of ownership patterning is one of the key culprits.

From Containment
to Community

A decade after the collapse of Soviet communism, U.S. foreign policy still lacks a post–Cold War theme. Policymakers can look back on a full half-century since George Kennan published his celebrated essay "The Sources of Soviet Conduct," in which he identified the Soviet empire's internal contradictions and predicted its eventual collapse, provided the democratic West maintained a "patient but firm and vigilant containment."[10] Though Kennan spent the next five decades disavowing strategies evoked by his analysis, containment quickly emerged as the dominant foreign-policy theme both for us and our Cold War allies. As events later proved, confirming Kennan's worst fears, containment led the United States to prop up corrupt and disreputable regimes worldwide (the Realpolitick of Pinochet in Chile, Noriega in Panama, the contras in Nicaragua, etc.) as we became embroiled in conflicts we could afford neither to lose nor to win. A tense stalemate typified the decades required for the Soviet Union to implode. That period will long be remembered for its rampant militarization as untold resources, both human and financial, were conscripted worldwide to pursue what conservative commentator Walter Lippman called a strategic monstrosity. Kennan agreed, dismissing Vietnam as a strategic folly.

Containment's critics often forget that its insights were intended not to be strategic or operational but moral, psychological, even spiritual. The most effective response to Soviet expansionism, Kennan insisted, lay not in the realm of military counterforce. That was seen as essential but insufficient, whereas conquest was viewed as transitory, even immoral. The long-term solution lay in mounting a moral and ideological counteroffensive designed to negate the very rationale for communism. Despite the demise of the immensely flawed Soviet system, our policymakers continue to put us at risk by neglecting the core of Kennan's counsel, namely, that U.S. leadership must demonstrate "the responsibilities of moral and political leadership that history plainly intended them to bear."

Does Victory Mean Vindication?

Instead of demonstrating this leadership, the conventional wisdom suggests that the Soviet collapse marks a vindication of U.S.-style individualistic capitalism. After all, they say, we now stand triumphant, basking in the glow of a record-breaking stock market, capitalism's most visible symbol of global leadership. The problem with this smug critique is that it fails to offer a moral standard of performance against which our version of capitalism can be measured. Meanwhile, the Soviet's discredited collectivism is plagued by a hugely corrupt and painful transition stuck somewhere between a discredited socialism and a dysfunctional capitalism. If the Soviet Union was destined to collapse of its own inconsistencies, as Kennan argued and as containment assumed, its collapse is not a vindication of our system but only an invalidation of a system that we fully expected to fail.

Our reluctance to address this discrepancy shows up in our inability to define for ourselves a foreign-policy theme for a post–Cold War world. Some would have us believe that the way forward is to dwell ad nauseum on the shortcomings of an ill-conceived system doomed from the outset. That's inane. The relevant task is how to identify policies capable of advancing the national interest in a far more complicated world.

To succeed in this globalized era, I suggest that those policies must point the way to a more peaceful and prosperous future *worldwide*— what I think of as "community without the communism."[11] With 3 billion members of the human community struggling to get by on less than $2 per day and more than 2 billion people anemic, the time has arrived to adopt a genuinely humane and aggressively global foreign policy that reflects the very best that democracy has to offer. From the perspective of the world's poor, the United States appears to have embraced a foreign policy intent on scouring the world for financial returns when what we need is to send out a search party to find our humanity.[12]

Kennan offers some clues about how we could establish a genuinely humane foreign policy. A decade after publishing his initial analysis, he urged that U.S. policymakers counter the Soviet threat by looking not to containment but to "our American failings, to the things we are ashamed of in our own eyes, or that worry us." That advice merits a fresh appraisal in light of the worrisome trends in economic disparity chronicled in earlier chapters.

Global leadership comes in many forms. At present, the United States leads the developed world with some of the worst rates of child poverty, teen suicide, violence, drug use, crime, family breakup, imprisonment, functional illiteracy, and homelessness. Our disparities in wealth and income surpass the class-ridden societies of Europe, though with a key difference: Although those nations inherited their disparities from a feudal past, we chose it. And not only do we continue to choose it, we're widening those disparities at an accelerating pace. This indefensible domestic policy undercuts any semblance of moral stature to which we might aspire in foreign affairs.

Developments in the former Soviet Union at the turn of the twenty-first century suggest that as the alleged victor, the United States should offer its assistance to address an emerging human crisis of stunning proportions. A recent UN Development Program report (*Transition 1999*) documents that the largest single human cost of the transition is the loss of lives among young and middle-aged men. The report documents 5.9 million "missing men" in the Russian federation alone and another 2.6 million in Ukraine. The total loss for the transition economies is 9.7 million. The causes are multiple and complex, including skyrocketing suicide rates, declining life expectancy, deteriorating health care, and an increase in self-destructive behavior. Widening poverty and an accelerating rich-poor gap are also key culprits, with the number of people living on US$4 a day rising from 2 million to 60 million by 1994. As of July 1999, one-third of Russians were living below the official poverty line of $38 per month. Many diseases that could be contained in a functioning health-care system are reemerging, among them tuberculosis, polio, and diphtheria. Tuberculosis cases are expected to top 1 million by 2002, along with 2 million projected HIV/AIDS cases (human immunodeficiency virus, which causes the acquired immune deficiency symptom), overwhelming an already-failing health-care system. Cancer and heart death rates for fifteen- to nineteen-year-olds are double the U.S. rates, as are suicide rates. New incidents of syphilis have increased seventy-seven-fold since 1990. A proud people need assistance in a situation in which asking for help may be politically impossible.

Missing: A Moral Foundation for Global Leadership

The fast-widening gap between our own haves and have-nots makes it difficult for us to protest as Russian policymakers create among their politically elite a private-property elite. Through a privatization process widely and rightly characterized as "grabification" and "mafia-ization," Russia's newly propertied kleptocracy has steadily displaced a discredited state.[13] Yet given our own plutocratic ownership patterns, how can we credibly object as Russian ownership patterns begin to resemble those of the czarist era? Novelist Alexander Solzhenitzyn insists that *never* in Russia's history has the gap been greater between ruler and ruled.

To justify the unjustifiable, Russian leaders need only point to their former adversary, now their capitalist mentor. Or they can (and do) point to ownership patterns in other nations that qualify for U.S. support, be it the crony capitalism of south Asia, the oligarchic capitalism common to our hydrocarbon allies in the Middle East, or the family aristocracies we've long pampered in Latin America and the Caribbean. Writing two years before Kennan published his article (originally a February 1946 "long telegram" to Navy Secretary James Forrestal), theologian Reinhold Neibuhr foretold the quandary in which we now find ourselves. In his classic *The Children of Light and the Children of Darkness*, he cautioned: "It may be found that the relation of economic classes within a state is more important than international relations." Therein lies our strategic dilemma as we confront a global marketplace not only in goods and capital but also in information, ideas, and ideologies along with a fast-emerging transparency that makes inequity, social injustice, and unsustainability ever more difficult to disguise.

When policymakers in Russia or elsewhere flaunt their rich-get-richer "reform" policies grounded in born-in-the-USA, Chicago-style economics, how can we credibly object? Where's our foundation of fairness on which to take a moral stand? Similarly, what advice can we credibly offer other countries struggling with racial or ethnic divides when our fast-widening rift is also racial and ethnic? If we hope to retain (or, more accurately, regain) our position as a credible world leader, we must lead not only with a clearly articulated global vision but also with a domestic policy that reflects at home what we advocate abroad. Our hard-earned mentor status has been seriously damaged, steadily reduced in stature and credibility, resigning us to the impotent role of a perky cheerleader for a social justice we lamely endorse but refuse to embrace. Meanwhile, the gap grows ever wider between the democracy we preach and the plutocracy we practice.

Who Lost Russia?

The "Who lost Russia?" debate has muddied the 2000 presidential campaign waters, particularly among those most concerned not with what was accomplished but with what we failed to achieve. Al Gore is taking the bulk of the heat. He earned it as co-chair of a coordinating mechanism (the Gore-Chernomyrdin Commission) that will best be remembered for the fact that the Russian cochair, then–Prime Minister Viktor Chernomyrdin evidently absconded with a sum that news accounts suggest may well tally in the billions. (Chernomyrdin was former head of Gazprom, the notoriously corrupt national gas monopoly.) Early euphoria at apparently quick success on the Russian reform front was followed by a deep angst, which became a "what have we wrought" introspection and now "whom do we blame?" Most of those involved hope to remove their fingerprints from anything associated with reform. That won't be easy.

In April 1999, Joe Stiglitz, World Bank chief economist, became the first of his stature to break ranks with the Washington–Wall Street consensus, aiming withering broadsides at Russia's U.S. advisers. What did they do wrong? Everything, he says, charging them with "a misunderstanding of the very foundations of a market economy, as well as a failure to grasp the fundamentals of reform processes." His conclusion: Due to their efforts, "the longer-run prospects of a market economy may actually be undermined."[14] Capturing the irony, he notes that communist China's gross domestic product (GDP) nearly doubled during the decade beginning in 1989 with the fall of the Berlin Wall, whereas Russia's GDP almost halved. Russia's GDP started out twice that of China's before reform and ended up a third smaller. Add to that "declining confidence in the economy and the government made the country even less attractive to foreign investors," and you have the ingredients for what has now emerged: a missed opportunity and a human tragedy amid rampant corruption.

As someone who conferred with Mikhail Gorbachev's first economic team and briefed Boris Yeltsin soon after he took office, I can confirm from firsthand experience that our reformers' academic credentials (largely University of Chicago and Harvard) were sufficient to trump my layman's appeal to common sense. My unconventional proposal for peoplizing capital was ridiculed by Russia's chief reform adviser, Harvard's Jeffrey Sachs, as the "Bolshevik-ation of capital" and a threat to what is now widely seen as an immensely flawed reform agenda that he and his lavish colleagues devised. Reportedly more than $300 million in advisory fees flowed through the accounts of those advisers whom Stiglitz dismisses as "misunderstanding the reform process." Among the many mistakes he cites was their insistence on "shock therapy" (a sudden change in the rules governing the economy in order to impose fiscal balance and introduce free markets). That strategy was useful as a way to reset expectations as part of an anti-inflation remedy in Bolivia (where Sachs made his reputation). On the other hand, the strategy was woefully inappropriate as a way to install the institutions needed for Russian reform—the rule of law, property rights, an independent judiciary, a bankruptcy code, reliable accounting and auditing systems, and other rules we take for granted. In Stiglitz's candid assessment, "their advice has sometimes contributed as much to the problem as to the solution." The political consequences not only hamper the reconciliation of Russia with the West; they may also reinstate hostility, threatening our vital interests.

The great irony, he points out, is that these academic superstars recommended not the practical path of gradualism but an idealistic root-and-branch blitzkrieg approach that, he charges, is "a reincarnation of the spirit and mindset of Bolshevism." Plus, rather than urging a decentralized economy that diversifies risk while improving incentives and accountability, the reformers instead left intact many of the very largest enterprises, which, as one would expect, continue to lobby the Duma for special treatment, much as our largest firms extract corporate welfare from Congress.

What would have been a better recipe? Stiglitz recommends a bottom-up approach to transformation, which would gain support for reform by getting more "buy-in" through broader participation. How? By relying less on abstract financial theories and more on common sense, steadily building social capital by decentralizing decision making and "rebuilding organizational relationships from the ground up." Citing *The Ownership Solution*, he urges instead "a strategy of privatization to stakeholders. . . . Had the *economics* of reform fared better, perhaps too would have the politics."[15] Unfortunately, there is no international tribunal for economic malpractice.

A Failed Experiment

The sad truth, Stiglitz concedes, is that this is "one of the most important experiments in economics ever to have occurred, a massive and relatively sudden change in the rules of the game," which went "wildly wrong." How did our advisers get it so dramatically wrong? Academic arrogance, self-righteousness, a profound lack of prudence, and by confusing means with ends. True to the Law and Economics consensus (embraced in Moscow as the Washington–Wall Street consensus), they obsessed on the creation of a market economy when the emphasis, Stiglitz argues, should have been on "the improvement of living standards and the establishment of the foundations of sustainable, equitable and democratic development."

How do you do that when there's very little "legitimate capital" in the country? You make owners of people who view the enterprise not merely as an abstract investment quickly to be harvested but as a day-to-day business relationship with some relevance to their livelihood. And you look for relationships in which ownership "might incubate and support entrepreneurial efforts." If you don't do that (as the reformers didn't) and you turn instead to conventional capital market-style absentee ownership (the Chicago ideal), ownership becomes disconnected, atomized, and dispersed—tempting the elites to gain control of the companies and strip out the financial value. That's precisely what they did, with an estimated $1 billion a month ($100 billion to $150 billion) taken out of the country during the 1990s. Some 12,000 firms in Moscow now specialize in money laundering and capital flight.[16]

This cowboy capitalism, or what the Russians call *dikiy* ("wild capitalism") fuels a particularly dark brand of wry Russian humor. One joke making the rounds these days goes like this: "Everything the Communists told us about communism was a complete and utter lie. Unfortunately, everything the Communists told us about capitalism turned out to be true." Unfortunately for the Russians, the operating credo among U.S. advisers remains "often mistaken but never in doubt." At the outset, it was an article of faith that if the Russians simply created a nation of property owners—regardless of the ownership patterns—everything else would somehow sort itself out. That naive prescription was dispensed despite a well-known legacy of authoritarianism, corruption, and avarice, plus monumental incompetence in the leadership, widely acknowledged problems in changing a national mind-set, and a culture steeped in generations of passivity, paternalism, cronyism, and criminality.

To indicate how bizarre was the thinking of our advisers, Charles Blitzer, chief World Bank economist in Moscow from 1992 to 1996, now concedes, "We were too willing to accept the Russian reformers' view that *it didn't make any difference who ended up with the assets initially.*" He adds that we "bought into the idea" that the new owners would push for a law-based society "because no one wants their sons to grow up to be the crooks they are."[17] With both the incentives and the structure fully aligned to facilitate massive rip-offs—per our advice—the Russians pushed forward with reforms whose predictably disastrous results we now owe a hand in finding some way to repair. After taking criticism for his candor, Stiglitz tendered his resignation in November 1999, conceding that when dealing with policies "as misguided as I believe these policies were, you have to either speak out or resign."[18] Indicating its keen displeasure at his articulate defection, the *Wall Street Journal* quickly moved to discredit this much-acclaimed economist, branding him a "gadfly."

The End of Delusion?

By all accounts, the thievery in Russia was simple and remarkably comprehensive. Some of the easiest parasitic activity occurred prior to privatization. For instance, in 1992, the Russian price of oil was still 1 percent of the world market price. A few state enterprise managers, with Chernomyrdin then head of the state energy lobby, reportedly amassed during that single year no less than $24 billion, then about 30 percent of Russia's GDP.[19] The swindle: Managers sold commodities (oil, minerals, timber) to their own private trading companies at state-controlled prices, extracted an export license and quota from a corrupt official, and then sold abroad for foreign currencies. Though most of those funds stayed abroad, some flowed back in to be laundered in privatization auctions, lending legitimacy to property acquired with stolen funds. In early 1990, a pack of Marlboros and a ton of crude oil sold for the same price—thirty rubles. Hypocritically, Chernomyrdin argued then that Russian industry would collapse if required to buy oil at world market prices.

Subsidized credits offered another avenue for easy pilfering. Arguing that bank credits were a useful "Keynesian stimulus," corrupt bankers stood by while industrial production plummeted as credit-induced hyperinflation ravaged the economy, wiping out personal savings as those credits enriched the elites. Their riches were enough that the oligarchs, in effect, bought the state, including financing Yeltsin's 1996 election campaign with financial support that critics charge totaled $500 million.

No pillage was too extreme for these pariahs. In 1995, a key oligarch (Vladimir Potanin) proposed a scheme so audacious that it embarrassed even our complacent advisor corps. In this infamous loan-for-shares program, the Russian government allowed shares in large enterprises (largely oil companies) to be placed in trust with oligarch-controlled financial institutions in return for loans to the state. When the government defaulted, as everyone knew it would, the trustees auctioned the shares to affiliates of the bank at knock-down prices. Some of the oligarchs even used the government's own money to bid in the auctions. For example, more than $512 reportedly disappeared in Potanin-affiliated banks, as did billions of dollars left in custody with the oligarch-controlled banks for the reconstruction of Chechnya, a key point fueling the uprising there in 1999. The theft was brazen and shameless. For instance, Yukos oil company had 1999 sales of $8 billion and sits on proven reserves of 11.5 billion barrels (equivalent to British Petroleum prior to its merger with Amoco). It sold at auction for $159 million. Sibneft, with proven reserves equal to Texaco, sold for $100.3 million.[20]

In a fruitless and ill-advised attempt to support the ravaged ruble in an environment in which the nation's financial value was routinely being shipped abroad, the IMF released $4.8 billion to the Yeltsin government less than a month before the August 1998 collapse of Russia's currency and financial markets. Former prosecutor general Yuri Skuratov, suspended by Yeltsin when he brought corruption charges against a key oligarch, charges that the funds benefited a few banks that transferred the entire amount out of the country just before the financial crisis.[21] Investigations are ongoing of transactions conducted by those who rule a nation "too big and too nuclear to fail." Russian-style democracy was treated to yet another round of Kremlin political drama with the millennium-weekend resignation of Boris Yeltsin, enticed by the allure of pardon from criminal prosecution.

A Step Toward the Miraculous

Much of Russia's corruption is the symptom of a failure to create conditions that would motivate capital to remain at work inside the country. Now that the financial pillage has been so complete and corruption has replaced ballet as the skill for which Russians are best known, voluntary capital repatriation is impossible. Conditions in today's decapitalized Russia will never improve sufficiently that capital spirited abroad will choose to return—at least until rule-making and civil society become the norm. Based on the mistakes made, that repatriation could take a generation or more.[22] Over the past several years, Russia has received less foreign direct investment than Peru. Because so much of Russia's wealth was claimed with so little legitimacy, fundamental notions of fairness mandate that the international community work with honest elements of the Russian government to recover what was pilfered. Though Russia's oligarchs enjoy comparing themselves to turn-of-the-century U.S. robber barons, at least our capitalist pioneers built something and then left a legacy of philanthropy. Russia's criminal oligarchs simply stripped the nation and shipped the funds to their private accounts abroad, shifting to them control over more assets than even the largest international drug cartel.

Although it's altogether too one-dimensional to dismiss Russia as a gangster state, its lawlessness continues to invite duplicity of the worst sort. Even the corrupt earned a measure of sympathy when they spirited funds abroad to escape a dysfunctional tax system, political instability, rampant extortion, gangland-style murders, and blatant theft at the hands of their rivals. Russia's thieves could only be sure of keeping their ill-gotten gains if they got the funds out of the country, and for that purpose, they required the help of others in the global financial community.[23] Doubtless, my proposal to assist with the recovery of these funds will upset those Russian rogues (and their accomplices), who will lamely claim that they complied with what was then the law. That's nonsense. Common sense, international common law, and generally accepted norms of civilized behavior mandate that mere compliance with the letter of the law should never trump the spirit of equity and fair play that underlie the law. To suggest otherwise makes a mockery of the international rule of law.

A revealing joke is making the rounds in Moscow: There are two ways out of Russia's economic crisis: the natural and the miraculous. In the natural way, the archangel Michael and all the angels descend to Earth and work twenty-four hours a day to save the Russian economy. The miraculous way is that the Russians do it themselves.

Based on the advice they have received from us to date, including complicity in money laundering by U.S. banks, the Russians may soon conclude that the miraculous is the more reasonable route to recovery.[24] Former Treasury Secretary Robert Rubin rightly reminds us that at least Russia did not sink back into an authoritarian state-planning mode. Nor did it drift into chaos or anarchy or become a country marked by anti-Western nationalism.[25] At least, *not yet*. The ongoing exodus of banks (Barclays, NatWest, etc.) suggests a steady deterioration of the country's regulatory and financial systems as well as a serious breakdown of infrastructure that should concern those who fret about instability in this nuclear nation.

Instability remains a very real threat. Tax collection is a disaster. Domestic terrorism brought to the surface a latent xenophobia and nationalism that could feed on itself, just as it fuels a cruel war in Chechnya. Moscow's financial elites have now become distributors of largesse in Russia's restless regions where their control over local purse strings (including local tax revenues) has elevated them above the Kremlin in their influence. With huge swaths of Russia impoverished by the all-encompassing scope of their thievery, these plutocrats now operate as mafia-like patrons of even such basic social infrastructure as schools, hospitals and recreation facilities, negotiating social services in return for local influence. Their control of most meaningful media outlets currently maintains a lid on what would otherwise be a politically explosive environment. Markets remain, at best, rudimentary.

In truth the Cold War is not yet truly over—in part because the reforms we sought were so poorly conceived and pursued. Although much has been wrongly done, conditions require that we remain engaged until the values for which we fought take root. Many of the privatizations should be undone and redone. A precedent has already been set when a Russian court renationalized the famous Lomonosov porcelain factory in October 1999.[26] Looted funds simply must be recovered—no matter where they may be found. During the First Hundred Days of a U.S. populist administration, negotiations would commence on how best our engagement could help restore to Russia the capital desperately needs to complete its economic transition in a way that ensures a stable and sustainable future.

Foreign Policy Requires a Purpose

What's missing in U.S. foreign policy, including our policy toward Russia, is a well-articulated purpose, a clearly stated goal, the pursuit of which the American people can support. As our focus shifted from anticommunism to pro-marketism and to an opaque policy known as economic engagement, the United States lost not only any sense of direction but also the support of those at home who rightly perceive a lack of any principles against which our conduct might be measured. The First Hundred Days of a populist administration would see the crafting of a principled and pragmatic foreign policy which would continue to focus on the spread of democratic values. However, it would also recognize the importance of providing a helping hand from a nation willing both to typify and to teach how equity and sustainability are the only feasible principles that can hold together either a nation or a community of nations.

We know that national governments are too large to address small problems. That does not mean they need be too small in spirit to address large problems. As the world's economic and military powerhouse, the United States bears the responsibility of proposing the underpinnings of a twenty-first-century democratic capitalism. In so do-ing, we must ensure that no nation or peoples are victimized by mis-takes made in the past. That requires our commitment to help others build the infrastructure required for a more dramatically inclusive free enterprise.

Dean Acheson, former secretary of state, correctly noted that "you can get agreement on anything if you continue to raise the level of abstraction." That's the problem with vague assurances of democratic values, vacuous Third Way rhetoric about economic empowerment, and vapid promises of a just social order or a compassionate conser-vatism. The challenge is how to make explicit the implicit democratic promise of what is fast becoming a free-enterprise culture that encir-cles the globe. To further complicate matters, we must also address the troubling paradox of how best to fulfill the promise of democra-tic self-determination (for Kosovo, East Timor, Kashmir, Tibet, Chechnya, the Kurds) in an environment in which this core principle directly conflicts with the commitment to national sovereignty. Consider, for example, Clinton's statement on Chechnya in November 1999 that Moscow has "the obligation to defend its terri-torial integrity." Worldwide, we can identify five thousand ethnic groups while the UN includes only 187 member states. Absent initia-tives that assure greater equity, self-rule and sustainability *within* states, democratic self-determination and nation-state sovereignty are on a certain collision course in global policymaking.

The goal of universal human rights, the original mission of the UN, requires radical rethinking if that organization is to take on the nation-state building role forced upon it in places like East Timor. In addition to the string of humanitarian disasters to which it turned its attention in the 1990s (Haiti, Iraq, Somalia, Rwanda, Bosnia), it is now expected to marshal the skills required to help newly emerging nations establish enduring democracies. For the UN to succeed in that challenging task requires far better tools for the job than it now possesses. Although the establishment of administrative and judicial systems is well within the UN's expertise, it is not equipped to assist with comprehensive framework building.[27] For example, what can the UN do to help an emerging democracy in which an entrenched plu-tocracy owns almost everything, as in Haiti? Yet the stability that democracy requires is certain to remain elusive so long as a structure of rank injustice remains. Surely U.S. leadership in this international body could ensure that a vigorous commitment is made to assist na-tions—including newly emerging nations—in their embrace of funda-mental elements of equity and sustainability.

During the First Hundred Days, a populist president would propose an international charter that adds a new dimension of moral authority to our foreign policy by setting our sights on a higher state of unity within the human community. To endure, every alliance must have a purpose. Some of those alliances—forged in the white heat of a war fought a half-century ago—have lost their focus. Their purpose should be revisited, updated, and restated. Some alliances have evolved into economic blocs whose purpose shifts with the prevailing winds of global trade. It does little good to keep our allies together while losing sight of where we hope to go. Formerly united around opposition to political evils since largely dispersed, our alliances should now be mustered to vanquish a far more intractable foe: poverty.

The alleviation of poverty remains the implied but unfulfilled promise of global democracy. Its elimination offers the only conceivable moral focus of a post–Cold War foreign policy. Its eradication offers the best hope for a world united as humans rather than divided by ethnicity, nationality, and ideology. Although we may not be able to evoke a genuinely global prosperity, the stamping out of poverty is essential to the enduring peace and stability that progress requires in a globalizing economy. Certainly nuclear disarmament is unlikely without agreement on new political and economic relationships. Lasting peace is best achieved by alliances that wage war on this oldest of human enemies, as we seek a remedy for the human family's oldest affliction. Emerging political and economic alliances, increasingly regional in scope, could do much to coordinate the resources that this challenge requires.

Needed: A Generosity Strategy

The frontiers of foreign policy lie in lands where the human spirit remains trammeled by the forces of intolerance, ethnic hatred, and nationalist fervor. Of the sixty-one major armed conflicts fought between 1989 and 1998, only three were between nations; the rest were civil.[28] Multiple factors influence these events, but underlying all of them are the daily degradations of poverty that afflict two-thirds of the world's people, a condition worsened by the steadily widening gap between the haves and the have-nots. It is those challenges for which the United States should seek its allies, and it is in those spheres that we should wield our influence. If we mean to offer a leadership relevant to today's needs, it is toward the sound of those battles that we must march. If we fail to pursue that higher level of humanity and global harmony when there's so little now stopping us, the failure can only reflect a lack of historical perspective and a profound failure of wisdom.

Given the widespread deprivation, degradation, and disease that afflict the human community, we must ground our foreign policy in *our unwillingness to allow others to suffer*. Not only is that the best way to secure the foundation of our own happiness, it also offers the only theme on which our national honor can reliably be based. In addition, it provides the best offense we could mount against terrorism, the most immediate threat to national security. Only an unassailably *moral* agenda can isolate those who justify their violence on moral grounds. Although it's not essential that we make life easy, we must at least do our part to make life possible. Even more fundamentally, the more attention that we as a nation give to *giving*, to actions motivated by our heartfelt concern for others, the more we will address the mental and emotional afflictions of modern society. That national effort could help remedy the isolation, the sense of hopelessness, the anxiety, the cynicism, and the pervasive lack of commitment and contentment that stands like a shadow between us and our happiness as a people.

If we can but master this path, as I'm confident we can, we will steadily gain the international support required to evoke a genuinely global democracy. History has proven time and again—twice in the twentieth century alone with two horrific world wars—that we are most fully a democracy when we lose ourselves in service to others. Fully absorbed in our pursuit of a higher calling, we consistently rediscover the generosity that lies latent in this nation's soul. The fruit of that service is a clear and peaceful national conscience. The fruit of that clear and peaceful conscience will be a world more widely characterized by peace. And peace, I suggest, is the only admissible evidence of the wisdom of our foreign policy because peace is essential in order for the institutions of democracy to work. The next world war must be waged in our hearts, with *applied* altruism our strategic weapon and a culture of generosity our battle plan. We know that democracy, despite its imperfections, is the system of government closest to humanity's essential nature. If we follow Gandhi's sage advice ("Let us become the change we want to see in the world."), we'll find that the essential groundwork for lasting peace lies in providing our people an opportunity to participate in initiatives that feed a national appetite too long starved of nourishment for the democratic soul.

Escape from Poverty

We've only just begun to identify methods with a proven track record of success in assisting entire nations to escape from poverty. Rather than simply giving poverty a new name every four years, the First

Hundred Days would declare war on it—both here and abroad. Now that we've won everything for which we fought, it's time to fight for what we really need. That requires not only a beefed-up Peace Corps but also a vibrant "Prosperity Corps." As a result of U.S. investment in education over the past half-century, including educating many from other lands, we now have access to a worldwide network of knowledge and practical skills that can be mustered to improve life in other countries. Today's profound disproportion in knowledge distribution is itself one of the key imbalances in economic development between rich and poor, as Amartya Sen, Indian-born professor at Cambridge and Harvard and 1998 Nobel economist, points out in *Development as Freedom*.[29] Without a well-educated workforce, globalization opportunities are useless (or worse) because people lack the skills to seize those opportunities. Communist China invested in education and now thrives in the world economy; democratic India did not and languishes.

Even our lesser-educated people could make a valuable contribution by helping others meet pressing needs for food, sanitation, clean water, primary education (especially for women), disease prevention, primary health care, transportation, and environmental restoration. As Sen points out, development must guarantee certain liberties, including freedom from hunger, from illiteracy, from premature death from lack of health care, and from the tyranny of undemocratic governments, which tend to ignore the poorest. That was the promise of the Universal Declaration of Human Rights adopted by the UN in 1948. You don't need to be a member of the "learning class" to be a force for positive change in Third World countries. What's required is good intentions, modest training, and the support of governments (including ours) willing to abandon today's radical laissez-faire attitude toward the alleviation of global misery. Surely hunger must rank as the clearest indicator of a lack of democracy. No famine has ever occurred in a democracy, according to a much-circulated account by Sen. No one has yet produced evidence to refute him.

The risks that accompany inertia are rising. The common denominator in those countries that have experienced war, famine, and upheaval in recent decades has been some combination of population growth and poverty accompanied by urban overcrowding or a severe strain on natural resources.[30] That was the case in Haiti, Ethiopia, Iran, Algeria, Nicaragua, Indonesia, Sierra Leone, Somalia, Yemen, and Rwanda.

Pakistan is the most recent country to suffer from these deprivations. Its 135 million people are drawn to vast cities and fetid urban slums with inadequate electrical, water, sewage, and transportation systems. Or they remain on farmland, where alkaline, nutrient-depleted soil and a fast-receding water table make the shantytowns look attractive by comparison. Education is nonexistent for many youth, as are job prospects. With impersonal urbanization comes weakened family links and the loss of social cohesion found in village life. Extremist religion often fills that void, along with the tensions that accompany regional and ethnic pride. Without a unifying force, governance becomes ever more difficult absent tyrannical means. Three hundred families (who openly call themselves the feudals) own the bulk of anything worthwhile and dominate Pakistani politics. With the state increasingly unable to provide expected services, the people (and the politicians) turn to ethnic and tribal patronage for support. Yet the urban poor grow ever more ambitious and angry because they've become dependent on a failing state (they can't grow their own food). They're also crowded together in a way that makes communication easy, and in-the-streets revolt an everyday possibility. Picture this: the unraveling of a nuclear Yugoslavia with a birth rate that could double this unstable nation's population in one generation.

Reforestation and Remediation

There is much that can be done, both in Pakistan and elsewhere, using proven and inexpensive development tools. In Africa, for example, portions of the sub-Saharan desert—a region notorious for endemic poverty—could be made fertile, much like how the Israelis converted many square miles of desert into green valleys. Our mothballed troop transports (hundreds of them lie idle in Virginia's James River) could be refurbished as the vanguard of a reforestation fleet for transporting seedlings and trained personnel to needy locales, whether to create orchards in Africa or to reforest poverty-plagued Haiti. Rather then fund defense-oriented bombing fleets, we could fund offense-oriented desalination and water purification plants, providing people with the fresh water needed to become self-sufficient (as mentioned in Chapter 2, 1.3 billion people lack access to fresh drinking water). The magnitude of the funds that could be converted to such uses is staggering. For instance, if we cut money for the entire F-22 and FA-18 E/F fighter jet program, we would liberate enough funds ($112 billion) to rebuild or repair every school in the United States.[31] Imagine what even a small portion of those funds could do abroad if directed to a global prosperity offensive.

Breakthroughs in ecological design suggest enormous potential for demonstration projects that could be showcased by the Prosperity

Corps working in conjunction with what might well mature into an "environmental remediation fleet." For example, biologist John Todd's "Living Machines" use eco-technologies to biologically purify and recycle wastewater. Using no chemicals (too expensive for developing countries) and producing small amounts of recyclable sludge (useful for fertilizer), a Living Machine wastewater treatment facility borrows its design from estuary ecosystems and includes a variety of organisms, from bacteria to plants and animals, including mollusks, snails, and fish. Contained in a medium-sized greenhouse, the Living Machine on display in Providence, Rhode Island, consists of a series of interlocking tubs through which wastewater flows in successive order, with various living organisms biologically degrading contaminants by treating them as food. Thus wastewater becomes not a nuisance but a habitat. Where sewage systems (versus, say, on-site composting toilets) are prevalent, Todd's Living Machines provide a way for Prosperity Corps recruits to demonstrate sustainable development strategies while also providing a focal point for ecological education.

Another of Todd's ecological contraptions was designed to clean up a polluted lake. On a raft, he mounted a wind- and solar-powered windmill that generated electricity to charge batteries which, in turn, drive two air compressors. The compressors lift huge volumes of water—up to 100,000 gallons per day—off the bottom of the lake and deposit it in the first of a series of nine cells. The cells contain a diversity of microorganisms, including beneficial bacteria, and nutrients to compensate for those lacking in the lake. In addition, specialized plants are mounted on racks, their roots allowed to hang into the water. Passage of water through each of the cells improves the water quality while removing the toxic chemicals and other pathogens attributed to chemical-laded groundwater leaching from a nearby landfill and sewage contamination. As an electricity-driven propeller stirs up pollutants that settled to the bottom, they are slowly absorbed into the plants' roots. Todd's eco-technology, which was physically and mechanically rather simple, quickly reestablished in the lake a symbiotic community of organisms that, in concert, cleaned up the water. Despite the continuing infusion of contaminated groundwater, the lake was soon reopened for swimming and even the bottom-feeding fish tested OK for cleanliness. Called restorers, these low-cost, low-tech devices proved that the biorestoration of water is both viable and cost-effective, substituting ecological technology for chemical and mechanical means. Restorers are now employed in a broad array of cleanup assignments worldwide.[32]

Paul Stamets adds to Todd's water purification system the notion of using mycelia (masses of microscopic, rootlike fungal structures) as an upstream biological filter. Because of their extensive branching, more than a mile of mycelia can permeate a cubic inch of soil. Fungal mats are the planet's largest biological entities; some cover more than 20,000 acres. Surrounding and penetrating the roots of grasses, shrubs, and trees, these organic sponges increase the soil's water absorption capacity ten- to a hundredfold. That assists plants in their quest for water by increasing the moisture-holding capacity of soils and forming buffer zones around streams to filter runoff from farms, highways, and suburbs. Mycologically rich zones attract insects, many of which lay larvae (food for fish) and foster bird life.

Mycelial mats also produce enzymes and acids that break apart hydrocarbons, the chemical structure common to petroleum products, polychlorinated biphenyls (PCBs), and pesticides. A recent test of bioremediation methods in Washington State (what Stamets calls mycoremediation) found that the living mycelia of oyster mushrooms broke down the toxic alkanes in petrol-contaminated soil (the mushrooms were later tested and found free of any petroleum products). Flies were attracted as the mushrooms rotted away. The flies drew other insects, which attracted birds, which brought in seeds, converting the previously toxic pile into an oasis of rich topsoil that could serve as a host to plants, which in turn use photosynthesis to manufacture their own food. "I am continually bemused," Stamets notes, "that humans 'discover' what nature has known all along."[33]

It is just this sort of eco-tech-intensive applied knowledge that could empower people in other countries to empower themselves. Soil is the most essential and the least understood of nature's many assets. In sub-Saharan Africa, once home to over one hundred forgotten grains and over two thousand forgotten crops, the *wealth* (from the Latin for "well-being") of farmers there may initially be measured in terms that Stamets recommends—in the yield of nutrient-rich soil and adaptive organisms that they can identify under their feet. With the help of living-systems' eco-technologies, their prosperity can be restored.

Poverty and Sustainability

Clean water, fresh foods, and adequate sanitation are essential components of any development strategy. Without those—and without ecological stability and vitality—disease is certain. The notion that poor health reinforces poverty is less well known than the idea that poverty causes ill health. Both are true. Early deaths present a huge impediment to development. Yet a 1999 report by the World Health Organization (WHO) found that just six ailments—AIDS, tuberculosis, malaria, measles, diarrheal disease, and pneumonia—killed 90 percent of those who died before their forty-fifth birthdays in 1998. All of these diseases are preventable, most quite cheaply. Yet governments spend sixty times as much on armaments as on disease prevention. Six times as many people have died of AIDS, malaria, and tuberculosis than in all the military conflicts of the last half-century. More than 150 million people are dead from these diseases just since 1945. That compares with 23 million who died in combat. More than 5 million Americans died of infectious diseases during that period. For nine countries in AIDS-infected Africa, life expectancy is projected to drop seventeen years by 2010, back to the levels of the 1960s.[34]

We share one world with two very different fates. Of children who die before age five, 98 percent are in the developing world. One-third of all children under five in these countries are malnourished and physically stunted—with profound implications for them, for the societies in which they live, and for those of us who turn a blind eye to their plight.

With the emergence of a genuine global village, it's difficult to overstate the potential threat posed by the spread of infectious disease, particularly in light of the rising worldwide resistance to antibiotics. The WHO report documents that tuberculosis drugs no longer work effectively in one of five patients in Eastern Europe, while anti-malaria drugs have lost much of their punch in Asia and Africa. An estimated one-quarter of childhood malaria deaths could be prevented if children in affected areas slept under mosquito netting treated with insecticide. Netting and a year's supply of insecticide cost about $11, "less than one hour's parking in New York, Paris, or Tokyo," the report notes. To be sustainable, development must be paired with disease control and prevention. Because of the fundamental interconnectedness that lies at the heart of globalization, what was previously "their" problem has now become ours. Sardines are now infected with the herpes virus, Antarctic seals have contracted canine distemper, and reefs are being destroyed by what was previously soilborne fungi.[35]

We've reached a point where we can best look out for our own good by contributing wholeheartedly to a common good. As the Dalai Lama advises: "Be selfish, think about others."[36] Indeed, we may yet discover—as all the world's wisdom traditions avow—that the greatest happiness flows from acting out of concern for others in the realization that the distinction between self and others is in some sense an exaggeration. For those who find this concept idealistic, I suggest that ideals have always been the engine of progress. Certainly that was the case with the founding of this nation, as reflected in its remarkably idealistic charter. My hope is that this book may help restore faith in our idealism.

A 1999 survey conducted for the *Wall Street Journal* and NBC News confirms that our deeply ingrained feelings of isolationism and nationalism remain intact. By a three-to-one margin we worry more about becoming "too involved" in world affairs than about being "too isolated."[37] At the same time, however, by a 69- to 19-percent margin, we worry more about too much immigration than about too much population growth here at home. I suggest that a foreign policy focused on fostering prosperity for others is the most sensible middle road—boosting living standards abroad to control immigration here while also fostering social equity in other nations to forestall flare-ups that may entice us into foreign entanglements. Paradoxically, isolationism only works when combined with an engaged globalism.

Low-Tech Prosperity

I offer here a few more examples of the tools we could offer to advance shared prosperity and sustainability—the principal uses to which I suggest that we put "America's primacy," as foreign-policy experts artfully phrase it. For instance, since 1988, Ralf Hotchkiss of San Francisco–based Whirlwind Wheelchair International has been training people how to locally fabricate wheelchairs to assist with the social integration of people with disabilities.[38] He found that more than 20 million people in developing countries are confined to their homes because of a lack of affordable and suitable wheelchairs. Responding to that need, the company designed a prototype rough-terrain, lightweight, low-tech, high-performance wheelchair that can be fashioned largely from locally sourced materials. It is that sort of heart-felt human-touch response to local needs that should become the hallmark of this World War on poverty.

We would do well to replicate the best examples of what people are already doing, taking our guidance from what's known in development circles as "positive deviants," that is, cases of unexpectedly good outcome within an area of adversity. Jerry Sternin, director of Save the Children's Egypt office, was the first to introduce me to that notion through his work on malnutrition among children in Vietnam. In devising a program, he starts not from needs but from a respect for current resources and successes—what he calls indigenous wisdom. His research found that 15 percent of Vietnamese children were well fed and healthy. That's because their parents supplemented the diet of these positive deviants with protein-rich shrimp and crabs from nearby rice paddies along with the nutrient-rich green tops of sweet potatoes. By replicating that positive but deviant practice more generally and supplementing it as needed, nutrition levels were raised such that 93 percent of the children were rehabilitated. The lesson here is that the problem itself often evokes a self-correcting response—in this case as parents were motivated to grow wiser.

Part of the development challenge lies in identifying that embedded wisdom—what poet Alexander Pope calls "consulting the genius of the place"—as therein may lie a solution available to everyone. This development strategy qualifies as "populist" because it recognizes that if people are granted respect—and provided information and tools—they will assume responsibility for solving their own problems. No neat formula for development fits every country. That remains one of the key fallacies in trying to spread cookie-cutter solutions around the planet in the name of economic growth, usually with a high dose of hydrocarbon-intensive industry as its core component. Each country needs support for identifying its own formula for development consistent with its traditions, capacities, and resources.

Innovative financing offers another opportunity in need of our attention. As the epicenter of global capitalism, the United States enjoys a native intelligence, primarily found in our remarkable financial skills. That national asset, the "indigenous wisdom" of a capitalist culture, could be tapped as a force for the common good. For instance, with quite modest amounts of capital, microcredit-financed entrepreneurs have become a major stimulus for development in many countries, fostering dignity, confidence, and economic self-reliance in ways never before seen. With the intensive application of financial, organizational, and information skills—abundant in the United States—small-scale, locally owned enterprises could become a key ingredient of the policy mix needed to eradicate poverty in an environmentally sound fashion. With our assistance, those loans could be bundled into securities for sale in global capital markets, vastly expanding the amount of funds that could be drawn into microenterprise development.

The Spirit of Sustainability

Demonstration projects could also play a key role, particularly when replicable on a low-cost basis utilizing abundant local labor. For example, environmental artist and activist Betsy Damon traveled on her own initiative to the Sichuan province of China to propose and then lead a project resulting in a six-acre "Living Water Garden." Constructed alongside the filthy Fu-Nan rivers, where 60,000 cubic meters of raw sewage are dumped every day, the park is designed to underscore the vital link between water and human health. Water drawn from the river circulates through a series of pools, its quality slowly improving as it trickles through settling ponds, aerating flow forms, wetlands, and fish ponds before flowing into a stone fountain landscape, where children play in the cleaned-up water before it returns to the river. Like all good design, it combines aesthetics and practicality. By combining education, recreation, and art in one project, Damon provides a model of real solutions for urban environments with the goal of ensuring that successive generations grow up knowing how water works and what's required to keep it healthy. The riverfront park, completed in 1998, has been designated a national tourist site and now serves as a source of local pride for a population of 9 million in the city of Chengdu. Easily replicable and scaled up, Damon's Living Water Garden would make an excellent entrée on a menu of projects that the Prosperity Corps could offer abroad.

Because such projects are hugely labor-intensive, they provide an appealing way to transform unemployment into environmental sustainability, a much-overlooked component of long-term prosperity. The International Labor Organization reports that more than 1 billion people worldwide need and cannot find work. With 2 billion people under age twenty entering the global workforce over the next two decades, the "demonstration potential" of such eco-projects is enormous.

The range of potential job-creating environmental-restoration projects is vast. In China, for instance, trees now cover only 14 percent of its huge land mass, well below the world average of 25 percent. Logging, overgrazing, industrial development, and poor irrigation have left 28 percent of China as desert, useless for farming until the soil is restored. Less than 20 percent of China's municipal waste receives any treatment, creating some of the foulest rivers on earth. The Pearl River has been popularly renamed the Black Dragon River because pollutants have turned it the color of night. Host to some of the world's worst air pollution, China can now claim respiratory disease as its leading cause of death, according to the World Resources Institute.

Many of the needs that could be met with modest aid from the United States have to do with matters that directly touch the human spirit. In many countries, women are taking the leadership role. Take Zimbabwe, for example. For Zimbabwean women watching their neighbors succumb slowly to AIDS, deaths are not statistics but friends with children facing lonely futures. An estimated 22.3 million people in sub-Saharan Africa are HIV-positive, 55 percent of them women. The UN reports that AIDS has already left 11 million orphans, mostly in southern Africa. Unable to wait for outside solutions to flow to the "forgotten continent," these women devised their own. At great personal sacrifice, they volunteer time to care for the ill and watch over their children, often traveling great distances to clean beds, cook food, wash clothing, console the dying, and comfort the living. Sustained by group singing and community spirit, they care for hundreds. What do they need? Not much. With the help of New York–based Synergos, one of our most creative nonprofits, they were provided uniforms to mark their new roles and bicycles to help them travel the long miles between homes.

What could we and our children learn from our support for such activities? We'd learn again what it means to bind together as a caring community and to expand the scope of community. We'd learn the art of giving and intergenerational caring. We'd learn how diverse cultures view the suffering of others as their own. Through exposure to poverty, deprivation, and other pain, we'd learn to open our hearts (and our wallets) and to cherish again the enormous blessings with which we've been graced in this country. We'd experience the mystery of premature death the challenge of raising an orphaned child, and the unique tenderness required in caring for a dying infant. And, if we're lucky, we'll learn to touch again through song the soulful spirit that animates all things worthwhile on this side of death. In short, we'd learn better how to *truly* prosper because it's only in giving full expression to the generosity of the human heart that we'll rediscover what lies at the heart of democracy.

Toward a Principled Foreign Policy

There comes a time in every great nation's history when it must revisit its purpose, restate its principles, and craft anew the values to which its people intend to be bound. For us, that time is now. We can look back with justifiable pride at the courageous stands we've taken against oppression and aggression, and at the costs we've borne in support of the transcendental values we share—freedom, equality, tolerance, self-determination. The question now becomes how do we redefine the national interest in a way that has resonance and relevance for today's fractious, interdependent, and increasingly global world? I suggest here that the issue is no longer how to make the nation-state stronger; it's about how to make our hearts grow larger. It is less about how to change the outside world and more about how we shift our personal values. That shift is essential if we are to sustain the resolve required to remedy conditions such as poverty, which people have assumed were intractable throughout history. I'm confident that our nation is populated by people who will rise to the challenge of ending poverty worldwide. We've proven time and again that when we set a goal, we can attain it, whether it's putting a man on the moon, defeating communism, or making obscene amounts of money in globalized capital markets. We have this annoying habit of believing that we really can change the world. With proper leadership, this "impossible" challenge is certain to summon America's optimistic, can-do spirit.

One aspect of this new post–Cold War era in foreign policy is crystal clear: History's sovereign-centric version of foreign policy requires something new. Although state-to-state relations must remain a key focus of foreign policy, the role of nongovernmental organizations must increase, particularly those that foster people-to-people exchanges. While protection, restoration, and remediation of the natural environment must be a linchpin of any principled foreign policy, the preservation and celebration of the world's cultural environment should also have priority in our foreign engagements. For that purpose, the First Hundred Days should include a statement of principle indicating how the United States—comprising many cultures yet one people—would pursue a post-sovereign foreign policy, directed not just from Washington but also from local communities. In sharing the richness of our melting-pot cultures through a community-initiated Culture Corps, we would learn how better to appreciate the wide spectrum of personal experiences that make up the human community.

In a world inhabited by more than five thousand cultures, including those of some three hundred indigenous peoples and a vast variety within those (the United States is home to more than five hundred Native American tribes), we must abandon the stingy isolationism and the naive nationalism that have been the hallmark of recent Congresses. Our notion of community is contracting, precisely when it most needs to expand. In the same way that two stones cannot occupy the same space but a single fragrance can, two sovereign states cannot occupy the same physical space, but mutual respect and a love of liberty can.[39]

U.S. financial dominance abroad has been accompanied by a form of cultural imperialism that others, including many among our allies, find obnoxious. In most any toy store worldwide you can now find the same blonde, blue-eyed Barbie dolls and Rambos with machine guns. In 1999, the French opposed what they call "McDomination" when the United States levied high tariffs on Roquefort cheese, pâté de foie gras, and other French imports in retaliation for their policy disallowing the import of our hormone-treated beef. Jose Bove, a French farmer, emerged as a national hero when he was jailed for leading a protest that trashed an under-construction McDonald's in Millau. "There have been three totalitarian forces in our lifetime," observed Bove, who supplies sheep's milk to makers of Roquefort cheese. "The totalitarianism of fascism, of communism and now of capitalism. How can people try and tell us we must import hormone-enhanced beef? What is that?"[40] Our answer: that's our Chicago-style version of free trade.

Culture-nomics

Today's flow of culture—movies, music, television, fashion, fast food— is unbalanced, heavily weighted in one direction. Writing in *Foreign Affairs*, Harvard's Samuel Huntington warned that elites in countries representing two-thirds of the world's population—Chinese, Russians, Indians, Arabs, Muslims, and Africans—view the United States as "the single greatest threat to their societies." They view us not as a military threat but a political and cultural threat—intrusive, interventionist, and hypocritical, engaging in financial imperialism and intellectual colonialism. In all human relations, politics and otherwise, few things are as damaging as conveying a sense of superiority. Bemoaning the trashy nature of much of the so-called culture that we export and cautioning that "these effusions become the laughingstock of intelligent and sensitive people the world over," George Kennan laments that we must "appear to many abroad, despite our military superiority, as the world's intellectual and spiritual dunce, until we can change our image of ourselves we purvey to others."[41]

In addition to sending our variegated cultures and our prosperity-inducing emissaries abroad, a modern-day populist president would also use the White House as a venue for showcasing (and televising) the world's diverse cultures. As the home for its First Family, the White House could serve as the congenial setting from which viewing audiences worldwide could deepen their understanding of the rich diversity of human culture. As Mahatma Gandhi expressed so eloquently, "I do not want my house to be walled in on all sides and my windows to be stuffed. I want the cultures of all the lands to be blown about my house as freely as possible. But I refuse to be blown off my feet by any." The celebration of native dress, dance, and music is a universal theme. Sustained, in-depth, and ongoing exposure to the richness of the human family's diversity can only enhance tolerance and deepen appreciation of other ways of life. That's a key missing ingredient in improving the quality and the stability of our foreign relations and in advancing the values that underlie democracy.

Like incense, democracy has powers of diffusion and penetration. Its values need not be spoken so much as shown. Yet there's a fine line here that must not be crossed. In Kennan's view, "This whole tendency to see ourselves as the center of political enlightenment and as teachers to a great part of the rest of the world strikes me as unthought-through, vainglorious and undesirable." The challenge lies in our ability to undertake this initiative with grace, humility, and heartfelt hospitality—and in the spirit of simply enabling the human family to celebrate itself. The worldwide embrace of human diversity requires that we learn to suspend judgment and put aside the culture-specific filters through which we view the world. Any process advancing that perspective is destined to enhance international harmony as the global community learns to embrace the similarities underlying our external differences. As we begin to live as if we are a global family, we will become one. Members of the Native American Muscogee tribe from southern Alabama use the greeting *Ash-te-he* ("I am you being me"). South Africans have a similar phrase (*Ubuntu*) to denote that a person becomes a person through others. Likewise Mayans in whose language *In lake'ch* means "I am another yourself." It is in that spirit that I suggest we turn to culture as a doorway to advancing global harmony.

For a nation that aspires to play a leadership role in a globalized world, we remain strangely removed, even provincial. Fully a third of our members of Congress do not have passports. Some even brag about it. No wonder our perspective appears to others so narrow and our ignorance of interdependence so very profound. In today's complex world, we narrow the scope of our national interest at our peril.

Kenny Ausubel, founder of the Santa Fe–based Collective Heritage Institute, notes that "one of our greatest strengths is our ability to grow culture very quickly."[42] With appropriate leadership and institutional support, we could within a single generation evoke a world-wide Earth-honoring culture. Keep in mind that the industrial era represents only 10 generations out of some 17,000–35,000 generations of human history. Ten generations from now, the culture that emerged alongside the industrial age might well be considered a curious aberration. Certainly there is much that we could learn from exposure to cultures that have long lived in a sustainable relationship with their environment. This cultural exchange could help us realize that what needs to be sustained is not mindless economic growth and ever-expanding consumption but the mindfulness essential to sustaining the web of life.

Prosperity Policy

During the First Hundred Days of a populist president's administration, a founding charter for the Prosperity Corps would be crafted. The goal should be not just to liberate people from material deprivation but also, where appropriate, to address the educational, social, and cultural isolation from which many seek liberation. Long term, it is those steadily thickening webs of personal, cultural, and commercial relationships that will serve as the best means to ensure our national security. Abraham Lincoln phrased the challenge best: "Do we not destroy our enemies when we turn them into our friends?"

Our national interest is best pursued by going well beyond today's shallow goal of creating export markets for U.S.-made goods. Although that may prove the economic icing on our foreign-policy cake, the more promising challenge lies in how best to create opportunities for Americans to give of themselves to others. While our material wealth has grown, our spiritual wealth as a nation has atrophied as our national interest became far too closely identified with our financial interests. The Prosperity Corps and the Culture Corps offer the potential for American youth, including those so cruelly marginalized, to discover the richness available in giving of themselves to others. In return, that gift could qualify them for vouchers redeemable in education, training, and affordable housing, much as the G.I. Bill provided it a half-century ago. National service has much to recommend it. As head of America's Promise, a volunteer-based organization, General Colin Powell sums up the potential advantage to our youth: "It helps them learn the joy of serving others, but at the same time it gives them a chance to exercise responsibility, to discover new strengths and talents within themselves and to feel that they are important and that their lives matter."

An Unaffordable Agnosticism

Fundamental to all this is the need to reject the ownership-pattern indifference that has long epitomized our foreign policy, ensuring that even the most outrageous results escape criticism. When it comes to ownership, an embarrassed and awkward agnosticism silences us. For example, during George Bush's Gulf War, a tight-lipped "no comment" prevailed while American lives were put at risk to secure not only our energy supplies but also the property of our suppliers, the region's oil oligarchs. Rather than dare hint at the need to reform ownership patterns that leave the vast majority of the world's 1.2 billion Muslims living lives plagued by poverty and bereft of democracy, we in the Islam-phobic West point instead to fundamentalist fervor as the cause rather than the effect of growing discontent in this long unstable region. George Kennan cautioned a half-century ago that the real challenge for the United States is to possess "a spiritual vitality capable of holding its own among the major ideological currents of the time." That still rings true. That's why our national security must be grounded not in force but in influence based on fairness. Any sustainable strategy for advancing global security *among* nations must include support for initiatives that strengthen social solidarity *within* nations. As Pope John VI put it, "If you want peace, work for justice." A global democracy requires global justice.

Our current foreign-policy corps chooses instead to divert its eyes, deflecting criticism at rampant economic injustice worldwide while dithering away opportunities to propose a morally sound and socially just form of global free enterprise. Instead, the very limited values of financial capital and the very narrow dictates of free trade have become the measures by which we gauge our foreign-policy success. From the perspective of others, our push for open markets looks like a convenient justification for quickening the pace at which more efficient U.S. firms dominate global markets. With finance-led capitalism now ascendant, the New World Order is steadily reshaping itself to the dictates of Wall Street. Add to that a world in which the domain of dollars has achieved priority in both private- and public-sector decisionmaking, and we can see the clear outline of a global financial architecture that's being rebuilt to Wall Street's building codes. Even among our major allies in London, Paris, and Berlin, there is "increasing disgust," says commentator Stephan-Goetz Richter, with the "quasi-imperialist dominance of the United States in all matters financial."[43] The disgust is even more understandable in light of the policies embraced by an isolationist-inclined Congress that has only reluctantly funded a portion of our agreed-to component of the UN budget while steadily cutting back on the quite modest funds provided for the State Department's U.S. Agency for International Development (USAID).

Disillusionomics

Rather than address the steadily widening gulf between the haves and the have-nots, the United States proceeds as though this disparity is a regrettable but unavoidable consequence of the otherwise beneficent spread of free enterprise and the unfettered flow of funds worldwide. Although this ideology, routinely disguised as economics, is gleefully parroted by the haves, the growing legions of have-nots, both domestically and abroad, find it increasingly unpersuasive.

Citing this widening rich-poor gap as evidence of a "failure of American leadership," former USAID Director Brian Atwood predicts that "you'll see democracies being defeated and radical leaders coming into office. . . . Clearly you could see more countries becoming anarchies in Africa. You certainly could see that as a possibility in Russia."[44] After serving six years as head of USAID, longer than all but one other person, Atwood insists that U.S. foreign-aid policies should spread the benefits of development throughout poor societies rather than restricting them to former ruling classes, which is the case now: "When only a small percentage of a population enjoys the benefits of democracy, disillusionment sets in."[45]

Atwood elaborates in a remarkably candid interview before he returned to private life in June 1999:

We hear a lot about the democratic revolutions around the world. But what we don't hear about is this growing gap between rich and poor, and that is a poisonous mix. That is going to create crises in the future. What will it take to wake up our political leaders? More failed states? More wars? More south-to-north migration? More transmission of infectious diseases? More terrorism? . . . [The government's international affairs budget is] a joke. There is no money to do anything. It's outrageous.[46]

The current Congress is profoundly out of touch with what the public expects in the way of aid we provide other countries. Nearly 60 percent of Americans believe that Washington spends more on foreign aid than on Medicare, when in reality Medicare accounts for 13 percent of the federal budget, and foreign aid less than 2 percent. (The survey respondents thought that foreign aid consumed 26 percent.) When asked how much of the budget *should be* allocated to foreign aid, the average response was 13 percent, fully six times more than what we now spend.[47] Americans are prepared to address today's destabilizing and inhumane gap between rich and poor. If we hope to avoid the crises that Atwood foresees, we need only do what the public thinks we're already doing: devote more resources to improving the living standards of others.

A World Awash in Capital and Bereft of Capitalists

Kennan cautioned fifty years ago that "the issue of Soviet-American relations is in essence a test of the overall worth of the United States." With the Dow Jones Industrial Average surging beyond 11,000 in May 1999, it's worth noting that Kennan made his point by citing Thomas Mann's classic novel *Buddenbrooks* and its warning that "human institutions often show the greatest outward brilliance at a moment when inner decay is in reality farthest advanced." An apt analogy is a star whose light shines brightly when in reality it is the afterglow of a distant constellation that has long since ceased to exist. Keynes made a similar point a decade before Kennan did, predicting that the grandchildren of his generation (i.e., today's baby boomers) would be able to recognize as vices those things then proclaimed as virtues.

If the very limited concerns of financial capital are to continue to play such a dominant role in foreign affairs, then the human community needs—at the very least—to be protected from two of capitalism's most well-documented weaknesses: its tendency to concentrate ownership, and its tendency to regard as inconsequential its impact on a broad range of nonfinancial values. On that score, it's fair to say that capitalism's chief adversary is now capitalism itself. Shortly before his death, futurist Willis Harman, founder of the World Business Academy, posed a haunting question, "If capitalism were dying, would we recognize the signs?"

Communism collapsed when no one expected it. The CIA missed it completely. Should we continue to ignore clear signs of fragility, smug in our Chicago-school certainty that financial markets will somehow make all things right? In the same way that health care is moving toward promotive and preventive measures, we need to do the same for capitalism. The G-8 (the United States, Germany, Japan, the United Kingdom, Italy, France, Canada, and Russia) acknowledged as much in October 1998, calling for a "new international financial architecture." Britain's Tony Blair urges a new Bretton Woods conference to rewrite the international rules that gave us the World Bank and the IMF. In the same way that we're creating designs to remove environmental toxicity from our production technology, shouldn't we create designs to remove toxic ownership patterns from our financial technology—particularly as we export that technology abroad? After all, those patterns create the social and economic context in which democracies are embedded.

The stakes are extraordinarily high. In Kennan's words—still relevant today—what we face is a "struggle for the very soul of America." If the United States is to regain its moral leadership, as distinguished from its lead in military and financial affairs, it must jettison its indifference about today's fast-widening economic disparities. Despite the central role played by private property in the success of free enterprise, the global community has yet to see the United States work at extending the ownership benefits of capitalism universally—either domestically or abroad. In the eyes of the global community, that makes our motives highly suspect. It must appear to others that we would be delighted with a world in which we own everything—while everyone else should be delighted to work for us.

In much the same way that colonialism insisted on keeping nations dependent on foreign-manufactured goods, the Washington–Wall Street consensus insists that developing nations (1) emphasize exports as a way to generate foreign exchange (to buy our products), (2) welcome foreign investors (including us) as increasingly dominant owners, and (3) agree that the World Trade Organization should overrule local policies that interfere with the free flow of goods and capital. Local elites, of course, are happy to rely on export earnings and foreign borrowing to keep their fortunes intact and to maintain low tax rates. Our patently self-serving policy mix must also make it seem to others as though we care nothing for the fate of the natural world as we promote the spread of free markets with no concern for whether pricing signals reflect the true costs imposed on the environment.

We know that anti-private-property Marxist/Leninist systems do not work. History has proven time and again that they cannot endure absent the force required to hold them in place. Yet history is also clear on another point: Capitalism does not *naturally* create capitalists. The capital is there. So is the capitalism. The missing ingredient has long been the capitalists. For capitalism to become a creator of capitalists, foresighted leadership is required not only among those in the private sector—corporate directors, managers, and labor leaders—but also among those in the legislative corps worldwide who have long condoned a policy environment that perpetuates today's unconscionable disparities and unsustainable practices. Continued inaction is a decision in favor of eventual political destabilization. The world community needs to convene a populist-inspired international assembly to commence negotiations on the cooperation required for a global financial architecture that ensures progress in these crucial areas. Time is of the essence; the best time to set the stage for such an assembly would be during a populist president's First Hundred Days.

9
Restoring the Free in Free Enterprise

If a free society cannot help the many who are poor, it cannot save the few who are rich.

—JOHN F. KENNEDY

The abolition of private property is a monstrously flawed way to share our wealth. The result, so apparent in the Soviet Union, combines economic and political power in the same hands—an invitation to inefficiency, corruption, and totalitarianism. Yet today's ownership-pattern agnosticism is also tragically flawed. Most of us are routinely denied the dignity of owning a stake in a system we may well be called on to defend. That both undermines democratic values and endangers their defense. The goal, I suggest, remains as George Kennan articulated: The United States must demonstrate its "spiritual vitality" and its ability to "hold its own among the major ideological currents of the time." Private property lies at the center of both free enterprise and democracy, providing an essential framework for economic, personal, and intellectual freedom. What's missing is a foreign policy that plays to this core strength in a sensible way. A palpable sense of community achieved through shared prosperity is the logical successor to containment in a post–Cold War world. Anything less invites inequity and its political partner, instability.

We live in an age when capital markets can topple governments. That makes for a difficult choice. On the one hand, U.S. foreign policy appears to bully other nations to open their borders so that our financial sophisticates can acquire companies at bargain-basement prices. That runs roughshod over the historical fact that some of those nations, many of them allies (such as South Korea), have dedicated decades of creativity and financial sacrifice to develop their economies, pulling themselves up by their bootstraps to become world-class competitors. On the other hand, it's clear that the rampant crony capitalism common to many of those countries (including South Korea) inhibits the "creative destruction" required for them to take the next step needed to compete in the global economy. That's not to suggest that our foreign policy should make the world safe for American-style, return-maximizing capitalism. We must, however, acknowledge that capital markets serve a useful role in nudging companies—and entire economies—to meet international standards while also exposing cronyism and unresponsive oligarchies and subjecting monopolies to competition. In that sense, globalization is an engine of modernization—but only if linked to rules governing the fair treatment of people and sensible regard for our environment.

What's the answer? I suggest that the future of nations and their cultures—and of democracy—is safest when a nation's ownership resides broadly in the hands of its citizens. That insulates them from the worst abuses of crony capitalism while also enabling them to decide *for themselves* how much deference they care to grant the peculiar dictates of global financial flows, and how rapidly the insistent winds of modernism are allowed to blow across their landscapes.

The benefits of higher financial returns are not without costs, many of them quite personal. For instance, the stress associated with Japan's recession, along with the intense sense of shame provoked by record unemployment, has proven too much for many. In 1998, approximately ninety people a day committed suicide, a total of 32,863, up 34.7 percent over the previous year. It's a cruel joke to suggest that a rising tide lifts all boats. Some are certain to sink, and not necessarily in silence or in suicide. That leaves elected officials of many countries floundering to explain why they care more for this very new phenomenon of global capital markets than for the old certainties of local culture. Or why voters should tolerate the sale of the crown jewels of their economy to foreigners while many citizens continue to live below the poverty line. Add to that the volatile populist sentiments and rising nationalist concerns. For instance, given Poland's history, it's not surprising why some Poles are less than thrilled at the prospect of key Polish companies passing into the hands of German investors.

For the sake of stability, a peoplization strategy may become essential if negotiations resume on the Multilateral Agreement on Investment and its announced intention to put the force of international treaty behind the unconditional cross-border flow of financial capital. A component of genuinely peoplized and localized capitalism could counter the Chicago-inspired policy mix that suggests economic efficiency should reign supreme and that money should be free to seek its highest return regardless of what communities may think of the results. Peoplization would also provide a counterbalance to the Chicago school ideology that suggests free capital flows should take priority over transparency and democratic accountability.

Opportunities abound to collaborate on a people-first foreign policy. In the year 2000, the year of the Jubilee, considerable financial creativity could be applied to negotiate debt restructuring that would benefit the poor. According to many faiths, debts should be forgiven every fifty years; hence the Jubilee. In Tanzania, half of whose population is illiterate, a third of the budget is spent on debt payments. That's four times the amount devoted to primary education. Niger, whose population has a life expectancy of forty-seven years, spends more on debt payment than on health and education combined. Working with the Vatican and other groups affiliated with Jubilee 2000, the United States should ensure that the poor become the direct beneficiaries of much-needed debt relief. In total, forty-two so-called Heavily Indebted Poor Countries owe approximately $127 billion to the World Bank Group, international banks, and governments of rich countries.

Debt Swaps for Sustainable Development

The bulk of this debt is owed by the world's 700 million poorest people living on an average of $4 a day. In June 1999, the G-8 agreed to a program from which thirty-three mostly African countries would benefit from about $65 billion in debt relief, requiring that the resources freed be used for health and educational programs, particularly AIDS programs in Africa.[1]

About $6 billion is owed to the United States. I recommend that during our next president's First Hundred Days, 80 percent of that debt be forgiven.[2] The balance should be repaid in local currency set-asides dedicated to in-country development through microcredit, environmental projects, and education. For example, Muhamad Yunus, founder of the microcredit-pioneering Grameen Bank of Bangladesh, proposes that debt relief be linked to the willingness of countries to commit local funds for microenterprise financing. Such debt-for-development programs have enormous promise. Similar debt-swap programs should be used to acquire nature preserves, both as a way to safeguard them for posterity and as a means to generate foreign exchange through ecotourism. Education offers another opportunity. I am confident that a high-profile, people-first foreign policy would attract enthusiastic support from many U.S. teachers who would be thrilled to live abroad to share their knowledge and experience. Salaries paid in local currency could be funded with debt-for-education programs. The dollar component (for transport, U.S.-based pension funding, etc.) could be paid from a combination of federal, state, and international funds.

Education is crucial. Singaporean efficiency engineer Eng Lock Lee offers one striking example of the potential payoff from upgrading a nation's "mindware." If, for instance, an engineer specifies for a building $3 million worth of HVAC (heating, ventilating, and air conditioning) equipment, the building might raise a utility's peak load requirements by a megawatt. The increased load, in turn, requires that a utility invest several million dollars in infrastructure. If better engineering education could make the equipment 20–50 percent more efficient (a readily achievable goal with what we now know), the utility would avoid $6–15 million in present-valued investments *per engineering brain*.[3] That's at least a hundred to a thousand times the cost of the engineer's education. And that's without taking into account any savings in operating energy or foregone pollution or what could happen if the efficiency were combined with the use of renewable energy. Even one sustainability-educated engineer could train or mentor many others. That constitutes a powerful formula for sustainable development, particularly when consumers are also educated to insist on ecologically sound design and utilization. Eng relies on a well-known design adage: "All the really important mistakes are made on the first day."

One of the best things that education could do is persuade people in developing countries *not* to purchase our outdated, capital-intensive power plants such as coal-fired facilities. Once a country decides to purchase these outdated plants, it has locked in 80–90 percent of the life cycle and environmental costs. Far better that a country invests in labor-intensive factories that produce energy-efficient building materials, lamps, and appliances, reducing their *need* for energy while creating more jobs and liberating the one-quarter of global development capital now claimed by the energy-inefficient power sector—one of our chief exports.

We in the United States know better. For instance, more than 1 million low-energy fluorescent lamps were given away by Southern California Edison. Saving energy with what Amory Lovins of the Rocky Mountain Institute calls "negawatts" was far less expensive than generating megawatts.[4] The money saved is better invested in buying up obsolete, energy-gobbling household appliances (refrigerators, for instance, consume one-sixth of U.S. households' electricity, the output of thirty large power stations); retiring energy-inefficient industrial motors (which typically consume three-quarters of the electricity used by industry); and introducing cogeneration plants that recover and use the heat that accompanies power generation (coal-fired power stations average 34 percent electricity and 66 percent wasted heat). Energy savings are also better invested in developing alternative energy sources such as biomass, wind, and solar energy (sunlight is most plentiful in those countries where most of the world's poorest live).

Again, the elimination of poverty is a design challenge. Much of that design has to do with the generation, distribution, and use of the energy required to sustain an acceptable standard of living, a perspective best appreciated from a sustainability-oriented education. That's consistent with the World Bank's *Wealth Index*, which found that human capital should be valued at about three times that of all other capital combined.

A Closer Look at the Capital Commons

The eradication of poverty is a very new goal for U.S. foreign policy. It's clear we cannot do this alone. Before we let our lofty aims outrun our limited means, we must recognize that many nations, including the United States, suffer from donor fatigue. Circumstances require that we be creative in mobilizing the resources required to move this agenda, particularly if we hope to achieve this goal within the fiscal constraints of today's political environment and the physical constraints of the natural environment.[5] Yet it can be done and done within the span of two decades dedicated to the task. We've made it possible for democracy to spread; we now need to create the environment required for it to flourish. A military analogy suggests the scope of what's required. "To win a military campaign," Colin Powell points out, "you need clear objectives, you need public support and you need to go in with sufficient forces to do the job."

Let's focus on the last requirement—the forces needed, particularly the financial forces. A global ownership survey would prove useful, as it would generate global support for a "capital commons user fee"—mustering financial support from those who presently most benefit from global capital markets. As I mentioned in Chapter 2, a modest 3.5 percent annual fee assessed on the assets of the world's two hundred most well-to-do people (average 1999 wealth: $5 billion) would suffice to fund the six core essentials for *all* those in developing countries: adequate food, safe water, sanitation, primary education, basic health care, and reproductive health care for all willing couples.

Financial markets are a commons, not unlike a commonly shared pasture where all the residents of a village graze their cows. No one owns the pasture, yet each profits from its use. No one owns the financial commons, yet theoretically at least, everyone benefits from it. There's a reason, after all, that we use the term "securities" to describe stocks, bonds, and other financial instruments: Their security is due largely to international treaties that underwrite the worldwide enforceability of property rights—from which a remarkably small proportion of the world's population pocket the bulk of the financial benefits.[6]

It's widely agreed that financial instability is a "public bad" that adversely affects innocent people worldwide. The question remains, however, just who should harvest the benefits from this public good, the financial commons? What we've learned about public goods—health, schooling, defense, infrastructure, national parks—is that their reach usually stretches across generations and that their provision usually requires partnership with others, both with taxpayers and with local and national governments.[7] We also know that prevention is usually easier than crafting a cure, in the same way that it's cheaper to build a fence at the top of a cliff than station an ambulance below. Healthy environments are cheaper than expensive health care and hospitals; vaccines are a bargain compared to plagues; diplomacy less troublesome than war; social justice preferred over revolution; financial stability over expensive bailouts. That suggests the need for certain standards for how people behave when operating in our financial commons. Just as we would not allow a few to dominate the benefits harvested from other global commons such as the atmosphere, the sea beds, the electromagnetic spectrum, and the Internet, we must address the financial commons—where monopolization is rampant.

Yet there's even more at work here. The financial value of securities traded in this commons is greatly enhanced by the liquidity that the commons provides. The ability to freely buy and sell reduces investment risk. As a general rule, capital market liquidity boosts by 35 percent the value of a security when measured against a comparable company whose shares are not readily tradable. Thus, a 3.5 percent user fee for use of the commons recovers only 10 percent of the *increase* in value attributable *solely* to the liquidity provided by the commons. How could anyone credibly object?

The issue is a simple one: Should those who benefit from this global commons contribute to its upkeep? It's largely their livestock that are fattened up in this pasture. If that seems a fair and reasonable proposition, then the next question becomes: Should that fee be paid in cash or in kind? For example, should security holders sign over a portion of their securities to contribute to the maintenance of the commons from which a sizable portion of the value of those securities arises?[8]

This user-fee strategy is meant to provide a fair and easily understood means for funding a legacy of human decency, one to which surely there would be no objection from these two hundred people and their descendants. We should convene hearings to solicit the views of those descendants, as they will have a far longer period in which to experience the costs and the benefits of such an approach—as well as the repercussions should we fail to address today's dehumanizing and destabilizing trends. During the First Hundred Days of a populist administration, hearings would be held to solicit the views of those among those affected who live in the United States as well as those from abroad who wish to share their views. In addition, international negotiations would commence to reach agreement on how best to proceed. Legislation would be introduced to clarify the objectives and focus public debate.

Emerging Market Funding

Should the power of international law enforcement be required for collection, nations will need to apply an unprecedented degree of cooperation, including agreements ensuring at least limited access to the world's financial havens that the rich have long used to remain beyond the reach of financial responsibility.[9] If this user fee is not readily tendered, an initial fee of 10 percent may prove more appropriate, not only to cover enforcement costs but also to compensate whistle-blowers who assist in identifying scofflaws.[10] An initial "capital commons legacy fee" in the 10 percent range is certainly justifiable based on the benefits conferred to date by the capital commons. Yet it's a fee that no country can collect alone, because it will drive uncooperative people to uncooperative jurisdictions, as proven by the legendary appeal of tax havens. "Money goes where it's well treated," notes former Citibank chair Walter Wriston, "and stays where it's well treated." You can't get any better treatment than in tax havens like the Cayman Islands—no income tax, no capital gains tax, no value-added tax, no sales tax, no inheritance tax, and, most critically, no tax treaties.

Imagine the potential for relieving both human misery and the tax burden on people worldwide if this effort were to identify owners of the $8 trillion-plus in tax-haven wealth now sloshing around in the world's financial underground (estimates run from as low as the IMF's estimate of $4.5 trillion to as high as $13 trillion). Either a specialty unit of a reinvigorated United Nations or a newly established international entity could be enlisted to coordinate an effort to collect a "freeloader levy," assisted by Interpol and overseen by the Switzerland-based Bank for International Settlements, a coordinating arm of the international banking community. A demonstration effort undertaken with the British could have a major impact. For example, the Cayman Islands are a British dependency whose governor and attorney general are UK appointees. The Cayman government Web site brags that of the 575 banks and trust companies "based" in the islands, 106 have a presence in the United States.[11] Yet if a U.S. bank inspector attempts to audit a bank there, he or she will be arrested. That's the rules. A coordinated U.S.-UK effort could get bank inspectors in for a look at the books.

A portion of the proceeds from the capital commons user fee and the freeloader levy could pay for UN peacekeeping, economic development, and refugee relief efforts, including the UN Development Program, through which I suggest proposed relief efforts be coordinated. The extent to which the proceeds from these two levies could pay for such efforts is outlined in Chapter 2.

Without a basic foundation of stability (peacekeeping, famine relief, refugee resettlement, environmental restoration, etc.), poverty will persist, as will political instability. Both the capital commons user fee and the freeloader levy could periodically be recalibrated to ensure that the UN's budget for peacekeeping, development, and the environment is funded from this source in perpetuity. This shift in development funding would be consistent with a change in development philosophy occurring in the 1990s. During this time, international financial institutions such as the World Bank have steadily transformed their role from capital provider to capital catalyst, relying ever more on the encouragement of global capital markets and cross-border capital flows ("emerging markets") as a source of development funds. In essence, the provision of development capital is being privatized as development banks focus more on building the institutional capital (laws, regulations, court systems, etc.) essential to the workability of capital markets.[12]

Prosperity-Sharing Development Funding

To minimize initial cash costs, those benefiting from the commons could donate a portion of their tradable securities to a Capital Commons Fund, a bit like a dog breeder offering the pick of the litter to a neighbor who provides the sire required to impregnate his female. Given the potential magnitude of the funds involved, some combination of cash and in-kind contributions may be sufficient, in time, to capitalize both the United Nations and the development banks. That would tap the financial offspring of emerging capital markets as a means to support the capital commons from which the offspring arise. This "organic," self-financed approach could also address donor fatigue. This fund might also be granted warrants in those companies utilizing the global commons, with those warrants dedicated to an intergenerational purpose, such as children's health, primary education, environmental restoration, or other public goods such as research on tropical diseases.[13]

A precedent is found in the United States. In return for the federal government's providing the Chrysler Corporation with a $1.2 billion loan guarantee in 1979, Chrysler was required to provide the government with warrants to buy Chrysler stock. That agreement recognized that U.S. taxpayers were taking a risk by guaranteeing the loan. Initially valued at $6 per share, those warrants were later exercised at $72, with the proceeds dedicated to general revenues.

The international treaties that underlie the security of global capital markets are a type of guarantee. The treaties assume that at least a minimal level of social justice will accompany the operation of those markets. Otherwise we undermine the public support that treaties require for their stability. Worldwide trends in wealth and income disparities suggest that this crucial element is now at risk. Those treaties also underwrite the liquidity component of capital markets, providing a huge financial benefit to those who own securities. The rapid increase in funds flowing through this commons have generated massive windfall gains for capital owners. That process is far from over. Research by John C. Edmunds, professor at Babson College, found that the total dollar value of all investment-grade securities that could potentially be issued worldwide is upward of $150 trillion. He estimates that only 40 percent of these securities ($60 trillion) have been issued.[14] To whom does that additional $90 trillion belong? Absent a dramatic change in the financial environment, the workings of today's closed system of finance—like software running invisibly in the background—ensure that today's rich-get-richer trend is certain to accelerate, destabilizing the very commons on which today's development strategy is based.[15]

Absent policy input and international cooperation, it won't be long before we're subjected to the unsettling spectacle of the world's first trillionaire (Bill Gates). That promises to be a truly astounding human spectacle in a world where 2 billion people are anemic (perhaps 3 billion by then). In the process of reaching agreement on a funding source to sustain this financial commons, the question will certainly arise: *For whom* are we supporting the security of this commons? An economic boom for whom? The answer to that question will generate a healthy and long-overdue debate that should improve the durability and robustness of free-enterprise democracy by ensuring that it becomes dramatically more inclusive.[16] My hope is that we'll begin to think of capital markets as what they are: a social invention whose properties (security, liquidity, diversification, etc.) we can draw upon to relieve poverty while lowering investment risk and enhancing political stability. That approach may yet prove to be the best financial risk insurance that global free enterprise could have. It also offers the hope of relieving poverty with only minimal building of new institutions worldwide.

Creative Capitalism

The global prosperity envisioned here is eminently achievable. The challenge lies in drawing on capitalism's many strengths while better managing its weaknesses, particularly its environmental impact and its tendency to limit the bulk of its benefits to the already wealthy, the financially sophisticated, and the politically well connected. This nation is rich in financial know-how. During the First Hundred Days, the United States should draw on input from its best and brightest to advise on how to put the global financial commons to work for the

common good. We know, for instance, that we must find ways to reduce investment risk to attract more private capital into developing
countries. A common component of the Asian financial crisis was
cozy credit terms alongside impenetrable accounting systems. That
combination deprived investors of conventional market signals that
could have alerted them to trouble. By consciously creating "up-
close" capitalists (managers, employees, suppliers, distributors, customers, etc.), investors could be assured that someone is minding the
store. If a little capitalism is so good, developing countries can rightly
ask, why not a lot? And if a few foreign capitalists are so good for us,
wouldn't lots of indigenous capitalists be even better? [17]

For intergenerational purposes, we also need to get much smarter
about how capital markets can be used to advance environmental sustainability. That's another place where our legendary financial creativity could be put to good use. For instance, in 1997, the Department
of Energy, joined by several top finance firms, created the
International Performance Measurement and Verification Protocol,
since embraced by more than twenty other economies. By standard-
izing the savings from reduced water and energy costs on a voluntary
industry-consensus basis (largely in buildings and industrial
processes), those savings can be aggregated and then treated as securities, in much the same way that the Federal Housing Administration
(FHA) standardizes home mortgages and bundles them for sale in
the securities market as mortgage-backed securities.

This creative use of capital markets means that loans to finance
water- and energy-saving projects can be organized more quickly and
at less risk, because they can be sold into the secondary securities
market. That new source of capital will enable companies to finance
energy savings more affordably and with fewer of the trade-offs that
usually guide business decisionmaking when other investment needs
are also at stake. This financial innovation also helps level the playing
field somewhat for energy-saving investments (which require short-
term returns) over energy-generation power plant investments (typically recovered over twenty and even thirty years). The higher returns
required for saving than for producing energy have long skewed energy policy as financial signals told us to consume when conservation
was the far better course. This misallocation of capital, years in the
making, will require years to correct. That suggests an obvious preferred investment for long-term investors such as pension trustees. If
combined with creative ownership-spreading mechanisms, there's
enormous potential here for advancing both equity and sustainability.

Ownership Patterns Matter

As with domestic policy, the impact of ownership patterns abroad is a huge blind spot for policymakers. Yet it's clear that ownership patterns matter: domestic versus foreign, concentrated versus broad-based, remote versus up-close and personal. If we've learned nothing else from the history of capitalism, hopefully we've at least learned that it must meet certain requirements for its sustainable success. For capitalism to succeed, international conventions must commit countries not only to common values (private property, the rule of law, etc.) but also to common constraints such as fair labor practices, environmental standards, and limits on ownership concentration.

During the First Hundred Days of a populist administration, a revised foreign policy would indicate how our development strategy could better advance our democratic values.[18] The lack of an inclusive free enterprise within the United States undermines the foundation on which our foreign-policy resolve must be built, including the popular support required for a robust defense. Gen-Xers already harbor a negative attitude toward the United States, placing little importance on either citizenship or national identity.[19] It may prove difficult to advance a more inclusive development strategy abroad as growing legions of Americans realize they've been excluded here at home. Americans have long shown a preference for a foreign policy that combines altruism with self-interest. Any program meant to spread prosperity abroad should include a counterpart policy here at home, particularly if we hope to engage Gen-Xers' support for political initiatives from which they now routinely tune out. Recapturing the support of the politically disengaged requires leadership able to project a renewed sense of national purpose and a reconceived global mission.

Divisive economic trends, both here and abroad, undermine U.S. ability to play a leadership role at this historic juncture, when ninety-five nations are in the process of making the transition from command to market economies. Many countries are well advanced in the transition. Egged on by the allure of images available worldwide through advertising, global product branding, telecommunications, and the Internet, people everywhere are now agonizingly aware of the potential for material prosperity. Their prosperity largely depends on their embrace of the right sort of free enterprise. With what we now know about how wealth is created and distributed and the environmental costs that development entails, the United States can lead the world toward broad-based prosperity while taking its citizens along for the ride. Within twenty years, we should be able to look back in wonder and disbelief at why we didn't start this commonsense effort much sooner. As we may require two full decades to achieve this goal, it would be a tragedy to be forced to wait another election season to begin. The trends accompanying today's wired world suggest that there's not a moment to waste. For instance, a Pricewaterhouse-Coopers survey of corporate executives, published January 2000, found that more than half of the 1,020 respondents feared that the Internet would widen the wealth gap between industrialized and developing nations, and possibly increase the risk of social unrest.[20]

Bioterrorism:
The Worst Possible Terror

Current U.S. leadership has taken its eye off the ball when it comes to the most significant threat to national security. Although nuclear weapons remain a looming menace, biological weaponry and a stealth attack of ideologically motivated madness may yet be our undoing unless we quickly mobilize resources to address the threat. We intuitively know this. A 1999 *Wall Street Journal/Newsweek* poll confirmed that the threat of terrorist acts is a concern of almost all groups surveyed. What follows is a brief description of one such danger and the profoundly inadequate response elicited to date.

Bioterrorism is the most likely bioterrorist tool, and smallpox (or anthrax) its most likely agent. Smallpox killed at least 300 million people during the twentieth century. A bioterror event is no longer just possible; the experts insist that it's now likely. In 1965, President Johnson endorsed the idea of smallpox eradication, largely as a way to improve U.S.-Soviet relations. By tracking outbreaks worldwide and quickly mobilizing to vaccinate people in a ring around any incident, the World Health Organization's Smallpox Eradication Unit was able, by 1977, to isolate the last natural case of smallpox, halting its life cycle in the human population.

That's the good news. The bad news is that during the Cold War, the Soviets produced twenty tons of weapons-grade smallpox, using industrial-scale pharmaceutical tanks known as bioreactors. The status of that inventory remains uncertain, though we know that many of Russia's scientific elite are among those now attempting to survive on less than $38 per month. With poverty like that among people in the know, the temptation to sell bioterroristic material may be great.

What does D. A. Henderson, who served as head of disease surveillance at the Center for Disease Control during the Johnson administration, say about the likelihood of smallpox bioterrorism? "The way air travel is now, about six weeks would be enough to seed cases around the world. Dropping an atomic bomb could cause casualties in specific areas, but dropping smallpox could engulf the world."[21] How likely is that? "I don't think there is any higher biological threat to this nation than smallpox," says Peter Jahrling, principal scientific adviser at the U.S. Army Medical Research Institute of Infectious Diseases in Fort Detrick, Maryland.[22] How could it happen? The silicon-chip industry has numerous devices that could do the job. Michael Osterholm, a leading epidemiologist and bioterrorism expert, describes a readily available credit-card-sized device that sprays an invisible mist of particles in the one- to five-micron size range, the sort that hang in the air for hours and get into the lungs. It can run for hours on a camcorder battery. Conceal one of these at each of several international airports; load each with two tablespoons of infectious fluid; and the devices could, he says, "fill a whole airport terminal with particles."

Smallpox spreads in fourteen-day waves of cases, reflecting the incubation period of the virus. Historically, each wave has been from ten to twenty times as large as the last, so the epidemic gathers force exponentially as each carrier infects an average of ten to twenty more people. By the third wave, it spreads with the strength of a biological tsunami. However, the historical rate of infection would now be both faster and broader, because of the combination of lower worldwide immunity and the advent of air travel, which provides an opportunity to infect immense airline terminals with planeloads of people traveling to dispersed locations worldwide, where they can infect others. The use of unsuspecting international travelers as disseminators provides the ultimate terrorist weapon, particularly with the freedom of travel now available in an increasingly borderless environment. That's truly globalized, high-tech terrorism.

Containing the Threat

The only way to contain smallpox is the same now as in the 1970s: isolate the victims and vaccinate everyone around them. Yet even if it were possible to identify and isolate everyone, the stock of smallpox vaccine worldwide is impossibly small and much of it is out of date. Which countries do we now suspect have either clandestine stocks of smallpox or seem to be trying to buy or steal the virus? Though the list is classified, reports suggest it includes China, India, Pakistan, Israel, North Korea, Iraq, Iran, Cuba, and Serbia. The list may also include terrorist Osama bin Laden and Aum Shinrikyo, the Japanese sect whose 1995 nerve gas release in a Tokyo subway served notice of the ease with which such attacks can be staged. Japan has almost no smallpox vaccine on hand and no known ability to cope with a bioterrorist attack.

What has been the response? In 1997, the Department of Defense hired a contractor to make smallpox vaccine for 300,000 military troops. Delivery is scheduled for 2006 at $75 per dose. That tightly targeted effort ignores the contagious nature of smallpox. The White House directed the Department of Health and Human Resources (HHS) to produce a stockpile of vaccine large enough (now conservatively estimated as 40 million doses) to protect the U.S. civilian population. The only possible way to combat this sort of warfare is to have fresh vaccine prepositioned on pallets, ready to disburse worldwide on a moment's notice. The HHS "request for proposals" (to produce the vaccine) closed March 16, 2000.

Yet even if an effective response is crafted to this particular agent, others may soon emerge through the modern miracles of biotechnology. The shift to highly specialized, single-species, continuous-crop agriculture leaves our food and fiber stocks particularly susceptible. Not only are today's genetically identical monocultures far more brittle and at increased risk from the growing volatility of weather, they also provide a veritable Valhalla for any agroterrorist able to design, say, a crop-crippling enzyme, germ-plasm toxin, or fast-spreading contagion. Agroterrorism was deemed "easy and likely" in the June 1999 issue of *Scientific American*.

High-tech farming may prove our own undoing before an outright terrorist effort can happen. Our petrochemical-addicted farms now use 2.2 billion pounds of pesticides each year plus 20 million tons of anhydrous ammonia fertilizers (160 pounds per person). The result: Although pesticide use is up 3,300 percent since 1945, crop losses to pests are up 20 percent. Meanwhile, more than five hundred pests have developed resistance (requiring more pesticides), the soil has become less productive (requiring more fertilizer), and illness among farm families is well above the median (leukemia and lymphoma from pesticides; miscarriages from nitrates). Moreover, the skyrocketing expense of oil-based inputs ($2.70 for every $4.00 of crops) means that we spend ten kilocalories of hydrocarbons to produce one kilocalorie of food (each of us eats the equivalent of thirteen barrels of oil each year).

Now that farming is nine parts oil and one part farmer—leading critics to charge that crops are grown not so much in soil as in oil—a majority of our farmers rely on off-farm revenues for half their income. Those who can't make it sell out. Eighty-five percent of our food and fiber now comes from 15 percent of our farms. Today's vast farms are viewed as machines, modeled after industry, not nature. They are managed at mega-acreage biofactories, whose absentee investors generate financial capital as they liquidate our ecological capital, weaken our soil, foul our water, and sicken our farming families—all the while consuming ever more nonrenewable resources. Scarcely what you'd call either a hardy or a sustainable food supply.

With the huge dangers accompanying biotechnology, we may destroy our agricultural system ourselves. We could have, for example, a mass plant die-off because of biogenetic drift, whereby a biotech-designed sterile seed or a superbacterium crosses over to other species. As natural resilience is bred out—so that more financial yield can be built in—our food and fiber supplies will become steadily more vulnerable, both to mishaps and to mischief. The United States is not alone in opting for humankind's modern cleverness over nature's ancient wisdom: India is replacing its 30,000 varieties of native rice with one supergrain, ensuring that this enormous nation is made dependent on identical plants with identical vulnerabilities. From a biological-vulnerability perspective, it's akin to giving a thief the key to every house in a community.[23]

Crafting a Response Equal to the Threat

What's at issue here is not just our clearly misplaced policy priorities—such as directing scarce fiscal resources to capital-gain tax cuts versus the production of smallpox vaccine or the preservation of our biodiversity. We must realize that the scope of our politics remains far too cramped for the realities we face. The modern-day convergence of economics, technology, and culture requires that we very quickly generate global awareness of how many people now share a limited space and what's required to live responsibly and in a way that benefits the next generation. At present, the United States lacks a political philosophy (or a national security strategy) equal to the challenges we confront.

For the global community to protect itself from human inventions that threaten us all, we must quickly infuse the human family with a keener sense of the responsibility—and the nobility—of being human, along with an awareness of the inescapable unity of all life. That requires people worldwide to utilize today's telecommunication capabilities far more creatively so that our best insights quickly become part of the common sense of humankind. That, it seems to me, is the most promising way to isolate (and eliminate) those who would endanger the whole of humanity.

More so than ever, we require a politics that can evoke genuinely global values as a counterbalance to the many perilous forces that now threaten us. There was a time when we could enjoy the luxury of turning minds, one at a time, against our blind spots and our vain ambitions. The perils we now face suggest the need for a conversion of perspectives en masse. There seems considerable cause for optimism, as the means are at hand to advance this agenda if only we embrace a politics willing to put to creative use our instruments of education, entertainment, and global communication. The margins of the world's cultures have never before been so porous and the means at hand never before more powerful for fostering worldwide awareness. I turn in Chapter 12 to propose an example of the global initiatives I have in mind.

PART THREE

The Path from Here to There

10
Education for Democratic Capitalism

Thus the task is not so much to see what no one yet has seen, but to think what nobody yet has thought about that which everybody sees.

—SCHOPENHAUER

No policy is sustainable without public support. If the voting public doesn't know that something is possible, the people can't choose it. To properly frame the choices requires an education initiative that is bold in tone and comprehensive in scope. People simply have no idea that there's a feasible alternative to today's highly exclusive economic system. They've yet to hear an appealing and practical vision for a system designed to include them. Nor have they been presented a clear picture of how the various components fit into a global whole. Instead, they've been so often promised more and so routinely left with less that they feel estranged both from politics and from a government they no longer consider theirs. Many have concluded there's little they can do to about it. That inertia, in turn, strengthens the powerful forces of exclusion. Filling that political void today are two equally ineffective alternatives: progressives and conservatives. Both labor under false assumptions.

Progressives work at marginal improvements to a system from which people are routinely excluded, in the ill-founded belief that inclusion will come simply with more education and training. Meanwhile, conservatives lavish more benefits on those already included, in the ill-founded belief that inclusion will come about simply by granting more freedom to market forces ("a rising tide lifts all boats"). Rather than revisit their false assumptions, both camps periodically redouble their efforts—as witnessed by such policy spasms as the Reagan-Bush rich-get-richer supply-side initiative in the 1980s and the Clinton-Gore education initiative in the late 1990s—which is certain only to further widen the gap between the learning class and the working class.

With trickle-down a certifiable failure, populists suggest that it's time to spread prosperity directly and widely. Because the two major political parties now ride on very narrow-gauge tracks, populists could pick up support from both. Party loyalty is elusive, as both parties know and rightly fear. Ross Perot's Reform Party presidential campaigns proved this in 1992 and again in 1996, as did professional wrestler Jesse Ventura's successful 1998 gubernatorial campaign in Minnesota. Political creativity is the key to electoral success.

The Raw Deal for Generation X

Voters are frustrated. Gen-Xers have every reason to be fed up, as there's *no* leadership on issues of most concern to them. Since 1973, median earnings for men aged twenty to thirty-four have fallen by almost a third. Even during the early boom years (1989–1995), the earnings of recent college graduates fell by nearly 10 percent. A 1999 survey by Peter D. Hart Research Associates found that 60 percent of workers between age twenty-five and twenty-nine believe that employers are failing to meet their end of the bargain when it comes to sharing profits with workers and providing upward mobility.[1] Of the 44.3 million Americans who the Census Bureau says lack basic health insurance, Gen-Xers are the least insured of all.[2] Many received a public education in schools weakened by budget cutbacks as fiscal resources were siphoned off into tax cuts instead. Government spending on education, infrastructure, and research plummeted from 24 percent to 14 percent of the federal budget since the mid-1970s and is poised to decline further as baby boomer retirement, military remobilization and Medicare commitments put more pressure on fiscal resources.

The in-school generation is also threatened by our steady reordering of public priorities. As we move into the twenty-first century, with its increased demand for communication and reasoning skills, educational achievement levels now reflect two decades of skewed fiscal priorities. Only one-quarter of elementary and secondary students write at a proficient level, according to a September 1999 report released by the National Center for Education Statistics. Arizona found that just 11 percent of high school sophomores could pass a state math test administered in 1998. Only 7 percent of Virginia's schools could show that 70 percent of their students met minimum state testing requirements. Los Angeles school administrators calculated that they would have to hold back nearly half their students if they ended automatic promotions in all grades.[3]

A closer look reveals that our poor across-the-board results mirror our widening economic divide. Whites and Asian Americans performed best on what's known as the nation's report card, with 24–36 percent scoring at the proficient level in tests given to 160,000 fourth, eighth, and twelfth graders. That compares with 8–11 percent of black, Hispanic, and Native American test-takers.[4] What's the response to date? Furious backpedaling. Rather than holding to standards to ensure that students in rich and poor schools cover the same ground—and mustering the fiscal resources to help students meet those high goals—schools instead are lowering their standards.

The standards that the schools *are* adhering to are those involved with cracking down on misconduct. Rather than the patience historically afforded adolescents and their usual, if annoying, behavior, the Justice Department reports that the vast majority of schools now have zero-tolerance policies not only for crimes like gun possession but also for infractions like tobacco use and noncompliance with dress codes. So although our schools have become factories of failure, at least we've found the funds to convert spirited and unchallenged teens into docile adults.[5]

Gen-Xers rightly sense that the social fabric is fraying and that, absent fundamental change, they will continue to face deep-seated economic insecurity. About 75 percent of young workers today lack a college degree. The Peter Hart survey confirms that the oft-touted promise of a high-tech career is typically little more than a fading dream for a large percentage of young workers who can't afford the additional training or education to upgrade their skills. While most young college graduates have full-time, permanent jobs, only half of young workers without degrees have such standard employment. The rest are working part-time as temps or in other substandard arrangements, the survey found. Mobility makes people more tolerant of inequality. Gen-Xers are slowly learning that they enjoy only the perception of mobility—within a very tight range of low-paid jobs.

Debtors for Life

This generation is also about to inherit a daunting array of fiscal, social, and environmental debts (chronicled in Chapter 4), including nearly $2 trillion in international debt as the United States went from being the world's largest creditor nation to its largest debtor.[6] That's certain to lead to reductions in both investment and consumption as Gen-Xers find themselves faced not only with extreme demographic strains (one Social Security recipient for every 2.1–2.3 workers) but also a tab for foreign indebtedness incurred to fuel the boom of the 1980s and 1990s. Fully 61 percent of this generation agree with the statement "Politicians and political leaders have failed my generation." That shows keen political insight. They're now faced with the spectacle of Republican congressional leaders who claim (with a straight face) that tax cuts are essential because, otherwise, politicians will spend any surplus. These same legislators propose tax relief for the well-to-do as a way to return projected budget surpluses to those "to whom they belong"—while passing along deficits to Generation X like some high-stakes intergenerational shell game.

Exposed to such disingenuousness, it should come as no surprise that Gen-Xers have record-low trust both in institutions and in elected officials. They also show an increase in materialism and individualism, traits that tend to weaken social bonds and further isolate people. Unless quickly addressed, their apathy, absenteeism, and disengagement will make it even more difficult to address the common good. No more than a third of today's young adults identify with either political party, whereas 44 percent of eighteen- to twenty-nine-year-olds think of themselves as independents. Theirs was among the strongest support registered both by outsider Perot and by upstart Ventura.

The reason both political parties need massive campaign funds to tout their message is easy to understand: Their campaigns don't *have* a message. Substance has been displaced by vague sloganeering and slick emotional appeals. The voters realize that. Certainly Generation X does. The party regulars know it too. They have good reason to be worried. Neither party can win with its core supporters alone. Political victory requires a complex weave of values and constituencies. In today's volatile mix of politics, personalities, and demographics, a well-conceived, upbeat, populist campaign could catch both parties off guard. Among Gen-Xers, who view both parties as corrupt to the core, a simple, straightforward, and pragmatic theme could bring them out in droves. Their widespread cynicism and political disengagement could shift quickly in response to a blunt-talking populist. At present, their materialism is mixed with an interest in spiritual quests along with a passion for the environment. Properly motivated, they have the potential to emerge as the nation's next swing-vote coalition with the capacity to redirect democracy. As the mainstream discovered in Minnesota in 1998, the right blend of message and messenger could galvanize a key constituency that pundits too quickly write off as not interested in politics.

Innocence and Ignorance

Three things are required to advance a more democratic capitalism. First, there must be a nationwide education campaign. In that always mysterious dance of leadership and "followship," the missing ingredient is our failure to ask the right questions. That makes the rollout of a populist education campaign essential. The capacity to think politically across the full tableau of history is uniquely *populistic*. That scale of thought is precisely what this education effort must help people to grasp. We must quickly *learn to learn* about the forces at work in today's endangered democracy. The reality of globalization requires that we educate ourselves to think both locally and globally. But we must also think historically so that we don't repeat the mistakes of the past. That's particularly the case on the sensitive issue of ownership patterns, for which naive and impractical reforms have long been the rule rather than the exception. And we must proceed with a profound sense of obligation to future generations, an element long absent from mainstream proposals.

For the most part, there's widespread innocence and enormous ignorance about the cruelly exclusive financial structure that underlies democracy. The workings of economics and politics are a mystery to many. That the two are inherently one is a revelation for most. Today's widespread political and economic illiteracy makes for a dysfunctional democracy that feeds a fast-spreading cynicism as people feel increasingly frustrated—both about their inability to change the system and about just what needs changing. Few Americans are in the position to take the time required to study these matters. Yet without some way of closing today's education gap, it will be difficult to muster the political support required for needed structural change.

Escape from today's intellectual and political servitude requires a corps of trained populist lecturers along with educational materials and nationwide venues to match instructors with interested people. These instructors need to be equipped with simple explanations that use flow charts, story boards, learning maps, and other highly visual and entertaining means to convey knowledge about issues long notorious for putting people to sleep. We must speed up a democratic learning process already very short on time. The tone should resemble that of a friendly campfire, or what Native Americans call a medicine council, in which people come together to learn, to share their experiences, to expand their thinking, to affirm their values, and to rekindle the spirit of community and commitment.

Second, we must restore our political confidence. This common-sense way of thinking will be labeled by some as radical. Those who oppose it will attempt to deflect these ideas from serious discussion. And they'll certainly attack the messenger (watch for the *Wall Street Journal* to apply its all-purpose put-down "gadfly"). Demagogic rhetoric should be expected, especially from those who see demands for inclusion as a threat to an exclusive system they've long portrayed as the natural consequence of free enterprise. Candidly, what these ideas most need is creative marketing. As people gain the confidence that accompanies understanding, we'll see the resurgence of a more robust democracy, one in which people *demand* their rights. The pride that people take in the rediscovery of the political and historical legitimacy of populist principles will generate the commitment required to *insist* on a more inclusive system. Political success requires that populists refuse to take no for an answer.

Third, there must be something for people to do. In politics, that's called mobilization. Shared effort in the pursuit of freedom and prosperity has a grand ring to it. And certainly camaraderie can be its own reward, as can education. Yet to succeed, this movement must be different from anything we've seen in this country since the turn-of-the-century agrarian populists. People will need to be courageous enough to heed their own common sense and to listen to lecturers from their own ranks rather than passively accept as true the conventional Wall Street thinking that has led us so far astray. The populist concept, deeply rooted in democracy, must itself be their guide. That's why self-generated educational materials are essential, along with self-trained lecturers. In the two traditional political parties, credibility means looking for validation to that echo chamber that constitutes the Washington–Wall Street consensus: academics, think tanks, popular pundits, and like-minded policymakers. Populists don't yet have that. For now, their support network is their own sense of purpose and their dedication to democratic principles. In modern politics, that makes for a very new version of political unity—and a very new challenge for political mobilization. The excitement at what might emerge from the populist possibility must be converted into political action: What are people *to do*?

The Doing of Populism

An informed, confident, and engaged electorate would be a very new phenomenon in U.S. politics that could open this country to the possibility of change unlike anything seen in recent history. We must consider too the potential impact of this movement on those in similar circumstances abroad, where economic exclusion is even more pronounced. Word of such a populist initiative in the very heart of capitalism has the potential to catalyze a genuinely democratic century, particularly with the aid of today's global telecommunications. The global spread of a U.S.-originated populist movement would be ideal, from a democratic perspective, as it would repair our much-tarnished image as a leader in democratic development.

What are people to do? They need first to educate themselves and others, and then mobilize to change the policy environment—starting from wherever they are. A broadening of the nation's prosperity should top the list of legislative priorities. This book and my previous one (*The Ownership Solution*) are replete with policy initiatives. There's no shortage of ideas, only an absence of education, initiative, and courage.

What will ensure political momentum is the capacity to maintain multiple methods of internal communication among those involved in this movement. Support systems must be created—to share experiences, to urge each other on, and to celebrate signs of progress. With the emergence of a broadly connected high-tech, high-touch society, the ability to maintain communication and momentum is far greater now than a century ago, when populism last had a chance at catalyzing significant change.

To maintain political viability, these ideas must engage people in dialogue in order to effect structural change. There must be the constant give-and-take of perceived problem and proposed solution. Vigorous exchange lies at the core of any genuinely democratic movement. Much of that can happen not only through conventional media but also through new communication channels, including the Internet, videoconferencing, and linked Web sites. Videoconferencing is now available by connecting a digital camera to a computer. Digital compression will soon allow the transmission of film clips over the Internet, opening another new vista for communication and mobilization, both here and abroad. For example, Republican presidential candidate John McCain convened a February 2000 cyber-conference and fund-raiser, complete with live video, on-line streaming of pictures and charts, and real-time polling on various subjects.

The roots of populism are found in a combination of personal self-respect and mass self-confidence. Self-respect requires self-assertion. People must know that their input can effect change. They must experience firsthand that democracy can work. Although the fellowship of like-minded people has a certain value, the emerging populist community—sometimes operating as a virtual community—requires a constantly renewed sense of accomplishment as the fuel to maintain its collective effort. A sense of accomplishment requires, at a minimum, a base of support through which a populist agenda can be advanced and from which populist candidates can emerge and be elected. A community cannot sustain itself simply because some think it should; it must show movement toward self-generated goals. Those goals must be realistic and the progress palpable. To achieve the goals requires an upbeat mix of passion, pragmatism, and persistence.

Populist Activism

There's an enormous amount that can be done through local initiative, including a vast array of projects in the environmental arena. Take the following examples:

- The establishment of wind farms in the Midwest was driven not by market forces or by a groundswell of public opinion but by a few concerned local legislators.
- In Minnesota, the legislature required that if Northern States Power wanted to continue storing spent nuclear fuel on its controversial Prairie Island site, it also had to provide renewable energy.
- In Iowa, the legislature mandated that at least 1.5 percent of energy be produced from renewable sources.

There are rules everywhere you turn. That's the real world of free-enterprise democracy. Populists must insist that the rules be rewritten so that they're equitable and sustainable—in other words, sensible. If you look through the recommendations in this book and then look through the list of committees in your state legislature, you'll find an issue of relevance for every committee on that list. Likewise for Congress. Populism is about bottom-up democracy. A democracy unlived is no longer a democracy. Look for what's needed and do it. Be demanding. Insist that your elected officials hold hearings. And that those hearings lead to new rules. Stop fighting the system; become a change agent in the system.

Engage in local action, whether in the streets or behind closed doors. Follow your passion, whether it's blocking retail chains, lobbying for bicycle lanes, insisting on better pay for child-care workers, petitioning grocery chains to label genetically modified foods, or pushing your pension plan to invest responsibly.[7] If you're at a private school with an endowment, make certain it's invested sensibly. Urge design retrofits for outdated buildings, organize a water conservation program, or spearhead experiments in recycling, restoration, or alternative energy. As a youngster growing up in Athens, Georgia in the early 1960s, I replanted fairways and greens at a local golf course using Milorganite, a pungent fertilizer made from reprocessed sewage that's still sold today by the city of Milwaukee. It smelled awful, but it worked great. What's your community been doing with its waste for the past four decades? What will it do for the next four? There may be a business there. Think like business. As ecologist-author Hunter Lovins suggests, take your values from your customers, your designs from nature, and your discipline from the marketplace.

Change local codes and ordinances so they incorporate the principles of living systems like John Todd's Living Machines or the use of landscaped swales rather than storm drains to handle water runoff. Use the saved money to beautify the landscape with shade trees and edible vegetation. Set standards. Publish a directory of local values-attuned firms. Urge the adoption of local indicators for sustainability. Support efforts to incubate small businesses. Don't worship the market; work with the market. Recognize it for what it is: a useful tool. For instance, Amory Lovins advocates "feebates" that encourage people to beat community standards and qualify for rebates while laggards pay higher fees. Properly designed, they're revenue-neutral.[8] Use time as your ally (that's what finance-savvy people do); constantly upgrade community standards. If change seems too daunting, convene a community medicine council and reflect with others on what can be done. Create a parallel economy in your community that supports local businesses. You'll be surprised how many people are already doing that. Use the media. Write op-eds and book reviews. Engage your local faith communities. I don't know of any faith that endorses today's grotesque inequality or unsustainability—or that suggests allowing people to starve. Most faiths consider it theft to withhold from others what they need to become productive members of society. Reach out. Act up. Have fun. Use ridicule, satire, slogans. Keep it simple.

Given the trends chronicled here, civil disobedience is highly appropriate, provided it's undertaken in a Gandhian manner: with a clear moral purpose, with concern for your opponent, with discipline, and with a willingness to take responsibility for your actions. You enjoy the full protection of the law so long as your actions are aimed not at overthrowing authority but at changing laws and practices. That's what people protesting the WTO (World Trade Organization) discovered in Seattle in December 1999. You'll be heartened at how sympathetic judges and juries agree. A Scottish judge threw out charges against antinuclear campaigners who damaged a *Trident* nuclear submarine installation on the grounds that such weapons are illegal under international law. The San Francisco–based Ruckus Society provides tactical training in nonviolent dissent, ranging from how to rappel down a building, to how to build a high-tech blockade, to how to dress in court for your arraignment. The group's emphasis is on creating obstructions to injustice, attracting media attention, and using this media wedge to impact public opinion—an essential tool for changing the rules. Use private court cases to outflank entrenched industries and their well-financed lobbyists. The hundreds of billions of dollars wrung from the tobacco industry has spawned copycat lawsuits against lead-based paints at DuPont and handgun makers at Colt. The courts provide an underutilized forum in which to sound a wake-up call. The latest activist koan is this: What is the sound of one unsustainable industry collapsing?

Do something. Start networking and dialoging. Dialog is how democracies learn; that's why free speech is essential for any functioning democracy. You'll be amazed at how many individuals and organizations are working on equity and sustainability (certainly the WTO was surprised in Seattle). Worldwide there's an estimated 100,000 nongovernmental organizations working on environmental issues. One of my favorites is Vancouver-based Adbusters, which publishes a magazine by that name with the telltale subtitle *The Journal of the Mental Environment.*[9] The organization's specialty is culture-jamming—using humor, art, and satire ("uncommercials") to skewer product pitches that glorify sex, violence, and pornography while eroding self-images, degrading human dignity, and encouraging shop-till-you-drop consumption that's wasteful, unhealthy, and unsustainable. Their knockoff cigarette ad of a wan Joe Chemo hooked up to an intravenous drip in a cancer ward is now a collector's item. Help locally by organizing Adbusters' next Buy Nothing Day (always the Saturday after Thanksgiving). Sponsor an uncommercial contest in local schools. Make change inviting and fun for people drawn to new ideas but stuck in an old model. Fight back against the consumer culture. Give your time to charity and send your friends "gift-free" certificates next Christmas (available from Adbusters). Stay optimistic. With passion and participation, we're just two short decades from a profound turnaround. Be careful that your actions don't feed today's rampant pessimism and cynicism. Engage people in upbeat, solutions-oriented behavior. That's the way to create a social multiplier effect. Whining doesn't work. Position yourself as a solutions maker, not a troublemaker.

At the same time, however, be realistic about what change requires. Keep in mind that the last time economic inequality was this extreme was in 1929, just prior to the Depression. Washington's response, many painful years in the formulation, was the job-generating New Deal. Yet even that modest and largely ineffectual political assistance (leaving ownership patterns intact) came only after major agitation in the streets. It's for good reason that democracy protects the rights of free speech and assembly. That clever "cybernetic" design ensures that backup feedback loops are available when, as now, the system's traditional circuits fail to produce sensible results. Given the extraordinary inertia that consumes Washington—along with the absence of leadership on an array of crucial issues—populists must activate those backup feedback loops to turn this around. Activism, boycotts, protests, litigation—those designed-in pressure points are meant to be used when, as the founders anticipated, democracy's operations periodically fall short of what it promises to deliver.

There's enormous potential here to transform the business community with reforms that originate from both the inside and the outside. On the inside, we can create more insider-shareholders; on the outside, we can create more ownership-empowered stakeholders along with a policy environment designed to give priority to equity and sustainability.

The Internet is emerging as a potential sleeper in effective organizing. For instance, in June 1999, a London-based group calling itself the J18 umbrella group, operating anonymously through the Internet, organized a "Carnival against Capital" in the City (London's Wall Street). Few participants in this virtual campaign knew the identities of those who called them into the streets.

Today's volatile mixture of worldwide urbanization and instant communication suggests the potential for mobilizing vast numbers of people on short notice to coalesce around commonly shared populist themes. Given the fast-accelerating nature of the economic and ecological trends chronicled here—and the worldwide reach of their effects—a genuinely global, populist-inspired activist and community may emerge as democracy's next authentic manifestation.

The Key Dangers Facing Populism

Three key dangers need to be anticipated. First is the temptation to substitute one received wisdom for another. Populism will fail if, in the allure of the new, those involved simply swap one pattern of deference for another. That's not authentic autonomy. Nor is it self-actualized citizenship. Little progress is gained by exchanging one form of intellectual servitude for another, one set of autocratic leaders for another, or one hierarchical system for another. Genuine populism is a mutual collaboration, not a guru-disciple capitulation. To endure, this shift to a truly consensual democratic culture must be embraced individually—thus the key role played by education and the need for a very new, widely distributed style of leadership (described in Chapter 11).

Second, populists must resist the temptation of the traditional. Personal, societal, and organizational creativity must all be cultivated. Today's very new circumstances call for experimentation and innovation. Change-agents must be careful always that proposals are familiar enough to be heard but different enough to be listened to. Our federal system of independent but affiliated states lends itself extremely well to just this sort of innovation. That's why, in these volatile times of widespread voter discontent and unimaginative national leadership, we should expect to see a steady increase in the election of populist governors at the state level. Modern-day populists recognize that what is required now are coalitions that previously may have been unthinkable. For instance, Mitsubishi, long the target of activist attack by environmental organizations such as Greenpeace and Rainforest Action Network, now works with both to design a new strategic vision for the company. Monsanto even seeks input from biotech opponents. Foresighted business leaders are beginning to join nongovernmental organizations lobbying for stricter environmental regulation in the interest of maintaining a level playing field with less environmentally sensitive competitors.

Third, to succeed, this populist sentiment cannot be an isolated phenomenon. It must mature into a genuine mass movement that catalyzes change in all sectors of society, including change in our two key political parties. Both are dominated by seasoned party veterans with a hierarchical makeup similar to that found in traditional military units and the corporate workplace. Today's populists—of whatever party—have both an opportunity and an obligation to create genuinely participative party structures, the first ever in this country, either by reforming the two existing parties or by starting their own. The danger lies in the temptation of modern-day populists to be consoled with their novelty instead of organizing to take advantage of today's unique political opportunity.

Political Parties Losing Support

If this twenty-first-century version of populism is to succeed, it must from the outset change the way America thinks. The stakes are incredibly high. Pessimists may argue that democracy has already been lost in this country. Indeed, I was urged to title this book *Democracy Lost*. Certainly record-low voter turnout suggests remarkably widespread disillusionment and deep-seated cynicism. Today's plutocratic ownership patterns only reinforce that perception. The populist opportunity lies in the ability to reframe the debate so that people are offered a real alternative through a politics of national identity wed to local initiative. As the world's bastion of democracy, U.S. populists cannot afford to lose this fight, particularly not when so many in-transition countries are desperately in need of practical alternatives that can hold their nations together amid the tendency of opposing ethnic groups to rip them apart.

At present, the desire of U.S. officeholders to prevail at the next election has taken priority over the needs of democracy, global security, and the environment. Instead of a real political choice, we see a disheartening political fusion, with faint differences rather than clear distinctions being the focus of a flattened political debate. This vague and dangerous centrism masks problems rather than solves them. In a recent survey, only 50 percent of registered voters knew whether their U.S. senator was a Republican or a Democrat, the same result one would get from random guessing. That shouldn't be surprising in a political environment where articulate blather now fills in for forthright discussion. Even extremism is covered over with a veneer of well-coached pleasantries and finely honed sound bites so that "more of the same" is made to sound like positive change.

It's also clear that the so-called wedge issue (i.e., race) is poised to haunt those who have relied on it in the past (such as George Bush). Within the next ten years and perhaps sooner, Hispanics will become the nation's largest minority group. In 1997, the number of Hispanic children surpassed for the first time the number of African American children. By 2050, Hispanics will constitute almost one-quarter of the U.S. population, Asians will total more than 8 percent, and the African American population will grow to 13.5 percent. That leaves less than 53 percent classified as non-Hispanic whites. In a number of key states, this group will be in the minority. This will happen in California before the 2000 election.[10]

Neither of the major political parties listens well. Both are run by party regulars known to be well outside the mainstream, whether left or right. Conservative policymaking is frozen in an abstract and out-dated economic model whose gale-force winds of constant change destabilize the very communities and families on which conservative values depend. Progressives, on the other hand, find themselves stuck without an identity. In moving steadily rightward, they lost the affec-tion of their natural base, America's blue-collar workers, while picking up only lukewarm support from knowledge workers and the suburban middle class, whose swing votes are heavily courted by everyone. With few issues of substance to distinguish them from con-servatives, the progressives turn instead to record-breaking fund-rais-ing as their only way to stay in office.

Fund-raising has become easier as, over the past three decades, the number of interest groups increased fivefold, while the number of lobbyists grew eightfold. That's one reason Al Gore's campaign could confidently announce the intention to raise $52 million (as of this writing, the Bush campaign had raised more than $70 million). With more than 25,000 lobbyists now plying the halls of Congress, about fifty lobbyists per member of Congress can be tapped for campaign contributions. What's more, they all descend on the White House. As a general rule, U.S. senators must raise $10,000 each week to fund a viable campaign (the average winning candidate in 1998 spent $4.7 million). Those are just the table stakes. A contested Senate campaign in a major media market can cost upward of $20 million. It's not dif-ficult to understand why the system seems so compromised, coopted, and ineffectual. U.S. politics is enormously unsettled, more so than at any time in memory. Only two changes are required to cause both major parties to lose their base of support: (1) an appealing alternative, and (2) increased voter turnout—which depends on whether there's an appealing alternative. Today's weak political involvement offers an unprecedented populist opportunity.

Elections as Educations

With a well-executed education campaign, voters will learn that populists embrace the core values of both conservatives and liberals, yet with a straightforward and pragmatic program that takes the nation in a very new direction. To prevail, populists need only educate people on four key issues.

First is the extent of today's economic disparities and the certainty that they will worsen unless action is quickly taken. Voters don't fully realize how these trends work such devastation across a wide array of values that everyone shares. This issue alone could prove compelling, particularly when compared to the tepid messages conveyed by the other parties. Both parties have ignored this vexing issue for so long that they can now address it only by parroting the populists. That will be apparent to voters.

Second is the unmet obligations due our children—fiscal, environmental, social, cultural. Neither major party proposes genuinely long-term solutions. The populists are the responsible voice, offering the only political message with a theme of genuine intergenerational equity and a commitment to honor the rights of children. Chapter 12 looks at the environmental conditions that we are leaving our children and proposes how to address them.

Third is the antidemocratic nature of our current financial structure. People know that something is terribly amiss, but they're not sure just what. What they know is that present-day politics is not responding to their concerns or the concerns of those they know. A populist education campaign can change that. None of this is rocket science. It's easily explained, drawing on commonsense analysis and well-known historical facts. It's simple enough to name those who have led us so far afield. And those who failed to speak up. The populist message is one that's accessible and anti-elitist. Happily, populists only need speak the truth, something neither major party dares to do after embracing these trends for so many years. So long as the education campaign remains accessible to those with a modest education, it cannot help but trump the simplistic appeals and superficial sloganeering that dominate the airwaves for the other parties.

Fourth is the threat that economic centralization poses to the democratic tradition. The very remoteness of today's business sector—its globalization, its finance-dominant culture, its megamergers, its community-insensitive practices, its hierarchical management structure, its plutocratic pay practices—all combine to create a sense of people being cut out, left out, even driven out. Though management theorists wax eloquently about the proliferation of Internet entrepreneurs working in the e-lance, e-commerce economy, or in virtual consulting firms from their spare bedrooms, the stress and uncertainty that surrounds such isolated and disconnected lifestyles is taking a huge toll, both financially and psychologically. Much as the centralization of land ownership was the dominant characteristic of feudalism, the centralization of capital ownership has come to define—and endanger—modern-day American democracy. As financial efficiency gained dominance over societal effectiveness, democracy was the loser.

A populist education program can provide the intellectual and rhetorical firepower that people need to express their anxieties politically. At present, there's no culturally sanctioned way to make their views known. That's because there's no political party offering a platform with any hope of significant change. Instead, people complain. They turn cynical. And occasionally violent. Americans are hungry for a distinctive presidential platform around which they can coalesce that will take this country in a very new, very inclusive direction. What's missing is a campaign that casts old problems in a new light—and offers the hope of new outcomes infused with vitality and meaning.

At present, the stature of our elected officials ranks close to the bottom on the scale of societal respect. They've earned it. Yet that's the very opposite of what a vibrant democracy should be. Those who stand for political office brought this on themselves with their lack of creativity and vision and their tightly pinched concept of what the public wants and what democracy can deliver. At the same time, however, voters realize they're co-conspirators in this sad waltz of public-sector mediocrity and popular passivity. The pot drips what's in it. Voters know that their involvement has been less than robust. What they don't know is that, absent their engagement, it's impossible for social change to keep pace with technological change and with the fast-paced transition to globalization. Instead, they've deferred to others, undermining their political self-confidence by so doing. It's time they become directors of a system that up to now has directed them. They're ready for a wake-up call. The twenty-first-century populism outlined here is intended to be that call.

Tapping into Wisdom

The chief remaining legacy of U.S. democracy is our capacity to have quite significant democratic aspirations. Americans aren't unique in that regard, but we have far more faith in our ability to change than do citizens of most other countries. We know that democracy can work, despite its current atrophied state. We've seen dramatic shifts come about through inspired and thoughtful leadership that emerged from within our ranks, most recently in civil rights and in ending an unpopular war in Southeast Asia. We know that the wisdom embedded in the system can respond. If we work it, democracy really does work. My goal here is to provide some tools for working it.

My generation (the baby boomers) has an unusual advantage that should work to the benefit of populists. We are the first generation in history who routinely have parents still alive when we are in our fifties. Our elders are a remarkable, untapped resource. A nation with the longest-lived elders ever known should not let that asset go to waste. That unexplored realm is a potential gold mine for learning how we might do things differently based on what they know. Their testimonials on populist themes could prove enormously persuasive—what they think about economic disparities, the multidimensional obligations owed their grandchildren, and similar hypersensitive issues that the major political parties avoid like the plague. That may prove the best strategy for restoring ethics to the nation's political dialog as our elders explore their dreams and ponder our responsibilities. Those testimonials should be paired with those of their grandchildren and their great-grandchildren to address issues that have long gone unmet by either party, particularly in such key areas as the environment, health, education, civil cohesion, racial harmony, nuclear disarmament, and such. What intergenerational obligations are due? And which ones haven't the major parties met? That's just the sort of personalized grassroots sentiments on which populism is fueled.

In addition, the power of the older voter cannot be overlooked. Their influence has long been magnified because of a simple fact: They turn out at the polls. That's why it's so difficult to reform Social Security and why today's politicians spend so much legislative time focusing on senior-sensitive issues such as Medicare benefits, prescription drug coverage, and long-term care.

Our elderly population is doing reasonably well. According to the Census Bureau, the poverty rate for Americans sixty-five and older dropped to 10.5 percent in 1997, from 35 percent in 1959. We now spend nine times more per capita on those over sixty than on those under six, an issue that our seniors might also care to address. Their median income, in constant dollars, more than doubled between 1957 and 1992. Because many of today's elderly were in their prime working years during the Reagan-Bush era, they can be expected to respond to a conservative approach to financial matters. That's all the more reason why intergenerational fiscal obligations—a key plank in any populist platform—should prove particularly appealing to this key constituency. Also, they're quite aware that neither major political party is seriously engaged in crafting a solution for Social Security. Instead, both parties are obviously jockeying for political advantage, hopeful that a misstep will provide an opening to demagogue the issue for political gain. Seniors need only be educated about the intergenerational ethics that underlie the populist sentiment. They've been around long enough to know what's missing and who is likely to supply it.

Education for Democracy

Education for democratic capitalism also requires a curriculum that can be adopted by secondary school and university faculty nationwide. From my work as an instructor in the MBA program at Emory University, I can attest from firsthand experience that today's narrow, finance-dominant, shareholder-value-focused, Chicago-inspired "economism" has been systematically and successfully drilled into the heads of degree candidates. The United States is now home to 748 graduate business schools, up from 125 at the end of the 1950s, which churn out 100,000 MBA degrees each year. The next generation of business leaders must be educated to think more comprehensively, more holistically, more pragmatically, more commonsensically—and more intergenerationally. That requires a concerted effort to break through the intellectual smog that the Law and Economics movement has spread nationwide.[11]

"The real world is by nature interdisciplinary," educator-diplomat Harlan Cleveland points out.[12] In a world where influences are interwoven and interactive, the education challenge for "the global century," he notes, lies in helping people "construct homemade ways of thinking about the whole."

If we are to have a sustainable free-enterprise democracy, we need an educated populace who understand the complex mix of relationships in which our commercial values are imbedded. Economic growth for the sake of growth is not the path to a viable democratic future. Yet change requires a populace willing to challenge whether endless economic growth and ever-expanding consumption can be sustained as our nation's central purpose. At the very least, a property-based system must be populated with people who know how to become owners and then to think like owners and to exercise their rights as owners. At present, there's no curriculum anywhere in the world that educates secondary-school and undergraduate students to become owners. Instead, they're educated to become employees. Trained and retrained, mind you, but *as employees*. This antidemocratic, dumbing-down anomaly must be addressed.

To evoke a leadership corps equal to this challenge, a true populist must show how to turn abstract ideas into everyday, concrete action. I address this question of everyday reality in the next chapter.

11
Leadership for
the Populist Century

If you expect to see the final results of your work, you have not asked a
big enough question.

—I. F. STONE

Populism is the soul of democracy. Like democracy, populism insists
that people be allowed an impact on those systems that have an impact on them. That's why modern-day populism strives to ensure
that small-unit democracy exists alongside large-unit systems of production. To suggest that such a personalized free enterprise might be
possible raises eyebrows within the mainstream. Yet that is precisely
the sort of intimate capitalism we need. Egalitarian in political spirit
and practical in economic design, today's populism aims to break the
mold of present-day politics. It's essential that our children not pay
the price for the tightly constricted range of today's political debate.
Yet if we are to have a productive debate about substantive change,
we must dramatically broaden the ranks of those leaders willing to
engage in that debate. Broad-based leadership is consistent with the
populist resistance both to traditional hierarchies and to political
elites. Populist leadership organizes not around personalities or political status but around principles and purposes. Its success is measured by its capacity to evoke local leadership excited about the
prospect of taking on more personal responsibility for the future of
their community.

The genuine populist leader creates an environment in which the genius of others can emerge. That's the only sensible way to govern a nation that prides itself on being a patchwork of diverse perspectives. It also recognizes that the breadth and depth of leadership required to mobilize needed change is vast and that no single leader can possibly suffice. Much like the way that geese in flight relieve the leader from time to time, this approach also acknowledges that we need depth in our populist leadership as many of the tasks require an intergenerational perspective. The goal here is not to prioritize an agenda in some top-down fashion but to "passion-ize" it—by empowering those who are enthusiastic about making change work from the bottom up. That's how we identify those who are ready to move from concept to reality and from advocacy to action. That means less top-down "dominator" democracy and more bottom-up "partnership-ocracy"—encouraging people to seize the initiative and to work within steadily shifting coalitions, crafting constantly evolving solutions to ever-changing challenges.[1] That's the real world. We just need to get smarter about how to cope with it.

Democracies are learning systems. Schools can't equip students with answers, but they can develop their capacity to learn. Educators have long known there's no such thing as a stupid child, only stupid systems of education. The same is true for democracies. Markets too. Both have imbedded within them a natural intelligence. The challenge lies in removing obstacles to its emergence. For instance, populists need only expose today's unconscionable economic disparities, and this nation's democratic intelligence will find its way to a political solution. Neither major party has any semblance of a workable plan for addressing today's inequity and unsustainability. Indeed, as of this writing, they've yet even to acknowledge that there's a problem. Populists offer the only genuine political alternative. Exposure to that alternative requires a national education campaign. That's the first and most urgent task in need of leadership.

Soulful Activism

Part of that leadership is already emerging in the form of traditional civil protest, often with an edge, or a sense of humor. Boycotts, protests, teach-ins, newsletters, community activism, Web sites—these are but a few. Boston-based Responsible Wealth sponsors shareholder resolutions asking that corporations adopt pay standards restricting their chief executive's pay to some multiple of the company's lowest-paid employee. Today's executive pay excesses are unlike anything ever seen. I mentioned earlier that Disney chief executive Michael Eisner's 1998 compensation was 25,070 times the average Disney worker's pay. Chief executive Michael Dell of Dell Computer rewarded himself $33.5 million in stock options in 1998—in a company in which he already owned stock valued at $16.4 billion ($20 billion in 1999). In May 1998, Computer Associates, a Long Island software company, awarded its top three executives 20 million shares worth $1.1 billion. Had the stock been divided evenly among the company's 9,850 employees, each would have received shares worth $113,000.[2] The prevailing Wall Street sentiment is reflected in the fact that Richard Grasso, a Computer Associates director who voted to approve the award, is chief executive of the New York Stock Exchange.[3] These trends scream out for a populist response.

Chuck Collins, codirector of Boston-based United for a Fair Economy, has a knack for adding humor to his activism. He made a point of showing up in New Hampshire in the spring of 1999, when Steve Forbes announced his presidential candidacy. As "Flat Tax" Forbes was about to speak, Collins and colleagues, dressed in business suits, unfurled a large banner reading, "Billionaires for Forbes—Because Inequality Isn't Growing Fast Enough." Other activists raised placards proclaiming "Free the Forbes 400" and "Tax Breaks for Me, Not My Maid," holding themselves out as members of the "Rich People's Liberation Front" (the flat tax would save Forbes an estimated $174,000 annually). When shoved to the side by Forbes's campaign staff, the demonstrators fought back with several chants: "Make workers pay the tax so investors can relax" and "Who needs day care, hire an au pair." Naturally, Collins and his supporters made the evening news. With so many inane ideas swirling around today's political scene, satire and ridicule have seldom been more appropriate. As comedian Steve Allen once observed, "satire is tragedy plus time." Those who bear the brunt of such populist humor should be thankful that they have not (as least not yet) become the focal point of popular rebellion.

A Boom for Whom?

Considerable creativity is called for if these sensitive issues are to pierce the hard shell of conventional news coverage. For that purpose, Collins also developed a compact disk that lets you "hear" inequality. Designed for radio spots, this audio CD features a voice-over describing how each BB dropped into a large metal pot represents $500 of personal wealth. You first hear the typical family's wealth, which sounds like a few plunks of only a very few BBs bouncing noisily around in the bottom of an empty pot. You then hear the wealth of the top 0.5 percent. The Niagara-like torrent of BBs takes about forty-five seconds to noisily fill the pot to overflowing.

The audio segment represents a form of leadership that populism much needs—devising entertaining, provocative, and humorous ways to alert people to the insanity of today's Law and Economics policy environment. If you don't like the news, go out and make your own. That's a populist style of leadership.[4]

Think Again, a Boston-area arts group, sponsors a series of innovative billboards, including one with the message "Top executives now make more in a day than the average worker makes in a year." Above that appear four shoulder-to-shoulder suit-and-tie torsos with chalkboard heads featuring four words: "Economic Boom for Whom?" Newspaper stories about the billboard campaign leveraged its impact across Massachusetts.[5] Think Again codirector S. A. Bachman explains that the group's strategy is "to put up images that talk back to other images" with a thought-provoking slant as a counterpoint to the mindlessly incessant "buy, buy, buy" message found on other billboards. The group's populist-inspired goal, he explains, is to raise the question "Who's manufacturing the rosy picture of the economy and to what end?"

At Citigroup's April 1999 shareholders meeting, activists from Responsible Wealth rolled out a "Weill-barrow" filled to overflowing with 5,500 "fortune" cookies representing Citigroup CEO Sandy Weill's 1998 compensation of $167 million. A second Weill-barrow carried just one fortune cookie, representing the $30,000 annual salary of the typical Citigroup bank teller.

A new quarterly publication (Too Much) features on each issue's back cover the Petulant Plutocrat of the Month.[6] The summer 1999 pick was media baron Rupert Murdoch. Despite his $23 billion in personal wealth, Murdoch has been handed some recent setbacks, detailed in a story titled "The world's biggest press lord just can't get any respect." Those include the UK government's blocking Murdoch's purchase of the legendary Manchester United soccer team after British fans went ballistic. Then his New York neighbors refused to grant him permission to renovate his $6.5 million Manhattan penthouse. Owner of everything from Fox TV and the Los Angeles Dodgers to the largest-circulation newspaper in the English-speaking world, he was also rebuffed in his attempt to buy a stake in Russia's top TV channel. Meanwhile, the Chinese turned a cold shoulder to his proposed satellite network. A global citizen carrying a tax haven passport, he pays virtually no U.S. taxes, even though 70 percent of his News Corporation's operating profit originates here. The steady spread of this freeloader's multimedia empire (this book is distributed by HarperCollins, one of his companies) led a *London Evening Standard* writer to observe that we may soon look forward to a world where "everyone will have a fantastic, amazing and truly liberating amount of choice: Murdoch, Murdoch or Murdoch."

Other activists are moving into cyberspace. In addition to the Web site that tracks Bill Gates's wealth (see Chapter 2), cyberspace also provides a handy home for others to lampoon curious aspects of our current political landscape. Longtime activist and satirist Paul Krassner describes Warren Apel's interactive Web site called the Flag-Burning Page, where Web surfers can click on images of a burning flag, with comments such as, "Well, now you did it. She's blazing and Newt's not gonna like it." A tag line indicates that "no actual flags were harmed in the production of this page."[7]

On a global scale, Philadelphia activist Judy Wicks has a knack for combining the lighthearted with the deadly serious. A successful restauranteur, Wicks has converted her lifelong interest in poverty and hunger into a sister restaurant program she calls A Table for Six Billion Please. With delegations to poverty-stricken foreign locales (Mexico, Cuba, Nicaragua, etc.), she takes concerned Philadelphians and others to see firsthand the challenges facing people in other countries and the effect of U.S. foreign policy on their lives. She runs her upscale gourmet restaurant, the White Dog Café ($4.5 million in annual revenue), as a center for social activism that combines high purpose with high jinks—sponsoring speakers, block parties, rollerblade outings, and a variety of community-building activities. With a leadership style that joins fun with education, activism, and enthusiasm, hers is soulful populist leadership at its best.

Vanity Rules

U.S. leadership over the past two decades has stoked the fires of human avarice like no other era in the history of democracy. Happily, the excesses of today's rich have reached such an extreme that they are easily lampooned by those with sufficient moxie to do so. In the 1980s, we saw Susan Gutfreund, wife of the CEO of Salomon Brothers, spending $20 million to redecorate their Manhattan apartment and booking two seats on the Concorde to fly a cake to her husband's birthday party in Paris. One of my favorites is the fifty-room, 60,112-square-foot Georgian mansion (three-quarters the size of the White House) built in the 1990s for Leslie Wexner, founder of the Limited (which owns or has spun off Abercrombie & Fitch, Victoria's Secret, Express, etc.). The floor of Wexner's lavish ballroom operates like a mammoth dumbwaiter so that it can be lowered into the cellar, where servants set the banquet table before it's raised into place. Another for the annals of our time are the estate owners in the Hamptons, whose trophy homes have long been the subject of curiosity. The residents have now taken to building their tennis courts six feet below ground level so that they won't be disturbed by the ever-so-annoying sound of bouncing tennis balls.[8] If the well-to-do get sick, they can repair to any of at least ten medical centers around the nation that, the *Wall Street Journal* reports, now offer "entire luxury floors or corridors with everything from chefs and concierges to high-end beauty products in the bathroom." For instance, New York's Memorial Sloan-Kettering Cancer Center opened in 1998 its "wealth care" facility, catering to the rich with resortlike facilities that cost up to $2,800 a day over the standard room rate. When they're ready to leave, the men can slip into a custom Brionis suit ($20,000) fashioned with 22-karat gold pinstripes and accented with a 24-karat tie from Paris shirtmaker Charvet ($185).

None of this opulence is new. Thorstein Veblen addressed it in describing the leisure class of the last Gilded Age, with their profound narcissism and their pathetic bids for immortality given expression in their "conspicuous consumption" and their "unremitting demonstration of ability to pay." The pleasure lies not in the consuming, he points out, but in the proof offered of one's capacity to pay for such superfluity. The more wasteful the expenditure, the more heightened the experience, as even more social credit accrues in their vanity account. To poke fun at this societal pornography, author Tom Wolfe dubs a newly lucrative publishing arena "plutography," the graphic depiction of the lifestyles of the rich and shameless. Though most major metropolitan areas have real estate listings catering to the high end, we now see a spate of national magazines such as the *Robb Report* dedicated to the luxury lifestyle. With displays that would make the Great Gatsby blush, these top-end-targeted publications feature everything from $3.2 million Patek Philippe watches to reviews of the latest, in what yet may become the rage among the architecturally sophisticated well-to-do, such as the "Neo-Fortress Movement," featuring towers and turrets, walled yards, massive gates and tall, narrow windows. That image epitomizes the paradox of what now passes for American democracy, as out-of-control capitalism begets neofeudalism.

Knowledge versus Knowing

Modern society grew out of a belief that democratic progress lay in the direction of reductionist knowledge—the idea that we could engineer our organizations so that you pull a lever over here and get a result over there. A vote over here ensures you a democracy over there. That mechanical notion also lies behind the appeal of hierarchical command-and-control leadership. The Newtonian-age "deterministic" approach to organizations assumed that everything could be understood as machinery, a clockwork universe reduced to simple cause-and-effect relationships. We now know that's simply not true. The more appropriate metaphor is organic, living systems with their complex, interwoven webs of constantly interacting parts. In a living system, dynamism is the reality and equilibrium is achieved only at death. There's no omega point in free enterprise where everything suddenly clicks into balance. Similarly, democracies are highly dynamic, constantly adapting organisms. So are markets. What makes such systems organic is that the parts communicate with the whole and their wisdom resides in the whole. Much in the same way that the body's immune system is distributed throughout the body, the wisdom of both democracies and markets is whole and irreducible. Although much adaptation in the system is information-based, other components are intuitive, even visceral, based less on knowledge than on a certain inner knowing. Albert Einstein agreed, advising that we learn to think with the feelings in our muscles. We do that naturally. First impressions are usually correct, even though they're based more on intuition than information.

Today's money-myopic, Chicago-inspired version of capitalism is based on an outmoded mechanistic assumption: Maximize financial returns over here and—just trust us—the results will be terrific over there. Looking back, it's extraordinary that such a simplistic, reductionist paradigm has enjoyed credibility for so long. Capitalism needs ways to learn with something more than just financial feedback, because that alone fails miserably to advance the sort of multidimensional learning now needed. Relying on finance to appraise the needs of a democracy is like trying to interpret the constitution by analyzing the ink it's printed in. Both markets and democracies now face the fast-rising costs of coping with a "democracy deficit" because both have failed thus far to engage *people* in a sufficiently robust fashion. In addition, neither system has yet figured out a way to ensure that we live for the benefit of the next generation and beyond. Or how to bring a global perspective to decisionmaking, even when operating at a local level. This global, multidimensional, and intergenerational learning requires a very new sort of leadership—one that distinguishes the external knowledge provided by markets from the inner knowledge within each individual and community. The challenge facing populist leaders lies in helping people regain the self-confidence required to translate their democratic instincts into institutions and rulemaking. Success in that domain is what gains social traction for people's democratic sentiments—and for their commitment to future generations.

A key reason that democracies and markets defer to individual and collective sentiment is that it's simply so much easier to rely on a system able to correct and repair itself. That's the genius in self-correcting systems and in democracies. They're governed from the inside out, not from some higher authority such as a bureaucratic elite or a politburo or a Washington–Wall Street intelligentsia. Democracies take whatever information comes from without and process it based on past experience before crafting a response. How the information is processed is key. The problem with placing so much reliance on market signals—particularly capital markets—is that they operate with a far more narrow set of values than those on which the democratic sentiment is built. Plus they're virtually blind when it comes to seeing beyond a few years or evaluating the impact on nature. Capital markets provide a valuable viewpoint, yet their input needs to be kept in perspective. Psychiatrist-author James Hillman suggests that we need to develop enough character to act like ancestors:

> Ancestors sit at the edge of the tribe and protect us from evil spirits: injustice, sham, hypocrisy, exploitation, destruction of the planet. Ancestors are individuals and ideas that help the tribe continue for seven generations. It is in humility (not hubris) and the force of character (not delusions about engineering the future) that we find lasting life.[9]

A Question of Perspective

Paul Hawken, coauthor of *Natural Capitalism*, tells a revealing story stemming from his work with Monsanto, best known for its pesticides, herbicides, biocides, and biotechnology products. He divided a group of Monsanto engineers and MBAs into five separate teams, asking each to design a spaceship that would leave the Earth and bring its inhabitants back, happy and healthy, a hundred years hence. They would then vote on the winning design. The winning team's design included two very revealing features. First, they agreed that virtually none of Monsanto's products would be useful. Second, they were asked if it was OK if 20 percent of the people on the spaceship controlled 80 percent of the resources on board. They immediately and vociferously rejected that notion as unworkable and unfair.

In other words, in small groups with appropriate goals and challenges, we know what to do. That's the populist point. Societies are large and abstract, whereas community implies human scale and hands-on. Trustworthiness correlates highly with face-to-face relationships, the real source of social order. If society doesn't work at this one-on-one level, it doesn't work at all.

Genuine democracies reject the notion of entrusting any one leader or organization or any single category of influence with the power to make sweeping change. That's why unbridled financial forces endanger democracy. The commercial corporation, a creation of money, quite naturally puts the interests of money first. That's what makes global capital markets potentially so very dangerous to democracy. And what makes Monsanto's engineers seem so schizophrenic. As employees of Monsanto, they create highly toxic agricultural chemicals to enhance financial returns for Monsanto's shareholders. Often those chemicals are then sold to corporate farms operating in a similar framework of values set by remote investors interested only in maximizing money-denominated returns. Those farms, in turn, supply food to corporate grocers. Yet as individuals in a limited, holistic environment (a self-contained spaceship), the engineers' point of reference shifted from making money (maximizing shareholder value for remote investors) to what is necessary to sustain a healthy living community for all stakeholders. Suddenly their focus shifted to *optimizing* a range of values. Their shift to a human-scale framework evoked a wholly different set of values. They began to think like ancestors. Different framework, different values. The paradox that confronts us in today's abstract, impersonal, and finance-obsessive capitalism is captured in a revealing remark by the CEO of U.S. Steel, who conceded, "We don't make steel; we make profits for our shareholders." Like the people at Monsanto, he could be producing *anything*.

Aligning the Corporate Purpose

Abraham Lincoln worried greatly about the dangers to democracy implied by the money-myopic nature of the corporate entity and its potential corrupting influence. Writing near the end of the Civil War, when government spending on the war had brought fantastic wealth to the defense contractors of his era, he cautioned:

> We may congratulate ourselves that this cruel war is nearing its end. It has cost a vast amount of treasure and blood. . . . It has indeed been a trying hour for the Republic; but I see in the near future a crisis approaching that unnerves me and causes me to tremble for the safety of my country. As a result of the war, corporations have been enthroned and an era of corruption in high places will follow, and the money power of the country will endeavor to prolong its reign by working upon the prejudices of the people until all wealth is aggregated in a few hands and the Republic is destroyed. I feel at this moment more anxiety for the safety of my country than ever before, even in the midst of war. God grant that my suspicions may prove groundless.[10]

Earlier, Thomas Jefferson had similar concerns: "We must crush in its birth the aristocracy of our moneyed corporations, which dare already to bid defiance to the laws of our country." James Madison, Jefferson's Charlottesville, Virginia, neighbor, was similarly apprehensive: "We are free today, substantially, but the day will come when our republic will come to impossibility because its wealth will be concentrated in the hands of the few. When that day comes we must rely on the wisdom of the best elements in the country to readjust the laws of the nation to the changed conditions."

The populist response to this recurrent concern is straightforward and democratic: Ensure that *people* are connected to the economy (and to the corporate entity) in a way that empowers them to resist what's not working and to create something that will. That's how systems learn—information and knowledge wed to the capacity to effect change. That's hardly a novel idea; Gandhi promoted it six decades ago. Feed that which leads to fairness and freedom, he advised, and starve the other. Soon enough, the other will disappear. Today's challenge lies in ensuring that we have a reasonable idea of just where it is we mean to go and the types of organizations likely to get us there. Making money is not the goal; making money is required for the organization to stay in the game. Populists need to articulate the point of the game because that should determine the rules within which corporations are allowed to operate and the feedback to which they are required to respond.

The questions involving how much power is granted to whom are important questions best answered by people granted the capacity to have an impact on forces that have an impact on them. More fundamentally, however, even that democratic sentiment misses the point. This nation was founded for clearly stated transcendental purposes—liberty, equality, dignity, posterity, self-determination, the pursuit of happiness. Commercial practices whose results prove inconsistent with those goals must be reformed or the firms closed down.

Collective Foresight Through Collective Leadership

Democracy is grounded on the fundamental premise that liberty is never safe except in the hands of the people themselves. Both democracies and markets rely on highly distributed forms of leadership because both assume that the decisions of the many will ultimately become the decision of the one—the organization. Both operate through engaged dialogue. The language of finance provides to the dialogue a useful but quite limited source of insight. It tells us whether the organization is successfully generating money-denominated benefits but it often tells us nothing about associated costs—social, fiscal, cultural, political, environmental.

In a true democracy, there is no *dominant* feedback loop. And no dominant leader. Because wisdom and expertise are scattered throughout any group of people, a democracy relies on extensive networks of engaged dialogue to achieve collective wisdom and expertise.[11] Dialogue is what brightens up those networks with clarity and opens democracy to more possibilities. Success in creating those engaged networks is the key to whether populism succeeds as a democratization movement. That's where leadership is most needed. Happily, that's a direction in which trends are already headed, as people are developing more loyalty to networks than to particular

firms or organizations. That tendency is destined to grow as occupa-
tions take on a more cellular structure held together less by hierarchy
than by mutual interests and by communication networks. In
Connexity, British author Geoff Mulgan explains the difference:

> In a stratified society what matters is your position on a vertical
> hierarchy which is recognized by everyone else. In a cellular or-
> der what matters is your membership in a number of different
> cells—a profession, sport, religion, family network, political
> party—and their relationship to the larger society. Indeed, it is
> one of the paradoxes of connexity that the more things intercon-
> nect, the more people want to be members of self-contained
> compartments.[12]

Toward a Wired World

Social indicators point in the direction of a more connected and
relationship-based world, whether at work or elsewhere. For example,
the number of employed people in California who could be classified
as wired workers—those who regularly use computers on the job and
work in self-directed teams—grew from 31 percent to 37 percent just
from 1996 to 1998 (California now boasts the world's seventh largest
economy). It's important to understand that networks, once they
achieve a critical mass, become powerful in themselves and are often
able to move an agenda. Former President George Bush proved the
power of networks over a few short weeks in the summer of 1999,
mobilizing the Bush clan's donor network to raise more than $50
million for his eldest son's presidential campaign, practically preempt-
ing the Republican presidential primary before it began. The quick
mobilization of moneyed networks was intended to ensure that his
boy's nomination was more a coronation than a contest. Lousy for
democracy but good systems logic.

As Kevin Kelly, executive editor of *Wired*, points out, the real value
in today's connected world is the connections themselves. That's
where the investment pays off. For genuine prosperity, he argues,
"feed the web first."[13] Build the platform of relationships. For instance, with on-line securities trading now taking off, seats on the
New York Stock Exchange lost half their value in 1998. People can
now handle that relationship in a very different way because they're
wired into the Web, while those who built that platform of new relationships made a bundle (eBay founder Pierre Omidyar's 1999

wealth is estimated at $4.9 billion).[14] In December 1999, Pittsburgh became the first city to offer municipal bonds over the Internet.[15] While consumer e-commerce is expected to grow from $7.8 billion in 1998 to $108 billion in 2003, business e-commerce is expected to rise from $43 billion to more than $1 trillion, according to Forester Research.

Relationships are not only how systems connect, but also how they learn and how they're held accountable. Serendipitously, the only possible way that robust democracies can work is through networks of people-empowered relationships. That's a key reason that the new global trading regime—the North America Free Trade Agreement (NAFTA), the General Agreement on Tariffs and Trade (GATT), and its successor the World Trade Organization (WTO)— has so many people worried. To make national economies attractive to the forces of economic globalization, these agreements press nations into competing with each other to lower production costs by weakening local rules on pay rates, health standards, environmental regulations, social safeguards, capital mobility, and so on. There's little opportunity for those affected to have any input in this global trading regime. The actors are largely multinational corporations from which those affected are disconnected. The agreements typify a system that assumes that enhanced financial returns and a rising GDP are desirable, regardless of who reaps the benefits or who bears the costs. The political embrace of this perspective by the WTO's 135 nation-state members offers compelling evidence of a leadership corps delighted to sacrifice democratic values to finance-denominated values.

Public reaction to the commencement of the WTO's Millennial Round of meetings in Seattle in December 1999 was, I suggest, just the tip of the iceberg. People are only slowly awakening to the very limited standards embraced by what WTO former director-general Renato Ruggiero calls a "new constitution for a single global economy." In their scope and impact, trade-related economic accords are the equivalent of the arms control agreements of the 1970s and 1980s. The difference is that only one value is reflected in this global constitution: the uninhibited flow of goods and capital. Lurking behind these global economic accords is the simplistic rationale "a rising tide lifts all boats," an assumption with no factual support. The WTO's judicial system is a three-member "dispute resolution body" staffed by former corporate or government trade officials that operates in secret (no press, no public). As a European trade minister conceded, "It's not undemocratic, it's *anti-democratic.*"

How so? For country after country, the chilling effect on democratic decisionmaking is palpable.

- The first WTO case affecting the United States ruled that we must amend our Clean Air Act to permit the import of dirty Venezuelan petrol that did not meet federal standards.
- Japan was told to lift its ban on the import of fruits known to carry certain invasive insects, even though such products require heavy doses of harmful pesticides at the border.
- The European Union was instructed to stop favoring bananas from small Caribbean growers over Chiquita-brand bananas grown by corporate-sponsored, plantation-style agriculture.
- Rather than fight the WTO, Guatemala lifted its ban on advertising by Gerber Infant Formula that claimed that it was healthier than breast milk.
- Thailand ceased its manufacture of a low-cost AIDS (acquired immune deficiency syndrome) drug after the Clinton-Gore administration threatened a WTO suit at the urging of one of our pharmaceutical companies.

Such cross-border deregulation ratchets down the standards for health, safety, and the environment *everywhere*—regardless of what people in affected countries may choose. If the WTO revives negotiations on the Multilateral Agreement on Investment (suspended in 1998), it could become illegal, for instance, to favor locally owned businesses when building infrastructure projects funded with local tax revenues. Likewise prohibited would be any requirement that some portion of local savings or profits be reinvested locally rather than flowing abroad. A state's pension plan investments could no longer be screened, say, to protest against companies that sell food containing genetically modified organisms. Or companies that clear-cut rain forests. Or use slave labor. Nelson Mandela might still be in prison had the WTO been fully in operation a decade ago as the widespread practice of antiapartheid screening of investments was clearly a form of financial discrimination that would be forbidden under this global Law and Economics–inspired constitution. Under the "investment rights" chapter of NAFTA, the Virginia-based Ethyl Corporation is suing Canada for forgone profits that Ethyl claims it could have made on the sale of a gasoline additive

that the United States has banned. Because the Canadian government didn't ban the additive until after Ethyl commenced sales
there, the company claims that it should be compensated for lost
sales. Is democracy at risk? Even if you're a committed earth keeper
or a concerned ancestor, the WTO insists that the community's
edges be permeable to trade and finance. The effect is to outlaw any
local initiative that aims to protect the safety of your food, your job,
your health, your family, your local businesses, or your environment. Do not be deceived by rhetoric: The WTO is not about
democracies regulating trade; it's about regulating democracies so
they don't interfere with trade.

Toward a Connected Global Capitalism

Whereas a key flaw of communism is its failure to protect the individual, the fault of finance-myopic free enterprise is its failure to respect
the communities in which those individuals reside.[16] A half-century
ago, conservative Austrian economist Friedrich Hayek foresaw that
centralized economies had no future, because the bulk of information
generated in a modern economy is local in character and requires ever
higher degrees of sophistication to account for the concerns of the local within the whole. Odd though it may seem, the colossal, centrally
run, multinational corporation—the most visible manifestation of
Hayek's laissez-faire economics—operates in clear defiance of
Hayek's keen insight, as does the WTO. The typical multinational is
run with a top-down, finance-driven agenda that ignores the nuanced
intelligence and locale-specific sensibilities unique to each community
and country. And now a global "constitution" emerges, insistent that
international law *enforce* worldwide deference to that very narrow set
of values regardless of local concerns. The political implications are
far too dangerous to describe as merely antidemocratic. It has all the
hallmarks of a fast-emerging twenty-first-century financial authoritarianism.

What's the appropriate response? How do we protect posterity
from this Chicago-inspired mechanistic model and craft in its stead a
democratic system suitable to today's complex and interdependent
world? Hayek, a Nobel laureate, offers a clue: "To the naïve mind
that conceives of order only as a product of deliberate management,
it may seem absurd that in complex conditions, order and the adaptation to the unknown can be achieved more effectively by decentral-

izing decisions."[17] Hayek's systems-insight suggests that the answer lies in the direction of more connexity. Where there are few peoplized connections, build them. Wire systems for inclusion. When building the platform of relationships, include a preference for the local and the broad-based. Build clusters of relationships around common interests. Use property as a way to link people to the pulse of particular places so that business orients itself to the needs of people and the bioregions they inhabit. View human relationships as a way to overcome the utter abstraction with which the finance globalists regard our earthly surroundings. Spread the word that a movement is loose in the world that would force us to live in a plutocratic, unsustainable, dehumanized world. Regardless of how many official facts this eloquent voice of unreason amasses in support of its operations, any force that fails the test of sustainability is a force that betrays democracy. Its promises must be portrayed as false, and its policies must be resisted with all the might that democracy can muster.

Thousands of organizations worldwide have taken a stand in favor of widely defined notions of sustainability (London-based SustainAbility, the Rocky Mountain Institute, the Switzerland-based World Business Council for Sustainable Development, The Natural Step, etc.). Though the organizations are diverse in focus and scattered across the globe, their statements of principle and purpose are remarkably consistent in both tone and content. They offer evidence of a fast-emerging, affinity-based network destined to steadily gain in strength. In an environment where commerce is king, 54 million disabled Americans are currently mobilizing their $1 trillion in buying power to command greater quality of life. We Media offers an example of a multimedia company focused on meeting affinity-group needs through an on-line community (www.wemedia.com).

These are early examples of an emerging form of leadership that is highly distributed, often affinity-group-based and passionate in its beliefs. Just as Seattle saw an alliance between hard hats and greens ("teamsters and turtles"), this connect-the-dots commitment to a web of common values is poised to become a populist model of how nongovernmental organizations (NGOs) become a force for positive change. Their emergence is evidence that, absent a global government with genuinely democratic values, such networks offer the most practical way for consensus to emerge that represents the breadth of society, particularly among its more activist elements. Delighted at the show of in-the-streets-democracy on display in Seattle, John Sweeney, president of umbrella trade union organization AFL-CIO, argues that it showed a "stunning breakthrough in the public debate over globalization" and punctured the WTO's "veil of secrecy and insensitivity."

Such shared-principle, shared-purpose, networked efforts have enormous potential for catalyzing the institutional change that a sustainable future requires, one that respects not just property people and the environment. They're in the vanguard of an emerging twenty-first-century populist politics—local yet international, diverse strategies yet similar principles, underfunded yet influential, tenuous yet tenacious, disjointed but doggedly determined. This is the newly emerging human (versus financial) face of globalization. It is from such passionate partnership and grassroots globalism that our populist future will emerge.

Values Barriers

This networked, relationship-based view of globalization (and leadership) also suggests the need to construct not trade barriers but values barriers. That requires a very new type of leadership. For instance, according to the late Pakistani development expert Mahbub ul Haq, south Asia alone has 134 million children working sixteen-hour days for eight cents a day.[18] A 1998 report by the International Labor Organization (ILO) documents that 250 million children between the ages of five and fourteen are working, mostly in Asia and Africa. Although the use of child labor ensures cheap products, it also cheapens human life and robs children of their childhood. Biologists know that unless a songbird hears another songbird in its first few months of life, it cannot sing. Any system that condones childhood employment in the interest of cheaper products and enhanced financial returns deprives us of the songs of children, robbing both them and us of their joy.

Populist leaders recognize that blind allegiance to a national identity can convert us into the poorest rich people on earth. We are all impoverished when a child misses its childhood. We are all the poorer when a member of the human community is not educated, or when a child is born into poverty. Yet one such child is born every minute. Everyone suffers when a child is born to a child, yet that also happens every minute. We are all impoverished when a child dies of hunger, yet 24,000 people die of hunger every day; three-fourths are children under five.[19] These facts and others like them suggest why democracies must take guidance from values other than financial values and those values associated with free trade. Alice Tepper-Marlin, founder of the Manhattan-based Council on Economic Priorities, established in 1997 a social accountability accreditation agency to provide a universal standard for consumers who no longer want their spending to contribute to human degradation. Using certified "social accountability auditors," the council issues Social Accountability Standard (SA8000) certificates in much the same way that companies now have their financial statements certified by public accountants.[20] U.S. firms well along in the accreditation process include Avon and Toys "R" Us. Though the concept originated in the United States, European firms are pushing ahead most rapidly, including Promodes, the $30 billion French hypermarket chain. SA8000 certificates are destined to take their place alongside audits for quality (ISO 9000) and environmental management (ISO 14000). Simply put, in an information age, people want to know.

Institutional investors can't afford *not* to know. The "precautionary principle," the hallmark of prudent business practice, mandates that companies avoid risks that cannot be identified and quantified. The potential for retroactive exposure to product liability claims (even human rights claims) suggests that values-free free trade may be hazardous to your financial health, as investors in companies making asbestos, tobacco products, and breast implants can attest, and as manufacturers of handguns and biotech products may soon discover.[21] Some of these corporations are like errant teenagers run amok. Relying on trend data suggesting that almost half of U.S. males (and one-third of females) will contract a non-smoking-related cancer, Samuel Epstein, a physician specializing in cancer prevention, documents as the causal factor our non-optional exposure to carcinogenic elements, which also results in a particularly high incidence of cancer among children.[22] Documenting a long history of deception and cover-up, he argues that we are losing a winnable war against cancer because we won't prosecute clear commercial wrongdoing. His solution: a "public health crimes tribunal," including prison sentences for those corporate executives found guilty of crimes of economic motivation that have a known adverse impact on public health. Regardless of whether you agree with that strategy, civil society clearly must find some way to cope with business leaders and firms that offload costs onto society.

To date, the greatest growth in corporate standards-setting has been in the environmental arena where numerous certification firms emerged in the 1990s. Eco-friendly certification is available for environmentally sensitive forestry practices from the Forest

Stewardship Council, based in Oaxaca, Mexico. Some electricity providers now sell appliances certified as climate-safe. September 1999 saw the launch of the Dow Jones Sustainability Group Indexes (DJSGI), which will rank thousands of companies from twenty-two countries and sixty-eight industry groups according to their commitment to sustainable development. According to Dow Jones calculations, DJSGI companies have substantially outperformed world index benchmarks, as sustainability-driven firms consistently generate better financial performance.[23] Although this steady growth in values-setting activities will doubtless have a positive effect, the First Hundred Days of my proposed populist administration should explore the adoption of international values barriers to displace trade barriers as the focus of trade negotiations. Free trade, yes. Values-free trade, why should we allow it?

Trading Values

During the New Deal era of the 1930s, FDR urged merchants to display in their shop windows the National Recovery Act's "blue eagle" to designate local business leaders who supported national political leaders in making the transition out of a very difficult time. A similar logo could prove useful internationally to "brand" companies and products that meet agreed-to standards of equity and sustainability. The rules governing international trade could require such labeling, ensuring that consumers have the information they need to choose.[24]

Current rules of international trade assume that consumers are well informed. That's simply not true. "Free trade" (i.e., exchange based on prices alone) is a misnomer when costs are either hidden, dumped onto an unwitting public, or passed on to the next generation. Prices provide profoundly misleading signals when externalities are not accounted for. Trade should be free only when it's beneficial, not when it's deceptive or abusive.

I get huge amounts of unsolicited third-class junk mail every day. It goes directly into the recycling bin. Why not allow a preferred postage rate for "green" versus regular third-class mail? For instance, Hanna Anderson, a catalog company that sells children's clothing, plants three trees for every one felled to print their catalogs. Founder Gun Denhart figures that's the responsible thing to do. Why not use pricing to *encourage* such social responsibility? We could issue "green eagle" stickers for certifiably sustainable mail order merchants. Or charge others a higher postal rate and earmark the proceeds to deploy a reforestation corps staffed by job-hungry youth. If prices are to mean anything, we must raise prices on what we want less of and subsidize what we want more of.

Effective global leadership must include a diverse array of innovative ways to persuade people to change their behavior, because the solutions now needed require that literally hundreds of millions of people do something—or stop doing something—united behind common values. That includes, for example, ensuring that homes and office buildings worldwide are rated for energy efficiency, a process already under way in the United States with the anticipated release in 2000 of the U.S. Green Building Council's LEED (Leadership in Energy and Environmental Design) rating system.

The Prosperity Corps (see Chapter 8) could serve a monitoring and a mentoring role in this equation, both here and abroad. For instance, many children working in developing countries will never have a chance to play with the dolls, soccer balls, or action figures that they produce for U.S. children. Youth-to-youth exchanges could prove hugely valuable. For example, U.S. at-risk youth could teach sports skills and math to Pakistani or Brazilian or Malaysian youth while also monitoring work sites for inhumane, unsafe, or environmentally insensitive conditions.

Another part of the equation is a "clean clothes" standard so that customers can know whether their clothing purchases are sweatshop-free. For instance, when Ava-Line president Irwin Gordon was asked by *Business Week* to explain the firm's success, he described how easy it was:

> We have a factory in China where we have 250 people. We own them; it's our factory. We pay them $40 a month and they work 28 days a month. They work from 7 A.M. to 11 P.M., with two breaks for lunch and dinner. They eat all together, 16 people to a room, stacked on four bunks to a corner. Generally, they're young girls that come from the hills.[25]

Do the values reflected in Ava-Line's financial success deserve the support of free-trade in a democracy? Both domestically and abroad, the Prosperity Corps could be in the vanguard in the education, skills-training, and standards-setting effort needed to move us toward a global system that affects equity and sustainability.

Because populism is about human dignity, a populist trade policy *must* screen for human values. Ownership patterns are destined to play a role. For instance, what possible sense does it make to endorse free trade in clothing or sports equipment or natural resources when the revenues generated by those companies are used to further enrich and entrench local plutocrats? Or to support military dictators? Access to our markets is far too critical a development tool to be used in a way that undercuts both democratic values and sustainable development.

Take another example. Investors in developing countries are often required to have local partners, a reasonable requirement except that it's regularly used to feather the nests of corrupt politicians. Indonesia's Suharto clan is but one of the more visible examples of this prevalent practice. What is gained by our compliance with such arrangements without an assurance that this partnering results in genuinely broad-based ownership?

The Populist Political Climate

On the home front, it's clear that new networking technologies fit well with current political sentiments. And with the need for a more distributed leadership. The politics of the past half-century have made us rightly skeptical both of centralized solutions and of large institutions in general. Yet polls confirm that we remain receptive to a more modest government that fosters individual opportunity.[26] Baby boomers, raised on a diet of both idealism and disillusionment (assassinations, Vietnam, Watergate), tend both to distrust authority and to believe in the power of collective action motivated by ideals. We can add to that confusing mix the formative experiences of Gen-Xers and their brush with economic insecurity, rising crime, and unprecedented family instability. Their experience with ineffective and immoral government has led them to embrace entrepreneurship and self-reliance. While supportive of government efforts in education and the environment, they're far less prone to participate in national politics than the boomers, though Gen-Xers are more likely to be involved in their local community. The common denominator here suggests that the political climate is ripe for a populist approach with its focus on an idealistic, people-first, community-focused agenda that draws on entrepreneurship—both in business and in advancing societal reform, particularly in the environmental arena.

The transformational leadership required to mobilize this wide-ranging agenda must be, like the forces behind markets and democracies, highly distributed. We learned from Einstein that no problem can be solved from the same consciousness that created it. Populists must therefore educate people in how to *see* the world in a very new way. We must empower each other to understand the multidimensional whole.

Both democracies and markets wrongly assume that people already have the relationships necessary for advancing their respective interests. In truth, democracies rely on often sparsely attended spasms of participation (periodic voting) interspersed with extended periods with very little day-to-day constituent input or feedback. Meanwhile, markets rely on pricing, with few other opportunities for the system to be genuinely people-responsive. We don't have an environmental problem; we have a lack-of-relationship problem. And a lack-of-connectedness problem. And a lack-of-communication problem. Most fundamentally, we have a systems-wide learning problem. People are simply too disengaged, disconnected and, as a result, often even disinterested and disillusioned. That presents populist leaders with the additional challenge of making their case for change not only compelling but also entertaining, even uplifting.

Quantum Populism

Populist leaders must evoke a new architecture of human relationships so that we learn better how to care for the intergenerational interests at stake across these various "nested" domains—economic, social, environmental. Both democracies and markets, by definition, are always a bit out of control. That's as it should be. Like nature itself, that's the source of their dynamism. The goal of both is to ensure a *healthy* state of ongoing adaptation in which the only constant is constant change and the only equilibrium is a dynamic equilibrium. Democracies and markets are verbs, not nouns. That also explains why granting too much leadership to any one set of values is inherently suspect. The response becomes simplistic, even mechanistic. We don't live in a world of billiard balls careening one off another at predetermined angles. What governs change is steadily shifting patterns of relationships. In nature, there are no kings, only kin. Therein lies the challenge of populist-inspired political leadership—to ensure that people are connected to the system through high-quality relationships—yet in a world where those relationships are constantly in flux. The critical focus for a populist is the relationships that people have—based on the steadily shifting settings in which they find themselves. The goal is dignity, confidence, and solidarity in every setting. That's the test of a living democracy. On the ownership-pattern front, Confucius captures the capitalist paradox: "Where wealth is centralized, the people are dispersed. Where wealth is distributed, the people are brought together."

It must also be said that financial markets exhibit an inherent irrationality from which protection should be sought by populist leaders. Financier George Soros labels this trait "reflexivity." Expectations, he argues, are themselves a key player in capital market behavior. That's because participants in financial markets base their decisions on their expectations. Yet the tomorrow they anticipate depends on the expectations they hold today. Decisions become reflexive when they have no independent source but arise solely from the expectations themselves.[27]

Every market watcher knows that a failure to meet analysts' expectations can tank a firm's stock. As can anything that changes analysts' expectations. Thus, for instance, technology stocks plummeted on September 23, 1999, after Microsoft's president, Steve Ballmer, cited the industry's gold-rush mentality. His personal stake lost $1.2 billion, whereas Bill Gates had a one-day paper loss of $5 billion, leading the Dow Jones Industrial Average to shed almost 4 percent of its value, the largest one-day decline in six months.[28]

In financial markets, the outcome reflects expectations. Financial markets are notorious for being described in very human, even emotional terms: apprehensive, gleeful, wary, nervous, relieved, upbeat, jubilant, depressed. A well-known Wall Street jibe helps keep financial analysts in proper perspective, including their blind obeisance to the wisdom assumed in securities markets: "How many financial analysts does it take to change a light bulb? Answer: none, because the change has already been discounted." The market's one-sided obsessiveness makes for a surreal world. For example, environmentalists report themselves at odds with financial analysts who claim that there can't possibly be a positive return on a green investment, because finance theory predicts that such savings are already anticipated in the stock price. These light-bulb-changers need on occasion to be reminded that the real world organizes itself not just around financial abstractions but also around physical realities.

Best known for pocketing $1 billion over a few days in 1992 when he bet that the British would be forced to devalue the pound sterling, Soros dismisses today's doctrainaire economic theories that espouse efficient markets and rational expectations. He notes that Myron Scholes and Robert Merton, joint winners of the 1997 Nobel prize in economic science, were advisers to Long Term Capital Management in September 1998, when the hedge fund lost more than $4 billion in a bizarre six-week financial panic. The fund had leveraged $4.1 billion in funds into $125 billion in arcane financial instruments, using computers and complex, rational-markets, Chicago-inspired math to identify temporary pricing anomalies among similar securities. News reports suggest that these leading financial theorists lost a portion of their Nobel prize winnings, even though the New York branch of the Federal Reserve organized a bailout after its president William McDonough concluded that collapse of this tax haven-based scheme posed "unacceptable risks to the American economy." Hedge funds remain largely unregulated, even though they're now a quarter the size of commercial banks and a fifth as large as mutual funds (daily trading in currency markets and financial derivatives now exceeds $1.5 trillion).[29] This illustrates another key reason why populist leaders need quickly to evoke more "up-close" ownership patterns. When remote and abstract *financial* value is the only value associated with what you own, that value is exposed to risks totally outside your influence. At present, policymakers favor a financial system that favors the financially sophisticated and the politically well connected. They may get bailed out. You won't.[30]

Information-Based Capitalism

Information is the real change agent; voters are the means through which information ripens into the concern that eventually results in change. Populist leadership is about evoking and analyzing that information—generating it, sharing it, and helping organize it in such a way that it creates better results. Democracies can learn, but they rely on people to insist on change. Because modern populism is about facilitating positive change, it may not be essential that populists become a majority in each of the legislative branches. It's conceivable they may serve their purpose as catalysts, becoming more effective than the majority simply by injecting clarity and common sense into policymaking systems now sorely deficient in both. I do, however, believe it's essential that a populist occupy the Oval Office. Someone must set the tone, point the way, and nudge things along.

The information age has about it a curious element not easily reduced to the numerical quantities favored by number-crunching "quants" in the financial domain. For instance, as I look out my window at woods that appear unchanged for nearly a century, my understanding of those woods is changed by what I've learned about how they are affected by other forces at work—climate change, atmospheric gases, aquifer levels, and so on. My understanding is very different from that of my grandfather. Today's information-intensive environment has had a powerful and productive impact on the way I interact with my physical environment, yet that may not register financially. It enhances my "intergenerational productivity," but in ways that are not measurable—at least not yet. It also enhances my ability to be more responsible to posterity—to which capital markets respond, "So what?"

That's why populists oppose abstract, detached, and top-down leadership systems because they quickly become stupid—communism, fascism, feudalism, hierarchically run corporations, de-peoplized capital markets. Such systems soon lose the capacity to sort good information from bad, useful feedback from clutter. They can't possibly know enough. Or know it at the right time. Or in the right sequence. Often the individual is viewed as subservient to the organization or to the market. Over time, the information generated becomes mindless (versus mindful), useful only for maintaining the organization rather than enabling it to become more responsive to genuine needs—human, societal, ecological, and intergenerational. Ultimately, such systems destroy even the values they pretend to protect, as their lack of flexibility and foresight ensures their demise or, like out-of-touch bureaucracies, guarantees that the costs they impose outpace the benefits they deliver.

The populist goal is to smarten up and loosen up today's dumbed-down and up-tight organizations by generating more useful information and by ensuring that the information is acted upon. That's best done by creating new relationships or better-engaged ones. As populists succeed in building layer upon layer of participation, what will emerge from that more finely textured system is a new depth of understanding. People will better see the totality. And organizations will better reflect the needs of those they affect. As leadership theorist Meg Wheatley says, "Life opens to more possibilities through new patterns of connection."[31] The self-correcting design that underlies free enterprise will smarten up as it's reconfigured to become populated with more self-motivated capitalists.

Smartened-Up Systems

For those addicted to order or to hierarchy, this change to a more open system may seem threatening, undisciplined, even chaotic. It's not. But nor is it specialist-driven, or top-down controllable. We've learned hard lessons about why not to put our lives in the hands of a few experts (recall the confident assurances of nuclear engineers as we built power plants). Control-crazed CEOs and hierarchy-obsessed policymakers should identify and articulate what fears arise when they contemplate organizing in this new way, particularly when the goal here is to bring society's dispersed intelligence to bear to address problems too long ignored. An institutional design capable of generating more two-way information—through peoplization—is essential if we are to smarten ourselves up. It's worth it. A richly feedback-fueled system is certain to be far more supportive of dignity, adaptability, and sustainability. The principal purpose of old-style, hierarchical leadership was to manage information and power efficiently (and forcefully). Societal design needs to catch up with advances in our capacity to gather and process information in a radically decentralized fashion.

This may sound like a new sort of politics or a new approach to business organization. It's actually quite old. Its emergence was anticipated by our more visionary and democratically inclined founders, particularly Thomas Jefferson, one of the most articulate advocates for systems of widely distributed control. Yet emergence in its present cyber-populist form only recently became possible—made so by remarkable technological progress in information processing, communications, and networking.

Like it or not, we now live in a connected world, one in which events such as the dread accompanying Y2K are awakening us both to the promise and to the peril of that connectedness. And to the reality that there's no longer any such thing as either individual preparedness or solitary learning. If my neighbor is not prepared, neither am I. Even if I'm an environmentally attuned consumer, one insensitive neighbor can offset my best efforts, even wreck my neighborhood. Independence is an illusion, as is the democratic ideal of personal autonomy. Interdependence is the reality. The paradoxical populist challenge lies in how best to foster self-sufficiency within overlapping networks of interdependence. Because the technology of cyber-connectedness is so very new, most people remain attached to its superficial busyness, overwhelmed by e-mail or wasting time surfing the Web, unaware as yet of the potential richness offered by this newly connected world.

Tim Berners-Lee, a key player in developing the World Wide Web, confirms that our maturity in using the Web is a long way off. If it is properly handled, he believes that the next stage of the Web holds promise of greatly increasing our "intercreativity and group intuition," enabling creativity to emerge across diverse groups of people, including such commercial projects as mapping the relationships and dependencies among rivals and suppliers.[34] Creativity comes from placing good minds in environments rich in information that might prove useful in solving a problem. With the Web's steady proliferation comes access to a very new information environment of extraordinary richness and potential.

I am hopeful that twenty years hence, we'll be able to look back on a much-changed and much more sustainable world and marvel at the source of the change. By then the cause will be all but invisible. That's because today's situation only developed step-by-step and it can only peacefully be remedied by changing one step at a time as opportunities arise. Many contributing factors and cycles of learning (education initiatives, new feedback loops, expanded access to information, institutional innovations, distributed leadership) will be all but invisible except to those who lived through each stage. We will not evolve to a higher level of economic order; instead we'll *coevolve*, with content and context, humans and technology, engaged in a waltz of steady progress toward sustainability. I expect the pace of progress to accelerate as a supportive foundation is built, much like bamboo grows slowly for three years and then enjoys a growth spurt in the fourth. This more organic approach to economics should not be expected to bear fruit overnight any more than an apple orchard would be expected to bear fruit in the first few seasons after planting.

This new strategy for social progress may initially sound muddled, even strange. It is not. This nation was founded on the notion of *E pluribus unum* ("One from many"). Although some suggest that the motto was merely a marketing slogan devised by the founders, it aptly describes what we as a nation remain—an amalgam of viewpoints. We've struggled for more than two centuries with how best to tap the genius that we know lies latent in our melting pot of viewpoints. We've long needed a way to meld that distributed intelligence into a coherent, cohesive, and harmonious political system. Only recently have we gained the analytical savvy and the organizational wherewithal to make that goal a practical reality. Therein lies the populist promise.

12

Democratic Capitalism and the Environment

Man, according to the Stoics, ought to regard himself, not as something separated and detached, but as a citizen of the world, a member of the vast commonwealth of nature . . . and to the interest of this great community, he ought at all times to be willing that his own little interest should be sacrificed.

—ADAM SMITH

A more intimately connected, information-infused world offers the best hope yet for addressing the world's environmental challenges. People will change their behavior as they gain a better understanding of their interdependence with nature and their place in it. We shouldn't be surprised that global understanding lags behind our scientific knowledge. After all, it's been only three decades since we first saw a photograph of our entire habitat from outer space. From that vantage point, We the People takes on a very different meaning. Yes, the United States is a sovereign nation, but so what? From that perspective, we're forced to think of ourselves not as independent states but as interdependent communities. That implies a scope of environmental responsibility that transcends nation-states. The adoption of a *post-sovereign* perspective is the only way to ensure that the human community coalesces around a global democracy designed to meet the needs of future generations. As we mature into that viewpoint, concern for the environment is destined to become the context for all policy decisions.

A planetary image of ourselves makes for a far more ambiguous policy environment. At the very least, it presents a challenge to the workability of unrestrained self-interest when there are far larger interests at stake. And it directly challenges the relevance of short-term financial values when intergenerational values are now so clearly at risk. We are faced with the disturbing spectacle of a species that insists on prospering at the expense of others. Humankind seems determined to alter the climate and its degrade the natural capital that rightfully belongs to future generations. Well over half the world's fisheries are overfished or severely depleted (about half the world's protein comes from marine species). More than a million acres of farmland is converted to urban sprawl each year in the United States alone. Freshwater tables have declined precipitously. The emission of greenhouse gases continues at an unsustainable rate. By "double-glazing" the upper atmosphere with the residue from fossil fuels, development ensured warmer air with more capacity to hold water. Scientists report that 1998, the warmest year on record, triggered the worst drought in three decades across the mid-Atlantic. Russia recorded its highest-ever summer temperatures in 1999, while China reported its second consecutive year of record flooding. Drought and deluge have emerged as the twentieth century's environmental legacy as the 1990s went on record as the warmest decade in a century of recordkeeping. The northward migration of warm-weather pests brings with it not only mosquitoes but also the diseases they carry, such as malaria and dengue. During the summer of 1999, Manhattan sprayed for mosquitoes carrying a deadly strain of West Nile virus, a sickness never before seen in the Western Hemisphere (the virus is transmitted to humans from mosquitoes that have bitten infected migratory birds).[1] Commentators seemed relieved to discover that the virus was not the work of terrorists but *only because humans had altered the climate of the planet.*

Meanwhile, political paralysis is the rule even though some environmental challenges can be solved locally. We have long known, for instance, how to clean up our rivers: Just place a community's discharge pipe upstream from its intake pipe. Try running a hose from your exhaust pipe inside your car, and notice how smart you suddenly get about what sort of pollution abatement system you should have. There's nothing quite like immediate feedback to speed up systems learning. Communities could be required to dispose of their solid waste on their own land. That shifts the feedback into a very different pattern. I'm not aware of any community that does that. Instead, we pretend that downstream is somehow separate and distinct. Downstream or downwind isn't "us," so it doesn't count. Nor, apparently, does the next generation. They're downstream too, just as we're downstream of the choices made by our ancestors. Given an informed choice, none of our descendants would choose today's environmental conditions. Yet we choose by our actions today the legacy we'll leave them tomorrow. Such is the intergenerational challenge of democracy.

Happily, the forces of synergy are at work—the tendency toward ever-greater association, communication, cooperation, and awareness. Doubtless that's because for 99 percent of human history, we have lived in small communities. When there's an opportunity for connection, people will often take it. Witness the Internet. That modern technology reflects the ancient human desire for connection and for community. It also provides a very new image of what humankind can be—a worldwide web of relationships. That's a very handy metaphor at a time when we desperately need to displace the myth of the isolated and separate self. Today's technologies of connectedness and communication offer a hopeful means for fostering a new image not only of the individual self but also of that larger self we think of as We the People.

As people begin to see how they're connected to everything, they're likely to feel more responsible for everything—or at least for their little piece of it. Yet much of today's increased connectivity is impersonal and dispirited, abstract and remote—as reflected in people's widespread ignorance about their place in the physical world. That too requires an educational effort. Ecological illiteracy is rampant. Many people are clueless about how they're imbedded in their world. Heat comes from the furnace. Gasoline? From the gas station. Water from the faucet. Food from the kitchen. Or McDonald's. A rapid greening of our education curriculum, and of our consciousness, is essential. We must also tone down today's strident individualism and jettison its political companions—nationalism and isolationism—so that we can tend to the real-world requirements of an inescapably interdependent world. We do that by steadily maturing our worldview.

Viewpoint 2000

We have the means available for a dramatic shift in our perspective. That shift is essential if we are to embrace the changes needed in today's finance-obsessed economic model. Our economic institutions, laws, customs, and traditions operate like a "cultural DNA," forming the societal memory with which we bequeath to future generations the insights of our own. The most immediate economic challenge is how we affect today's dumbed-down capital flows so they don't continue to wreak environmental havoc. We do that by steadily upgrading our grasp of interdependence and by constantly updating our mental imagery of the relationships we have with our world. For instance, it wasn't that long ago we thought the sun spun around the earth. Exposure to a more realistic perspective gradually changed our behavior. That's the power of a proper perspective. Thirty years ago we didn't know that pollution contributes to global warming. The challenge lies in finding ways to ensure that everyone understands that everyone's activities affect an ecosystem now under siege. I suggest here a very low-tech means for helping advance a collective shift in our cultural DNA by engaging worldwide youth in a project I call Viewpoint 2000.

The origins of this idea can be traced to my relationship with two individuals on opposite coasts. While living in San Francisco during the 1970s, I was a member of the San Francisco Sidewalk Astronomers. For $125, founder and neighbor John Dobson would teach you how to make your own large, very high-quality telescope. On nights when something interesting was visible in the Bay Area sky, the membership—children and adults—would roll its telescopes onto the sidewalk and urge passersby to take a look. Hence the name. It was *very* 1970s San Francisco.

The second person is Kenny Schaffer of Manhattan, who years ago did public relations for rock legend Jimi Hendrix. I first met Kenny in the mid-1980s, not long after he'd figured out how to bring live Soviet television into the United States by intercepting a satellite transmission between Moscow and Siberia. As a rock-and-roll techie, he invented both a cordless guitar and a cordless microphone, including an early version used by the Rolling Stones, who picked up a passing police cruiser during an early performance.

Kenny was the first person to alert me to the high-resolution optics used in U.S. spy satellites. From four hundred miles out, while moving at $4\frac{1}{2}$ miles per second, the best of our satellites boast an optical resolution measured in inches. In other words, you can almost make out the manufacturer's name on a basketball. The world of satellite observation was turned upside down in September 1999 with the launch of *Ikonos,* a 1,600-pound commercial imaging satellite owned by Space Imaging. The company will offer the finest-grained satellite photos ever sold on the open market, with black-and-white resolution to one meter and only a thirty-minute delay.

What do home-made telescopes and high-tech satellites have to do with finance and the environment? Only this: Imagine if our Culture Corps, staffed by American youth, provided the materials and the know-how for children worldwide to construct their own low-tech telescopes. With the benefit of that perspective, they could quickly learn to better grasp their place in the universe—using their telescopes to gaze outward into space. In my mind, that experience alone is worth our effort if we can assist the next generation in accessing wonder, mystery, and a sense of awe, even sanctity, at the vastness of creation.

Now imagine combining that viewpoint with the inward-looking, high-tech observation capacity of satellite technology and linking both to telecommunications technology. Now we can broadcast those images (both satellite and telescopic) anywhere on earth. Those images could enable youth to observe both outer space from earth and themselves on earth from outer space. With modest support, this project could become a fun hands-on science project for youth worldwide. The project is doable. While I was constructing my 12-inch telescope, a ten-year-old girl was building a huge 16-inch reflector telescope with an 8½-foot focal length.

What's the point? Imagine an observation satellite broadcasting an image of a ten-year-old Russian (or Rwandan or Haitian) standing beside her homemade Culture Corps–sponsored telescope, through which she has just spotted *Ikonos* speeding overhead in its twice daily north-south axis. Imagine *Ikonos* spotting her community and beaming the satellite-generated image to a receiving station for relay to a computer screen, where she can make out herself and friends as viewed from outer space.[2] Provide her a computer print-out of that image and never again will her viewpoint be the same. She will have instantly become a twenty-first-century global citizen. A citizen of a specific nation (culture, tribe, etc.), but never again *only* that. One set of blinders will be forever removed. "Perception is not whimsical but fatal," Ralph Waldo Emerson mused. "If I see a trait, my children will see it after me and in the course of time all mankind."

By enlarging the scope of their perception, widening their worldview, and opening their minds about the scale and dimension of the work that needs to be done, tomorrow's adults will be far better equipped to make sense of their world and to identify those tasks into which they choose to sink their life's hours. It is, after all, from the thoughts and dreams of its children that a nation's destiny emerges, and perhaps now the destiny of earth as well.

During periods of needed paradigm shifts, intensive education is essential.[3] We face an array of unsustainable human behaviors that must quickly be addressed. Dysfunctional conduct is best solvable when people grasp the situation as a whole so they can see their part in it. Environmental sustainability falls in that category. Recalling the adage that genius is a fresh approach to the obvious, my hope is that Viewpoint 2000 serves as a useful catalyst to genius as participants are transformed by their vision of what's possible—stimulating the formulation of solutions that are more creative and more holistic. Viewpoint 2000 could also provide a fresh and entertaining project—combining low and high technology—on which we can focus international cooperation that engages the next generation in realizing that the balance of nature is ultimately far more important than the balance of power.[4]

Twenty years from now, we may find that a disproportionate share of our leadership is drawn from those who participate in this new-perspective new-paradigm project. Two decades hence, our leaders may have learned to spend less political capital on the abstractions and distractions of nation-states and financial markets and more time on nurturing and defending those places that physically sustain us.

Updating Our Worldview

By providing a new way of seeing ourselves, this holistic framework offers a new platform for dialogue to negotiate a very new political reality in the global community. As the relevance of political barriers fades into the background and other challenges, including ethnic and environmental challenges, rush in to take their place, tomorrow's leaders must be exposed early on to the scope of what's at stake and the scale at which remedies must be pursued. Although nationalism will likely retain its appeal as a sweet indulgence, and ethnic and tribal identities will certainly maintain their innate allure, we badly need a generation of savvy globalists prepared to tackle the issues that now confront us. Sustainability requires nothing less than a generation educated in a worldview equal to the challenges we face. We don't need a global government so much as we need a global perspective that informs our governments. If those governments are to be genuine democracies, we need global populations educated to think of themselves as both local and global citizens, because that's what they inescapably are.

With the population of our shared habitat now expanding at the pace of 10,000 people each hour, according to the UN Development Program, the icon of our era should be the image of our common home hovering like a pale blue jewel in the vast darkness of space. That's the inescapable common ground on which our diverse cultures and interdependent life forms must make a go of it. That's why a twenty-first-century education requires more than just literacy and technical skills. Those are the bare bones minimum. Education also requires perspective. A sound education should open each child's eyes to the lives lived by others—humans, plants, and animals—so that knowledge is accompanied by empathy, tolerance, common sense, and, above all, compassion, the most crucial capacity for becoming truly human. Empathy is a way of opening the heart of compassion through ways of knowing or imagining connections that may not yet be fully explicit.[5] It is those "human sympathies" that serve as the animating force found at the heart of Adam Smith's moral philosophy. There also, I suggest, lies the key to overcoming ethnic and interreligious conflict, as our youth develop tolerance and understanding and as the United States settles into a more wizened and less militarized role, leading more often *from behind* as educator and facilitator. There too lies the commonsense road to nuclear disarmament.

In the same way that a new type of foresight brought us Yosemite and Yellowstone National Parks, we need a new sort of foresight in the domain of the human psyche if we are to effect the global shift in perspective required to protect the values we hold most dear. George Kennan, looking back from the vantage point of ninety-four years, notes simply: "This planet is never going to be ruled from any single political center, whatever its military power."[6] That suggests, he says, the need to

cut ourselves down to size in the dreams and aspirations we direct to our possibilities for world leadership. We are not, really, all that great. We have serious problems within our society these days; and it sometimes seems to me that the best help we could give to others would be to allow them to observe that we are now confronting those problems with a bit more imagination, courage, and resolve than has been apparent in the recent past.[7]

Sage advice. He might well have added that besides not being ruled by a single political center, the world will never be ruled by any single perspective—political or otherwise. That would be the most profoundly antidemocratic notion imaginable.

Yet a healing is now needed,— not only between peoples, cultures, tribes, ethnic groups, and such,— but also between humankind and the natural world. Part of our leadership role should be expressed by finding some way to heal the many rifts that history has left in its wake—most obviously those between rich and poor and between the developed north and the struggling south—but also the separation that modern, high-tech humankind feels from its surroundings and from nature. Indigenous peoples have much to offer on that score. The original meaning of healing is "to make whole." Everyone from psychotherapists to mystics has long advised that we are best healed of our sense of separateness through our contact with wholeness.[8] Everyone knows that intuitively. Although the Christian faith suggests that the meek will inherit the earth, the Greek word for *gentle* includes the meaning "well trained." Consequently, our education must include training in wholeness, keeping reductionism and mechanical thinking in perspective while embracing a more organic and holistic understanding through the mental pictures (and icons) we carry around in our heads and in the stories we tell our children.

Culture and Perspective

In *The Alphabet versus the Goddess*, Leonard Shlain suggests that before alphabetic literacy, cultures were largely egalitarian and oriented toward visual images for communication.[9] As more analytical and left-brained cultures became dominant, so did more masculine god figures, pushing aside what were previously female images of the divine and a more intuitive, right-brained perspective. The author hypothesizes that the spread of modern-day image-based technologies (movies, television, computer screens, and now the Internet) is opening the door for a more balanced perspective that engages both the linear left lobe and the more holistic right lobe. Living in a world awash in images, he argues, eases the way for a return to more whole-systems-attuned thinking, including the respect, even the reverence, granted such feminine images as Mother Nature and Mother Earth. That analysis helps open our thinking to such concepts as the Gaia hypothesis, developed by scientist James Lovelock, suggesting that the earth functions as a living, self-correcting organism whose interconnected components make ongoing adjustments in weather patterns, ocean currents, cloud cover, plankton populations, and so forth.[10] Although reverence for the earth may be a stretch for some, it's at least time we upgraded the mental imagery of our habitat from the purely reductionist concept of life clinging to an inert rock third in orbit around the sun. If we are to have a higher order of meaning around which humankind can focus the restorative efforts now required, we need unifying themes grounded in our common identity and based on imagery (and icons) that all can embrace.[11] Like it or not, we're an inescapably interdependent and global species.

If we can but elevate the level of the dialogue and broaden our frames of reference, many of today's nation-state problems will fade into insignificance as we join other peoples in improving the human condition while also restoring the conditions essential for the sustainability of life. Holistic thinking requires that we close the gap between the personal and the global, between the self and nature, and between humans and humankind. What's badly needed is some hands-on, entertaining ways for people to stretch the limits of what they know about themselves and their world. Viewpoint 2000 suggests one of many ways we can encourage our communion with a broader spectrum of realities. As artist-author Frederick Franck reminds us, icons have long served as a "window into the sacred," an invitation to reflection and self-confrontation.[12] The challenge facing global democracy and sustainability lies in enhancing our capacity to transcend the limits both of the sovereign state and of the individual.

New Perspective, New Protection

Worldwide television bandwidth could be dedicated to broadcasting the imagery from Viewpoint 2000, with photos *from* space interspersed with images *of* space taken from Culture Corps–sponsored telescopes—making every day Earth Day. That perspective could do much to smarten us up, by ensuring that the next generation is more realistic about environmental issues than today's out-of-touch policymakers.[13] Youth could also use this technology to become satellite-assisted, on-site environmental monitors, providing policymakers a next-generation voice with a personal stake in ensuring that global environmental standards are met. Dedicated satellite capability could be utilized by youth to monitor environmentally sensitive areas and to identify new areas in need of protection. For instance, highly sensitive hyperspectral satellite imagery can detect camouflage, identify underground minerals, and may someday even detect genetically distinct strains of crops. Similar imaging capacity could help enforce environmental treaties. Or make the case for new ones. The ongoing sharing and analysis of global environmental intelligence is the only conceivable way to identify, protect, and restore endangered ecosystems.[14]

Psychologists agree that one of the most common psychological wounds is a feeling that one's voice was lost in childhood. This project could help the world's children discover early on that their voice counts, as well it should when it comes to the condition of their environment. For example, we only discovered in 1999 that a layer of smog covers virtually all of the Indian Ocean for much of the year. Atmospheric residue from industrial development fills the skies with an acrid cloud that drifts out over the water until the monsoon season blows it back onshore, where it is converted to acid rain that dumps on both land and sea. Are the youth of that region fully aware of how intimately they are connected to that phenomenon, regardless of their nationality or their standard of living? Do they fully grasp that development in the region directly impacts their lives and their futures, regardless of whether they realize its benefits? Do they understand the intimate linkage of development, weather, and water quality? The connection between hydrocarbon-fired energy and the availability of edible fish? An enhanced sense of interdependence is certain to breed social concern and political activism, essential preconditions for genuinely robust democracies. This is not an issue just for developing countries. Do Swedish children understand that they're subsidizing the British, whose furnaces belch acidic fumes that destroy Swedish forests and turn Swedish lakes too acidic to support aquatic life? The world's children are the most appropriate intergenerational accountants; let them do what adults have never dared to do: create international balance sheets in which the stock and flow of the earth's resources are fully charted and valued. Children have a remarkably well-developed sense of justice.

For those of you sick of today's small-beer variety of reform, I suggest we encourage the globe's children to create their own economic indexes and social indicators. I wager that, unlike us adults, they won't misidentify themselves as "consumers." Or conveniently forget that they're citizens who are destined to become ancestors. Most likely the children want to know how the sea turtles are faring. And the redwoods. And the butterflies. And what sort of toys the typical Rwandan child has. Or what Serbian schoolchildren have for lunch. After spending some time with Viewpoint 2000, I wager they'll want to know why adults put unborn children at risk by producing goods with the use of toxic chemicals that show up in the fatty tissue of nursing mothers. Their curiosity—and their willingness to ask innocent questions about crises we refuse to confront—could put a human face on economic and environmental issues. That could prove a powerful means for mobilizing a shared sense of human citizenship. Once their perception is no longer limited by the physical confines of their immediate community, I'm confident that they'll insist on a world saturated with kindness. That's their nature—until we wean their humanity out of them and convert their innate generosity into market-myopic self-interest. If we are to have a consensual decisionmaking process appropriate to a global democracy, we must find ways to inform our decisions with the dreams of those who will succeed us. Posterity demands of us no less. The commitments now required for restoring the health of "place" are not going to be simply legislated into existence. This is the work of multiple generations as we learn how to raise community standards and have to operate free enterprise with an inclusive etiquette.

Toward an Ancestral Capitalism

What about the youth of the United States? Are they aware that the smog that supports their lifestyle can blow hundreds of miles from its source? The long-distance migration of polluted air means, for example, that mountaintop trails in the East may be at the same altitude where pollution from the Midwest drifts by. A hiker from Cleveland hoping to escape polluted city air with a trek along the Appalachian Trail may encounter even dirtier air as prevailing winds load up with pollutants in various cities along the way, baking them in the summer heat on their journey eastward. To get pollutants out of sight, our electric utilities built ever-taller smokestacks during the 1970s (429 are taller than 200 feet). Many are more than 700 feet. That's high enough to ensure that prevailing winds carry them enormous distances. During the summer of 1999, the tip of Cape Cod had more smog violations than the city of Boston. The Jersey Shore tied with Newark for smog alerts, whereas the Great Smoky Mountains National Park had more pollution than any city in the South except Atlanta.[15] Wild horses along Georgia's shorelines often now die within two years, their intestines rotted from grazing on acid-laden grasses. Georgia's fish and wildlife personnel caution that fish caught in our once-pristine mountain lakes and streams may now be inedible once they've grown to more than eight inches in length. Of course that assumes the water is merely toxic and not acidified to the point of complete sterility. Surely a well-informed youth generation would persuade their parents to smarten up. The anti-tobacco ads designed by teenage ex-smokers were enormously effective, and in ways that government agencies (or adults) could never have fathomed.

The 56 million kids known as Generation Y are positioned to catalyze a profound social transformation. In the same way that television defined my generation, the Internet is defining theirs. There are already 16 million teens on-line, a number expected to double by 2002. What's the number one activity on the Net? Talking to their friends. Young people put a particularly high premium on authenticity. That's bad news for today's uncreative and co-opted politicos, and very good news for those who see the Net as a means for advancing much-needed change. Though every retailer is scrambling to grab a piece of the hottest segment of this on-line group, the market here is not so much the money ($250 billion in disposable income) as the minds—engaged kids and young adults looking for some way out of what they know is an imperiled future. They're smart enough to know they're not getting it straight from today's leadership. They hunger for an upbeat, fun, solutions-oriented, truthful politics.

The Values Environment

Youth may also be the most effective monitors of compliance with child labor standards and a potent force for more effective standards. Anyone who thinks I expect too much of our youth has never met Canadian Craig Kielburger, who as a fifteen-year-old founded Free the Children. Craig traveled the world documenting the exploitation and abuse of children and promoting their rights. Although his stories are harrowing to hear, their impact would be far greater if a means were available to broadcast evidence of what he discovered. Imagine, for example, a ten-year-old chained to a loom producing fine carpets for your living room. Or an eight-year-old standing barefoot on a pile of medical syringes that she is forced to disassemble for reuse, totally oblivious to the potential of contracting AIDS. Imagine beaming into your home the plight of twelve-year-old boys working sixteen joyless hours each day to manufacture the toys that give our children such joy. Or sixteen-year-old Thai girls watching televised cartoons while they wait their turn with a tourist in a Bangkok brothel. With the proper support, global youth could emerge as a powerful voice insistent that we create an environment of broad-based prosperity as the only effective remedy to the global sickness of child labor. Although child labor is often justified on the basis that the children's families need the funds, the argument only confirms that endemic poverty is the real culprit, with child labor a disturbing symptom of a much deeper malady.

The word *educate* traces its origins to the merger of two Latin words, *e* ("out of") and *ducere* ("to lead"). Equity and sustainability require a radically broader and longer-term perspective if we are to *lead ourselves out of* the prevailing worldview—abstract, insular, self-absorbed, short-term, values-deficient, and finance-dominant. Our descendants deserve a perspective better able to address the shocking reality of fast-spending human and environmental degradation. For too long, we have stressed our separateness as individuals, as cultures, as nations—and as generations. We now know that this perspective is false. No people can freely choose their future, not when left a degraded and depleted past. We need quickly to get on with the business of transforming our perspective so that we work together to address an array of issues that threaten us all—from hunger to disease to terrorism to human habits that endanger not only our habitat but also, as in the case of child exploitation, our hearts. In *Disposable People*, Kevin Bales identifies at least 27 million slaves worldwide.[16] Pakistani slave labor may have made the shoes on your feet. Caribbean slaves may have harvested the sugar in your coffee. Or fashioned the Brazilian charcoal that tempered the steel for your lawnmower blade. Slavery is a surefire way to keep costs low and financial returns high—the epitome of financial efficiency.

Altruism and Capitalism

Only on the basis of shared perspectives can we become genuinely wise institution-builders capable of addressing in law, custom, and practice the human and environmental challenges of our times. A widely agreed-to perspective is required if we are to live in right relationship with the world around us and with those who will inhabit this world after us. Yet that global cooperation can only be sustained if it is grounded in a *personally* integrated worldview rooted in each individual's psyche. That's a very tall order. Absent that internalized change, we'll be forced to rely on regulatory efforts that run the risk of imperial overreach if any one nation assumes too dominant a role. For global cooperation to be sustainable, both leaders and citizens worldwide must "own" this perspective in the same way that we now own the perspective that the earth circles the sun.

Several experienced change agents assure me that people can't be reformed and that our only hope is to replace them. My hope is that poet Gary Snyder is correct and that instead we can issue "Tibetan army knives" guaranteed to open even the most closed of minds. However, *if* reform of our current leaders in business and politics is impossible, that makes it even more essential that we expose the next generation to a worldview grounded in the challenging reality they face. In the meanwhile, it's quite understandable that so little caring and compassion is extended to those with whom we have so little contact. For example, Princeton University ethicist Peter Singer points out how difficult it is to consign a child to death when the child is standing in front of you, though it may be quite easy to ignore, say, a written appeal for funds to help children you'll never meet. The genius of global telecommunications, properly utilized, lies in its ability to put people in relationship with one another in ways never before envisioned. That could help release our compassion from the coldness of distance and close the "caring gap" that typifies today's international relations. Our ability to bridge this relationship gap may determine whether worldwide communication technology—including the Internet—emerges as a genuine tool for human advancement or remains simply a high-tech toy. In a world where only $200 would help a sickly two-year-old become a healthy six-year-old, offering safe passage through childhood's most perilous period, people in well-to-do nations see such children as too remote to relate to in a personal way.

My hope is that Viewpoint 2000 and similar efforts will play a role in nudging us in a more humane direction. For instance, Singer urges individuals to redirect their spending on luxuries to children's relief agencies such as Unicef, Oxfam America, and others dedicated to ensuring that children are spared preventable deaths.[17] Instead of that pricey new suit, $1,000 could save five children's lives. That high-minded moral ground may be beyond the reach of many in today's me-centered, high-consumption era. Yet with more effort put into creating relationships with these children (such as through our youth engaged in Prosperity Corps missions abroad), we should at least be able to muster the public support required for meeting the modest UN target of 0.7 percent of our GDP to support such efforts. As of this writing, U.S. contributions lag well below that, at 0.09 percent, not even half of Japan's 0.22 percent or a tenth of Denmark's 0.97 percent.

At Least Now We Know What We're Doing

Microbiologist Theo Colborn documents five hundred measurable chemicals in our bodies that were absent from anyone's body before 1920.[18] Those include a particularly nasty array of endocrine-disrupting chemicals (EDCs) linked to a litany of health effects, including weakened immune systems, reproductive anomalies, and metabolic disorders, along with functional deficits in intelligence, behavior, and sexuality (bioaccumulative EDCs are also known as "gender benders"). They're largely a by-product of plastics derived from oil. Their most frightening aspect, she tells me, stems from potency: They're dangerous not in parts per million or parts per billion but in parts *per trillion*. Plus the effects are multigenerational. They affect not only our children but also our grandchildren and their grandchildren, putting our estrogen and testosterone receptors into a state of overdrive and leading to cancer. Unlike a reprogrammable computer system, we cannot reprogram damaged endocrine, immune, or mental systems.

Other researchers point to similarly disturbing trends, including a 300- to 400-fold increase in cellular levels of heavy metals and dioxins from herbicides and pesticides since they were first measured. The rise corresponds with huge increases in conditions such as chronic fatigue, allergies, and chemical sensitivity. Swedish scientists uncovered a link between disease and commonly used crop sprays, suggesting why non-Hodgkin's lymphoma has increased 73 percent since the mid-1970s.

The data can be unnerving, even depressing. In a world where pesticide-laden rainfall means that even falling water may be unfit to drink, I asked Colborn to tell me, please, what is the silver lining in this horrifically dark cloud, with 70,000 manmade chemicals now loose in the world and destined to end up *somewhere*. Her answer: "At least now we know what we're doing." That's a good credo to recall as we contemplate the inequity, the unworkability, and the unsustainability of present-day free enterprise with its multitrillions in unconscious capital sloshing about the globe. Although that knowledge may not be salvation, it's at least an intermediary grace, because until we know what we're doing, we can't take corrective action.

Timeless Capitalism

Capitalism and ecology are an unnatural mix. Financial values lose all relevance absent a dimension of time, whereas nature's recurrent cycles are timeless. My fear is that today's money-obsessed economic model will insist that we put a present value price tag on every environmental impact before we address the problems. I sat through seven years of Senate testimony during which the experts would periodically assure us that the environmental impact of hydrocarbon use would eventually work its way into prices at the gas pump, causing us to use less and pollute less. Expert testimony aside, we have yet to see this happen. The same argument could be made for the EDC-laden compounds that coat the insides of soda cans. Or for asbestos, tobacco, or biotechnology. Even handguns. That's the conventional wisdom of today's economism: Let the market sort it out.

The problem lies, in part, in the financial model embedded in the very concept of capitalism and its notion of discounting future revenue streams to put a present-day monetary value on a decision. Thus, for example, if I borrow $1,000 today with the promise to pay it back at 7 percent annual interest, at the end of ten years, I will owe $2,000. Thus, a dollar ten years from now is worth only half what it is now. In twenty years, it will be worth just one-quarter as much, and so on. Fifty years from now, it's worth hardly anything. Yet that same model is used to put a value on fishing grounds. Or to estimate the cost of felling an eight-hundred-year-old old-growth forest. The model is what it is: It discounts the future. In commercial settings, it provides a useful yardstick—but only for measuring certain things. And only in a very limited way.

Ecologist Paul Hawken argues that since we've never really practiced capitalism, we really don't know whether it works. To make his point, he suggests we distinguish finance capitalism from natural capitalism. "In a true capitalist system," he argues, "you preserve your capital, create income, and invest it. In the present system, we spend our human, natural and social capital—everything that we have—to increase our financial capital."[19] In other words, we focus on the value-added element of economics rather than the value-retained criteria of ecology.[20] No one would dare run a business without accounting for its capital outlays. Yet that's what we do every day with the capital provided by nature, treating natural resources as though they were a business in liquidation—and then scoring it as income. Rather than design within nature's constraints, we pick entrees from a financial menu on which the environment does not yet appear. Or where it appears to be free.

German parliamentarian Ernst von Weizsacker, coauthor of *Factor Four* with ecologists Amory Lovins and Hunter Lovins, documents how we could live twice as well using half as much material and energy if we only focused on increasing our resource productivity.[21] In addition to offering fifty practical examples of quadrupled productivity, the authors suggest even greater savings available through, for instance, shifting information storage from filing cabinets to CD-ROMs (a factor of 10), eating only seasonal vegetables (a factor of 100), and cutting back on air travel in favor of videoconferencing (a factor of 1,000). They show how a shift of emphasis toward resource productivity would also help in the struggle for more and better jobs in a business model that currently pretends people are scarce and nature abundant. Although an increase in labor productivity typically commands huge amounts of capital, an increase in *resource productivity* frees up capital for use elsewhere, including for increasing labor productivity. Practitioners of resource productivity also discovered an unexpected benefit: This ecological focus gives employees a new sense of purpose as their activities at work become better aligned with what's in the best interest of their families and their descendants.

The margin of needed improvement is mind-boggling. Bruce Cranford at the Department of Energy cleverly divides the economy into product output and "non-product output"—everything that isn't the intended outcome of production. Every system has a flow of energy and materials going in and coming out. An anomaly arises because production is physical and real while business decisions are made on the basis of money, which is an abstraction. In the U.S. economy, Cranford calculates that only 6 percent of our physical output is product output. The rest—94 percent—is non-product when measured on the basis of mass rather than money. Thus, as Hawken notes, one ton of paper requires the use of 98 tons of various resources. Two quarts of gasoline and a thousand quarts of water are required to produce a single quart of Florida orange juice. "For all the world to live as an American or Canadian," Hawken computes, "we would need two more earths to satisfy everyone, three more if population should double, and twelve earths altogether if worldwide standards of living should double over the next forty years."[22]

Natural Capitalism

In *Natural Capitalism*, Hawken carries the resource productivity argument to its logical conclusion. Along with coauthors Amory and Hunter Lovins, he urges that we rediscover the common sense that's been lost in this financial age.[23] For example, most companies expense each year the full cost of their raw material consumption, whereas the cost of any resource-saving expenditure is written off over several years. That makes the wasting of resources more tax-efficient than efforts to improve their efficiency. Today's financial model badly needs revision—both by companies in the way that they allocate capital and by the Washington-Wall Street consensus in the way that tax policy forces that allocation. Our current system penalizes what we want more of—resource-conserving jobs and income—while subsidizing what we want less of—resource depletion and pollution. It's time that we deepen the environmental debate to ensure that the otherwise sound logic of economizing on our scarcest resources can logically operate within sensible financial and accounting rules. Output is now more often constrained by the supply of trees than by logging trucks, by fish rather than fishing trawlers, by fertile topsoil rather than tractors and plows. Until reformed, today's financial rules and accounting conventions will continue to run roughshod over widely agreed-to environmental common sense.

Hawken and the Lovinses serve up an array of examples of how whole-systems thinking and life-cycle cost accounting could dramatically transform resource productivity by extracting the same amount of work or utility from a product or a process while using less material and energy. For example, they point out that about 100,000 twenty-year-old glass office towers in the United States are ripe for low-cost improvements in glazing, lighting, and office equipment that would save 75 percent of their energy use. Life-cycle savings from fourfold more efficient air-conditioning could pay for the new windows and other improvements.

Some changes are quite simple, such as amending the use-it-or-lose-it water laws that ensure inefficient water usage in our arid western states. Setting the default on office copiers and printers to double-sided mode reduced AT&T's paper costs by 15 percent. Reclaiming even half the discarded wooden pallets from our fifty largest cities could provide 2,500 inner-city jobs and save 765 million board-feet of lumber, equivalent to 152,000 acres of timberland (nationwide we have an estimated 1.5 billion pallets).[24] Imagine, they suggest (and offer examples), intelligent design such that a kilowatt or a board-foot becomes ten or a hundred times more productive while also reducing the initial capital investment. Enormous progress could be made simply by ensuring that waste is no longer rewarded and resources are no longer underpriced.

Selling Services versus Products

Imagine an economy in which customers lease services rather than buy the products that provide those services. If, for example, manufacturers were made responsible for their products *forever*, that would dramatically change the usage of (and demand for) consumer durables such as refrigerators, cars, computers, carpets, and the like. Imagine a shift from offering quantity and mass to offering quality and service, focusing on the performance that customers want (cooling, transport, information, comfort under foot, etc.) rather than the products that manufacturers now offer for sale. By the end of 1998, twenty-eight countries had enacted legislation encouraging "extended product responsibility." Known as take-back laws, they cover everything from packaging to batteries. Such product life-cycle responsibility raised Germany's recycling rate for packaging from 12 percent in 1992 to 86 percent in 1996, while plastic recycling is up 1,790 percent. Reverse logistics is slowly working its way into our business schools as MBA students learn about not only distribution but also "dedistribution" as disassembly and *re*manufacturing become mainstream profit centers. Herman Miller, the Michigan furniture maker, takes back and reconditions its room dividers. Steelcase does the same for its filing cabinets.

Atlanta-based Interface has emerged as a global leader in this trend, offering an "Evergreen Lease," under which the company sells not carpet but floor covering services provided by the carpet—warmth, beauty, ambiance. The firm retains ownership along with an agreement to replace worn-out carpet tiles in perpetuity while drawing on the best know-how so that recovered carpet becomes, as the Interface annual report puts it, "the technical 'food' to be reincarnated by recycling into the product's next cycle." The goal, says CEO Ray Anderson, cochair of the President's Council on Sustainable Development, is not just zero scrap and zero emissions ("cradle-to-cradle" production") but a *restorative* company "that will grow by cleaning up the world, not by polluting or degrading it."[25] Dreamy-eyed? Four years after commencing this quest in 1994, Interface's revenues had doubled (now more than $1 billion), its profit had doubled, and the company had doubled the number of jobs it provides (though at this writing, its stock is struggling). Interface no longer thinks of itself as a seller of products but as a deliverer of services provided by upgradeable durables. The company now sells results rather than carpets. Its goal is to market in performance and customer satisfaction rather than in tons of nylon that no one really wants and the disposal of which our landfills can't handle (used carpeting enters our landfills at an estimated rate of 10 million pounds a day).[26] Anderson's goal is to sever the link between the oil head at the front end and the landfill at the back end. With that in mind, Interface engineers designed a carbohydrate-based product (Solenium) that gradually displace their hydrocarbon-based nylon carpet. Reflecting on our profound lack of ecological awareness, Anderson muses, "We must be the youngest species of all, because everything else seems to know what to do."

In a survey of North American and European business leaders, consulting firm Arthur D. Little found that 83 percent believe that they can derive "real business value from implementing a sustainable development approach to strategy and operations." The key reason for delay is the instruments companies use to set targets, measure performance, and pass out rewards. If our accounting systems included in their measurements the expenditures that subsidize, encourage, and attempt to remedy resource inefficiency and damage that ought not to have occurred in the first place, we may be no better off today than we were in 1980, according to University of Maryland economist Herman Daly and his colleague John Cobb.[27] The trade-off between nature-intensive production and low-cost labor suggests that we shift to a set of rules that steadily "lays off" unproductive natural resources—in the form of tons, gallons, kilowatts, and such—while putting to work more of our human resources at better wages. At present, we tax jobs—something national policy says we want more of—and leave untaxed what national policy says we need to use less of—natural resources. Because finance is the language that business understands, commerce proceeds as though the pricing signals associated with natural capital work like any other input that simply needs to be plugged into the conventional financial model. That's like looking for a lost key under the street lamp, not because it's there but because that's where the light is best. Plus business tends to chase ecological shadows, focusing not on where environmental impacts originate but where they end up. A wholly new approach is required that combines education, ecological design, intelligent technologies, realistic accounting, and policy intervention.

Governing for Posterity

It would help if future generations became involved in this dialogue. That presents a problem. It's impossible to engage the unborn. And the law deems those under age eighteen not yet sufficiently mature. Yet it is they who must cope with the effects of our demonstrably immature decisions. Thus, during the First Hundred Days, I suggest that the attorney general in a populist administration join a lawsuit brought by minor children to represent their own and future generations under the doctrine of *intergenerational equity*. That legal strategy has a hopeful precedent. In April 1999, the Philippine Supreme Court upheld the standing of forty-one children and one adult who brought just such a suit to ensure "the judicious disposition, utilization, management, renewal and conservation of the country's forests, mineral, land, waters, fisheries, wildlife, off-shore areas and other natural resources to the end that their exploration, development and utilization be equitably accessible to the present as well as future generations." A populist president would have little choice but to support such a suit under the Constitutional mandate requiring that he or she "provide for the general welfare, and secure the blessings of liberty to ourselves *and our posterity*." In approving the Philippine suit for further disposition, their supreme court took a courageous yet commonsense stance, holding that "the right to a balanced and healthful ecology" need not be found in the law because "it concerns nothing less than self-preservation and self-perpetuation." Further, the court held that environmental sustainability "may even be said to predate all governments and constitutions. As a matter of fact, these basic rights need not even be written in the Constitution for they are assumed to exist from the inception of humankind."

The legal (and moral) issue concerns the right of children and the unborn to *insist* that policymakers work to maintain an earth capable of sustaining life. That's as fundamental a posterity issue as I can imagine. Such a suit could help change our image of who we are as a nation ("We the People—Born and Unborn") by establishing a precedent that recognizes the interconnectedness of the present and the future in legal terms. The impact on decisionmaking in the financial domain could be profound, rejecting today's use of ridiculously short-term financial models in favor of an obligation to use valuation techniques with an intergenerational focus. It's essential that we devise more creative ways to protect the rights of children, particularly as the number of children in the United States is expected to exceed 90 million in 2050, versus just 70 million today. More than 90 percent of this increase will come as the result of immigration (mostly Hispanics and Asians). At the same time, however, the number of families with minor children is projected to decline to only 20 percent of total households by 2010, making such families a distinct minority.[28] That suggests the need to ensure in political and financial decision making the principle of shared responsibility for all children in society. The fact that only one household in five will then include young children means that today's narrow appeal to self-interest alone will no longer suffice to support policies that honor those with legitimate needs.

Arrogance and Ignorance

Markets need to be kept in their place if we are to leave behind an "ancestral capitalism" of which our descendants can be proud. One way to think about these issues was captured in an article titled simply "Who Will Pay the Pollinators?"[29] What happens if nature's pollinators (bees, birds, butterflies) don't show up for work (one-quarter of our honeybee colonies have been lost just since 1990)? Do we offer to pay them more? Fire them and hire replacements? Retain an arbitrator? File an appeal with the National Labor Relations Board? Urge our R&D departments to design a substitute? Eighty percent of the 1,330 plant species that constitute our food supply are pollinated by wild or semiwild pollinators.

Today's markets make certain assumptions about nature that are wholly false. We now know, for example, that we are cutting 2 percent of the world's standing rain forests each year. That works out to 80,000 square miles a year—an acre each second.[30] Even where forests are not clear-cut, they are often fragmented into small "islands" that are *ecologically* damaged as they become separated from the whole. For example, the ruby-throated hummingbird previously migrated to the United States each year, stopping along the way in different rain forest habitats. Now that many of those habitats are destroyed or left in fragmented, more distant segments, suitable stopovers are now too far apart for the birds to successfully navigate the journey. Many now perish en route. Such is the fate of that particular pollinator, a priceless yet *unpriced* factor of production whose services are embedded in a fabric far broader than the concerns of finance.

Similar stories abound. For instance, in the spring of 1999, farmers in the U.S. Corn Belt sowed 10–20 million acres of genetically modified corn that protects itself from pests by generating a biotoxin in its tissues.[31] Biodesigned by Monsanto, this plant produces a windborne pollen that killed half the monarch butterfly caterpillars in a 1999

Cornell University study. The monarch butterfly claims our Corn Belt as the heart of its breeding range, as it migrates from Mexico and into Canada before returning south.

Such genetic tampering has untold human, ecological, commercial, foreign-policy, and intergenerational implications. For example, we don't know if inbred plant toxicity may detrimentally affect not only pollinators but also soil organisms, damaging soil fertility, one of the most complex of living systems.[32]

Curiously, this very new "life science industry" relies on old paradigm thinking. The prevailing biotech view assumes that genes are modular entities with a mechanistic one-to-one relation between gene and function, a sort of genetic reductionism. That's simply not true; the gene's function is context-specific. Also, genetic engineers routinely neglect second- and third-level consequences that could have disastrous results many levels up from the farm food web, such as the effect on birds (eaten by humans) that have eaten insects that feed on biodesigned plants. They also fail to take into account the unknown impact on subsequent generations. From a business perspective, these risks involve potentially severe and incalculable financial liability issues. Imagine the impact as genetic drift occurs and genes designed for one purpose mix with other plants. "The arrogance of human action in the face of human ignorance is unfailingly breathtaking," notes Chris Desser, an environmental lawyer and coordinator of the Biotech Working Group. I will be surprised (and disappointed) if the Mexican government chooses *not* to file a lawsuit against the United States, relying not only on intergenerational equity (per the Philippine suit) but also claiming, under the North American Free Trade Agreement (NAFTA), that bioengineered efforts to boost the U.S. corn crop endangers Mexican farmers, adversely affecting trade.

Intergenerational Values

The human community is not some finite "thing;" it's a partnership not only among the living but also between the living and those yet unborn. Democracies are founded on an implied covenant that each generation will operate in good faith to preserve for the next the natural heritage with which it has been entrusted. The wisdom of societies is rightly measured by how well they keep that covenant. Native Americans capture the spirit of that ethic by classifying the actions of people according to whether they are takers or keepers. "Earth

Keepers" is a phrase they use to denote the mission of those who live in harmony with the ways of the earth.[33] Judging by our actions as clear takers, future generations have good reason to be concerned that maturity, good faith, and wisdom are all now lacking.

Today's Chicago-inspired finance-focused economic model clearly conflicts with our constitutional obligations to posterity. At the very least, we need to slow the fevered pace at which we bequeath to future generations the excesses of our own.

The UN Environmental Program confirms the international dimensions of this failure of democracy in its sobering publication *Global Environmental Outlook 2000,* which identifies a number of "full-scale emergencies" on the environmental horizon. These include severe water shortages; reduced agricultural productivity due to the loss of topsoil; the unwanted growth of vegetation along the sea coasts; and vast algae blooms, caused by runoff from agricultural fertilizers.

A study of Atlantic and Gulf of Mexico coastal waters by Harvard Medical School's Center for Health and the Global Environment found that both area's waters and the people who live near them are getting sicker. Between 1976 and 1996, annual occurrences of harmful algae blooms, a leading indicator of health risks for marine animals and for humans, increased from 74 to 329. Strandings of whales, dolphins, and porpoises jumped from nearly zero in 1972 to almost 1,300 in 1994. Mass fish kills and disease outbreaks went from nearly unheard of before 1973 to almost 140 events in 1996. Human health problems also surged, including everything from swimmer's itch to memory loss and cholera induced by the toxic alga *Pfiesteria.*[34] Is all this simply a reflection of better reporting, as skeptics charge? In a particularly grim assessment, the report concludes that the destruction of rain forests has gone too far for people to prevent its irreversible damage and that it's already too late to regain the planet's former biodiversity. To give the developing world a chance to emerge from poverty, the report recommends that the developed world cut its use of natural resources by a whopping 90 percent. Recent and promising breakthroughs in alternative fuels, fuel efficiency, and ecological design suggest that may well be feasible.[35] Some frugality on our part is certainly called for, not in the sense of Aunt Jane's padlocked pantry but in its original meaning of *fruitfulness*—getting more out of little.

A shift in U.S. energy use may already be under way. The Federal Energy Information Agency reports that the amount of energy consumed for every dollar of GDP fell 4 percent in 1997, and another 4 percent in 1998, the biggest gain in half a century. About a third of the gain is due to the expansion of information technology, whereas the balance is due to increased energy efficiency. One heartening development suggests that the energy savings due to increased e-commerce could avoid the need for as much as 2 billion square feet of commercial building space, equivalent to almost 450 Sears Towers. The resulting energy savings from operations and maintenance alone could total 53 million kilowatt hours per year. That's the output of more than twenty-one typical power plants, preventing the release of 35 million metric tons of greenhouse gases into the atmosphere. Avoided construction of all those buildings saves the equivalent of ten more power plants. Add to that the savings from the ground shipping of Internet-purchased items, which uses an estimated one-tenth the energy of driving yourself to the mall.[36]

As for personal frugality, I am always struck on my return from overseas at the remarkable number of Americans who are overweight. Foreigners comment on it too. Yet health research suggests that we can maintain excellent health, weigh less, and live considerably longer by reducing our caloric intake by 40 percent.[37] Consider that the food we eat in this country has traveled, on average, 1,300 miles. That suggests far more hydrocarbon than food content in the prices we pay. The implications for energy savings are enormous. As any outspoken vegetarian will tell you, the environmental implications of meat-eating are profound. Those range from aquifer depletion (water needed to grow feed grains) to groundwater contamination (runoff from pigs, chickens, etc.), and from rain forest devastation (cutting trees to raise cattle) to destruction of ocean reefs (nitrate runoff from fields used to grow cattle feed). Germans were astounded to learn that a cup of their widely popular strawberry yogurt entails 5,650 miles of transportation as trucks traversed the country to assemble and deliver the various ingredients before they show up on the grocery store shelf.[38]

From an intergenerational perspective, the lesson is clear: We must become more mindful of the *full* implications of our consumption patterns and adjust them to meet the demands of sustainability and the needs of those in this and future generations. On that point, it's useful to recall that Adam Smith based much of his economic reasoning on the advantages of specialization, particularly his classic example of the pin maker who performed all the various manufacturing steps when it would have been more efficient to have various specialists work together—one to draw the wire, one to sharpen the point, one who attached the head of the pin. That eighteenth-century story, now apocryphal in the economics literature, forms the basis of modern-day labor productivity. Yet that antiquated example, persuasive in isolation, may lose all relevance if environmental costs are considered. From the perspective of *resource productivity*, the Germans (as well as the rest of us) may be better off if they became a bit less specialized and instead made their own yogurt. That, of course, qualifies as rank heresy among the Chicago-anointed and their puckered-up notions of money-measurable productivity.

Big-Picture Capitalism

There are no easy answers here. Regardless of the fate of those downstream or downwind, or of the ruby-throated hummingbird, the monarch butterfly, the rain forests, or those yet to draw their first breath, there remains $17 trillion-plus in the hands of U.S. money managers. That money *will* be invested—somehow, somewhere. Some critics suggest we'd be better off with more women investment managers because they've a more keenly developed sense of caring. Compared to men, they demonstrate more capacity to see the big picture. They're also better at conferring about their investment decisions with others, ensuring that they understand the broader implications. Men, on the other hand, are more likely to look for a shortcut. Women do business. Men try to make a killing. Women are more likely to hold on for the long-term compared to men who, according to one study, trade 45 percent more often than women, their trading commissions eroding returns.[39]

While it's tempting to read too much into such research, there's clearly a need for an investment decisionmaking process that takes into account a broader range of nonfinancial measures. Though "nonfinancial indicators" are presently a hot topic among investment analysts, Wall Street's interest stems not from any concern for equity or sustainability but from an attempt to identify additional criteria in the search for heftier financial returns, regardless of the broader impact. The last time I looked, thirty-nine nonfinancial indicators had been identified including employee voice, management effectiveness, and the ability to bring ideas quickly from concept to market.

In short, no methodology is yet available for incorporating environmental or intergenerational costs into investment decisionmaking. Even to suggest that we do so strikes some as foolhardy, arrogant, even obscene. How, they ask, can you put a price on a tree for only its board-feet when it's an eight-hundred-year-old fir and an integral part of one of the continent's last stands of ancient forest? Some things (including certain relationships in nature and in society) simply cannot be separated, commoditized, and capitalized. Yet what's even more obscene is a system that assigns to such values *no value at all*. What's needed is some way for the future to eavesdrop on today so that the interests of tomorrow are protected. In this effort, the courts can play a constructive role. That's also why I advocate the notion of up-close ownership as one way to create personal, long-term, we-live-in-the-neighborhood relationships with those companies likely to do environmental mischief. Things look far different when it's your family, your neighbors, your community, and your descendants who are at risk instead of just your financial return. Similarly, a component of local ownership of natural resource extraction operations (mining, fishing, lumbering, oil drilling) would bring to decisionmaking a useful new mix of place-sensitive concerns. However, regardless of the ownership pattern, regulation is the only feasible avenue to address many environmental challenges. When the whole is at risk, involvement by the whole is essential. To suggest otherwise is either naive or disingenuous.

Now that we know economics is intertwined with the environment, the question becomes how best to evoke a capitalism with more collective foresight. Pricing signals have clear limits. So do financial valuation techniques. At the very least, we need to ensure that we grant less credence to signals we are struggling to be less driven by. As a general rule, as systems get larger they need more signals. If we hope to stop endangering our environment, we must recognize that financial returns are but one set of signals; others are required. We will find our way through this environmental impasse by realizing that this is a transition phase during which we need to reformulate the feedback to which free enterprise responds. While financial signals are certain to remain important, even crucial, we will always be suspended somewhere between mystery and mastery when it comes to preserving nature. Short-term, the best that we can hope for is that our decisionmaking is ethically alert. Unless our commercial decisionmaking becomes broadly peoplized, that's unlikely to be the case. That's why modern-day populism holds such great promise for the future of the environment.

PART FOUR

Share Our Wealth 2000

13
Share Our Wealth

Those exertions of the natural liberty of a few individuals, which might endanger the security of the whole society, are, and ought to be, restrained by the laws of all governments.

—ADAM SMITH

During Mahatma Gandhi's time in South Africa just after the turn of the twentieth century, he developed as a weapon of social justice, a notion known in Sanskrit as *Satyagraha*, literally, "firmness in truth." When faced with South Africa's apartheid system, in which he was considered "colored," he sought ways to wage nonviolent warfare as a way of defeating the enemy without harming him and without arousing feelings of hatred on either side. There lies the modern origins of civil disobedience used so effectively by Martin Luther King, Jr., and others in the U.S. civil rights movement of the 1960s, which gained for blacks the right to vote and other key elements of their previously denied citizenship.

What we face today is very different. We don't find ourselves without a vote. Or on the losing side of a vote. We face conditions on which no one has been *allowed* to vote. And we face circumstances—vast and fast-expanding economic inequality and tragic environmental degradation—that would never be approved *if put to a vote*. As a democracy becomes less and less democratic, the obligation to abide by its rules diminishes in kind. That's the quandary we now face. And a key reason why democracy is in such jeopardy.

I'm not certain that we can design our way back to a sane and sustainable system in a peaceful way. I know we must try. For a nation founded on the notion of inclusion and dedicated to posterity, we've gone a very long way down the path of exclusion and unsustainability. Now we must find our way back and, if necessary, fight our way back. Though I hope that we can evoke rather than mandate a more just ownership result, any fully voluntary method for sharing our wealth would, in effect, reward yet again those whose wealth is already profoundly unjust. That's because any proceeds from voluntary sales are certain to favor those already unjustly favored. Plus we'd be buying at highly inflated prices—and be required to borrow the funds from them for the privilege of making the purchase.

This book and my previous one, *The Ownership Solution*, aim to stimulate the creative thinking required to move us off today's stale, repetitious, and unproductive debate. Other ideas can be solicited through congressional testimony. I've been at this now for twenty-seven years. I've yet to hear even a word of disagreement concerning the desirability of the *goals* outlined here. Indeed, if I could harness the energy of all the nodding heads I've encountered along the way among policymakers and their staffs—both Republican and Democrat—I could drill for oil in east Texas. Yet still no one takes the initiative. No one. The leadership is simply not there. That suggests the time has come for more direct action. That's the purpose of this and the next chapter.

Here I make two proposals. First, I offer the outline of a practical plan for ensuring that more Americans have an opportunity to share in their nation's prosperity. These ideas draw their inspiration from the Long Plan proposed by Louisiana's Huey P. Long in the 1930s. His Share Our Wealth proposals were conceived as an answer to the rampant greed of the 1930s, the last time extreme avarice enjoyed political support in such a comprehensive fashion. Second, it must be recognized that we live in what can most charitably be called leaderless times, particularly when it comes to issues of intergenerational consequence—the future of democracy, civil cohesion, fiscal foresight, environmental conditions, and so forth. If our political leadership proves unwilling to lead us in this direction—as I anticipate will continue to be the case—what then? I propose in Chapter 14 that civil disobedience and "firmness in truth" is the essential next step required to advance this agenda.

These are critical times with crucial decisions that *must* be made—and soon. Demographics don't wait. Cascading crises—not only fiscal crises but also political, social, cultural, health, and environmental crises—confront us. If these long-festering issues continue to be left unattended, those of us committed to democracy must take the actions required to take our democracy back.

The agenda I suggest is not one that ages well. It cannot be put off for leisurely study and academic reflection. Or set aside for lengthy review by presidential commissions, congressional task forces, or official boards of inquiry. Action is needed now. Procrastination is its greatest enemy. The next greatest is incrementalism. Today's circumstances call for change that is both comprehensive and quick. That presents a particularly daunting challenge for a democracy designed to ensure that even rapid change is pursued in a deliberative fashion. A wealth-sharing agenda must and will be pushed along to enactment—if not by the forces of today's sadly stunted democracy then, let us hope, by the democratic forces of one newly established by the people for this purpose. For those who agree that this is an agenda with relevance to them and their children, it's essential that you assist in rousing others to action. Yet that arousal is only possible if the larger public has a chance to hear this message. That's the democratic way.

Share Our Wealth

Louisiana's Huey Long, for all his flaws (and they were many), viewed his plan as "destined to save America from Communism and Fascism."[1] While other politicians of his era were promising to remake America, he was promising to "sustain" it. Though the collapse of communism, let us hope, has saved us from any resurgence of that ill-conceived notion, it's not at all clear that this nation will be spared the yoke of fascism. If we hope to live in a country where healthy dissent, diversity, and political equality are celebrated rather than barely tolerated, we must find a way to ensure the widespread economic self-reliance so essential to individual liberty. That's a key reason Ronald Reagan declared himself an early advocate of these ideas, characterizing them in the mid-1970s as "the answer to the stupidity of Karl Marx." And, he might have added, to the perils of a Benito Mussolini. In a similar vein, I recall walking into the Senate Finance Committee with Russell Long and Bob Dole in 1984, when Long asked that Dole, then chairman, call for a vote on a Long amendment encouraging employee stock ownership plans, which Dole agreed to do. Dole prefaced that vote in a way that should resonate with those who may wonder why I dare speak highly of Huey. "I don't know much about ESOPs," Dole quipped, "but Russell reminds me that when people own property they vote Republican, and I'm for that." Long's proposal received a unanimous vote in the committee.

Therein lies the paradox for conservatives who would embrace too radical a version of laissez-faire capitalism. "The problem with capitalism," Russell Long often reminded his colleagues on the committee (many of them multimillionaires), "is that it doesn't create enough capitalists." Thomas Jefferson understood that. Back when land was the most important form of capital, he included in his draft of the Virginia Constitution of 1776 a provision that every person of voting age "neither owning or having owned 50 acres of land shall be entitled to an appropriation of 50 acres."[2] In a democracy founded on the rights of private property, he knew that provision must be made to ensure the broad-based personal autonomy that accompanies the ownership of property. That's why the Long Plan seems in retrospect quite conservative, albeit populist. What he proposed was a variation on a point first raised by Plato, who cautioned that the republic is endangered when its policies allow personal wealth disparities to exceed five to one. Long proposed a far more generous one hundred to one. Nor did his proposals suggest that wealth be redistributed—in the sense of being taken by the government and spent by politicians on their pet programs. Quite the contrary. Like his conservative son Russell, Huey sought a way to capitalize individuals, not bureaucracies.

Share Our Wealth, Huey Long–Style

Unlike his son, Huey was not a financial sophisticate. But he had a feel for politics, as Franklin Delano Roosevelt soon discovered. It was Huey's credibility as a political candidate that lent political substance to his populism. Plus he had the gift of gab. And he didn't mind playing in-your-face politics with someone he considered a patrician and who, in turn, viewed Long as a back-country rube. However, Roosevelt, the New York sophisticate, soon discovered that this white-suited former Southern governor posed a serious political threat. When Huey announced his Share Our Wealth program on nationwide radio in a February 1934 speech titled "Every Man a King but No Man Wears a Crown," Long received 140,000 letters from a Depression-weary public whose plight, he assured them, was worsened by the unbridled greed and policy-endorsed excesses of that era's pampered rich.

"A New Deal?" Huey thundered, incredulous at the narrow scope of FDR's plans for economic recovery. "It looks like the Same Old Deal to me." Truth is, he wasn't far off the mark, at least from an ownership perspective. The country was sinking deeper into the Depression, and Roosevelt was uncertain where to turn. At one point, he engaged Huey in debate, quickly retreating when his opponent received more than 30,000 letters of support each day over a twenty-four-day period. Long also had his eye on what remains the heart of the problem: the financial system. When FDR proposed consolidating the Federal Reserve's powers in Washington, Long supported the notion, but only if the central bank was controlled by directors elected by the people. "After all," he charged, with all the irony present in the midst of the Depression, "the people make fewer mistakes than those which can be charged to private bankers." Long's solution: authorize a Federal Reserve Board with one director for each state; fix their terms at six years and elect one-third of them every two years. When bankers objected on grounds that this move would result in the popular control of banking, Long ridiculed their opposition as "the most unpatriotic, greedy, and heartlessly selfish thing in America today."[3]

By the time Huey was ready to prepare seriously for a presidential campaign, he could claim that 7.7 million people had joined 27,431 Share Our Wealth clubs nationwide. By April 1935, his office was receiving 60,000 letters a week. In his book, with the attention-grabbing title *My First Days in the White House* (published posthumously), he laid out his political strategy for implementing Share Our Wealth if he won the 1936 election. He proposed to appoint John D. Rockefeller, Jr., chairman of a National Share Our Wealth Committee, assisted by Andrew Mellon, Charles Schwab, Bernard Baruch, and others among the Gilded Age's masters of finance, as he depicted them. Their charge: to devise a plan for sharing wealth through the imposition of a "capital levy" on family fortunes in excess of $5 million ($62 million in 1999 dollars).[4] By appealing to their patriotism, he was confident that Rockefeller and the others would cooperate. Certain that J. P. Morgan's firm would not, Long banned from the process both the Morgan and the Drexel firms.

Anticipating the plan that he expected the committee to propose, he urged that this "surplus wealth" (in the form of corporate stock) be turned over to a corporation that, in turn, would issue its stock for distribution "among the peoples according to any plan deemed suitable by the Congress." Ironically, the structure that Huey envisioned is remarkably similar in form to Warren Buffet's investment strategy whereby the Omaha-based multibillionaire invests long term in a portfolio of securities, with investors sharing the wealth through their individual stakes in Berkshire Hathaway, a Buffet-founded holding company. Huey didn't lay out the full mechanism for Share Our Wealth; he just knew that something had to be done and that the democratic process was uniquely well suited to sort it out once the question was properly framed. That remains the challenge today. The timing seems propitious. For instance, a 1998 Gallup News Service survey found that nearly half of Americans agree that the government should redistribute wealth by hefty taxes on the rich.

Every Man a King

Huey also began to lay plans for a vigorous presidential campaign for which he was well positioned to raise funds from banks and corporations that anticipated he might dislodge FDR, allowing Republicans to regain the White House. Conspiracy theorists of that era charge that Huey's hidden agenda was to unseat Roosevelt in 1936, confident that four years with another Republican in the White House would plunge the nation into an even deeper depression, paving the way for Long's landslide election in 1940. By early 1935, Roosevelt's New Deal was at a crossroads. Programs spawned by his vaunted First Hundred Days had fizzled. Criticism was mounting. Although he continued publicly to ignore the Louisianan's fast-growing political insurgency, his anxious brain trust commissioned the nation's first rigorous presidential public opinion poll. Its sole purpose: to gauge Huey's political appeal. Devised by James "Big Jim" Farley, chairman of the Democratic National Committee, the postcard ballot was accompanied by a six-paragraph cover letter dated April 30, 1935, from the editorial department of a fictitious *National Inquirer* magazine. With Farley serving double duty as postmaster general, return postage was prepaid. Distributed to 150,000 people, the poll posed a presidential horse race question: If the presidential election were today, would you vote for (1) Franklin D. Roosevelt, (2) a Republican candidate (unnamed) or (3) Huey P. Long.

The results confirmed their worst fears. Though Farley limited the tally to only two-thirds of the ballots returned, ignoring those from people on relief (who were doubtless even more sympathetic to Huey), FDR's populist nemesis polled 10.9 percent of the vote. That put this brash dissident in the clear spoiler position, ensuring him the balance of power in the upcoming 1936 election. To their horror, the poll also documented Long's popularity well outside the rural South, showing substantial support in key industrial states, enough to transfer five major states to the Republicans, including Roosevelt's native New York, with 122 electoral votes. Even in California, Share Our Wealth was poised to pick up the pieces of the "End Poverty in California" campaign after Upton Sinclair's failed bid for governor in 1934.

Share Our Wealth or Tax Our Paychecks?

Though historians hotly debate Long's impact on what emerged in June 1935 as Roosevelt's Second Hundred Days, a close adviser to Roosevelt confirms FDR's comment that he intended for his proposal to "steal Long's thunder."[5] Certainly Long's fingerprints are all over what emerged. The legislation included not only a "soak the rich" tax but also a hike in inheritance taxes, a graduated corporate income tax, and the Wagner Act (already under consideration), which guaranteed the rights of labor (Huey advocated a minimum wage and a thirty-hour work week). Looking back, these measures marked the nation's first embrace of a genuinely progressive agenda, permanently changing the face of national tax and labor policy. The most radical, even socialist proposal was Roosevelt's endorsement of social security.

Russell Long shared with me a revealing anecdote from that era. He said that Arthur Altmeyer, the nation's first social security commissioner, had once told him about a meeting that Altmeyer had with FDR concerning social security. According to Altmeyer, he left their meeting uncertain whether he had been summoned to discuss Russell's father or to discuss Social Security. That's because whenever FDR mentioned Social Security, Altmeyer said he could hear him mutter under his breath, "That damn Huey Long."

Is that comment significant six decades later? You bet. Instead of Long's Share Our Wealth, we got FDR's Tax Our Paychecks. Social Security payroll taxes now account for one-third of the federal government's tax revenues. That progressive-era levy is now the largest tax paid by a majority of Americans and the single greatest tax paid by 90 percent of Gen-Xers. It's also our most regressive tax, computed at a flat 12.4 percent rate on income up to $72,600 (thanks but no thanks, Steve Forbes, we already have a flat tax). Social Security is now the only pension for more than half those in the private sector. Thus, the most significant "wealth" for most Americans is an assurance that someone else will be taxed on their behalf. Adding insult to injury, the tax is levied on jobs, the sole link that most Americans have to their capitalist economy. Adding outrage to insult, rather than asking why so many Americans remain dependent on social security more than six decades after its inception, Washington instead debates how to finance it. You can bet something is fundamentally amiss when a program designed as a Depression-era social safety net becomes instead most Americans' largest "asset."

Adding stark terror to outrage, insult, and injury, the same economists who defend today's brutishly exclusive private property system now serve as favored advisers to ninety-five fledgling economies worldwide that are struggling with the transition from socialism to capitalism, a political feat roughly equivalent to unscrambling an omelet. These finance fundamentalists conveniently forget that many of those in-transition nations embraced socialism precisely because of harshly exclusive ownership patterns. Yet with high-paid advice from our academic and financial elite, those plutocratic patterns are again emerging worldwide. Rather than embrace a capitalism designed for inclusion, they instead divert the debate—ensuring that any discussion of design is limited to crafting the most financially efficient safety net to accompany a capitalism certain to remain highly exclusive.

Why Not Share Our Wealth?

We'll never know whether the Long Plan would have worked. On August 9, 1935, Huey Long presented his shocked Senate colleagues with a transcript indicating a plot to assassinate him, including an unidentified voice bragging, "I haven't the slightest doubt but that Roosevelt would pardon anyone who killed Long." A month later, Huey was gunned down in a hallway of his vaunted statehouse in Baton Rouge, shot by the son-in-law of a state judge Huey planned to remove from the bench. He died two days later at the age of forty-two. Russell, age sixteen when his father was slain, assures me that Huey (he typically referred to his father that way) was murdered by an obscure "them," implying that it was those who viewed his presidential ambitions for what they were: a credible electoral threat.[6] Others aren't so sure. All we know for certain is that the Roosevelt Treasury ordered an investigation of Long's tax returns as well as returns of many of his allies, a common political harassment both then and now. We also know that FDR had long denied federal patronage to Huey's allies, lavishing it instead on his enemies, another political tool that remains in widespread use. Historical records also confirm that after Long's death, federal funds for Louisiana flowed in such abundance that ousted Share Our Wealth supporters labeled it the Second Louisiana Purchase.

That's the last time a U.S. office-seeker dared address our ownership patterns. No one other than Huey Long has since advanced an agenda to turn capitalism into a system broadly populated with capitalists. I don't know why. Perhaps it's because the world's two most-quoted and least-read economic theorists, Marx and Keynes, excluded that possibility from their analysis. In his foreword to *The General Theory* (1935), Keynes mused: "In so far as the distribution of wealth is determined by the more or less permanent social structure of the community, this also can be reckoned a factor, subject only to slow change and over a long period, which we can *take as given* in our present context." What if the distribution of wealth were no longer regarded as "given"? What then of Keynesian economics? Similarly, a close reading of Marx suggests that broad-based personal ownership rather than state ownership would have provided an equally satisfactory solution to the evils of concentrated capitalism that he found so repugnant. As Marx put it: "You are horrified at our intending to do away with private property. But in your existing society private property is already done away with for nine-tenths of the population; its existence for the few is solely due to its nonexistence in the hands of those nine-tenths." What then is the point of socialism if capitalism is rewired to share the wealth with those nine-tenths? What then of Marxist economics? I suggest that the only sensible and sustainable defense of free enterprise must be based on the appeal of inclusive design rather than on the threat of nuclear weapons—with a mix of populist policies that ensure ownership is spread among those nine-tenths.

Wealth must be both generated and distributed. Either one in isolation is insufficient. The political left typically limits itself to vague proposals to redistribute wealth (tax the rich), ignoring what's required to generate wealth. Meanwhile, the political right limits itself to vague proposals to generate wealth (laissez-faire), ignoring the need for policies to distribute it (a rising tide lifts all boats). As events since the collapse of communism have made clear, there are no major ideological alternatives to free enterprise. The question is how to ensure it works in an optimal fashion. The alternatives to free enterprise don't work, as those who now reject them will readily attest. When all else fails, perhaps we'll finally turn to common sense and design capitalism for inclusion.

No Person Wears a Crown

In November 1998, I traveled to the Old Statehouse in Baton Rouge to participate in Long Day. The commemoration brought out the historians, the pundits, and the politicians, both retired and current, plus a gaggle of press. Many of us had a few stories to add to the Long legend, arguably the nation's most colorful political dynasty and certainly its most controversial. Huey alone generated enough material to spawn both a 926-page Pulitzer Prize–winning biography and a Pulitzer Prize–winning novel, *All the King's Men* by Robert Penn Warren.[7] During his time as governor, Long was both reviled by the rich for his heavy-handed politics (giving populism a bad name that lingers still) and praised by the poor for his many social welfare programs, including roads, bridges, hospitals, schools, and even free schoolbooks, a radical and much-needed political innovation in a state that then ranked forty-seventh out of forty-eight in literacy.

Though the times are now very different, Huey remains correct on his key point: Ways must be found to Share Our Wealth. Despite Huey's many detractors and his controversial politics, he could claim thousands of formerly dispossessed Louisianians who gratefully recalled him decades later as simply "the Kingfish," their poverty-plagued lives improved by someone willing to confront the forces of capital during an earlier, similarly radical laissez-faire era, and bend those forces to the common good.

Russell Long, now eighty-one, still frets about the prospects for a free-enterprise democracy once "those on the taking down end begin to outnumber those on the putting up end." Yet without a Share Our Wealth program, that's where we're headed. Every seven seconds for the next ten years, an American will turn age fifty. In 1998, we had thirty-four workers for every ten social security beneficiaries. By 2030, when our last baby boomer turns sixty-five, the Social Security Administration projects that we'll have about twenty-one to twenty-three workers for every ten beneficiaries. Yet even that fails to capture the full extent of the challenge, because 80 percent of boomers expect to continue working during retirement, either part-time, full-time in a new career, or by going into business for themselves.[8] That will put additional downward pressure on Gen-Xers' job prospects. By 2050, an unprecedented 21 percent of the population will be sixty-five and over, compared with 12 percent today. Why that demo-graphic wake-up call has not yet been heeded should concern us all—and should give pause to anyone who thinks well of today's political leadership. We can wait no longer. The policy environment must be redesigned to ensure a broader sharing in our nation's economic well-being. Whether voluntarily or otherwise, we must begin *now* to share our wealth.

14
The First Hundred Days

Men are qualified for civil liberty in exact proportion to their disposition to put moral claims upon their appetites.

—EDMUND BURKE

What I propose here is similar both in process and structure to the Long Plan, which never received consideration during the Roosevelt era. Though social security should remain as our somewhat tattered safety net, the best way to shore it up is to ensure that people need it less. Plus, it must be said that social security was always intended as a means for leveling economic outcomes. Anyone who fails to acknowledge that goal denies both its history and its effect. To date, policymakers have focused on incentives for personal saving and for participation in employer-sponsored pensions. The national debate continues to cluster around this conventional three-legged stool of retirement security—personal saving, pensions, and social security.

However, two other key areas need attention. The first area deals with how to finance tomorrow's capitalism so that more Americans become capitalists. Today's system ensures success for the successful. The more money you have in the bank, the more interest you earn, and thus the more money you have in the bank. Once you're included in the "closed system of finance," you accumulate more capital each year—automatically. That self-reinforcing feedback loop will destroy both free enterprise and democracy if allowed to continue unchecked. The symptoms are there for all to see. There are many ways to slow that phenomenon by redirecting financial flows in a way that steadily broadens ownership. That's a key theme of *The Ownership Solution*. Although that's helpful, experience to date suggests that redirecting financial flows won't be nearly enough, particularly after two full decades of legislation designed to make the rich far richer while leaving most everyone else either stranded or sinking. For instance, despite an array of tax incentives for employee stock ownership plans (ESOPs) that were routinely attacked as too generous, ESOP transactions in 1998 totaled only $1.16 billion in a year when capital investment nationwide was $932 billion and mergers and acquisitions exceeded $1.6 trillion.[1] Something more must be done.

That brings us to the second area and to the heart of the matter. How does a democratic nation founded on the twin pillars of private property and political equality recover from a policymaking environment that has for so long been indifferent about its property patterns? That's the unavoidable issue. Most critically, what do we do about *current* ownership patterns, particularly when, absent action on our part, we can foresee their steady worsening? If you agree with what I propose here, it's essential that you let your opinion quickly be known because silence serves as an endorsement of trends that are dangerous and unsustainable.

To kick off the national dialogue required a resoluton to this troublesome issue. I suggest that we proceed along the same lines as those Huey Long proposed in 1935. As he suggested, we should seek the advice of those most experienced in finance and business. Though opinions may differ about who is best suited for this task, during the First Hundred Days a list of two dozen qualified people would be proposed for a National Share Our Wealth Committee. Certainly investor Warren Buffet, the "Oracle of Omaha," should be involved, perhaps as chairman (*Forbes* lists his 1999 wealth at $31 billion). Other potential candidates I suggest be considered include the following:

Peter Lynch, founder and CEO of Fidelity Securities
Bill Gates, former CEO of Microsoft, and world's richest man
Ned Regan, former comptroller of New York
Colin Powell, former chairman of Joint Chiefs of Staff
Tom Jones, former president of TIAA-CREF
John Whitehead, former deputy secretary of state

Mary Bush, former board member of International Monetary Fund (Reagan appointee)

David McLaughlin, president emeritus of The Aspen Institute

Muriel Siebert, first woman with seat on New York Stock Exchange

Ted Turner, founder of CNN, and vice chairman of Time Warner (AOL–Time Warner)

Bob Beyster, CEO of Science Applications International Corporation

Lynn Williams, president of United Steelworkers (retired)

George Soros, financier, and founder of the Open Society Foundation

Robert Rubin, former secretary of treasury

Jack Kemp, former U.S. congressman, and former secretary of housing and urban development

Mark Hatfield, U.S. senator, retired (R.–Oreg.)

David Pryor, U.S senator, retired (D.–Arkansas)

Jack Danforth, U.S. senator, retired (R.–Missouri)

In today's finance-dominant political environment, Wall Street's financial skills should be sought from the outset. The committee should be particularly keen to seek the counsel of those whose expertise was applied so successfully over the past two decades for the benefit of so few. Surely those same talents could be utilized to spread the benefits of free enterprise more broadly. Huey Long was not certain what the National Share Our Wealth Committee would recommend. He anticipated that it would propose a Federal Share Our Wealth Corporation that would "operate as a steward and trustee for the American people in the redistribution of wealth." As a conservative, he argued that the private sector should retain full authority for the *allocation* of economic resources while policymakers focused solely on questions of *distribution*:

We propose that the government, in seizing wealth, shall leave management of every industry or business in the hands of those people now controlling it. . . . We propose that the surplus of wealth in every family owning more than five million dollars shall be converted into the form of securities, which in turn shall be turned over to this corporation to hold in trust for the American people. This corporation shall then issue its own stock, which can then be distributed among the peoples according to any plan deemed suitable by the Congress.[2]

He offered as an example what might happen at the firm of J. P. Morgan where, say, the government has imposed a capital levy of $175 million on a partnership valued at $200 million, leaving its five partners with a total $25 million in assets. That's $5 million apiece or, for the five, $310 million in 1999 dollars. The partners would issue two classes of stock bearing equal dividends. The stock with voting powers would be issued to the Morgan partners, whereas the balance of the shares, all nonvoting, would be turned over to the Federal Share Our Wealth Corporation. "In this manner," he explained, "the assets of the corporation would be seized, but the management of it would temporarily remain with Mr. Morgan and his partners." Rather than suggesting that the corporation issue stock directly to people, he proposed that the shares be retained in the corporation in order to gain the benefit of diversification.[3]

While this would mark a vast improvement on how we presently share the nation's prosperity, it begs the critical issue of how the interests of stakeholders will find a voice in corporate operations. Doubtless that will pose for the committee one of its most contentious issues, particularly when what I suggest here is that the elite of Wall Street advise on sharing wealth and decisionmaking, that they've henceforth been happy to reserve for themselves and their well-to-do-clients. Democratizing the nation's wealth is a relatively simple matter of designing more inclusive channels of distribution. The more challenging issue concerns how citizen-shareholders in this vast holding company can have their voice heard in the corporate realm. By combining the spotlight of public scrutiny with an appeal to the national interest, I'm hopeful that this skilled cadre can devise a workable plan that includes appropriate mechanisms for public accountability.

Ways and Means

Huey Long also described his criteria for setting a cap on personal wealth: "I have felt that this moderated program which allowed enough wealth to any family to inspire effort, service and achievement, but such a limit as would curb needless greed, would create a proper balance between wealth and poverty, thereby insuring the maximum inspiration of all our people." As mentioned earlier, although Plato argued that democracy is at risk when economic disparities are allowed to exceed five to one, Long proposed a ratio of twenty times as large, suggesting that wealth holdings of the "bloated plutocracy" of his time gradually be reduced from $5 million ($62 million in 1999 dollars) to $2 million ($24.8 million).

There is no correct cutoff limit. Inaction is the only wrong answer. Criticism is assured for any personal wealth cap proposal, no matter what limit is set. Some will see any limit as too low; others too high. The radical right will claim that any limit smacks of communism, whereas the loony left will whine that this proposal legitimizes the inequities of capitalism. For purposes of setting an interim benchmark to catalyze debate, I suggest that personal wealth disparities in the range of one hundred to one be the standard. Let the critics argue otherwise, including what they define as wealth as well as appropriate exemptions. Commentators are certain to describe this proposal as either too generous or too stingy. Ridicule and harsh reactions are guaranteed. Such is the dialogue of democracy. Long put it simply:

> We do not propose any division of property. We propose that no one man shall own too much, and that no one family shall have too little for comfort. There is a sane limit to the amount of water that a horse can drink; to the number of miles that a man can run; to the length of time which one can live. There is also a sane limit to the amount of wealth which it is healthy for one to own. It may be that the proportions which I suggest are too high or too low, but for the present I ask that law-makers provide that when a man gets enough wealth so that he has one hundred times as much as the average family in the country, then we say he has reached his limit.[4]

What's Wrong with Greed?

Someone might ask what, really, is the point of wealth accumulation beyond the dreams of avarice? Although one would think there's a limit to how much someone can consume, the construction of super-luxury yachts (more than 150 feet in length) is now at historic highs, with all our shipyards operating at full capacity. Spending on luxury goods grew by 21 percent from 1995 to 1996, while overall merchandise sales grew only 5 percent. What rationale, other than ostentatious consumption, might there be for unbridled greed? Despite clear evidence to the contrary, economists continue to advance the outdated notion that the savings of the well-to-do are needed to fuel the economy. That's nonsense. As I show in Chapter 6, the closed system of finance has long been the principal source of funds. Plus firms now have access to quite robust capital markets, including the ability to sell corporate bonds, even high-yield junk bonds. At one time the savings of the rich played a role as the well-to-do were persuaded by financial innovators such as J. P. Morgan to employ their wealth rather than hoard it—underwriting roads, canals, railroads, ships, and factories. That's all changed. Wall Street innovations now allow the rich both to employ their wealth *and* to hoard it—using capital markets to vastly expand their holdings.

Others argue that motivation is the key to innovation and human progress and that mandated prosperity sharing will, in some vague fashion, de-motivate entrepreneurs, deter economic growth, and retard rising standards of living. Nonsense. Any system that makes it easier for this nation's four hundred richest people to accumulate another $1.3 million *per day* over the 1997–1999 period than it does for the typical African American to accumulate $200 in financial wealth over a working lifetime is buying a lot of rubbish about what it takes to motivate people and what's required to sustain a vibrant democracy. Far better that we give hope and encouragement to the ambitions and aspirations of the many than feed the greed of the few. Huey offered a homespun way to think about it: "If America for its greatness must depend on exciting super-greed for the sake of modern and greater development, then we have set a bad example to the great inventors, to our great scientists, and to those of us here who manage the country for a mere living."[5]

What's the point of unlimited wealth accumulation? Is it to snatch someone else's opportunity, ensuring that he or she is excluded from even that modest accumulation essential to human decency and dignity? That's been the result to date. One might conclude that some of the wealthy plan on taking it with them, but I've yet to see a hearse pulling a U-Haul. Property is a social convention meant to benefit the living. It's time we insist that some live it up a bit less so that others can have a decent life.

Identifying the Means to Share Our Wealth

The question that Huey put to the lawyers of the well-to-do of his day remains the relevant question to ask again now that ownership patterns parallel that earlier era: "What are your suggestions for putting the Share Our Wealth program into effect with the least disturbance to commerce, business and industry?" That seems to me sufficient as the question to pose to this cadre of people experienced in the ways of commerce, business, and industry.

The principle of prosperity sharing is sound, particularly in a nation of political equals. Today's prosperity hoarding strikes me as a remnant of feudalism that any vibrant democracy must oppose. I've stated here the case for *why* we must share our wealth. The question for the Share Our Wealth Committee is largely one of process—*how* do we do it? For those who believe that this is an impossible task, I suggest the same response offered by Huey, when, as he envisioned in *My First Days in the White House*, he was informed by the well-to-do of his era that they had no plan for accomplishing this goal: "If that is true, and God forbid it, it would only go to prove that the public was being cheated when men of such inferior intelligence amassed so much wealth."[6]

The constitutionality of this proposal is certain to be challenged, no matter what form it takes. That's to be expected. Given the remarkable spread of the Law and Economics ideology, even the nation's highest court has been seduced by its allure. Thus, I suggest that the solicitor general in a populist administration advise in the preparation of a brief in defense of Share Our Wealth. All of the court's filings should be posted on an Internet Web site, and a White House hot line staffed round-the-clock to monitor public input. I also urge that the Supreme Court's proceedings be televised live, including the arguments of all those who might oppose the people's plan for decentralizing and democratizing their nation's prosperity. Per Long's plan, I also suggest that the nation's chief executive (i.e., the president) argue the people's case before their court. Members of Congress should be urged to attend, particularly the leadership of both parties and those chairing committees responsible for the nation's financial health.

These unique times present a unique political challenge to guide us through a difficult period of transition. Although the United States has an avowedly representative political system, we face the daunting task of undoing the impact of several decades of intense indoctrination in what can only be called radical market ideology. The Supreme Court was envisioned as a body that could stand back from the political fray with it's divisive rhetoric and help guide the nation's course in a way that nudges us ever nearer to the unifying transcendental goals that all three branches of government are pledged to pursue. If, after reflecting on this nation's long history, the Supreme Court concludes that broad-based sharing in the nation's prosperity is inconsistent with Americans' pursuit of happiness, then the people may need to mobilize to reclaim today's democracy as their own. Huey Long envisioned that the Supreme Court would decide the case favorably, albeit on narrow grounds, upholding his capital levy as a revenue source to fund armies in time of war and support the general welfare in times of peace.[7] My hope is that this case might evoke from today's conservative Court their somber reflection on the conservative doctrines of self-preservation and self-perpetuation that predate the Constitution and serve as its conceptual core. That, I expect, is what most resonated with Ronald Reagan, Jack Kemp, Mark Hatfield, Jesse Helms, Michael Novak, and other conservatives who have long endorsed these prosperity-sharing ideas.

An Old Wrinkle on a New Idea

As a key part of his political strategy, Long proposed that the mechanism devised for his plan be announced by the National Share Our Wealth Committee, its architects. As he envisioned it, the national media would carry banner headlines indicating that "the barons of Wall Street were content at last to accept democracy in America." Allowing the committee to announce the mechanism remains a sound strategy. Huey remained silent about what he meant by "more effective distribution later." However, in reserving that option, he mentioned an alternative approach that he embraced in an imaginary conversation with Henry Ford and his son, Edsel. In professing support for Huey's goals, Ford mentions that the automaker family has "ore mines, steel mills, glass works, and a vast assortment of other interests." Conceding they could not possibly estimate their wealth, the elder Ford proposes that the family be allowed to redistribute their own wealth to keep their organization intact:

> We plan to retain control of our properties by dividing their ownership among long-term Ford employees. We propose to use the money invested outside the Ford organization to construct homes for loyal Ford employees not now owning their own homes. That will be a free gift to the Ford employees. . . . We propose, further, to issue stock against the physical value of our properties, placing a fair capitalization—as fair as our economists can fix it—on each property, and issue stock against it. Then we propose to divide that stock among our workers.

Foreshadowing Russell Long's ready embrace of ESOPs four decades later, Huey hoped that all the wealthy would follow Ford's example.

Finally, those enamored of the current megamerger craze can take solace in Huey's view of corporate giantism (reflecting also his easy embrace of finance-myopic free enterprise):

> We do not propose to break up big enterprises. All that we will do will be to provide that more people will share in the profits and ownership of big enterprises. In other words, instead of one man drawing down several million dollars out of the earnings in a year, the company will make just as much money as ever, but there will be thousands, maybe hundreds of thousands, perhaps millions of people drawing what formerly a few people drew in the way of profits. We do not care how big business grows so long as it is efficient for the country. Our concern is that their ownership should not be concentrated in too few people and that their profits should be shared by the people more widely.[8]

Huey's approach avoids the troublesome issue of out-of-touch corporations and the tendency of large, finance-myopic firms to lose sight of those issues that most concern stakeholders and the communities in which they operate. The committee may conclude that genuine democratization requires that today's megalithic firms become smaller, perhaps even sacrificing some short-term efficiency in the name of long-term equity and sustainability. That, in turn, suggests that the ownership of firms would be reengineered to include a substantial local ownership component so that they respond more effectively to legitimate local needs.

Firmness in Truth

If present-day political forces resist this modern-day approach to populism, other means must be sought to effect this change. Mahatma Gandhi's advocacy of *Satyagraha* ("firmness in truth") provides an inspirational model for what can be accomplished with devotion to nonviolent action against forces that are demonstrably unjust. Although I have taken several potshots at policymakers in these pages, I urge others to criticize the act and not the actors. I suggested at the outset that a Gandhian nonviolent revolution may be required. I fully realize that there are "multiple stable states" into which human society can settle. A certain superficial stability can prevail even when, as now, social injustice is rampant, poverty widespread, insecurity severe, and environmental destruction spreading. Even now, with more than 3 billion people living on $2 or less a day and 2 billion people anemic, we in the United States enjoy relative calm. And arguably the U.S. military commands weaponry sufficient to enforce today's stability should we choose that as our goal. I hope that through education and advocacy—and through *firmness in truth*—we can embrace instead a higher level of order.

Although I do not suggest the full panoply of strategies that might be advanced should the changes required not be enacted in short order, I remind readers that Thomas Jefferson wisely observed that "a little rebellion now and then is a good thing." No one else can know what form of rebellion is best suited to you or your circumstances. For some it may be picketing; for others praying. Perhaps you'll find that marching and shouting is your natural style, whereas others gravitate to meditation and singing. Comedic or somber, feasting or fasting, through influence or force, alone or in coalitions—all have their place as we awaken to the realization that democracy cannot be played successfully as a spectator sport. Both our prosperity and our posterity depend on our becoming creatively proactive so that the future envisioned here becomes not merely possible but inevitable. In the same spirit in which Mahatma Gandhi and Martin Luther King, Jr., sought justice through nonviolence, I urge that people devise their own strategies for opposing these trends and for electing to office people with heart and courage sufficient to oppose the forces we now face. Change requires of us sustained engagement so that we might smarten up both ourselves and our democracy and thereby build the support required to move this agenda. And move it we shall.

15
Common Questions

Democracy is dialogue. Here I respond to some of the most common questions that arise in the dialogue surrounding this subject. Please send any other questions to <www.sharedcapitalism.org>.

Q: This sounds to me like radical left-wing communism. Is it?

A: Communism is ownership by the state. This is ownership by you. Conservative Republican Ronald Reagan characterized these ideas as "the answer to the stupidity of Karl Marx." The eighteenth-century Virginian Arthur Lee may have put it best, noting simply that private property is "the guardian of every other right."

Q: This sounds to me like radical right-wing capitalism. Is it?

A: Capitalism involves the private ownership of productive capital. What we have now is a radically exclusive form of plutocratic private ownership. I propose instead a radically *inclusive* form of *democratic* private property capitalism. It's radical only in the sense that it gets at the root of the problem by reframing the problem. Proponents span the political spectrum, from Jesse Helms to Jesse Jackson.

Q: If this is such a good idea, why haven't we done it before?

A: If peace is such a good idea, why isn't it breaking out all over? More seriously, ownership patterning remains even now a blind spot in both economics and politics. Economists don't know how to think about it, policymakers refuse to talk about it, and the greedy don't want you to know about it. Yet surely patterns of private ownership must have relevance in a system built on the notion of private property.

Q: If we're in such trouble with just a few capitalists, why do we want to create more?

A: Have you ever seen a practical plan for eliminating capitalists? Attempts to do so have proven disastrous. I argue that it's not private ownership that's the culprit but a combination of concentrated and disconnected ownership.

Q: If the only mission of the corporation is to make money and yet you say that financial values are already too dominant, aren't you making a bad situation worse?

A: The mission of the corporation is to maximize shareholder value. The corporation has proven itself enormously effective in doing so. With ownership held largely by the few and by money managers, the pursuit of financial values has become the default mode in the pursuit of shareholder value. As more people become capitalists and hence stakeholders, those "up-close capitalists" can insist on the pursuit of a broader range of values.

Q: You concede that globalization is here to stay. And we know that free trade has long been a way to raise living standards and fuel economic growth. Isn't this some sort of "global-phobia"? Wouldn't this choke off trade?

A: Quite the contrary. Trade can be hugely beneficial. But don't let rhetoric replace reason. We know that rule-free trade can also degrade. We've seen it hollow out high-paid jobs, damage the environment, create multinational monopolies, and undermine the democratic process while also concentrating wealth in precious few hands and leaving countless millions exposed to a very Darwinian situation. We best capture the benefits of trade by addressing the inevitable tension between commercial freedom and the general welfare, mindful that democracy will always be plagued by some individuals (and firms) insistent that their financial interests should prevail over the common good. The goals of finance should never be allowed to prevail over democratic principles.

Q: You imply that some elected officials are pawns of the well-to-do. Is that so?

A: I can't judge those you elected. I suggest that you judge them by the results. The results chronicled here suggest that we've not yet realized the broad citizen representation envisioned in the Constitution. The Tibetans have a saying: "Roll all blames into one." The real fault lies in not seeing ourselves as an indivisible one. The culprit is not evilness but ignorance. Democracy is designed to reflect your interests. But you must insist on it. Get informed. And stay engaged in the dialogue so essential to a living democracy.

Q: Are you suggesting that we redistribute the wealth?

A: Wealth is already being redistributed—upward. As I document, it's not trickling down; it's gushing up. The market does the best job of allocating resources to produce prosperity. Most everyone agrees on that. The question is how to distribute the prosperity. The market directs income to whoever owns productive inputs. Finance those inputs into a few hands, and guess where the prosperity flows? Our many decades of reliance on income redistribution has been like trying to fix a leak with a bucket.

Q: Isn't this just envy run amok, an egalitarian, slippery slope that's certain to result in more government interference in our lives?

A: Quite the contrary. One key psychological goal is to remedy the self-blame that people feel in a system they know is unjust but in which they're told they've only themselves to blame. If a hundred-to-one ratio in wealth disparities sounds egalitarian, then I urge that you present your case for more inequality. Inequality per se is not what irks people; it's the combination of unearned rewards, unfair advantages, and extreme inequality. The goal is not an egalitarian society, but a sustainable democracy and a smaller government.

Q: In a free society, shouldn't all this be purely voluntary?

A: I've been advocating voluntary programs since 1973, when I was twenty-seven. I continue to do so now in my fifties. Inaction is purely voluntary. That's what we've had so far. Continued in action is certain to result in even more dramatic economic disparity. Take your pick.

Q: How would you describe today's economic scene now that we see so little difference between Republicans and Democrats on economic issues?

A: Disconnected, divisive, dumbed-down, demonstrably unsustainable, and rapidly becoming more so.

Q: Who are the best candidates to become populists?

A: Fed-up Democrats, reformed Republicans, loosened-up Libertarians, and any independent, whether Reform, Green, or otherwise.

Q: What makes you think the powers-that-be will let you get away with this?

A: In a democracy, *you* are the powers-that-be. If that sounds to you like a reasonable proposition, then get educated, get into action, support this agenda, and create your own agenda. Power concedes nothing without a demand. Be demanding.

Q: How do you define wealth?

A: I've been at this for twenty-seven years and I still have difficulty defining it. However, I do think I can define poverty. Poverty is being denied the capacity to give. A widespread sharing of prosperity provides a means for unlocking human generosity. Generosity, I suggest, lies at the heart of any genuine democracy.

Q: Aren't you buying into the growth model of economics? Won't this further endanger the environment?

A: Like Adam Smith, I expect people to look after their best interests once they have the capacity to do so. I point to today's *disconnected* capitalism as the environmental culprit because its values are too dominantly financial. A component of up-close capitalism changes the frame of reference by injecting personal, community, environmental, and intergenerational values into economic decisionmaking.

Q: How do we know this will all work out?

A: We know that current economic policies are generating horrific results. If we revisit core democratic principles, the notion of a genuinely peoplized free enterprise emerges as the most logical way forward.

Q: I was told, "If it ain't broke, don't fix it." The stock market is doing fine; why rock the boat?

A: I've documented here that it *is* broke and certain to get more so the longer we delay in enacting a policy environment that addresses today's widespread lack of household assets and rampant economic disconnectedness. Ecologically, we need to concede huge gaps in our knowledge regarding biotechnology, global warming, holes in the ozone, aquifer depletion,

bioaccumulative toxins, and the like. The precautonary principle suggests that operative credo in both economics and
ecology should be "If you don't know how to fix it, don't
break it." Today's "Wall Street Rapture" has overridden our
common sense.

Q: What makes you think that the average American is smart
enough to be a capitalist?

A: We can wait until everyone is smart about ownership and
then convert them into capitalists. Or we can make them
owners and use that relationship to smarten them up. Or we
can continue, as now, to do neither.

Q: I know people who will sell anything as soon as they get it.
What's the point of the Federal Share Our Wealth
Corporation?

A: The answer depends on what the National Share Our Wealth
Committee recommends. They may suggest that shares be
held in trust for a number of years, much like an individual
retirement account (IRA) or an employer-sponsored pension. Perhaps they'll suggest a sliding tax scale that rewards
long-term shareholding. In any case, let's use this period to
educate people on what's required to become an owner and
the benefits of long-term capital accumulation.

Q: By the time you share today's wealth with 274 million
Americans, there won't be much to go around.

A: We've got to start somewhere. At present, we're taxing each
other's jobs to fund an extremely modest social security benefit. The ratio of jobholders to retirees is worsening at a
steady clip. The goal is to start small and make it grow. If we
cap the wealth of the most well-to-do people, that alone ensures that our future prosperity will become more widely
shared, particularly as fast-expanding global capital markets
bring more financial wealth into being. Money is like ma-
nure; it works best when spread around.

Q: Your notion of community-responsive information flows and
people-empowered feedback loops sounds good in theory,
but some people simply don't want to be bothered.

A: Maybe that's because they've never experienced a system in
which their voice counts.

Q: If we attempt to reallocate the nation's surplus wealth,
won't the well-to-do simply transfer their wealth to foundations and other nonprofits?

A: That wouldn't surprise me. That's not necessarily a bad development. The IRS requires that foundations pay out at least 5 percent of their capital each year for public purposes. That would be an improvement over today, where wealth is accumulated only for the sake of more accumulation. However, we need to revisit that minimal pay-out requirement, particularly when the Standard & Poor's 500 has averaged 17.6 percent growth over the last two decades. In addition, we need to pay far closer attention to what passes muster as a public purpose. At present, a lot of vanity foundations qualify and arguably shouldn't.[1]

Q: Aren't you worried about the nonprofit sector getting too large?

A: Peter Drucker projects that soon one of three new jobs will originate in the nonprofit sector. My concern is that the nonprofit sector will continue its current practice of blindly entrusting their funds to capital markets, using their investment returns to address problems that would be far less severe if only the nation (and the foundations) invested funds to foster broader economic self-sufficiency and environmental sustainability. The nonprofit sector needs to do a much better job of questioning today's rules if they hope to get better results. At present, many foundations are part of the problem.

Q: Aren't you worried about people putting all their eggs in one basket, particularly if both their investment and their job are tied up in the same company?

A: It's amazing to me how this concern consumes commentators when so many people have neither eggs nor a basket. It reminds me of the adage "I started out with nothing and still have most of it left." Diversification is a terrific way to minimize risk once you've accumulated some capital to risk. In addition, what's proposed here goes well beyond the notion of employees' owning employer stock. Yet even there the evidence suggests that ESOP companies both pay better and provide better retirement benefits than the norm.[2] It's envisioned that Share Our Wealth portfolios will be quite diversified.

Q: Isn't this something for nothing?

A: Hardly. Something for nothing is when the average wealth of the four hundred richest Americans increases by $1,287,671 *per day* from 1997 to 1999. For those not yet capitalized, they can't possibly give any more than they've got. Many people are going full out already and are barely getting by. Yet we're expecting them to save their way to significant capital accumulation? That's not only impossible; it's insulting to suggest they could. And naive to suggest they would.

Q: Aren't people better off now than they've ever been—more cars, appliances, TVs, stereos, VCRs, personal computers, you name it? So what if the rich get richer so long as we see a rising standard of living?

A: Without a doubt we have the richest poor people in the world. And certainly the standard of living is higher now than it's ever been. Yet it's virtually stagnated for 80 percent of Americans for the past twenty-five years. Also it's clear that the immense baby boomer generation won't have the capital required to sustain themselves as they move into retirement. We have the means available in this country for widespread abundance and leisure. The more relevant question is Why should we allow a few to monopolize the nation's abundance?

Q: Isn't this risky? You can make money with stocks, but you can also lose.

A: Economists recommend that we limit risk to the well-to-do because they can better afford to bear the loss. If you limit risk to the wealthy, guess who gets wealthy? Plus, diversification within Share Our Wealth should address that concern.

Q: Ownership motivates business creativity. Aren't we endangering the nation's entrepreneurial spirit?

A: To suggest that ownership (or prosperity) be limited to entrepreneurs is like advising that inner-city kids become world-class basketball players. Although entrepreneurs will always be a valuable force in any dynamic economy, we now have substantial *overcapacity* in many industries. We need more creativity in how to share our prosperity, and how to extract more productivity from our natural resources. We also need to export our entrepreneurial talents to those nations struggling to escape from poverty, including the former socialist countries, where entrepreneurs are in such short supply.

Q: Why should public policy penalize success?

A: There's a fiction afoot in the land that all great fortunes are "earned" when, in reality, many are due to inheritance, good luck, and even antisocial behavior. The question also assumes that personal success is a solitary effort. Nothing could be further from the truth. Private fortunes are built on a foundation of public investment, ranging from educated workers, to paved highways, to government research, to court systems for enforcing contracts. We all contributed to the prosperity now harvested by a few. Or think about it this way: If a "flat tax" imposes a 10 percent tax burden on a worker's $30,000 income and the same tax on an investor's $300,000 income, the worker is left with $27,000 and the investor with $270,000. Whose success is really penalized?

Q: Wasn't this nation built on a foundation of great wealth?

A: What's the point of great "wealth" (from the Latin for *well-being*)? Spending the interest on $1 billion is a full-time job ($1 million per week if invested at 5.2 percent interest). If you can't spend it, what's the point? Do we really want to encourage the fortune-facilitated antics of recluse Howard Hughes or tobacco heiress Doris Duke, who gave two camels the run of her house? The well-being of democracy would be much improved if we made it "billionaire-free." Let's hear the argument for the other side.

Q: Is this notion liberal or conservative?

A: It's populist. A parable reminds us of how easy it is to give meat to a tiger but difficult to take it away. Once people have some ownership, they protect it. That's conservatism. But first a policy environment must make that feasible. That's liberalism. Why and how we do it is what makes it populism. It's done to assist people in living free and with a sense of confidence and dignity among political equals. That's the goal of any true democracy.

Q: Is this constitutional?

A: I've no doubt that Share Our Wealth will be challenged in the courts. Any number of grounds can be invoked on which it should be upheld. If it's found unconstitutional, then we'll need to amend the Constitution and, over time, replace today's jurists with people better attuned to the times—and to the Constitution.

Q: We live in a federal system. What if a state governor refuses to cooperate with Share Our Wealth?

A: If Share Our Wealth has the support of the people, any governor would look foolish opposing it. Imagine, for example, if a governor calls out the National Guard to resist. It would quickly become apparent just whose interest is being protected. That governor had better be careful. As we say here in the South, people may figure out which rabbit to shoot.

Q: The foreign policy elements seem particularly challenging. Why would other nations cooperate?

A: Because it's the right thing to do. And they've tried everything else. If we show how it can be done here, people will hear about it. Concentrated wealth is now the global norm. That must change if we are to have a global democracy and sustainable development. The question is how to make the needed changes with as little disruption as possible. There are many points of leverage that can be used. We should use them all. A key leverage point in foreign policy is to demonstrate our commitment here in the United States.

Q: You make this sound like a do-or-die situation for democracy? Are things really that serious?

A: Each generation is trustee for the next. We carry within us both the intentions of our ancestors and the hopes of our descendants. The choice is ours. This can be the age of wisdom or the age of foolishness.

Q: What can I do?

A: Talk it up. What's most needed at this point is ears and eyeballs. In today's hurried-up world, time and attention are our most precious commodities. I offer here a very new way to think about what it takes to create and sustain a modern-day democracy. If we are to make the changes required, people must know about this so that they can support it. Great things begin by the thinnest edge. Anything positive you can do to raise its profile will help. Stay tuned in to <www.sharedcapitalism.org>.

Epilogue

It really boils down to this: that all of life is interrelated. We are all caught in an inescapable network of mutuality, tied to a single garment of destiny. Whatever affects one directly affects all indirectly.

—MARTIN LUTHER KING, JR.

In good conscience, the United States should begin this new century of capitalism with a mea culpa. Our stature in the world community would be much enhanced if we simply concede what everyone already knows—that our pell-mell worldwide pursuit of profit has been accompanied by considerable human, political, and ecological damage. It's also true, of course, that much good has been done. Living standards have risen for some at a pace never before witnessed in human history. However, even this apparent victory has been accompanied by a palpable inner poverty—a spiritual vacuum—that has come to define our troubled, finance-obsessed times. We need to "own" that result and pledge our considerable creativity to its correction. The United States should also, as a nation, bear witness to the preventable misery that typifies life for most in the human family. That's not so we can be accused of the obvious but so we can motivate ourselves to move forward in helping bring to a close this self-absorbed era in human development.

As a nation, we would do well to have our dark side step out of the geopolitical shadows so that we can be candid about the imperfections of our system and about our own hidden difficulties. That includes not only the inequities we've ignored domestically and those we've fostered internationally but also the fact that we're shoving so many Americans into jobs too small for their spirits. Our overwrought, even strident pursuit of financial values should be acknowledged as often out of step with the values that underlie democracy. Our hyperconsumption lifestyle and our identification of value with monetary value have subtly become a sort of official idolatry, a disturbing reminder that the word *worship* means "to value."[1] By embracing Chicago-inspired financial fundamentalism with such enthusiastic naiveté, we created a category of value called "financial returns" and then began to craft our foreign policy from that perspective. Now we've allowed that notion to spin wildly out of control when what's needed is an increased capacity for empathy, compassion, and ecological common sense. Absent that, the market-myopic freedom we enjoy will continue to imperil both ourselves and others while degrading the shared commons in which all our activities are embedded. Today's unbounded capitalism is a danger not only to democracy but even to itself. Religion scholar Joanna Macy urges that we revisit our biblical tradition and its view that humans are destined to go on somehow to a better world. This view allows us to treat this world as though it were merely a handy backdrop for our moral battles—making our behavior akin to that of a traveler who plans never to pass this way again.[2]

The destructive trends revealed here need to be not just restrained but steadily reversed. The ownership patterns that now accompany the spread of democracy mock democracy, particularly when considered against the historical backdrop of what this nation's founders endured to ensure refuge from the economic royalists of *their* day. Of the fifty-six men who signed the Constitution, five were captured and tortured before they died; another nine perished from wounds or hardships of the Revolutionary War. Many others lost their homes, their fortunes, and their families. All were then British subjects who pledged to fight their own government so that their descendants might be free from forces remarkably similar to those at work today.

One can only wonder where the men and women of honor are today. What happened to the free thinkers and the skeptics? Where are the custodians, the caretakers, and the earth keepers—those concerned for what we leave our descendants? Where are the activists, the agitators, and the courageous troublemakers? Where are the labor leaders willing to insist on a place at the table of global trade rather than settle for a token footstool? Where are the political candidates whose principles rise above the parties that their political candidacy nourishes? The twin parties that constitute today's political duopoly deserve to fail unless they respond to this plea for an equity, a workability, and a sustainability that predates the notion of political parties. To any impartial observer, it looks as if both parties conspire to favor their high-income, campaign-contributing constituents—leading one pundit to urge that they combine their conventions to better accommodate their donors.

Lead by Example

In this post–Cold War era, we need to better articulate those values by which we intend democracy to be defined. And because democracy is a dialogue across the ages we need to demonstrate those values by our own example. John Quincy Adams urged that we lead not by preaching or by precept but by the force of our own example. Today's example is not one for emulation. It's clear that we've allowed ourselves to drift much too far to the political right. Perilously so. Although we need both Adam Smith's carrot and Darwin's stick, we also need a free enterprise that leaves enough of our humanity intact to make it a free enterprise worth having.[3] Governments fail when their results become inhumane and when they lose sight of the moral source of their legitimacy. As a nation, we've lost our bearings. We are all too willing to grant deference to the domain of dollars (the "level playing field") in lieu of principled leadership. In place of an economics that promotes good citizenship, per Jefferson's charge, we now have a citizenry struggling to cope with its economics.

Globalization makes it imperative that the scope of our national concern ("the general welfare") extend well beyond our borders. Precisely because it is *our* model of free enterprise that rules the global roost, it's essential that we take responsibility for conceding its limits, identifying its dangers, and urging corrective action. We must be scrupulously candid about the imperfections of markets. Finance capitalism must be bounded and market forces monitored to ensure that the commons is protected and that appropriate fees are charged for its use.

The state of world health offers a compelling example of a clear market failure. The World Health Organization estimates that more than $56 billion a year is spent on health research. Yet less than 10 percent of that sum is directed toward diseases that afflict 90 percent of the world's population. Monsanto's R&D budget is more than twice the amount available for R&D in the worldwide network of public-sector tropical disease research institutes. Although there's a robust *human* market for a malarial vaccine, there's very little *money-denominated* market because it's a disease suffered largely by the poor. What's required is the push of public-sector support plus the pull of market demand, an element that the Bill and Melinda Gates Foundation is helping address with support for tropical disease research. It is in the resolution of conflicts between altruism and markets, between human rights and property rights, that the future of free enterprise may well be found. If we fail to evoke a free enterprise capable of addressing today's fast-mounting human crises (including crises in education, nutrition, sanitation, the environment, etc.), the niceties of property rights will soon prove less compelling than the social realities.

Plutocratic Generosity

New York Times ethicist Randy Cohen takes issue with the noblesse-oblige spectacle of great personal wealth being funneled back into public works by modern-day monopolists: "When a thief, having stolen your wallet, hands you back carfare, it's tough to mutter much of a thank-you. Similarly, nice as it is that Bill Gates gives money to libraries, a decent country would tax Microsoft at a rate that lets cities buy their own books." [4] My personal peeve is my experience of CNN or, more accurately, my inability *not* to experience CNN when I'm traversing Atlanta's huge Hartsfield International Airport. No matter where you turn, CNN blares its revenue-generating programs at captive passengers at every gate in all six of its immense concourses. I find it obscene that my serenity is sabotaged because of a contract that some local politico inked with CNN, doubtless with campaign contributions easing the way. That agreement stole my quiet by leasing public space to further enrich a local multi-billionaire. It is difficult to applaud when Turner pledges $100 million per year of his Time Warner cable-monopoly profits to the United Nations Foundation. The pledge follows hard on the heels of the predictable market run-up in the value of his stock in the merged companies. *Forbes* puts his 1999 net worth at $6.9 billion, up from $2.5 billion in 1996, and since increased to an estimated $10 billion with the January 2000 announcement of Time Warner's $165 billion merger with America Online. So long as policymakers insist on serving lemons, maybe that's as close to lemonade as we'll get. At least until we revive our democracy and replace today's plutocracy-prone politicos.

Bill Gates and Ted Turner can position themselves to look relatively good only because most others in their position look so incredibly bad. Consider this: If your financial wealth is $225,000 (about twenty times the national median) and you give $1,500 to charity, how large a donation would be required for Bill Gates to experience a similar dent in his net worth? According to *Wired*, you would need to give away $6.7 billion, or almost seven times the amount he pledged in September 1999 to provide 20,000 minority student scholarships over the next twenty years.[5] When Gates made that pledge, the value of his Microsoft shares alone totaled about $100 billion (which jumped to $130 billion after the December 1999 completion of Windows 2000). That's almost twelve times the $11 billion or so in securities owned by all 33 million of our black citizens combined. "This disparity," notes *Washington Post* columnist Courtland Milloy, "suggests something so wrong that it's going to take much more than a billion dollars' worth of schooling opportunities to fix it."

If an entry-level Forbes 400 member gives away a cool $1 million of his or her income, how much would a median-level household need to donate to make a similar sacrifice? Less than $60. So who's being generous here? Can anyone identify a billionaire whose net worth has been significantly diminished by his or her generosity during that individual's lifetime? Warren Buffet (1999 net worth of $31 billion) claims that his talent lies in making money, not in giving it away. So where's his democratic generosity? Deferred. He claims that he'll leave the bulk of his estate to a foundation that may do some good deeds later. Maybe. Though, of course, he could change his mind. And only he knows for sure what the foundation might do, someday. Maybe.

The Hunger for Human Happiness

The rules of the global economy are what determines whether the setting is right for a genuine global democracy to emerge. As presently constructed, those rules are not conducive to a democracy that responds to legitimate human (versus financial) needs. Not only are key market failures routinely ignored, today's financial technologies undermine democracy, as we've seen them foster plutocracies worldwide. Rather than operating in the world as a model democracy, that is, using our experience and insight to save people from grief, our financing methods instead are causing grief. Meanwhile, the costs continue to mount—to the human community, to civil society, to democratic values, and to the environment—as what now passes for leadership—in both politics and business—insists on ignoring these dangerous trends.

The solutions have been hiding in plain sight. Yet for modern-day populism to prevail, the nation needs both a crash course in economic literacy and a program to evoke broad-based, grassroots leadership. People are only generally aware of the source of today's grotesque economic inequities and the many perilous trends threatening the environment. Never before has humanity had the ability to affect all life on the planet. Consequently, the responsibility to become fully human has never been so crucial. To support the reform effort now required, these issues must engage not just our intellect but also our conscience—not just our heads but also our hearts. That's the only way we'll muster the sustained commitment required.

The Hunger for Human Happiness

This nation was born in prophecy—the product of a gnawing hunger of a people in pursuit of goals far more grand than a steadily rising standard of living. That inner impoverishment calls out to us again. Historian Arnold Toynbee had it right, noting that "the ultimate function of civilization [is] to serve the unfolding of ever deeper spiritual understanding." More specifically, he described the essence of a civilization's growth as the "law of progressive simplification"—the ability of a society to transfer its attention and energy from the material to the nonmaterial side of life and thereby advance their culture, their sense of community, and their compassion—and strengthen their democracy. When the setting is right, the work of being fully human emerges spontaneously as humanity harmonizes with itself and its surroundings. That's when we see a Renaissance. Or an Enlightenment. We've the potential to evoke such an era—possibly on a worldwide basis. With a supportive environment, inner exploration emerges, connections are seen, patterns are recognized, unity overcomes separation, and the parts are again recognized as whole. As Paul Ray makes clear, the beauty of an information society is that the means are there to foster a "universal connectivity never seen before." With the proper policy context—support for which is readily available from 50 million Cultural Creatives in the United States alone—people are fully capable of tuning themselves to an inner unfolding wherein their happiness is found.

"As the Integral Culture comes upon the world scene," Ray notes, "it will succeed precisely to the extent that it solves the problems of the whole planet that is starting to be 'one world' for the very first time." Characterizing today as a "tipping point in civilization," he suggests that we take heart because "we're traveling in the midst of an enormous company of allies; a larger population of creative people, who are the carriers of more positive ideas, values, and trends than any previous renaissance period has ever seen. And they can probably be mobilized to act altruistically on behalf of our future."[6]

That's very good news indeed. Rapid passage to this new world requires what anthropologist Anthony Wallace calls cultural revitalization, that is, a willingness to accept that the old ways don't work and that more of the same (today's political prescription) isn't going to work any better. Progress requires that we invent for ourselves a new story about what makes us unique as a people. Cultural revitalization experts have found that we transform ourselves by inventing a new way of seeing ourselves (the sun no longer revolves around us). The creation of new perspective requires new symbols, new imagery, and new pictures in the mind. That's one of the key rationales for Viewpoint 2000, the Prosperity Corps, the Culture Corps, the Sky Trust, international collaboration on the capital commons, and similar undertakings with a global focus. Each of those projects is meant to help us see ourselves as an inescapable whole. The generosity that animates democracy cannot be forced; it moves through us when we feel deeply connected to others and when we allow ourselves to be sufficiently conscious that a sense of shared destiny rises in us as compassion and moves through us as grace.

Interdependent Democracies

If democracy were a symphony, its melody would make us all feel related in some undeniable yet mysterious way. Isaac Stern tells a revealing story about a question he was asked in a public forum concerning why so many violinists play the same notes in the same order as Stern, yet most don't sound nearly so good. After hesitating a moment, Stern objected, "But it isn't the notes that are important. It's the intervals between the notes."[7]

The revitalization of democracy must focus on fostering the connections, the spaces between the notes. That's where democracy lives;

that's where you discover the dignity of being able to look anyone in the eye. That's the space from which emerges the confidence that you feel just before drifting off to sleep. A living democracy gives you comfort knowing that you belong and that your heartfelt concerns have a forum where they will be heard. It's not just about what you can do; it's about who you're encouraged to *be*. The dignity of citizenship in a democracy is found not in things but in relationships. It resides less in our doing than in our "inter-being," as Vietnamese monk Thich Nhat Hanh puts it. "Everything you do, you do not for yourself alone," he notes, "you do it for all of us. . . . There is no 'I,' there is no 'you,' because I am in you, and you are in me. We inter-are."[8]

This popular Buddhist teacher, nominated for the Nobel Peace Prize by Martin Luther King, Jr., gives voice to a point since proven by quantum physics that no one—no person, no community, no nation, no component of nature—is a separate entity. We "inter-be." We live in relationships. In Buddhism, that's called "dependent origination" or "dependent co-arising." That ancient wisdom from the East is consistent with modern insights from systems science in the West. And also with the life sciences, where it's called *epigenesis*, or interaction-dependent causation. Indigenous peoples resonate with that notion as well. In languages spoken by Native American tribes, such as the Hopi and the Algonquin, a person can speak for days and never utter a single noun. Their language emerges from a people attuned not to things but to relationships, particularly their relationship with nature. The sweetness in sugar is found not in the individual molecules but emerges from their interactions; its taste lives in the relationships where change is the only constant.

The dynamic nature of democracy makes it essential that we constantly update our economic rules to reflect the ever-changing world of our day-to-day economic relationships. Democratic leadership for the global age requires that we craft a more mature, relationship-based version of capitalism and combine that with a more humane approach to foreign relations and a more sensible approach to the environment. The community of nations expects no less. Our descendants deserve no less. The United States is the dominant player on the world scene, yet it's playing its role poorly, with neither vision nor heart. Gandhi advised that our labors within the public sphere are not secular but sacred. As a people, we are at our finest when engaged in dialogue about how best we might realize those intangible values to which our founders pledged their lives, their fortunes, and their sacred honor. It is then that we know we are engaged in the genuinely soulful art of democracy. And it is then that we best remember that our obligations extend not only well beyond our borders but also well beyond this generation. It is *only* then that we fulfill our obligations to posterity. Anything less is a distraction, at best a means, not an end. Thich Nhat Hanh puts this intergenerational, community-building challenge in the proper context: "It is possible that the next Buddha will not take the form of an individual. The next Buddha may take the form of a community—a community practicing understanding and loving kindness, a community practicing mindful living. This may be the most important thing we can do for the survival of the earth."

Toward a Civilized Capitalism

Civilization, like democracies and markets, is a verb. It must constantly be recreated and replenished, each day infused and renewed with the values that enable us to extract meaning from the mundane and inspiration from the day-to-day. Toynbee felt that civilization would someday mature sufficiently that humankind could focus on the development of higher, less tangible values. That time, I suggest, is now. It only requires leadership equal to the task. Instead, today's leadership encourages a turning in on ourselves and a narrowing of democracy to mean merely markets. Rather than a future grounded in the reality of our earthly surroundings, we're told that acquiescence to the abstractions of finance is the way forward. That perceptual prejudice not only fails to acknowledge the mystery of life; it also reflects the naive notion that we need only live in harmony with our own values and our own designs, regardless of our impact on the biological fabric. Yet the means are at hand to shift to a perspective that advances humanity's highest values. The material, financial, institutional, and technological know-how is available to eliminate the scourge of poverty from the anguished face of humankind. The only barrier is today's poverty of political will. Indeed, the means are available *now*—in the United States and at least two dozen other nations—for widespread leisure, even genuine, broadly shared affluence. We don't need a new free enterprise, we need new forms of practice and engagement—*and new leadership*—so that we might formulate new convictions and new commitments and emerge from that reformulation with a new unity for the human species. What's required is new ways to tap democracy's hidden reserves so that we can evoke the can-do energy and the generous spirit that today lies trapped in stale and uninspired relationships.[9]

The business of ending hunger and eliminating poverty is an essential first step if we are to get on with the long-deferred business of civilization and the task of empowering humanity to realize its full potential. Yet somehow our focus has shifted away from the undeniable needs of all humanity and onto our personal desires as one small component of the human family. In addition, we know that the needs of nature transcend all notions of our free will as a people because the condition of the environment goes to the very conditions required for the possibility of life. On these intertwined issues—the condition of humankind and nature—we are thrown into what philosopher William James called "a live, forced, momentous option," where we are no longer at liberty to choose not to choose. In a democracy, we have the privilege of choice, yet we choose unwisely if we continue to ignore those concerns that now force their attentions upon us.

The Work of Being Fully Human

The real issue at stake is whether we mean to be true to our democratic values—and whether we have the integrity as a people to fulfill the intergenerational obligations that underlie those values. It's really as simple as that. This is not some naive notion of going back to a simpler time and place. Rather it's a question of democracy coming full circle to engage again with the local and the particular so that the character of place is reflected in the various faces that free enterprise displays as it assumes its many forms. For free enterprise to be truly democratic, it must be *reinhabited* by those whose values it is meant to reflect. Rather than today's adolescent obsession with such a restricted range of values (largely financial), a mature free-enterprise democracy must constantly attune itself to the ever-shifting needs of place and time, informed always by the distinct contours and rhythms of the lives it touches and the natural environment in which its operations are embedded.

In order for the full breadth of the human community to participate in the uniquely human pursuits—music, the arts, science, politics, sports, spiritual practices, raising a family, and so forth—civilization requires a global community that remains steadfast in its pursuit of that very democratic goal. Here in the United States, we don't need full employment so much as we need post-employment or affordable unemployment. We need a financial architecture that affords widespread leisure, personal development, and opportunities to be of service to each other and to the environment. Yet so long as we condone such staggering economic disparities here at home, that goal is destined to remain elusive, particularly if—as now—other nations follow our lead. The result will be more of what we now see as the bulk of humankind is denied the material means required to realize their full humanity in a meaningful way. Instead their lives will continue to be consumed by the pressing demands of the day-to-day.

In effect, today's rampant prosperity-hoarding denies most people the means to become fully human. That's a cruel twist indeed in a global political environment, ostensibly a *democratic* environment, that holds itself out as responsive to humanity's deepest needs and aspirations. Yet despite the global spread of democracy and its handmaiden, free enterprise, the gap grows ever wider between what is economically achievable and what people experience in their personal lives. Tragedy awaits us if people begin to equate their prolonged misery with the spread of democratic values. Or if needed reforms find a foothold not in the democratic spirit of generosity but instead in bitterness, recrimination, or revenge. People rightly expect more from democracy than the heartless right to choose poverty. Today's poor results are due in substantial part to the complicity of legislators who choose to allow a few to monopolize the means by which prosperity is achieved and leisure attained. When the voting public awakens to this reality, as soon they will, heads will roll in the political arena, as well they should. It's time for us to reclaim our democracy.

Is it so unreasonable to expect that we could have a leadership capable of guiding this nation's economic genius in a way that ensures genuinely broad-based prosperity? Is it really so strange that those in other countries would expect the same? Is it really so preposterous to insist that cyber standards of speed not be applied to the pace at which we live and work? Is it really so outrageous to insist on a policy environment that will lead us toward the only legacy of any consequence that we could leave our descendants: an equitable society and a suitable environment? If these goals are extravagant, then so too is the very premise of democracy, an idea that seemed *profoundly* unreasonable when first proposed during a period when the divine right of kings was considered sensible.

Today's finance-dominant economic paradigm exhibits an undeniable genius. Compared to the alternatives proposed to date, it has been a rip-roaring success, albeit not when compared to what might have been had it operated in accord with democratic principles. The time has come for the spirit of democracy to fuse with the capacities of capitalism to create a genuinely inclusive free enterprise where widespread prosperity provides the economic backdrop for a democracy that is just, robust, humane, and sustainable. Anything less leaves the promise of democracy unfulfilled and our human potential denied. What I've attempted to do here is clarify that we are not so much the source of that work as a community of relationships through which that work emerges.[10] The work of democracy is far from done.

Notes

Introduction

1. Edward N. Wolff, "Recent Trends in Wealth Ownership" (paper presented at conference on Benefits and Mechanisms for Spreading Asset Ownership in the United States, New York University, December 10–12, 1998). In 1992, the financial wealth of the top 1 percent was greater than the combined wealth of the bottom 90 percent. Research is based on the Federal Reserve's triennial Survey of Consumer Finances. For this purpose, wealth (or net worth) is the current value of all marketable assets less current debts. Assets include housing and other real estate, cash and demand deposits, savings, money market accounts, financial securities, life insurance, equity in unincorporated businesses, trust fund equity, and the cash value of individual retirement accounts, including IRAs and Keogh and 401(k) plans. Liabilities are the sum of mortgage debt, consumer debt, and other debts. For this purpose, consumer durables (furniture, appliances, vehicles) are excluded along with the value of social security benefits and retirement benefits from defined benefit pension plans, as these funds are not in the direct control of families and cannot be marketed. Financial wealth (net worth less home equity) is a more liquid concept since one's home is difficult to convert into cash in the short term.

2. Ibid. The period cited by Wolff 1983 to 1995.

3. The Forbes 400 wealth was $624 billion in 1997, $738 billion in 1998, and $1 trillion plus in 1999. From special annual issues of *Forbes* magazine, profiling the richest four hundred people in the United States.

4. Median household financial wealth was less than $10,000 in 1995. The $11,700 figure is based on the 12-percent growth projection in Wolff, "Recent Trends in Wealth Ownership." As of this writing, the latest wealth and income data are found in the Federal Reserve's 1998 triennial Survey of Consumer Finances. The results, based on 4,309 interviews, were released January 2000. The accompanying commentary states that stock-market-fed increases in net worth over the 1995–1998 period were "broadly shared by different demographic groups." However, the distributional analysis had not

yet been done. Nevertheless, although the Standard & Poor's index of five hundred stock prices registered a gain of 76 percent over the 1995–1998 period, median net worth rose just 17.6 percent among survey respondents—to $71,600 (i.e., including home equity, vehicles, etc.). The report also acknowledges that for all groups under age fifty-five, "the medians of net worth were still substantially below their 1989 levels." Arthur B. Kennickell, Martha Starr-McClure, and Brian J. Surette, "Recent Changes in U.S. Family Finances: Results from the 1998 Survey of Consumer Finances," *Federal Reserve Bulletin*, January 2000, pp. 1–29.

5. Median earnings based on U.S. Department of Commerce, Bureau of Economic Analysis, *State of Working America* (Washington, D.C.: U.S. Government Printing Office, 1998–1999), tables 3.2, 3.3, 3.6; labor's share of nonfarm business sector income based on U.S. Bureau of Labor Statistics, *Economic Report of the President* (Washington, D.C.: U.S. Government Printing Office, 1999), table B-49 at p. 384.

6. Juliet S. Schor, *The Overworked American* (New York: Basic Books, 1992), indicates that the annual work year increased by 139 hours from 1969 to 1989. The Washington, D.C.–based Economic Policy Institute found that the annual hours worked expanded by 45 hours from 1989 to 1994.

7. The poverty line for 1998 was $16,655 for a four-person household. The national child poverty rate grew 26 percent from 1970 to 1996. Laura Meckler, "Poverty Rising Among U.S. Kids," *Atlanta Journal-Constitution*, July 10, 1998; Tamar Levin, "Study Finds That Youngest U.S. Children Are Poorest," *New York Times*, March 15, 1998. The U.S child poverty rate is the second highest in the developed world (one-third of British children are living in poverty). Decca Aitkenhead, "Small Expectations," *Search* (published by the UK-based Joseph Rowntree Foundation), summer 1999, p. 12. According to U.S. Census Bureau data, poverty rates among all children fell a percentage point in 1998, to 18.9 percent. That level is well above the rate in the 1970s, and higher than in Canada or Western Europe.

8. U.S. Congressional Budget Office, *Estimates of Federal Tax Liabilities for Individuals and Families by Income Category and Family Type for 1995 and 1999* (memorandum, May 1998). The projected data includes the effects of tax cuts enacted in 1997 that phase in over time.

9. Isaac Shapiro and Robert Greenstein, "The Widening Income Gulf" (Washington, D.C., Center on Budget and Policy Priorities, September 4, 1999, typed report), citing Congressional Budget Office (CBO) figures. According to CBO, median before-tax household income for 1998 was $38,885.

10. "Forty-Ninth Annual Executive Pay Survey," *Business Week*, April 19, 1999.

11. United Nations, *United Nations Human Development Report 1999* (New York: Oxford University Press, 1999). See also Kerry A. Dolan, "Two Hundred Global Billionaires," *Forbes*, July 5, 1999, p. 153.

12. United Nations, *United Nations Human Development Report 1998* (New York: Oxford University Press, 1998), p. 30.

13. See "Rich Comparison," *Wall Street Journal,* July 30, 1999. See also *United Nations Human Development Report 1999.*

14. *United Nations Human Development Report 1999*, p. 3.

15. The International Monetary Fund (IMF) estimates that the amount in offshore tax havens grew from $3.5 trillion in 1992 to $4.8 trillion in 1997. But see Douglas Farah, "A New Wave of Island Investing," *Washington Post National Weekly Review*, October 18, 1999, p. 15; Alan Cowell and Edmund L. Andrews, "Undercurrents at a Safe Harbor," *New York Times,* September 24, 1999.

16. Lester Brown et al., *1998 State of the World* (Washington, D.C.: Worldwatch Institute, 1998).

17. See ,www.turnpoint.org..

18. Interview at <www.PaulaGordon.com>.

19. R. Lal, "Global Soil Erosion by Water and Carbon Dynamics," in *Soils and Global Change,* ed. R. Lal et al. (Boca Raton, Fl.: CRC/Lewis Publishers, 1995), pp. 131–142.

20. William McKibben, *The End of Nature* (New York: Doubleday, 1989).

21. Paul Hawken, Amory Lovins, and L. Hunter Lovins, *Natural Capitalism* (New York: Little Brown, 1999), p. 151, offer a definition of natural capital: "Natural capital can be viewed as the sum total of the ecological systems that support life, different from human-made capital in that natural capital cannot be produced by human activity."

22. *United Nations Human Development Report 1999*, p. 2.

23. Ibid., p. v.

24. Paul H. Ray, "The Rise of Integral Culture," *Noetic Science Review* (spring 1996), updated with results from January 1999 survey for the Environmental Protection Agency and the President's Council on Sustainable Development (unpublished). Personal correspondence, September 20, 1999.

25. Riane Eisler, *The Chalice and the Blade* (San Francisco: HarperCollins, 1987).

26. The ownership impact of supply-side economics ("Reaganomics") is analyzed in chapter 3 of Jeff Gates, *The Ownership Solution* Cambridge, Mass.: Perseus Publishing, 1998).

27. U.S. Geological Survey, *Status and Trends of the Nation's Biological Resources* (Washington, D.C.: U.S. Geological Survey, 1999).

28. Fritjof Capra, *The Tao of Physics* (Boston: Shambhala, 1975); Fritjof Capra, *The Turning Point* (New York: Simon & Schuster, 1992); Fritjof Capra, *The Web of Life* (New York: Doubleday, 1996).

29. Stafford Beer, "On the Nature of Models: Let Us Now Praise Famous Men and Women, Too," *Informing Science* 2, no. 3 (1999): 69. See also Warren McCulloch, *Embodiments of Mind* (Cambridge: M.I.T. Press, 1965); Francisco J. Varela, *Embodied Mind* (Cambridge: M.I.T. Press, 1993).

30. Candace Pert, *Molecules of Emotion* (New York: Touchstone, 1997).

31. Myron Kellner-Rogers, "Changing the Way We Change: Lessons from Complexity," *Inner Edge*, October/November 1998, p. 18.

32. Thomas Sowell, *The Quest for Cosmic Justice* (New York: Free Press, 1999).

Chapter 1

1. See Christopher Lasch, *The Revolt of the Elites and the Betrayal of Democracy* (New York: Norton, 1995). See also Mickey Kaus, "Compassion, the Political Liability," *New York Times*, June 25, 1999.

2. "Flat Tax Goes from 'Snake Oil' to Tonic for G.O.P. Presidential Contenders," *New York Times*, November 14, 1999.

3. See Frances Moore Lappe, *Rediscovering American Values* (New York: Ballantine, 1989).

4. Jeff Gates, *The Ownership Solution* (Reading, Mass.: Addison-Wesley, 1998).

5. See <www.skytrust.cfed.org>.

6. See <www.dfdpo.com>.

7. Joey Reiman, *Thinking for a Living* (Atlanta: Longstreet, 1998).

Chapter 2

1. *Forbes 400* (special issue of *Forbes* magazine devoted to the richest four hundred Americans), September 13, 1982; *Forbes 400*, October 12, 1998; *Forbes 400*, October 4, 1999. Note that the 1998 figures are based on a Dow Jones Industrial Average of 7827 (the Dow topped 11,000 in early May 1999).

2. Reported in Louis Uchitelle, "More Wealth, More Stately Mansions," *New York Times*, June 6, 1999, summarizing research by Edward N. Wolff.

3. Reported in David Wessel, "U.S. Stock Holdings Rose 20% in 1998," *Wall Street Journal*, March 15, 1999.

4. Edward N. Wolff, "Recent Trends in Wealth Ownership" (paper presented at conference on Benefits and Mechanisms for Spreading Asset Ownership in the United States, New York University, December 10–12, 1998), p. 10. "Indeed, median income between 1989 and 1998 rose appreciably only for families headed by college graduates." Arthur B. Kennickell, Martha Starr-McClure, and Brian J. Surette, "Recent Changes in U.S. Family Finances: Results from the 1998 Survey of Consumer Finances," *Federal Reserve Bulletin*, January 2000, p. 3.

5. Robert Frank, *Luxury Fever* (New York: Simon & Schuster, 1999). See also Tom Vanderbilt, "Prophets of Boom," *Wired*, September 1999, p. 164.

6. *Forbes 400*, October 11, 1999. See also <www.forbes.com>.

7. "Forty-Ninth Annual Executive Pay Survey," *Business Week*, April 19, 1999.

8. "State Income Inequality Continues to Grow in Most States in the 1990s, Despite Economic Growth and Tight Labor Markets" (Economic Policy Institute and the Center on Budget and Policy Priorities, Washington, D.C., January 18, 2000, report).

9. Sarah Anderson et al., *A Decade of Executive Excess: The 1990s* (Boston: United for a Fair Economy, 1999). CEO annual pay increases calculated by *Business Week* for annual executive pay survey, average of top two executives at the largest 365 U.S. corporations (by sales).

10. It was only after strenuous objection from institutional investors that Eisner agreed to remove his personal attorney from the compensation committee of Disney's board of directors (personal conversation with TIAA-CREF trustee and Georgia State University law professor Marjorie Fine Knowles, May 1999).

11. *New York Times,* July 4, 1999.

12. Evan L. Marcus, "The World's First Trillionaire," *Wired*, September 1999, p. 163. If Microsoft's stock value grows at the same rate that the Standard & Poor's 500 has averaged over the past twenty years (17.6 percent), then Gates would become a trillionaire in August 2015, at age 59, and his holdings would be worth $1 quadrillion in March 2058, at age 102. See <www.webho.com/WealthClock> for one of several examples of a wealth clock, which tracks the current value of his Microsoft shares.

13. Richard N. Goodwin, "Lost Opportunities Are at the Heart of the Clinton Legacy," *Boston Sunday Globe*, July 4, 1999.

14. *Nature,* May 15, 1997. The high estimate was $54 trillion. The highest annual value per acre was for estuaries, because of their nutrient-recycling services. The highest valued environments were wetlands and floodplains because of their importance in flood control, waste treatment, and water storage.

15. Wolff, "Recent Trends in Wealth Ownership," p. 10.

16. See <www.census.gov> ("income" at table H-2).

17. Data on Gates from Edward N. Wolff, cited in "A Scholar Who Concentrates . . . on Concentrations of Wealth," *Too Much*, winter 1999, p. 8.

18. Doug Henwood, "Debts Everywhere," *The Nation*, July 19, 1999, p. 12. Since 1992, mortgage debt has grown 60 percent faster than income, whereas consumer debt (mostly auto loans and credit cards) has grown twice as fast. The fastest-growing segment of the credit card market consists of low-income holders, with the average amount they owe growing eighteen times faster than income.

19. The ratio of total family debt payments to total family income is the highest recorded since 1989. "Recent Changes in U.S. Family Finances: Results from the 1998 Survey of Consumer Finances," *Federal Reserve Bulletin,* January 2000, p. 25.

20. U.S. Geological Survey, *Status and Trends of the Nation's Biological Resources* (Washington, D.C.: U.S. Geological Survey, 1999).

21. United Nations Environmental Program, *GEO (Global Environmental Outlook) 2000* (New York: Earthscan, 1999).

22. See Jeff Gates, *The Ownership Solution* (Reading, Mass.: Addison-Wesley, 1998).

23. Richard Goodwin, "Lost Opportunities Are at the Head of the Clinton Legacy," *Boston Globe*, July 4, 1999

24. "Tax Report," *Wall Street Journal*, July 28, 1999, p. 1.

25. U.S. Congressional Budget Office, *Estimates of Federal Tax Liabilities for Individuals and Families by Income Category and Family Type for 1995 and 1999* (memorandum, May 1998). The 1999 projected data include the effects of tax cuts enacted in 1997 that phase in over time.

26. Current tax law allows a personal income tax deduction on home mortgage interest up to $1 million. If that limit were reduced to $300,000, the Congressional Budget Office reports that federal tax receipts would increase by $40.8 billion over nine years. In 1998, 4 percent of new mortgages exceeded $300,000.

27. Of the nation's 103 million households in 1999, 66.6 percent occupy homes owned by a member of the household. Yet even among married couples in the under–forty-four age group (the most significant home-buying years), the rate of home ownership has not yet recovered its 1982 level of 82 percent. Home ownership among blacks rose to 45.8 percent in 1999, recovering ground lost since 1983, when the rate was 45.6 percent. Home owners are now much more highly leveraged than fifteen years ago, with down payments at record lows and mortgage amounts far higher. Lou Uchitelle, "In Home Ownership Data, a Hidden Generation Gap," *New York Times*, September 26, 1999.

28. Wolff, "Recent Trends in Wealth Ownership" Ibid.

29. Ibid., p. 41, table 6.

30. See Albert B. Crenshaw, "Taking Reduced Saving into Account," *Washington Post National Weekly Edition*, June 28, 1999, p. 21.

31. Shapiro and Greenstein, "The Widening Income Gulf.".

32. Ibid.

33. Charles Handy, *The Hungry Spirit* (New York: Broadway, 1998).

34. James K. Glassman and Kevin A. Hassett, *Dow 36,000* (New York: Times Books, 1999); David Elas, *Dow 40,000* (New York: McGraw Hill, 1999); Harry S. Dent, *The Roaring 2000's* (New York: Simon & Schuster, 1998); Charles W. Kadlec, *Dow 100,000: Fact or Fiction* (New York: Prentice Hall, 1999). See also Peter Schwartz, Peter Leyden, and Joel Hyatt, *The Long Boom* (Reading, Mass.: Perseus Books, 1999). At the heart of these projections lies a financial theory concerning the risk premium on stocks versus bonds and the narrowing of the extra return (historically 7 percent or so) that investors demand to compensate for the riskier volatility of equities. As that premium has narrowed, stock prices have soared.

35. Jacob M. Schlesinger, Tristan Mabry, and Sarah Lueck, "Charting the Pain Behind the Gain," *Wall Street Journal*, October 1, 1999.

36. Steven Greenhouse, "So Much Work, So Little Time," *New York Times*, September 5, 1999.

37. Critics of this analysis point out that the after-tax income of the poorest fifth rose nearly 13 percent from 1993 through 1999. Key demographic changes should also be considered, though they are not the main driver of the trend. For instance, the huge baby boomer generation is now in its peak earning years, accelerating income growth at the top of the scale while baby boomers' parents are retiring, pushing them down the income scale. George Hager, "While the Rich Get Richer, . . . " *Washington Post National Weekly Edition*, September 13, 1999, p. 12.

38. See Joel Blau, *Illusions of Prosperity: America's Working Families in an Age of Economic Insecurity* (New York: Oxford University Press, 1999).

39. Louis Uchitelle, "Devising New Math to Define Poverty," *New York Times*, October 18, 1999.

40. After predicting a $4.9-trillion surplus in February 1999, the administration picked up another $1 trillion in July by raising projected productivity growth from 1.3 percent to 1.6 percent, which helped raise new estimates of economic growth from 2.2 percent to 2.5 percent. On July 22, 1999, the Republican-controlled House approved $792 billion in tax reductions in which 79.6 percent of the individual tax cuts would flow to the top 20 percent of income earners. See "White House Says No to a $500 Billion Tax-Cut Proposal," *New York Times*, July 26, 1999.

41. "The Surplus Illusion," *Washington Post National Weekly Edition*, July 12, 1999, p. 24.

42. Reported in Near Karlen, "And the Meek Shall Inherit Nothing," *New York Times*, July 29, 1999.

43. Wolff, "Recent Trends in Wealth Ownership," pp. 30–31. Between 1983 and 1995 (the latest Federal Reserve Board figures), the bottom 40 percent of households lost 80 percent of their net worth. By 1995, 18.5 percent of households had zero or negative net worth (an average deficit of $5,600, down from a deficit of $3,000 in 1983).

44. Reported in Louis Uchitelle, "As Class Struggle Subsides, Less Pie for the Workers," *New York Times*, December 5, 1999.

45. United Nations, *United Nations Human Development Report 1999* (New York: Oxford University Press, 1999), p. 25.

46. United Nations, *United Nations Human Development Report 1998* (New York: Oxford University Press, 1998).

47. Stijn Claessens, Simeon Djankov, and Larry H. P. Lang, "Who Controls East Asian Corporations?" (Washington, D.C.: World Bank, 1999).

48. *United Nations Human Development Report 1999*, p. 28.

49. United Nations, *United Nations Human Development Report 1996* (New York: Oxford University Press, 1996), p. 4 (emphasis added).

50. United Nations, *United Nations Human Development Report 1996* (New York: Oxford University Press, 1996), p. 4 (emphasis added).

51. Mahbub ul Haq, "Charter of Human Development Initiative" (paper presented at State of the World Forum, San Francisco, October 3, 1996).

52. As of this writing, the Clinton administration is calling for a 50 percent increase in weapons procurement through 2004, whereas Congress is demanding even higher military spending. In the 1997 fiscal year, the last year for which figures are available, the United States shipped a record $8.3 billion of arms exports to nondemocratic countries. See Oscar Arias, "Stopping America's Most Lethal Export," *New York Times,* June 23, 1999.

53. *United Nations Human Development Report 1998,* p. 30.

54. *Times* (London), September 23, 1999.

55. Riane Eisler, *Tomorrow's Children: A Blueprint for Partnership Education in the Twenty-First Century* (Boulder: Westview, 2000); Riane Eisler, *The Chalice and the Blade* (New York: HarperCollins, 1987); Riane Eisler, David Loye, and Kari Norgaard, *Women, Men and the Global Quality of Life* (Pacific Grove, Calif.: Center for Partnership Studies, 1995).

Chapter 3

1. Robert G. Kaiser and Ira Chinoy, "How Scaife's Money Powered a Movement," *Washington Post,* May 2, 1999.

2. The distinction between expenditures and contributions was upheld on appeal to the Supreme Court in a January 2000 decision *(Nixon vs. Shrink Missouri Government PAC)* in which a failed candidate for state auditor complained that he couldn't mount an effective campaign with such low contribution limits (Missouri's limits parallel the federal caps). Some campaign finance reformers suggest that this opinion sends a signal that overall spending limits may be permissible. Some civil libertarians see any limit on contributions as a handicap for potential challengers (Senator Eugene McCarthy's 1968 presidential campaign was financed largely by a small handful of large contributors). One possible component of a remedy: restrict the use of personal funds to a small multiple of the median household's financial wealth. That would keep political candidacy more within the reach of what's economically representative.

3. Don Van Natta, Jr., "Democrats Aim for Record in Unregulated Donations," *New York Times,* July 25, 1999.

4. Don Van Natta, Jr., "Campaign Fund-Raising Is at Record Pace," *New York Times,* October 3, 1999.

5. "Mr. Gates Giveth," *Wall Street Journal,* July 23, 1999.

6. According to the Social Investment Forum, as of December 1997, investment portfolios, including mutual funds, using socially responsible criteria amounted to $1.3 trillion in the United States alone. However, such social screening of funds in tax-favored pension plans is generally permissible

only if the fiduciary can demonstrate that "social investments" are able to generate returns comparable to non-screened alternatives. See <www.wetv.com>.

7. Juliet S. Schor, *The Overworked American* (New York: Basic Books, 1992).

8. See discussion of caring labor at United Nations, *United Nations Human Development Report 1999* (New York: Oxford University Press, 1999), p. 7.

9. Cited in Charles Handy, *The Hungry Spirit* (New York: Broadway, 1998), p. 17.

10. Marvin Olasky, "Building Social Capital," *American Outlook* (The Acton Institute), summer 1999, p. 20.

11. See Steven Greenberg, "So Much Work, So Little Time," *New York Times*, September 5, 1999, p. WK1.

12. Ken Magid, *High Risk: Children Without a Conscience* (New York: Bantam, 1989).

13. *Economic Report of the President* (Washington, D.C.: U.S. Government Printing Office, 1999), p. 421.

14. Before the Joint Economic Committee, Federal Reserve Chairman Alan Greenspan testified on June 14, 1999, "I'm hard-pressed to see how we can maintain what is increasingly an intellectual-based output system [without a better education system]." Reported in Jacob M. Schlesiner, "Greenspan Warns on Productivity Gains," *Wall Street Journal*, June 15, 1999.

15. Richard G. Wilkinson, *Unhealthy Societies: The Afflictions of Inequality* (London: Routledge, 1996).

16. Joel Blau, *Illusions of Prosperity: America's Working Families in an Age of Economic Insecurity* (New York: Oxford University Press, 1999).

17. Sheryl Gay Stolberg, "Poor People Are Fighting Baffling Surge in Asthma," *New York Times*, October 18, 1999.

18. Peter T. Kilborn, "Health Gap Grows, with Black Americans Trailing Whites, Studies Say," *New York Times*, January 26, 1998.

19. Ibid.

20. Ibid.

21. Peter Passell, "Benefits Dwindle Along With Wages for the Unskilled," *Wall Street Journal*, June 14, 1998.

22. Various reports issued by the Employee Benefit Research Institute, Washington, D.C.

23. Cited in Deepak Chopra, "Opening the Doors of Perception" (presentation for State of the World Forum, San Francisco, September 28, 1995).

24. "Deaths Rise at Start of Month, Study Shows," *New York Times*, July 8, 1999.

25. James Lardner, "Deadly Disparities," *Washington Post,* August 16, 1998.

26. Dean Ornish, *Love and Survival* (New York: HarperCollins, 1998).

27. Decca Aitkenhead, "Small Expectations," *Search* (published by the UK-based Joseph Rowntree Foundation), summer 1999, p. 12. See also Jules Shropshire and Sue Middleton, *Small Expectations: Learning to Be Poor?* (York: York Publishing Services Ltd., 1999); Paul Gregg, Susan Harkness, and Stephan Machin, *Child Development and Family Income* (York: York Publishing Services Ltd., 1999). The Joseph Rowntree Foundation maintains a Web site with summaries at <www.jrf.org.uk>.

28. "A Sobering Report on CEO Greed . . . and a Plea from a Wealthy Mom," *Too Much,* fall 1999, p. 7.

29. "Deadlines, Dismissals and Health," *New York Times,* April 12, 1998.

30. See James Gleick, *Faster: The Acceleration of Just About Everything* (New York: Pantheon, 1999).

31. Lawrence Goodwyn, *Democratic Promise: The Populist Moment in America* (Oxford: Oxford University Press, 1976).

32. Robert D. Putnam, *Making Democracy Work: Civic Traditions in Modern Italy* (Princeton, N.J.: Princeton University Press, 1993).

33. Quoted in *Rachael's Environment and Health Weekly,* June 10, 1999.

34. Francis Fukuyama, "The Great Disruption," *Atlantic Monthly,* May 1999, p. 55.

35. Cited in M. Mitchell Waldrop, *Complexity* (New York: Touchstone, 1992), p. 265.

36. Louis Uchitelle, "Survey Finds Layoffs Slowed in Last Three Years," *New York Times,* August 20, 1998.

37. Michael Hammer and James Champy, *Reengineering the Corporation* (New York: HarperCollins, 1993).

38. Many of reengineering's most vocal proponents are having second thoughts, including Stephen Roach, Morgan Stanley's chief economist, once an outspoken advocate for the "rightsizing" of workforces as a means to revive American productivity. One of the key downsizing challenges, he now concedes, is to find a way to restrain costs without tearing out the innovative heart of a company, as much reengineering has risked doing. See "Jobs and Wages Revisited," *The Economist,* August 17, 1996, p. 62.

39. Erica Goode, "Sharpe Rise Found in Psychiatric Drugs for the Very Young," *New York Times,* February 23, 2000, p. 1.

40. Numerous organizations are at work attempting to shift consumption patterns in order to protect the environment and enhance the quality of life, including the Center for the American Dream <www.newdream.org>. There's a concern emerging that we may be creating yet another generation of hyperconsumers that threaten our environmental future. See the center's "Tips for Parenting in a Commercial Culture" on its Web site, with facts on advertising, consumption, and children.

41. Richard Morin, "We Gamble for Fun? Don't Bet on It," *Washington Post National Weekly Edition*, August 16, 1999, p. 34.

42. Brett Pulley, "Living Off the Daily Dream of Winning a Lottery Prize," *New York Times*, May 22, 1999. The National Gambling Impact Study Commission report in June 1999 concludes that lotteries are an "astonishingly regressive" tax, indicating that players with incomes below $10,000 spend more on lottery tickets (an estimated $597 each year) than any other income group. Reported in Anny Fawcett, "Alabama Gears Up for Showdown over Lottery Vote," *Wall Street Journal*, August 10, 1999.

43. Lawrence Goodwyn, *Democratic Promise: The Populist Moment in America* (Oxford: Oxford University Press, 1976).

Chapter 4

1. Gina Kolata, "Vast Advance Is Reported in Preventing Heart Illnesses," *New York Times*, August 6, 1999.

2. See Albert B. Crenshaw, "Taking Reduced Saving into Account," *Washington Post National Weekly Edition*, June 28, 1999, p. 21, citing Brookings Institution economist William G. Gale, who figures that if 60–80 percent of pre-retirement income is adequate, then roughly a third of the boomers are doing very well, a third are doing very poorly, and a third are in between, meaning their savings, including home equity, are barely adequate. Most studies include home equity in the computation of household wealth, suggesting that retirees must sell their home (and rent) or that we must see (very unlikely) a huge market in reverse mortgages.

3. Instead of allowing a personal tax deduction for funds set aside for retirement through an individual retirement account (IRA), a Roth IRA (named after Senate Finance Committee chairman William Roth of Delaware) allows an *after-tax* set-aside to a tax-exempt account that can be withdrawn tax-free. Clinton's USAs would devote 62 percent of projected federal budget surpluses over the next fifteen years to a plan designed to match (with government bonds) personal contributions to a savings plan that would be invested in the stock market. The plan is projected to direct between $650 billion and $1.2 trillion of taxpayer dollars into the stock market over that period.

4. That includes more than $2 trillion owed by the government to Social Security. It may be inherently counterproductive to attempt to maintain long-range actuarial balance for the Social Security Trust Fund, as funding is not essential for a public program that uses involuntary taxes as its revenue source. If higher payroll taxes are utilized for funding, that makes U.S. labor more expensive, putting domestic production at a competitive disadvantage and encouraging the substitution of capital for labor, possibly raising unemployment. Further, asset prices may be driven higher than without a surplus as those tax revenues flow into the stock market, heightening the likely drop

in asset prices as both private and public pension funds begin to sell assets to meet pension expenditure requirements, a situation that would be worsened by the simultaneous sale of Trust Fund securities. This could have a snow-balling effect because, as a result of the stock market run-up, many corporate pension plans are overfunded. As of June 1999, the ten U.S. corporate pension plans with the largest surpluses (General Electric, Bell Atlantic, GTE, IBM, AT&T, etc.) had combined surpluses of more than $100 billion. Because accounting rules allow the reporting of excess assets as a credit on the income statement, many companies are reporting higher earnings. For example, of GE's 1998 pretax profit of $13.8 billion, its pension plan provided more than $1 billion. As pension demographics shift from today's pay-in mode to tomorrow's drawdown mode, the drop in asset prices will erode these phantom earnings first, potentially shifting companies from apparent profitability to unprofitability which may drive stock values even lower. See Ellen E. Schultz, "Joy of Overfunding," *Wall Street Journal*, June 15, 1999.

5. Had they been properly accounted for, stock options would have lowered aggregate published profits by 56 percent in 1997 and 50 percent in 1998, according to research originated by London-based Smathers & Company. See [Richebacher@agora-inc>.

6. Paul Hawken, Amory Lovins, and L. Hunter Lovins, *Natural Capitalism* (New York: Little Brown, 1999), p. 196, report the following: "Around 1948, at the start of the era of synthetic pesticides, the United States used 50 million pounds of insecticides a year and lost 7 percent of the preharvest crop to insects. Today, with nearly 20-fold greater insecticide use—almost a billion pounds a year, two-fifths more than when Rachael Carson published *Silent Spring* in 1962—the insects get 13 percent, and total U.S. crop losses are 20 percent higher than they were before we got on the pesticide treadmill."

7. For a more complete chronicle of this phenomenon, see Jeff Gates, *The Ownership Solution* (Cambridge: Perseus Publishing, 1998).

8. Statistics cited in Phillip J. Longman, "The World Turns Gray," *U.S. News & World Report*, March 1, 1999, p. 30.

9. Rudi Dornbusch, "The Global Economy's Trouble Spots," *Wall Street Journal*, May 14, 1999.

10. Yumiko Ono, "An Army of 'Home Helpers' Is Ready to Descend on Japan's Seniors," *Wall Street Journal*, October 7, 1999.

11. Peter F. Drucker, *Management Challenges for the Twenty-First Century* (New York: HarperBusiness, 1999).

12. With jurisdiction over all matters dealing with taxation, trade, social security, Medicare, and Medicaid, the Finance Committee raises 98 percent of the federal government's revenue and disburses roughly 50 percent.

13. Supply-siders' reverse redistribution was comprehensive. Not only did the well-to-do own the assets financed with the deficits, they also owned the bulk of the debt securities used for the financing. Tax-exempt government

securities continue to be owned dominantly by upper-crust households. For example, the Internal Revenue Service (IRS) reports that tax-exempt interest was reported on 4.9 million individual returns for 1997 (the latest figures), down 2.5 percent from the prior year. That represented only about 4 percent of all returns in both years. Total tax-exempt interest income was $48.5 billion in 1997 (*Wall Street Journal*, July 21, 1999). In the obscure language of modern economics, the deficit financing of rich-get-richer tax cuts is known as the "reverse multiplier effects associated with bond-financing of budget deficits." Robert A. Mundell, "Mundell on Supply-Side Economics," *Wall Street Journal*, October 14, 1999.

14. Lawrence Goodwin, *Democratic Promise: The Populist Moment in America* (Oxford: Oxford University Press, 1976).

15. See Charles L. Black, Jr., *A New Birth of Freedom* (New York: Grosset/Putnam, 1997).

16. William Claiborne, "Tale of Two High Schools: An Object Lesson," *Washington Post*, September 11, 1999.

17. Results of 1991 Federal Reserve Board study analyzing 1990 Home Mortgage Disclosure Act data, reported in Chuck Collins, Betsy Leondar-Wright, and Holly Sklar, *Shifting Fortunes* (Boston: United for a Fair Economy, 1999). p. 56. See Chuck Collinsand Felice Yeskel, *Economic Apartheid: A Primer on Economic Inequality and Insecurity* (New York: New Press, 2000).

18. Reported in "Credit Gap in Black and White," *FOMC Alert*, Financial Markets Center, May 18, 1999, p. 11. See also Jeffrey A. Tannenbaum, "Small-Business Lenders Rebuff Blacks," *Wall Street Journal*, July 7, 1999.

19. Reuters, "15,000 Black Farmers File Claims in Racial Settlement," *New York Times*, September 21, 1999.

20. Dalton Conley, *Being Black, Living in the Red*, (Berkeley: University of California Press, 1999).

21. Through 1997, 43 percent of the judges appointed by Bill Clinton were millionaires. Just over 21 percent of those appointed by Reagan were millionaires, whereas the Bush administration figure was 33 percent. Alliance for Justice Statistics, reported in *Washington Post*, March 17, 1999.

22. For an account of this period in U.S. political history, see chapter 5 of Gates, *The Ownership Solution*.

23. Financial analysts have an array of yardsticks for measuring financial value, including profitability (and its growth), return on investment, earnings per share, capitalized earnings, and three of the latest entries in the financial sweepstakes: economic value added, market value added, and total shareholder return.

24. Hans Peter Durer, personal conversation, November 1998.

25. Steven Pinker, *How the Mind Works* (New York: W. W. Norton, 1997), p. 565.

26. Jeremy Rifkin, *The Biotech Century* (New York: Jeremy P. Tarcher/Putnam, 1998).

Chapter 5

1. As of the fourth quarter 1998, institutional assets totaled $15.4 trillion. Of that amount, $7.4 trillion (48 percent) is held by pension trustees. See The Conference Board, *Institutional Investment Report* 3, no. 1 (September 1999).

2. Assets under management in stock mutual funds soared 44-fold, to $3.2 trillion in the fifteen years ending in May 1999, according to data from the Investment Company Institute, the industry trade group. Index funds accounted for 43 percent of all new cash flows into stock funds during the first six months of 1999, according to AMG Data Services. Reported in Richard A. Oppel, Jr., "Fund Expenses: They're Going Down, Down, Down," *New York Times*, July 4, 1999, p. BU 1.

3. Shann Turnbull, "Employee Governance" (available through [sturnbull@mba1963.hbs.edu]).

4. Francis Moore Lappe, *Rediscovering America's Values* (New York: Ballantine, 1989).

5. Daniel Goleman, *Emotional Intelligence* (New York: Bantam Books, 1995). Emphasis added.

6. Sam Brittan, *Capitalism with a Human Face* (London: Edward Algar, 1995).

7. William Greider, *One World, Ready or Not* (New York: Simon & Schuster, 1997).

8. Louis O. Kelso and Mortimer J. Adler, *The Capitalist Manifesto* (New York: Random House, 1958).

9. Jacob M. Schlesinger and David P. Hamilton, "The More the Japanese Save for a Rainy Day, the Gloomier It Gets," *Wall Street Journal*, July 21, 1998. In November 1999, the Japanese government announced a $171.4 billion economic stimulus package that included not only an expanded loan program for small business but also a large increase in public spending on public works projects, including roads and bridges.

10. Alan S. Blinder, "Eight Steps to a New Financial Order," *Foreign Policy*, September/October 1999, p. 50.

11. Louis Uchitelle, "Global Good Times, Meet the Global Glut," *New York Times*, 16 November 1997, p. WK 3.

12. Jan Hemming, "Colin Powell: His Formula for Success," *Priorities*, September 13, 1999.

13. Voting could be a condition to qualify for participation in certain wealth-sharing arrangements such as allocations under the Sky Trust or in the National Share Our Wealth Corporation, both discussed herein.

14. Even longer voting hours, easier access to absentee ballots, and Election Day registration may do little to increase voter participation, because many nonvoters have simply opted out, whether because of alienation,

a lack of information, as a protest, or the assumption that elections won't affect their lives. Jack C. Doppelt and Ellen Shearer, *Nonvoters: America's No Shows* (New York: Sage Publications, 1999).

15. Basil Rauch, ed. *The Roosevelt Reader* (New York: Holt, Rinehart, and Winston, 1957), pp. 148-152

16. This historically loaded phrase came to mind when I saw a newspaper photo of Senate Majority Leader Trent Lott (R., Miss.) speaking at a political fund-raiser hosted by the Conservative Citizens Council. As a "son of the South," I recall the Council well. It was previously known as the White Citizens Council or, when I was a kid, simply the Ku Klux Klan.

17. Granting priority to financial signals is clearly a mixed bag. In an interview in conjunction with his resignation as managing director of the IMF, Michel Camdessus conceded, "We created the conditions that obliged President Suharto to leave his job." He then qualified this statement, saying, "That was not our intention," while quickly adding that soon after Suharto's resignation, he traveled to Moscow to warn President Boris Yeltsin that the same financial forces could end his reign in Russia. David E. Sanger, "Longtime I.M.F. Director Resigns in Midterm," *New York Times*, November 10, 1999.

Chapter 6

1. Reported in Richard Morin, "Have the People Lost Their Voice?" *Washington Post National Weekly Edition*, June 28, 1999, p. 34.

2. See George McGovern, "Are the Primaries Over Before They've Started?" *New York Times*, July 9, 1999.

3. For a mathematical theory predicting just such a result, see G. Spencer Brown, *Laws of Form* (New York: Bantam, 1972).

4. Jay Griffith, *Pip Pip: A Sideways Look at Time* (London: Flamingo, 1999).

5. Joseph Fletcher, *The Ethics of Genetic Control* (New York: Prometheus, 1988).

6. Lee Silver, *Remaking Eden* (New York: Avon, 1998).

7. Rich Hayes explains the difference between genetic manipulation in somatic and germ cells: "Somatic manipulation seeks to change the genetic makeup of particular body (somatic) cells that comprise our organs–lungs, brain, bone, and so forth. Changes in somatic cells are not passed on to one's children. Germline genetic manipulation changes the sex cells–that is, the sperm and eggs, or 'germ' cells–whose sole function is to pass a set of genes to the next generation." Interview with Rich Hayes, *Wild Duck Review*, summer 1999, p. 19.

8. Wendell Berry, "Thy Life's a Miracle," *Wild Duck Review*, summer 1999, p. 3.

9. Roger Cohen, "To Spur German Economy, Schroder Offers Veer to Right," *New York Times*, July 25, 1999. By late 1999, the Social Democrats were experiencing severe setbacks in local voting.

10. Tod Lindberg, "Why the 'Third Way' Is Winning," *Wall Street Journal,* May 26, 1999.

11. Cited in Paul Hawken, Amory Lovins, and L. Hunter Lovins, *Natural Capitalism* (New York: Little Brown, 1999), p. 112.

12. For a compilation of facts about advertising and marketing to children, see the Center for a New American Dream Web site <www.newdream.org>. For an assessment of our long-term responsibilities, see Stewart Brand, *The Clock of the Long Now* (New York: Basic Books, 1999). See also <www.longnow.org>.

13. Barbara Crossette, "In Numbers, the Heavy Do Not Match the Starved,:" *New York Times,* January 18, 1999, p.10.

14. Lester Thurow, *Building Wealth* (New York: HarperCollins, 1999).

15. Some banks will lend based on projected revenues, but most continue to require collateral as well—real estate, buildings, inventory, accounts receivable, etc.—that can be readily sold if the loan is not repaid.

16. Louis O. Kelso and Patricia Hetter Kelso, *Democracy and Economic Power* (Cambridge, Mass.: Ballinger, 1986).

17. *Economic Report of the President* (Washington, D.C.: Government Printing Office, 1999), p. 348.

18. The enormous sensitivities that surround these issues became apparent in the UK early in 1999, when UK pension funds reversed their opposition to government rules requiring that they disclose their ethical and environmental stance only after the Blair government assured them that the rules would go no further. The funds were concerned that this disclosure requirement might be extended to force them to avoid investments in firms seen to be ethically unsound, such as tobacco or arms companies. *Financial Times,* July 2, 1999.

19. "Employee-Owned Companies Continue to Significantly Outperform the Market," *Foundation Newsletter* (Washington, D.C.: Foundation for Enterprise Development) 11, no. 2 (1998). The index is maintained by American Capital Strategies, based in Bethesda, Maryland.

20. Quoted in Melody Petersen, "American and British Law Firms Set to Merge," *New York Times,* July 12, 1999.

21. Adam Bryant, "Free Lunch," *New York Times,* April 19, 1998, sec. 4, p. 1. By late 1999, Weill had pocketed more than $700 million over the past decade, much of it through appropriating a substantial portion of the shareholder value created by downsizing Travelers by a third from its 1987 workforce. In his post at Citigroup, *Business Week* ranks him as the nation's second-worst executive in delivering shareholder value.

22. Today's generally accepted accounting practices also fuel merger mania. For example, many mergers generate restructuring costs for everything from professional fees to employee layoffs. Also included, however, is the cost of executive pay packages, both for departing executives ("golden parachutes") and for those who remain. In 1998, U.S. corporations announced $76 billion in restructuring costs. Instead of requiring that those costs be

spread over a few years, current accounting (and tax) rules allow companies to write off those costs in a single taxable year. Thus, newly merged companies often appear to be less profitable in the first year following a merger (when stock options are often granted), only "bouncing back" in the next year, when the company's "superior performance" gives a boost to share prices, instantly making those options more valuable (while also providing executives a financial incentive to increase layoffs). Executive suite reengineering of pension plans is another favorite. The booming stock market has allowed plan sponsors to book plan surpluses as a credit to earnings, further boosting share prices. Many companies have not needed to make pension contributions for years. In 1998, for example, IBM showed a pension surplus of $450 million. In an attempt to fatten earnings to $650 million, IBM announced that it would convert most employees to what's known as a cash-balance pension plan in which older employees typically find they either lose a portion of their pension benefits or must work longer to earn their way back to their old level of final-average-pay benefits. After employees mounted an e-mail-organized protest, IBM relented. It's not known what impact those pension plan amendments would have had on the value of IBM's executive stock options. The IRS indicates that it approved several hundred such plans. Lawsuits are currently pending based on age discrimination issues arising under both federal pension law amendments enacted in 1986 and the Age Discrimination in Employment Act of 1967. Ellen E. Schulz, Jon G. Auerbach, and Glenn Burkins, "Boomer Backlash: Controversy Besetting New Pension Plan Rises with IBM's Retreat," *Wall Street Journal*, September 20, 1999.

23. On February 29, 2000, John Reed announced his retirement effective April 18, 2000.

24. See Jeff Gates, *The Ownership Solution*, Cambridge, Mass.: Perseus Publishing, 1998), pp. 138–141.

25. Cyrus Freidheim, *The Trillion-Dollar Enterprise* (Reading, Mass.: Perseus Books, 1998). As Freidheim points out, "[A]lliances require careful, partnerlike negotiation of a range of complex variables—valuation, ownership shares, mutual obligations, authorities, sharing the profits, transfer pricing, people, organization, systems, reporting, compensation, and so on." Alliances also require some anticipation and negotiation of terms and conditions for dissolution.

26. James Womack and David Jones, *Lean Thinking: Banish Waste and Create Wealth in Your Corporation* (New York: Simon & Schuster, 1996). See also <www.lean.org>.

27. Hawken, Lovins, and Lovins, *Natural Capitalism*, p. 131. See also <www.rmi.com> and <www.naturalcapitalism.com>.

Chapter 7

1. The tax code already includes one popular capital gain tax incentive for employee ownership. For sellers to an ESOP, proceeds received on the sale to an ESOP of unlisted shares may be reinvested ("rolled over") without tax. Since 1984, ESOP rollovers have encouraged thousands of business owners to sell some portion of their companies to their employees. To qualify, shareholders initially need sell only 30 percent of the company's shares to the ESOP. That allows founders to adopt an ESOP on a step-by-step basis, generating cash for some shares while maintaining control of the company. British ESOP law has a similar tax-free reinvestment provision, though with only a 10 percent minimum-sale requirement.

2. There's more than one way to skin the tax policy cat. Rather than use tax policy to inject dynamism into otherwise static ownership rights, Australian Shann Turnbull argues that ownership itself be made "dynamic." For instance, he would allow tax write-offs for depreciation only to the extent that a corporation's ownership is transferred to stakeholders at the same rate. In other words, tax write-offs would be paired with ownership write-offs. The company could either broaden its ownership or pay higher taxes. Many forms of property already incorporate such time-limited property rights—patents, leases, bonds, etc. Shann Turnbull, "Stakeholder Governance: A Cybernetic and Property Rights Analysis," *Corporate Governance: An International Review*, January 1997, pp. 11–23.

3. Paul Hawken, Amory Lovins, and L. Hunter Lovins, *Natural Capitalism* (New York: Little Brown, 1999).

4. The approach recommended here is very different from required "benchmarking," whereby compensation would be geared to certain predetermined performance standards. Although that may be an improvement over the current system, this approach suggests that fast-widening pay disparity is *itself* an issue.

5. Don Van Natta, Jr., "Republicans' Goal Is $1 Million Each from Top Donors," *Wall Street Journal*, August 9, 1999.

6. Jim Hightower, *If the Gods Had Meant Us to Vote They Would Have Given Us Candidates* (New York: HarperCollins, 2000).

7. Don Van Natta, Jr., "Looking a Gift House in the Mouth," *New York Times*, September 19, 1999, p. WK6.

8. Elizabeth Drew, *The Corruption of American Politics* (Secaucus, N.J.: Birch Lane Press, 1999).

9. Micah Morrison, "From Oil to Baseball to the Governor's Mansion," *Wall Street Journal*, September 28, 1999.

10. Micah Morrison, "Occidental and Oriental Connections," *Wall Street Journal*, September 29, 1999.

11. See Joanna Cagan and Neil deMause, *Field of Schemes: How the Great Stadium Swindle Turns Public Money into Private Profit* (New York: Common Courage, 1998).

12. Marc Fisher, "Taking Out the Old Ballparks," *Washington Post National Weekly Edition*, September 27, 1999, p. 30. Studies of the economic impact of sports facilities concur that the facilities can reduce the number of jobs in a city because much of the spending goes to a few players, coaches, executives, and investors, whereas if those same dollars were spent on other forms of recreation (museums, parks, bicycle paths, restaurants, etc.), the funds would support more employment and broader-based enjoyment.

13. Tim Smart, "Count Corporate America Among NATO's Staunchest Allies," *Washington Post*, April 13, 1999.

14. Tim Weiner, "Battle Waged in the Senate over Royalties by Oil Firms," *New York Times*, September 21, 1999.

15. LBOs are feasible only because of the self-financing logic of the closed system of finance ("productive assets can pay for themselves"). Any policy tinkering that enhances the funds flowing through this closed system (such as supply-side tax subsidies) enhances their feasibility and finance-ability. See John B. Shoven and Joel Waldfogel, eds., *Debt, Taxes and Corporate Restructuring* (Washington, D.C.: Brookings Institution, 1990).

16. See Jacob M. Schlesinger and Michael Schroeder, "Law Requiring Banks to Aid Poor Communities Faces Uncertain Future as Gramm Mounts Attack," *Wall Street Journal*, July 27, 1999.

17. Dee Hock, remarks made at Social Venture Network meeting, Oakland, Calif., October 1998. See also Dee Hock, *Birth of the Chaordic Age* (San Francisco: Berrett-Koehler, 1999) and <www.chaordic. com>.

18. Malcolm Wells, *Infra Structures* (Brewster, Mass.: Underground Art Gallery, 1994).

19. "ShopSop stock" should be distinguished from the growing interest in tracking stock. Unlike common stocks, tracking stocks don't represent an ownership interest except to the extent that they pay dividends based on the operating performance of specified businesses such as Staples, the office-supply chain, for which a tracking stock follows the performance of its Staples.com Web site. Tracking stock gives a company two financial statements, often so that stock options are available to attract and retain electronic-commerce professionals and to finance the acquisition of e-commerce companies.

20. See <www.dfdpo.com>.

21. Complexity theorist John Holland suggests a bucket-brigade algorithm for attributing value to each of many contributors. See John Holland, *Hidden Order: How Adaptation Builds Complexity* (New York: Addison-Wesley, 1995).

22. D. North, "Is Your Head Office a Useless Frill?" *Canadian Business*, November 14, 1997, p. 78.

23. United Nations, *United Nations Human Development Report 1999* ((New York: Oxford University Press, 1999), p. 5.

24. Christian Aid calculates that the developed world's bill on its carbon dioxide account is three times as large as its financial debt from the developing world, or $612 billion compared with $200 billion. To calculate carbon debt, the world population in 1990 is divided by the carbon dioxide emissions that scientists say would be permitted to hit the target of a minimum 60 percent reduction in the production of global-warming gases. This results in an annual allocation of 800 pounds per person, with each ton priced at $3,000 according to the contribution its use is estimated to make to the GDP. On that basis, the indebted poor countries are in credit on their "climate account" as a result of their underuse of fossil fuels. From a report titled "Who Owes Who? Climate Change, Debt Equity and Survival," reported in *Guardian* (London), September 20, 1999.

25. See Peter Barnes, "The Pollution Dividend," *American Prospect* (May-June 1999), p. 61.

26. See <www.skytrust.cfed.org>.

27. Some development experts suggest instead that a global tax on fossil fuels be used to finance an enhanced supply of public goods for developing countries, including vaccines to combat tropical diseases. Jeffrey Sachs, "Helping the World's Poorest," *Economist*, August 14, 1999, p. 16.

28. Ross Gelbspan, "Trading Away Our Chance to End Global Warming," *Boston Globe*, May 16, 1999.

29. "UK Firms to Pilot Greenhouse Gas Emissions Trading," *Environment News Service*, June 30, 1999 (on-line at [envdaily@ends.co.uk]).

30. William Clairborne, "Harnessing the Wind," *Washington Post National Weekly Edition*, September 27, 1999, p. 19.

31. To stimulate private-sector research and development, the initial project could be financed with a structure whereby the facilities are initially owned by the private sector with an agreement to transfer them to the GSOC over time. Private-sector contractors could retain an interest through repair and maintenance contracts and for research and development.

32. Ed Ayres, "Will We Still Eat Meat?" *Time*, November 8, 1999, p. 106.

33. Sandra Postel, *Pillar of Sand: Can the Irrigation Miracle Last?* (New York: W. W. Norton, 1998).

34. Unless governments commit to spending money on cleaner water supplies, 3 million to 5 million people, most of them children, will continue to die each year from diseases carried in dirty water. The UN estimates that the price of bringing safe water to those who need it would be $23 billion to $25 billion per year over eight to ten years. Current world investment in clean water supplies is only $8 billion. The $15 to $17 billion shortfall is about the same amount spent every year on pet food in the United States and Europe. *Environmental News Service* (ENS) release of July 20, 1999.

35. Employee ownership offers one promising component of this strategy, particularly to address today's outrageous executive compensation practices. For instance, union leaders at majority-employee-owned United Airlines negotiated a pay policy that ties executive compensation to employee-share-

holder satisfaction, as measured by an outside survey firm. This new system, effective for 2000, also makes bonuses for its 625 executives dependent on customer satisfaction and on-time performance.

36. Abramson pay package reported in *Wall Street Journal*, April 8, 1999.

37. Gary Strauss, "Parting Could Be Sweet Sorrow for Sprint CEO," *USA Today*, October 5, 1999.

38. Pfeiffer pay package reported in *Wall Street Journal*, April 8, 1999.

39. Teresa Wyszomierski and Pieter Bierkens, "Stock Options: Rewards Without Merit?" *Washington Post National Weekly Edition*, September 13, 1999, p. 23.

40. Mason Gaffney and Fred Harrison, *The Corruption of Economics* (London: Shepheard-Walwyn, 1994).

41. "Charles Handy Sees the Future," *Fortune*, October 31, 1994.

42. *Business Week*, September 20, 1999.

43. Gregory J. Millman, *The Day Traders* (New York: Random House, 1999).

44. Financial Markets Center, *The Federal Reserve and Local Economic Development* (Philomont, Va.: Financial Markets Center, 1999).

45. *Federal Reserve System Purposes and Functions* (Washington, D.C.: Board of Governors of the Federal Reserve System, 1994).

46. Laurence Zuckerman, "Firing on Fortress Northwest," *New York Times*, August 25, 1999. What the flying public doesn't yet realize is that today's huge cattle-car-sized airplanes were built not for passenger convenience but to reduce competition by monopolizing gates and air traffic at those key hubs. Instead of air transport efficiency (captured by profitable Southwest Airlines with its cheaper flights, smaller planes, and more direct routing), the major airlines resort to revenues generated by systems designed for less efficiency, including "self-sorting cargo" (i.e., you) as passengers rush to remote gates in huge terminal complexes in out-of-the-way cities whose residents underwrote the construction of these oversized airports.

47. Lock-ins are not limited to technology. In the case of airline gates (as well as takeoff and landing rights), control to airport tenants was often ceded during the 1950s and 1960s, when carriers agreed to help pay off airport revenue bonds. This often puts start-up airlines in a hugely disadvantageous position, particularly at hub airports. A congressional audit found that travelers pay a premium to fly from "gate-constrained" hubs with average fares on short-haul flights in 1998, for example, 90 percent higher at Delta Airlines' Cincinnati hub than at non-hub airports of similar size. "Majority-in interest clauses" give incumbent airlines virtual veto power over airport expansion plans. See Bruce Ingersoll, "Flexible Flier," *Wall Street Journal*, June 12, 1999.

48. Joel Brinkley, "U.S. Judge Declares Microsoft a Monopoly Stifling a Market; Gates Dissents, Favoring Talks," *New York Times*, November 6, 1999.

49. Kevin Kelly, *New Rules for the New Economy* (New York: Viking, 1998).

50. See Amy Harmon, "Gates Hits $100 Billion Mark, More or Less," *New York Times*, July 17, 1999, updated the following the announced completion of Windows 2000. See <www.webho.com/WealthClock>.

51. Donella H. Meadows, "Places to Intervene in a System," *Whole Earth*, winter 1997, p. 78.

52. Lawrence M. Fisher, "The Race to Cash In on the Genetic Code," *New York Times*, August 29, 1999, p. BU1.

53. "Scientists Discover 'Immortal' Genes," *Sunday Times* (London), July 4, 1999.

54. Mae Wan Ho, comments at Bioneers Conference, San Rafael, Calif., October 29–31, 1999 (<www.bioneers.org>).

55. Barnaby J. Feder, "Monsanto Says It Won't Market Infertile Seeds," *New York Times*, October 5, 1999. On December 17, 1999, Monsanto agreed to a merger with Pharmacia and Upjohn.

56. Stephan Labaton, "Accord Reached on Lifting of Depression-Era Barriers Among Financial Industries," *New York Times*, October 23, 1999.

57. William Greider, *One World, Ready or Not* (New York: Simon & Schuster, 1997).

58. Charles R. Morris, *Money, Green and Risk* (New York: Random House, 1999); David Korten, "Wealth versus Money," *Yes!* spring 1997, p. 15.

59. Germ plasm is the genetic heart of food crops. See Paul Hawken correspondence in *Rachel's Environment and Health Weekly* 667 (September 9, 1999).

60. Stephan Labaton, "Ownership Rules in Cable Industry Loosened by F.C.C.," *New York Times*, October 9, 1999.

61. See Sheryl WuDunn, "An Entrepreneurial Exception Rides the Internet in Japan," *New York Times*, July 26, 1999.

62. Reported in George Anders, "Eager to Boost Traffic, More Internet Firms Give Away Services," *Wall Street Journal*, July 28, 1999.

63. Robert Berner, "Merck, CVS Agree to Link Internet Sites," *Wall Street Journal*, October 6, 1999.

64. Cited in "Charles Handy Sees the Future," p. 17.

65. Ibid.

66. See Stacey Mitchell, "The Buck Starts—and Stops—Here," *The New Rules*, summer 1999.

67. Kent Whealy, "Weaving the World: Voices of the Bioneers," *Bioneers Letter*, autumn 1999, p. 1. See <www.bioneers.org>.

68. Cyrus Freidheim, *The Trillion-Dollar Enterprise* (Cambridge, Mass.: Perseus Books, 1998).

69. *Human Development Report* 1999, p. 78.

Chapter 8

1. This initial survey will also need to identify and recommend how best to resolve the barriers to transparency that are certain to be encountered. The U.S. Congress has periodically convened hearings on this matter, though with little discernible success in advancing disclosure in a system in which wealth is often held in trust, in "street names" (such as brokerage accounts), or in nominees beyond the reach of research by any democratic institution. See U.S. Congress, Senate Committee on Government Operations, *Disclosure of Corporate Ownership*, Staff Report of the Subcommittee on Budgeting, Management and Expenditure, 93rd Cong., May 4, 1974; U.S. Congress, House Committee on Banking and Currency, *Commercial Banks and Their Trust Activities, Emerging Influence on the American Economy*, Staff Report for the Subcommittee on Domestic Finance, 90th Cong., July 8, 1968.

2. Reported in Neil King, Jr., "Instead of Big Strikes, U.S.'s Terrorism Battle Focuses on Harassing Would-Be Troublemakers," *Wall Street Journal*, August 4, 1999.

3. In May 1999, *Time* reported the family's combined wealth at $15 billion.

4. Wayne Arnold, "Tough Guy at the Loan Office," *New York Times*, July 28, 1999.

5. "A Tycoon Nearly Sunk by Indonesia's Straits Lands on Solid Ground," *Wall Street Journal*, January 12, 2000; Robert Frank, "Teflon Tycoon—The Crony Capitalist: 'People Never Thought I'd Survive,'" *Wall Street Journal*, August 30, 1999.

6. Mark Landler, "First Lady's Squawk Hints at Dictator's Nest Egg," *New York Times*, December 22, 1999.

7. United Nations, *United Nations Human Development Report 1999* (New York: Oxford University Press, 1999), p. 5.

8. Jay Solomon, "Bali High Jinks: In Indonesia, Crisis and Corruption Create Financial Vigilantes," *Wall Street Journal*, September 21, 1999.

9. These include Antigua and Barbuda, Anguilla, Barbados, the British Virgin Islands, the Cayman Islands, Dominica, Grenada, Montserrat, the Netherlands Antilles, St. Kitts and Nevis, St. Lucia, St. Vincent, and the Grenadines.

10. [George Kennan], "Sources of Soviet Conduct," *Foreign Affairs*, July 1947, pp. 566–582.

11. See chapter 11, "Community Without Communism," in Jeff Gates, *The Ownership Solution* (Cambridge, Mass.: Perseus Publishing, 1998).

12. Jeff Gates and Patricia L. Gates, "From Containment to Community," *Perspectives*, September 1999, pp. 33–46.

13. Raymond Bonner, "Russian Gangsters Exploit Capitalism to Increase Profits," *New York Times*, July 25, 1999.

14. Joseph E. Stilitz, "Whither Reform: Ten Years of the Transition" (keynote address to World Bank Annual Conference on Development Economics, Washington, D.C., April 28–30, 1999).

15. Ibid., citing Gates, *The Ownership Solution*.

16. David Hoffman, "Russia's Capital Flight Problem," *Washington Post National Weekly Edition*, September 6, 1999, p. 16.

17. Michael Douglass and Paul Blustein, "The End of Illusion," *Washington Post National Weekly Edition*, September 20, 1999, p. 6.

18. Louis Uchitelle, "World Bank Economist Felt He Had to Silence His Criticism or Quit," *New York Times*, December 12, 1999.

19. Anders Aslund, "Russia's Collapse," *Foreign Affairs*, September/ October, 1999, p. 64.

20. Lee S. Wolosky, "Putin's Plutocrat Problem," *Foreign Affairs*, March/April, 2000, pp. 18-31.

21. Alan S. Cullison, "Russian Banks Gained Unfairly By IMF Loan Critic Says," *Wall Street Journal*, September 16, 1999. In early 1999, Skuratov issued an arrest warrant for business tycoon Boris Berezovsky on corruption charges. Shortly thereafter, the interior minister at the time, Sergei Stepashin, announced that he would not honor the warrant.

22. Meanwhile, Russians should consider the use of local currencies as a way to match productive needs and productive capacities. See discussion of "capitalism without the capital" in Gates, *The Ownership Solution*, pp. 155–161. Worldwide approximately 1,400 versions of local currencies help employ local people and clear local markets by providing an alternative source of locale-sensitive purchasing power.

23. To move funds abroad, many Russians established accounts in local banks that maintained "correspondent" relationships with banks abroad, such as the Bank of New York and others that pursued Russia's banking business. Funds can then easily be transferred from the Russian bank's correspondent account to an account of a shell company invented to conceal the account's ownership. Thus laundered, some of those funds reentered Russia. Much of the money presumably moved to secret accounts in tax haven jurisdictions, with nearby Cyprus emerging as a favorite location both for dachas and for money laundering. Martin Mayer, "Sunshine Disinfects Dirty Money," *Wall Street Journal*, September 24, 1999.

24. On money laundering by U.S. banks, see Michael Wines, "Yeltsin Son-in-Law at Center of Rich Network of Influence," *New York Times*, October 7, 1999.

25. Robert E. Rubin, "Don't Give Up on Russia," *New York Times*, September 21, 1999.

26. Jeanne Whalen, "Russia Ousts Foreign Owners of Prized Factory," *Wall Street Journal*, October 12, 1999.

27. Robert P. DeVeechi and Arthur C. Helton, "Are We Asking Too Much?" *Washington Post National Weekly Edition*, September 27, 1999, p. 21.

28. *United Nations Human Development Report 1999*, p. 5.

29. Amartya Sen, *Development as Freedom* (New York: Knopf, 1999).

30. Robert D. Kaplan, "Weakness in Numbers," *New York Times,* October 18, 1999.

31. Business Leaders for Sensible Priorities is made up of five hundred business leaders and military experts who lead a campaign to redirect military spending to education and health care. See <www.businessleaders.org>.

32. For Living Machines, see <www.livingtechnologies.com>. For restorers, see <www.oceanarks.org>.

33. Paul Stamets, "Earth's Natural Internet," *Whole Earth,* fall 1999, p. 74.

34. *United Nations Human Development Report 1999,* p. 4.

35. Thom Hartmann, "Have We Already Played the Game and Lost?" *Tikkun,* November/December 1999, p. 21.

36. See His Holiness the Dalai Lama with Fabien Quaki, *Imagine All the People* (Boston: Wisdom Publications, 1999).

37. Albert R. Hunt, "Americans Look to Twenty-First Century with Optimism and Confidence," *Wall Street Journal,* September 16, 1999.

38. See <www.whirlwind.sfsu.edu>.

39. Kabir Edmund Helminski, *Living Presence* (New York: Jeremy P. Tarcher, 1994).

40. Suzanne Daley, "French See a Hero in War on 'McDomination,'" *New York Times,* October 12, 1999.

41. Richard Ullman, "An Interview with George Kennan," *New York Review of Books,* August 12, 1999, p. 4.

42. Kenny Ausubel (comment at Bioneers Conference, San Rafael, Calif., October 29–31, 1999. See also <www.bioneers.org>.

43. Cited in Michael Hirsh, "At War with Ourselves," *Harper's Magazine,* July 1999, p. 150.

44. Philip Shenon, "Departing Foreign Aid Chief Says Cuts Are Dangerous," *New York Times,* July 6, 1999.

45. George Gedda, "Outgoing AID chief blasts US for foreign budget, policy on UN," *Boston Globe,* June 30, 1999.

46. Philip Shenon, "Departing Foreign Aid Chief."

47. "Tuned Out, Turned Off," *Washington Post National Weekly Edition,* February 5–11, 1996, p. 6.

Chapter 9

1. As of this writing, the funding aspect of this plan was uncertain. The original proposal suggested that the IMF sell a portion of its gold reserves, invest the proceeds, and use the income to fund debt relief. Responding to complaints from gold producers, the chairman of the U.S. House Committee on Banking, charged with oversight of the national interest in those reserves, announced his opposition to the plan. Note the ownership blind spot embodied in this otherwise well-intentioned plan, which includes

no mention of the impact on the value of those securities in which proceeds from the sale of IMF gold reserves would be invested. Thus, under this proposal, in order to assist the poor, the IMF would first further enrich the already-rich. In September 1999, President Clinton proposed that the United States forgive 100 percent of debt of the most indebted countries—mostly in sub-Saharan Africa—if they show that the savings were being used for education and fighting poverty. David E. Sanger, "Clinton Widens Plan for Poor Debtor Nations," *New York Times,* September 30, 1999.

2. To ensue that this relief does not reward corrupt officials who spirited funds abroad, it's essential that this program be combined with the induced transparency program, proposed in Chapter 8.

3. Cited in Paul Hawken, Amory Lovins, and L. Hunter Lovins, *Natural Capitalism* (New York: Little Brown, 1999), p. 112.

4. See <www.rmi.com>.

5. Dramatic savings in both energy and materials may well be available through "green" design. See Ernst Ulrich von Weizsacker, Amory Lovins, and L. Hunter Lovins, *Factor Four* (London: Earthscan, 1997).

6. This security also plays a key role in the run-up in stock market prices. James K. Glassman, coauthor of *Dow 36,000,* bases his projection on the notion that the risk premium for stocks over more secure bonds has been closing over the past two decades from 7 percent to about 3 percent. That falling premium means a rising price. James K. Glassman and Kevin Hassett, *Dow 36,000* (New York: Times Books, 1999).

7. Inge Kaul, Isabelle Grunberg, and Mark A. Stern, *Global Public Goods* (New York: Oxford University Press, 1999).

8. This idea was developed in concert with Peter Barnes, cofounder and former president of Working Assets and founder of the Common Assets Project, a Washington, D.C.–based effort that is part of the Corporation for Enterprise Development, an organization devoted to asset-building strategies in low-income communities. This proposal should be distinguished from the transaction-based "Tobin tax" proposed by Yale University professor James Tobin, who would impose a tax on currency exchange transactions rather than, as here, on the presence of securities in global capital markets. Although access to potential transactions has value, it is the presence of the commons itself that creates the value accessible by those transactions. In addition, the Tobin tax weds the beneficiaries to transactions that may well destabilize the commons (do we really want to encourage more leveraged derivatives financing?).

9. It is my hope that a portion of the funds raised would be dedicated to development efforts in those tax haven countries willing to cooperate with this effort.

10. Since much of this personal wealth accumulation was financed, in part, with public debt (as in the case of supply-side economics), we should also explore appropriate means for deferring the payment of interest on govern-

ment bonds held by recalcitrant wealth holders. Or, perhaps we could disavow the obligation altogether for those debt holders identified as refusing to participate in this arrangement. The prevalence of bearer bonds, however, complicates this approach.

11. Robert M. Morgenthau, "On the Trail of Global Capital," New York Times, November 9, 1999.

12. The development task is complicated by the fact that the globalization of capital markets has largely bypassed the poorest countries. With 20 percent of the world's people, these countries receive a meager 0.2 percent of the world's commercial lending. In addition, their share of world trade fell between 1960 and 1990, from an already low 4 percent to less than 1 percent. United Nations, Human Development Report 1996 (New York: Oxford University Press, 1996), p. 9.

13. Warrants involve the right to purchase shares at a price set today.

14. "The dollar value of unsecuritized income-producing assets is approximately $90 trillion. If securitized, the value of those assets could approach $150 trillion. Thus, an income-producing asset is worth about three times the value of its annual gross output if it is not securitized and five times the value if it is securitized. . . . Securitized assets are worth more than the 'lumpy' assets that collateralize them, partly because they are more liquid." John C. Edmundson, "Securities: The New World Wealth Machine," Foreign Policy 104 (fall 1996): 118. Securitization involves combining financial obligations with similar attributes of risk (such as home mortgages), creating a single security, and selling that security in the capital markets.

15. Although "securitization" removes certain risks (such as lack of liquidity), it also imposes others, depending on the security. For example, when banks securitize their loans, the credit system loses both the lender's knowledge of borrowers and their incentive to monitor the status of the loan. Whenever a loan is securitized, nobody has the credit watch. See Martin Mayer, "The Dangers of Derivatives," Wall Street Journal, May 20, 1999.

16. This process should also provide an appropriate venue to debate a diversity of views on what can and should be owned, from plant varieties to human genes. In addition, this should provide a forum for determining how best to address the ongoing commercial appropriation of centuries of knowledge of indigenous peoples in some of the poorest communities in developing countries. For example, in an attempt to reserve for the few that which was common, corporate patents have been filed for several of the more than sixty varieties of potatoes developed by indigenous peoples of the Andes.

17. Nobel laureate economist Robert Solow cautions that even where foreign investment enhances productivity and profitability, efficiency alone cannot sustain economic growth. There must also be robust market demand, and that demand must show up not abroad but in that country. Foreign investment typically results in a perpetual drain on a nation's foreign exchange

earnings as profits are repatriated to the investor's home country. An owner-ship-pattern-sensitive development policy can help reduce outsiders' claims on foreign exchange reserves while also dampening financial instabilities by anchoring assets in local hands, where investment returns can show up as domestic demand.

18. Exchange-rate stability, a key goal of the International Monetary Fund, is also undermined by the concentrated ownership patterns associated with traditional finance. With a practical and foresighted asset-accumulation strategy, public sector spending in developing countries can gradually be curbed as people become more economically self-sufficient. Absent such an ownerization strategy, populations will continue to be left dependent for their economic support on government-funded safety nets, a priority target of the IMF's hugely unpopular structural adjustment programs designed to restore fiscal prudence and address exchange rate stability.

19. Ted Halstead, "A Politics for Generation X," *Atlantic Monthly*, August 1999, p. 33.

20. Reported in Jane Perlez, "At Trade Forum, Clinton Pleads for the Poor," *New York Times*, January 30, 2000.

21. Quoted in Richard Prestion, "The Demon in the Freezer," *New Yorker*, July 12, 1999, p. 44.

22. Quoted at Ibid., p. 55.

23. Janine M. Menyus, *Biomimicry* (New York: Morrow, 1997).

Chapter 10

1. Frank Swoboda, "They'll Buy Their Own Gold Watch," *Washington Post National Weekly Edition*, September 6, 1999, p. 34.

2. Amy Goldstein, "Who Lacks Health Insurance?" *Washington Post National Weekly Edition*, October 11, 1999, p. 18.

3. Jacques Steinberg, "Academic Standards Eased as a Fear of Failure Spreads," *New York Times*, December 3, 1999.

4. Jodi Wilgoren, "Most Pupils Can't Write Well, Report Says," *New York Times*, September 29, 1999.

5. Dirk Johnson, "Schools Are Cracking Down on Misconduct," *New York Times*, December 1, 1999.

6. The current account deficit is the broadest measure of what we pay to foreigners for goods, services, and other things, less what we collect from them. As of fall 1999, the deficit was a record-setting 3.63 percent of GDP and was growing nearly a billion dollars a day ($80.7 billion for second quarter 1999). To date, foreigners have been willing to take our dollars (for oil, cars, software, etc.) and invest much of that in U.S. securities, providing yet more fuel for the stock market boom. As alternatives to investing here look more attractive, downward pressure on the dollar will grow, as will pressure for protectionist measures. Traditional analysis suggests that the Federal

Reserve will be feel pressure to raise interest rates to attract investment in our government debt. That will depress stock prices, causing more foreigners to flee U.S. securities. Mexico offers a example of how quickly such events can spiral out of control when in 1994 capital markets ceased providing the funds needed to finance their expanding current account deficit.

7. For information on fighting global retail chains, see <www.sprawlbusters.com>.

8. Paul Hawken, Amory Lovins, and L. Hunter Lovins, *Natural Capitalism* (New York: Little Brown, 1999).

9. See <www.adbusters.org>.

10. William A. Galston and Elaine C. Kamarck, "Five Realities That Will Shape Twenty-First-Century Politics," *Blueprint* (fall 1998).

11. Michael M. Weinstein, "Students Seek Some Reality amid the Math of Economics," *New York Times*, September 18, 1999.

12. Harlan Cleveland, "The Global Century," *Futures* (November-December 1999).

Chapter 11

1. Riane Eisler, *The Chalice and the Blade* (San Francisco: HarperCollins, 1987).

2. David Cay Johnston, "A 1995 Executive Pay Plan Led to Big Bonus This Week," *New York Times*, May 23, 1996.

3. The Delaware Chancery court ruled on November 9, 1999, that more than half of the shares must be returned—not because the award was excessive but because the compensation agreement lacked a clause authorizing alteration in the number of shares that could be awarded following a stock split. David Cay Johnston, "$558 Million Ordered Repaid in Stock Grants," *New York Times*, November 10, 1999.

4. See Andrew Boyd, *The Activist Cookbook: Creative Actions for a Fair Economy* (Boston: United for a Fair Economy, 1997).

5. Agitprop's billboards also urge those interested in sponsoring a billboard campaign in their community to call United for a Fair Economy at 1-800-JOIN UFE.

6. *Too Much* can be ordered by calling 1-800-316-2719.

7. Paul Krassner, *The Winner of the Slow Bicycle Race* (Los Angeles: Seven Stories Press, 1996).

8. *New York Times*, May 23, 1999, quoting Frank Newbold, vice president of Sotheby's International Realty, who manages the company's East Hampton office. Cited in *Too Much* (quarterly publication of Boston-based United for a Fair Economy), summer 1999.

9. Interview on *The Paula Gordon Show: Conversations with People at the Leading Edge* (November 13, 1999). See <www.PaulaGordon.com>.

10. The passage appears in a letter from Lincoln to Col. William F. Elkins, November 21, 1864. Archer H. Shaw, *The Lincoln Encyclopedia* (New York: Macmillan, 1950,), p. 40, traces the quote to Emanuel Hertz, *Abraham Lincoln: A New Portrait* (New York: Horace Liveright, Inc., 1931), vol. 2, p. 954.

11. For descriptions of this phenomenon, see Joseph Jaworski, *Synchronicity* (San Francisco: Berrett-Kohler, 1996), and Margaret J. Wheatley, *Leadership and the New Science* (San Francisco: Berrett-Kohler, 1992).

12. Geoff Mulgan, *Connexity* (Boston: Harvard Business School Press, 1997).

13. Kevin Kelly, *New Rules for the New Economy* (New York: Viking, 1998).

14. *Forbes 400,* October 11, 1999, p. 208.

15. Gregory Zuckerman, "Pittsburgh Bonds to Sell on Internet," *Wall Street Journal,* October 12, 1999.

16. Lon Smith, "Herman Daly and John Cobb's Vision: Person-in-Community," *Human Economy Newsletter,* June 1991.

17. See <http://www.brownsteingroup.org/letter/issue4.html>.

18. Mahbub ul Haq, "Charter of Human Development Initiative" (paper presented at State of the World Forum, San Francisco, October 3, 1996).

19. See <www.thehungersite.co>.

20. See <www.cepaa.org>.

21. For handguns, see Paul M. Barrett, "Colt's Cuts Role of Handguns in Revamping," *Wall Street Journal,* September 29, 1999. For an example of problems with biotechnology, see the discussion in Chapter 12.

22. Samuel Epstein, *The Politics of Cancer Revisited* (Fremont Center, N.Y.: East Ridge Press, 1998).

23. *Independent (London),* September 6, 1999.

24. Institutional investors should be screening their investments to ensure that financial values are not running roughshod over other values. Newly emerging indexes (such as the Domini Index of ethical investment) utilize rating systems. Wider media coverage of corporate behavior would also be helpful, along with Internet-accessible critiques of their behavior in developing countries. Support is growing for a movement known as SEAAR (social and ethical accounting, auditing and reporting). The Environmental Protection Agency sponsors a voluntary Energy Star standard for energy-efficient office equipment and home appliances that could save U.S. households as much as $100 billion over the next fifteen years.

25. Quoted in John Sweeney, "Dark Side of Global Economy," *Houston Catholic Worker,* p. 2.

26. William A. Galston and Elaine C. Kamarck, "Five Realities That Will Shape Twenty-First-Century Politics," *Blueprint* (fall 1998).

27. George Soros, *The Crisis of Global Capitalism* (New York: Public Affairs, 1998), pp. 40–43.

28. Robert D. Hershey, "Stocks Plunge over Remark on Microsoft," *New York Times*, September 24, 1999.

29. The 1998 Nobel Memorial Prize in Economic Science was awarded to Amartya Sen, who writes on ethics and poverty. Since awarding the prize to Friedrich von Hayek in 1974 and Chicago's Milton Friedman in 1976, the awards have shown a keen preference for Chicago-style neoclassical economists, a key element locking in today's finance-dominant paradigm.

30. Paul Krugman, *The Return of Depression Economics* (New York: Penguin, 1999).

31. Margaret J. Wheatley and Myron Kellner-Rogers, *A Simpler Way* (San Francisco: Berrett-Kohler, 1996), p. 69.

32. Tim Berners-Lee, *Weaving the Web* (New York: HarperCollins, 1999).

Chapter 12

1. Jennifer Steinhauer and Judith Miller, "In New York Outbreak, Glimpse of Gaps in Biological Defenses," *New York Times*, October 11, 1999.

2. The number of television sets per thousand people almost doubled between 1980 and 1995, from 121 to 235. *United Nations Human Development Report 1999* (New York: Oxford University Press, 1999), p. 4.

3. Thomas Kuhn, *The Structure of Scientific Revolutions* (Chicago: University of Chicago Press, 1962).

4. Wes Nisker, *Crazy Wisdom* (Berkeley, Calif.: Ten Speed Press, 1997).

5. Mary Catherine Bateson, "We Are Our Own Metaphor," *Whole Earth*, fall 1999, p. 14.

6. Richard Ullman, "The US and the World: An Interview with George Kennan," *New York Review of Books*, August 12, 1999, p. 4.

7. Ibid., p. 6.

8. See Kabir Edmund Helminski, *Living Presence* (New York: Jeremy Tarcher, 1993).

9. Leonard Shlain, *The Alphabet versus the Goddess* (New York: Viking Penguin, 1998).

10. James Lovelock, *Gaia: A New Look at Life on Earth* (New York: Oxford University Press, 1982).

11. Roy A. Rappaport, *Ritual and Religion in the Making of Humanity* (New York: Cambridge University Press, 1999).

12. Frederick Franck, "Pacem in Terris: A Love-of-Life Story," *Annals of Earth*, November 2, 1999, p. 8.

13. This interactive project is quite different from the various Web sites that carry pictures of the earth and from Al Gore's proposal (the Triana pro-

ject) to have (yet another) live video image of the earth transmitted twenty-four hours a day on the Internet. Note that multicultural public access television is already available (such as <www.wetv.com>).

14. Paul Stamets, "Earth's Natural Internet," *Whole Earth*, fall 1999, p. 74.

15. Matthew L. Wald, "An Ill Wind Blows at Vacation Sites," *New York Times*, August 6, 1999. In December 1999, the Environmental Protection Agency ordered 392 plants in a dozen midwestern and eastern states to cut their pollution by 50 percent.

16. Kevin Bales, *Disposable People* (Berkeley: University of California Press, 1999). Visit the Anti-Slavery International Web site at <www.charitynet.org>.

17. Peter Singer, "The Singer Solution to World Poverty," *New York Times Magazine*, September 5, 1999.

18. Theo Colburn, Dianne Dumanoski, and John Peterson Myers, *Our Stolen Future* (New York: Plume, 1997).

19. Paul Hawken, Amory Lovins, and L. Hunter Lovins, *Natural Capitalism* (New York: Little Brown, 1999).

20. See also David Wann, "Negotiating the Future by Design," *Whole Earth Review*, winter 1995, p. 14.

21. Ernst Ulrich von Weizsacker, Amory Lovins, and L. Hunter Lovins, *Factor Four* (London: Earthscan, 1997).

22. Hawken, Lovins, and Lovins, *Natural Capitalism*, p. 51.

23. Hawken, Lovins, and Lovins, *Natural Capitalism*.

24. Rainforest Action Network, *"Cut Waste Not Taxes"* (San Francisco: Rain Forest Action Network, 1995), available at <www.ran.org>.

25. Ray Anderson, *Mid-Course Correction* (New York: Chelsea Green, 1999).

26. Peter Warshall, "The Tensile and the Tantric," *Whole Earth*, summer 1997, p. 4.

27. For a new tool for assessing national trends, see Hazel Henderson, Jon Lickerman, and Patrice Flynn (eds.), *Calvert-Henderson Quality of Life Indicators* (San Francisco: Calvert Group, Ltd., 2000)

28. William A. Galston and Elaine C. Kamarck, "Five Realities That Will Shape Twenty-First-Century Politics," *Blueprint* (fall 1998).

29. For information on the Forgotten Pollinators Campaign, contact [fpollen@azstarnet.com].

30. Richard Leakey and Roger Lewin, *The Sixth Extinction* (New York: Doubleday, 1995), p. 237.

31. Carol Kaesuk Yoon, "Altered Corn May Imperil Butterfly, Researchers Say," *New York Times*, May 20, 1999.

32. Jane Rissler and Margaret Mellon, *The Ecological Risks of Engineered Crops* (Boston: MIT. Press, 1996).

33. See <www.earthkeepersmission.com>.

34. "Coastal Waters Have Big Problems," *Sustainability Review* 3 (October 4, 1999) (available at <www.eeeee.org>).

35. von Weizsacker, Lovins, and Lovins, *Factor Four*; Hawken, Lovins and Lovins, *Natural Capitalism*; Paul Weaver, ed., *Factor Ten* (New York: Greenleaf Publishing, 2000).

36. Jon Coifman, "Internet and E-Commerce Unleash Major Environmental and Energy Savings Throughout the Economy," available at <www.getf.org/pr1.html>.

37. Caloric restriction does not suggest a malnutrition diet. Rather, this notion is based on a long-standing theory of aging that says cells are damaged by oxygen-derived chemicals known as free radicals, which are created as a by-product of energy production. Fewer calories, less energy production, less damage to the cell's mitochondria, as its miniature batteries are called. Nicholas Wade, "Eating to Reach Your Life Span—Or, to Extend It," *New York Times*, September 26, 1999, p. WK5.

38. von Weizsacker, Lovins, and Lovins, *Factor Four*.

39. Andrew Bull, "I Am Woman, Watch My Stocks Soar," *(Winnipeg, Manitoba) Globe and Mail*, April 17, 1999.

Chapter 13

1. Huey Pierce Long, *My First Days in the White House* (Harrisburg, Pa.: The Telegraph Press, 1935), p. 3.

2. Thomas Jefferson, *The Papers of Thomas Jefferson*, vol. 1, 1760–1776, ed. Julian P. Body (Princeton: Princeton University Press, 1950).

3. Long, *My First Days*, p. 37.

4. Though Huey spoke frequently about this $5 million limit, which he proposed be gradually reduced to $2 million, the details of his capital levy provided for a graduated tax that accelerated dramatically for wealth holdings over $5 million. For example, he proposed a 16 percent tax on wealth between $5 million and $6 million, 32 percent on the next million, 64 percent on the next million, and 99 percent on all wealth above $8 million ($99.2 million in 1999 dollars). Where large quantities of properties could not be converted to cash to make an immediate payment, he envisioned that the person would be allowed to turn over property instead and pay the levy in installments. He also suggested that government should have the right to issue currency to be retired from the sale or disposition of properties. Ibid., pp. 144–146.

5. Edwin Amenta, Kathleen Dunleavy, and Mary Bernstein, "Stolen Thunder? Huey Long's 'Share Our Wealth,' Political Mediation, and the Second New Deal," *American Sociological Review*, October 1994.

6. With the fast-rising popularity of Adolph Hitler in Germany and Benito Mussolini in Italy, Huey's critics attempted to characterize him as an

American fascist. Often they supported that charge by pointing to his strong-armed rule of Louisiana that continued after he gave up his position as governor to take his seat in the U.S. Senate. Long contributed to that image by surrounding himself with some of the trappings of fascism, including a phalanx of heavily armed bodyguards. Yet that vilification also shifted public attention to his personality and away from his Share Our Wealth politics.

7. The biography was T. Harry Williams, *Huey Long* (New York: Vintage/Random House, 1969).

8. Robin Toner, "The Retirement Lobby Goes Va-Va Boom!" *New York Times*, August 8, 1999, p. WK1.

Chapter 14

1. The Washington, D.C.–based ESOP Association reports that its professional members tallied 1998 ESOP transactions totaling only $1.16 billion.

2. Huey Pierce Long, *My First Days in the White House* (Harrisburg, Pa.: The Telegraph Press, 1935), pp. 95–96.

3. Ibid., pp. 97–98. Note that some accommodation would be needed on the valuation issue because of the higher value accorded voting shares vis à vis nonvoting shares. In certain jurisdictions, the issuance of nonvoting shares may require amendment to state corporation laws. Under Long's proposal, the trustees would be empowered to petition the court for removal of management in any company in which mismanagement is apparent.

4. Huey variously argued for 100-to-1 and 300-to-1 limits. Note that there is a vast difference in gearing the limit to average rather than median wealth. The median would identify the wealth of the family in the middle of the wealth distribution, whereas the average would pull the threshold far higher when setting a benchmark. Although ten of us may have an average $1 million each, nine of us may have $50,000 each while one has $9.55 million.

5. Long, *My First Days*, p. 110.

6. Ibid., p. 83.

7. Ibid., p. 8114-115

8. Some might well argue that Huey was not a genuine populist, because he relied on charity as a key rationale for his redistributive policies. See Ibid., p., 114, where he cites 1 Cor. 13: "Though I speak with the tongues of men and of angels, and have not charity, I am become as sounding brass, or a tinkling cymbal."

Chapter 15

1. While it's tempting to celebrate competing visions of the public good and to embrace the notion of unfiltered pluralism that expresses itself through the tax exemption granted philanthropy, some recent donations

test the outer bounds of public tolerance, particularly for activities that operate with the support of public policy. In San Francisco, for instance, PeopleSoft cofounder David Duffield committed his private foundation to the goal of spending $200 million to ensure that a home is provided for every dog and cat in America—because of his love for his miniature schnauzer. In Madison, Wisconsin, toy maker Jerome Frautschi pledged $100 million to realize his vision of a downtown arts center. Equivalent to the annual budget of the National Endowment of the Arts, Frautschi's pledge dwarfs the total arts grants given annually by all U.S. foundations. Although drawing the line between the individual and the idiosyncratic will be neither easy nor popular, the magnitude of the funds now heading toward foundations mandates that the issue be raised and appropriate boundaries be set for giving that qualifies for public support. Standards are also required to curb charitable giving that supports the giver's commercial interests. The linkage was obvious when Microsoft's Bill Gates donated funds to bring computers to public libraries. Less obvious was the gift for tropical disease research, an area of keen interest to biotechnology firms, where Gates is reportedly one of the world's largest investors.

2. Reported in "Pay and Benefits Are Higher in ESOP Companies," in *Employee Ownership Report* (Oakland, Calif.: National Center for Employee Ownership, July/August 1998) based on 1998 report by Peter Kardas, Jim Keogh, and Adria Scharf for the Washington State Employment Security Department (based on 1995 data).

Epilogue

1. Harvey Cox, "The Market as God," *Atlantic Monthly*, March 1999, p. 18.

2. Joanna Macy, *World as Lover, World as Self* (New York: Parallex Press, 1990); Joanna Macy, *Coming Back to Life* (New York: New Society, 1998).

3. Charles Handy, *The Hungry Spirit* (New York: Broadway, 1998).

4. Randy Cohen, "The Way We Live Now: 6-20-99: The Ethicist; Uncharitable View," *New York Times Magazine*, June 20, 1999.

5. Evan L. Marcus, "The World's First Trillionaire," *Wired*, September 1999, p. 163. Former Congressman Bill Gray, president of the United Negro College Fund, which will be administering the Bill and Melinda Gates Foundation largess, indicates that this private-sector funding will enable African Americans to increase their proportion of Ph.D.'s in math by 40 percent, that is, from 1.0 percent to 1.4 percent. William Raspberry, "The Gates Family's Billion-Dollar Hurrah," *Washington Post National Weekly Edition*, September 27, 1999, p. 26.

6. Paul H. Ray, "The Rise of Integral Culture," *Noetic Sciences Review*, spring 1996.

7. Recited in Harlan Cleveland and March Luyckx, "Governance and Religions," *World Affairs* 3, no. 1 (Jan.–March 1999): 62–74.

8. Thich Nhat Hanh, "The Nature of Self," July 21, 1998, available from <www.plumvillage.org/summer1998/199>.

9. Peter Senge, et al., *The Dance of Change* (New York: Bantam, 1999).

10. Robert F. Lehman, "Our Common Work" (talk given at Spirituality and Philanthropy Meeting, Santa Fe, New Mexico, March 1, 1997).

Index

self-esteem
effect of economic insecurity on, 49
impact of inequality on, 47
self-reliance, interdependence and, 6
Sen, Amartya, 181–182
Seneca tribe, 34
seniors. *See* elders
services, emphasizing over products, 287–288
Share Our Wealth program, 300–304
control of allocation of wealth in, 313–314
implementing with least disruption, 316
plan for announcement of, 318
popular response to, 302
on setting limits on wealth accumulation, 315
sharing wealth. *See* wealth sharing
Shinrikyo, Aum, 215
Shlain, Leonard, 276
shopper stock ownership plan, 128–129
Silver, Lee, 90
Sky Trust, 134–135
Small is Beautiful (Schumacher), 109
smallpox, as bioterrorist threat, 213–215
Smith, Adam
Karl Marx and, 80
market ideological of, 71
misinterpretation of, 6
moral philosophy of, 275
people-based values of, 78, 324
on sacrificing self interest to greater community, 269, 299
warnings about market orientation by, 40
smog, long distance migration of, 279
Snyder, Gary, 282
Social Accountability Standard (SA8000) certificates, 258
social issues
bread-and-circus approach to, 27
disregard of social costs and, 161
health effects of social isolation, 46
social harmony and, 81
social issues as alternative to economic reform, 20–21
use of pricing to encourage social responsibility, 259–260
Social Security
costs of, 42

demographic challenges to, 63–64
FDR's role in founding, 305
lack of funding for, 62
political jockeying and, 237–238
racial inequalities in, 70
regressive nature of social security payroll taxes, 305–306
shoring it up by ensuring it is less needed, 311
society
changing from hierarchical to relational model of, 252, 266
impact of corporate mergers on, 110
sociopathic behavior
among youth of today, 57
as symptom of capitalist extremes, 54–55
soft money, 38. *See also* campaign finances
solar energy, 135, 205
solid waste, local disposal of, 270–271
Solzhenitzyn, Alexander, 171
Son, Masayoshi, 154
Soros, George, 263
sovereignty, global perspective and, 269–270
Soviet Union, U.S. foreign policy on, 168
Stamets, Paul, 184–185
standard of living, inequalities in, 327
Sternin, Jerry, 187
Stern, Isaac, 337
Stiglitz, Joe
controversial resignation of, 175
criticism of Russian financial reform by, 172–173
offers alternative approach to Russian reform, 174
Stockman, David, 29
stocks
customer stock ownership plan, 126
employee stock ownership plans, 122
as substitute for wages, 62
volatility of, 143
stress
as cost of high financial returns, 202
as symptom of capitalist extremes, 95
subsidies, tax incentives and, 114
Suharto, 261
supply and demand, balance of, 82–83
supply-side economics
effect on wealth distribution, 65–66